A D.H.Lawrence
HANDBOOK

Keith Sagar *editor*

A D. H. *Lawrence* HANDBOOK

MANCHESTER UNIVERSITY PRESS

BARNES AND NOBLE BOOKS New York

© Keith Sagar 1982

Published by Manchester University Press
Oxford Road, Manchester M13 9PL

First published in the USA 1982
by Barnes and Noble Books
A division of Littlefield, Adams and Company
81 Adams Drive, Totowa, N.J. 07512

British Library cataloguing in publication data

A D. H. Lawrence handbook.
  1. Lawrence, D. H. – Criticism and interpretation
  I. Sagar, Keith
  823'.912   PR6023.A93Z/

UK ISBN 0-7190-0780-1

US ISBN 0-389-20312-2

Photoset in Plantin by
Northern Phototypesetting Co., Bolton

Printed in Great Britain by
Butler & Tanner Ltd, Frome and London

Contents

Dennis Jackson

1
A select bibliography, 1907–79

This selective checklist of writings by and about D. H. Lawrence is meant primarily for the serious but non-specialist student of Lawrence's writings. Lawrences novels, and many of his shorter works of fiction, non-fiction, poetry and drama are listed, along with information on their publication, and some five hundred bibliographical entries are included on books and articles written about those works, or· about Lawrence's life and ideas. Because of limitations of space, many fine works about Lawrence have been excluded. No effort has been made to list all his poems and essays: only those which have individually received critical attention in articles or in substantial portions of longer works have been listed. With few exceptions, the secondary materials have been selected with an eye toward their *usefulness* to the student of Lawrence's works, and their *accessibility* (most are available through university or public libraries, or through major presses in England or America). Also, books on Lawrence have generally received priority over periodical articles.

The bibliography is organised in nine major sections:

    I   BIBLIOGRAPHIES
    II   BIOGRAPHIES AND MEMOIRS
    III JOURNALS DEVOTED TO LAWRENCE
    IV   BOOKS AND ARTICLES ON LAWRENCE: GENERAL
    V   FICTION
    VI   POETRY
    VII NON-FICTION PROSE
    VIII DRAMA
    IX   FILMS BASED ON LAWRENCE'S WORKS

All titles of books or articles on Lawrence are accompanied by bold reference numbers which have been assigned consecutively throughout the checklist. The final five sections (V–IX) offer separate alphabetical listings of Lawrence's individual works within each genre. Section VII lists most of Lawrence's major NON-FICTION PROSE in alphabetical order, with several special categories included therein: LETTERS; LITERARY CRITICISM (including separate entries on *Studies in Classic American Literature* and 'Study of Thomas Hardy'); PSYCHOLOGICAL ESSAYS (*Fantasia of the Unconscious* and *Psychoanalysis and the Unconscious*); TRANSLATIONS; and TRAVEL (including separate entries on *Etruscan Places, Mornings in Mexico, Sea and Sardinia*, and *Twilight in Italy*).

Each listing of a Lawrence work indicates when it was *published* and, for the shorter pieces, when it was first *collected* with other Lawrence items. That information is followed by a listing of the work's *recent printings* (which mentions only books included in British and/or American *Books in Print* for 1979) and by *criticism* on the work. The criticism is presented in two different listings for each Lawrence work: (1) the first list refers the reader by CRITIC'S NAME and a **bold number** to books or articles cited elsewhere in the bibliography, and gives page numbers in those sources where material concerned with the particular Lawrence work may be found; (2) the second list introduces books or articles written about that specific Lawrence work. Each entry in this list is assigned its own bold number, and that number may appear elsewhere in the checklist to refer the reader back to the specific item and its full bibliographical entry.

A Summer Research Grant from the University of Delaware aided the preparation of this bibliography.

I BIBLIOGRAPHIES

1 BEARDS, Richard D. 'D. H. Lawrence: Ten Years of Criticism, 1959–1968, a Checklist.' *D. H. Lawrence Review* 1 (fall 1968): 245–85. [Secondary bibliography updates 1959 list by Beebe & Tommasi **2**. See also Beards's 'D. H. Lawrence: Criticism: September, 1968–December, 1969: A Checklist'. *D. H. Lawrence Review* 3 (spring 1970): 70–9. That was the first of a series of annual bibliographies in each *DHLR* spring issue. The journal has also frequently published (*a*) checklists of DHL criticism and scholarship in languages other than English, and (*b*) lists of doctoral dissertations and masters' theses on DHL.]

2 BEEBE, Maurice, and Anthony Tommasi. 'Criticism of D. H. Lawrence: A Selected Checklist with an Index to Studies of Separate Works'. *Modern Fiction Studies* 5 (spring 1959): 83–98. [Updates McDonald **3**, White **7** bibliographies, lists secondary materials on DHL up to 1958.]

3 McDONALD, Edward D. *A Bibliography of the Writings of D. H. Lawrence.* With a Foreword by D. H. Lawrence (Philadelphia, Pa.: Centaur Book Shop, 1925). [See also McDonald's *The Writings of D. H. Lawrence 1925–1930: A Bibliographical Supplement* (Philadelphia, Pa.: Centaur, 1931). Two checklists rptd as *Bibliography of D. H. Lawrence with Supplement 1925–30* (NY: Kraus Reprint, 1969). McDonald's list was the first full-scale descriptive bibliography devoted to DHL's works. Some secondary works listed.]

4 ROBERTS, Warren. *A Bibliography of D. H. Lawrence* (London: Rupert Hart-Davis, 1963). [The definitive primary bibliography of DHL to that date. Also lists some 'Books and Pamphlets about D. H. Lawrence'. See also **123**.]

5 STOLL, John E. *D. H. Lawrence: A Bibliography, 1911–1975* (Troy, N.Y.: Whitston, 1977). [Book-length primary and secondary bibliography; many entries incomplete or inaccurate.]

6 TEDLOCK, E. W., Jr. *The Frieda Lawrence Collection of D. H. Lawrence Manuscripts: A Descriptive Bibliography* (Albuquerque, N. Mex.: U of New Mexico P, 1948). [Extensive description of DHL manuscripts.]

7 WHITE, William. *D. H. Lawrence: A Checklist. Writings About D. H. Lawrence, 1931–50,* with Foreword by Frieda Lawrence (Detroit, Mich.: Wayne State UP, 1950). [Lists over seven hundred items; 'takes up where Edward D. McDonald left off' in 1931. Mostly secondary sources compiled alphabetically within each year, with reviews listed under the book reviewed.]

II   BIOGRAPHIES AND MEMOIRS

8 ALDINGTON, Richard. *Portrait of a Genius, But . . .* (London: Heinemann; NY: Duell, Sloan & Pearce, 1950); also pub. as *The Life of D. H. Lawrence, 1885 to 1930: Portrait of a Genius, But . . .* (London: Heinemann, Readers Union, 1951); rptd as *D. H. Lawrence: Portrait of A Genius, But . . .* (NY: Collier, 1961). [Biography with critique of DHL's work.]

9 BRETT, Dorothy. *Lawrence and Brett: A Friendship* (Philadelphia, Pa.: Lippincott, 1933); rptd with additional material (Sante Fe, N.Mex.: Sunstone, 1974). [Recounts friendship 1915–26.]

10 BREWSTER, Earl and Achsah. *D. H. Lawrence: Reminiscences and Correspondence* (London: Secker, 1934).

11 BYNNER, Witter. *Journey with Genius: Recollections and Reflections Concerning the D. H. Lawrences* (NY: Day, 1951; London: Nevill, 1953). [Memoir of 1922–5 period when Lawrences were in New Mexico and Mexico.]

12 CALLOW, Philip. *Son and Lover: The Younger D. H. Lawrence* (London: The Bodley Head; NY: Stein & Day, 1975). [DHL's life 1885–1919.]

13 CARSWELL, Catherine. *The Savage Pilgrimage: A Narrative of D. H. Lawrence* (London: Chatto; NY: Harcourt, Brace, 1932).

14 CARTER, Frederick. *D. H. Lawrence and the Body Mystical* (London: Archer; NY: Warner, 1932). [Relates friendship with DHL, touches often upon his ideas, e.g., his attitudes concerning myth, the Apocalypse of St John.]

15 CHAMBERS, Jessie. *D. H. Lawrence: A Personal Record,* by 'E. T.' (London:

Cape, 1935) (American ed., NY: Knight, 1936; 2nd ed., with new material (London: Cass; NY: Barnes & Noble, 1965). [Valuable account of DHL's early intellectual development, by real-life 'Miriam' of *Sons and Lovers*.]

16 **CORKE, Helen.** *D. H. Lawrence: The Croydon Years* (Auston, Tex.: U of Texas P, 1965).

17 **FAY, Eliot.** *Lorenzo in Search of the Sun: D. H. Lawrence in Italy, Mexico, and the American Southwest* (NY: Bookman, 1953; London: Vision, 1955).

18 **FOSTER, Joseph.** *D. H. Lawrence in Taos* (Albuquerque, N.Mex.: U of New Mexico P, 1972).

19 **HAHN, Emily.** *Lorenzo: D. H. Lawrence and the Women Who Loved Him* (Philadelphia, Pa. & NY: Lippincott, 1975).

20 **LAWRENCE, Ada, and G. Stuart Gelder.** *Young Lorenzo: Early Life of D. H. Lawrence Containing Hitherto Unpublished Letters, Articles and Reproductions of Pictures* (Florence: G. Orioli, 1932); rptd with some changes as *Early Life of D. H. Lawrence Together with Hitherto Unpublished Letters and Articles*, 1st English ed. (London: Secker, 1932).

21 **LAWRENCE, Frieda.** *Frieda Lawrence: the Memoirs and Correspondence*, ed. by E. W. Tedlock, Jr. (London: Heinemann, 1961; NY: Knopf, 1964).

22 **LAWRENCE, Frieda.** *'Not I, But the Wind . . .'* (Sante Fe: privately printed by the Rydal P; NY: Viking, 1934; London: Heinemann, 1935); rptd (Carbondale & Edwardsville, Ill.: Southern Illinois UP; London: Feffer & Simons, 1974).

23 **LUCAS, Robert.** *Frieda Lawrence: the Story of Frieda von Richthofen and D. H. Lawrence*, trans. from the German original by Geoffrey Skelton (London: Secker & Warburg; NY: Viking, 1973).

24 **LUHAN, Mabel Dodge.** *Lorenzo in Taos* (NY: Knopf, 1932; London: Secker, 1933).

25 **MERRILD, Knud.** *A Poet and Two Painters: A Memoir of D. H. Lawrence* (London: Routledge, 1938); rptd as *With D. H. Lawrence in New Mexico: A Memoir of D. H. Lawrence* (London: Routledge & Kegan Paul, 1964). [Recounts L's relationship with Merrild and Kai Gotzsche, 1922–3.]

26 **MOORE, Harry T., and Warren Roberts.** *D. H. Lawrence and His World* (NY: Viking; London: Thames & Hudson, 1966). [Biography, heavily illustrated.]

27 **MOORE, Harry T.** *Poste Restante: A Lawrence Travel Calendar* (Berkeley & Los Angeles, Cal.: U of California P, 1956). ['Geographical biography', a year-by-year calendar of DHL's travels. 'Introduction' by Mark Schorer, pp. 1–18.]

28 **MOORE, Harry T.** *The Intelligent Heart: the Story of D. H. Lawrence* (NY: Farrar, Straus & Young, 1954; London: Heinemann, 1955; rptd 1962); rvd. and enlgd. as *The Priest of Love: A Life of D. H. Lawrence* (Carbondale & Edwardsville, Ill.: Southern Illinois UP; London: Heinemann, 1974) (further revised: Harmondsworth: Penguin, 1976). [See also Moore's *The Life and Works of D. H. Lawrence* **105**, 1951.]

29 **MURRY, John Middleton.** *Reminiscences of D. H. Lawrence* (London: Cape, 1933). [Section II reprints 'Reminiscences' from *Adelphi*, June 1930–March 1931; Section IV reprints Murry's pre-1930 criticisms of DHL's writings.]

30 **NEHLS, Edward** (ed.). *D. H. Lawrence: A Composite Biography*, 3 vols. (Madison, Wis.: U of Wisconsin P, 1957–9). [Unique, extremely useful biography

which traces DHL's life using his own writings, excerpts from memoirs and reminiscences written by DHL's acquaintances, numerous pieces of correspondence, and other sources.]

31 SCHORER, Mark. *D. H. Lawrence* (NY: Dell, 1968). [103-page biography precedes selections from DHL's works.]

32 TREASE, Geoffrey. *D. H. Lawrence: the Phoenix and the Flame* (London: Macmillan; NY: Viking, 1973). [Short, simple biography.]

III JOURNALS OR SPECIAL NUMBERS OF JOURNALS DEVOTED TO LAWRENCE

THE D. H. LAWRENCE REVIEW. [Ed. by James C. Cowan, at University of Arkansas, Fayetteville, Ark. three times per year since 1968.]

JOURNAL OF THE D. H. LAWRENCE SOCIETY. [Ed. by John S. Poynter, Pub. annually since 1976 by D. H. Lawrence Society of England.] The society also publishes, quarterly since 1975, *LAWRENCE COUNTRY NEWS.* Ed. by Peter Preston.

THE LAUGHING HORSE. 13 (April 1926) [Special 'D. H. Lawrence number'. Ed. by Willard 'Spud' Johnson. Included several works by DHL, essays on him by other writers.]

LITERATURE/FILM QUARTERLY I, No. 1 (Jan. 1973). ['D. H. Lawrence' number. Ed. by Thomas L. Erskine, at Salisbury State College, Md. Included eight articles on DHL and film.]

MODERN FICTION STUDIES 5, No. 1 (spring 1959). ['D. H. Lawrence Number'. Ed. by Maurice Beebe, at Purdue University, Ind. Included seven articles on DHL, plus extensive secondary bibliography.]

THE NEW ADELPHI (June–Aug. 1930). [Lawrence memorial issue. Ed. by John Middleton Murry. Included first of Murry's 'Reminiscences', articles by Rebecca West and others, and several pieces of DHL's own writings.]

PAUNCH 26 (April 1966). [Special Lawrence issue. Ed. by Arthur Efron, in Buffalo, N.Y. Included essays on DHL.]

IV BOOKS AND ARTICLES ON LAWRENCE: GENERAL

33 ALBRIGHT, Daniel. *Personality and Impersonality: Lawrence, Woolf, and Mann* (Chicago, Ill.: U of Chicago P, 1978), 17–95.

34 ALCORN, John. *The Nature Novel from Hardy to Lawrence* (London: Macmillan; NY: Columbia UP, 1977).

35 ALLDRITT, Keith. *The Visual Imagination of D. H. Lawrence* (London: Arnold; Evanston, Ill.: Northwestern UP, 1971).

36 AMON, Frank. 'D. H. Lawrence and the Short Story'. In Hoffman/Moore, *The Achievement of DHL* **76**, 222–34.

37 ANDREWS, W. T. (ed.). *Critics on D. H. Lawrence* (London: George Allen & Unwin; Coral Gables, Fla.: U of Miami P, 1971). [Chronologically arranged collection of reviews and critical essays on DHL, 1911–1960s.]

38 ARNOLD, Armin. *D. H. Lawrence and America* (London: Linden P, 1958; NY: Philosophical Library, 1959). [Extensively discusses *Studies in Classic American Literature* and offers bibliographical essay (pp. 163–223) on DHL's 'reputation' in America and Europe.]

39 BEAL, Anthony. *D. H. Lawrence* (Edinburgh: Oliver & Boyd; NY: Grove, 1961).

40 BEDIENT, Calvin. *Architects of the Self: George Eliot, E. M. Forster, and D. H. Lawrence* (Berkeley, Los Angeles, Cal., and London: U of California P, 1972), pp. 98–195.

41 BLACK, Michael. *The Literature of Fidelity* (London: Chatto; NY: Barnes & Noble, 1975), pp. 169–211. [Ch. 11 'Sexuality in Literature: *Lady Chatterley's Lover*', pp. 169–83; Ch. 12 'Lawrence and "that which is perfectly ourselves" ', pp. 184–98; and Ch. 13 'Tolstoy and Lawrence: some conclusions', pp. 199–211.]

42 BLANCHARD, Lydia. 'Mothers and Daughters in D. H. Lawrence: *The Rainbow* and Selected Shorter Works'. In Smith, *Lawrence and Women* **130**, 75–100.

43 CAVITCH, David. *D. H. Lawrence and the New World* (NY and London: Oxford UP, 1969).

44 CLARK, L. D. 'D. H. Lawrence and the American Indian'. *D. H. Lawrence Review* 9 (fall 1976): 305–72.

45 CLARKE, Colin. *River of Dissolution: D. H. Lawrence and English Romanticism* (NY: Barnes & Noble; London: Routledge & Kegan Paul, 1969).

46 COOMBES, H. (ed.). *D. H. Lawrence: A Critical Anthology* (Harmondsworth: Penguin, 1973).

47 COWAN, James C. *D. H. Lawrence's American Journey: A Study in Literature and Myth* (Cleveland, Ohio, and London: P of Case Western Reserve U, 1970).

48 CRAIG, David. *The Real Foundations: Literature and Social Change* (NY: Oxford UP, 1974), pp. 17–38, 143–67. [Includes comments on *Women in Love*, *Virgin and Gipsy*, 'Captain's Doll', 'St Mawr', 'Daughters of the Vicar'.]

49 CURA-SAZDANIC, Ileana. *D. H. Lawrence as Critic* (Delhi: Manoharlal, 1969).

50 CUSHMAN, Keith. *D. H. Lawrence at Work: the Emergence of the 'Prussian Officer' Stories* (Charlottesville, Va.: UP of Virginia; Hassocks: Harvester P, 1978).

51 DAICHES, David. *The Novel and the Modern World*, rvd. ed. (Chicago, Ill.: U of Chicago P, 1960), 138–86. [Material on DHL not in first ed of this book; assesses DHL's major novels.]

52 DALESKI, H. M. 'Aphrodite of the Foam and *The Ladybird* Tales'. In Gomme, *DHL: A Critical Study* **69**, 142–59.

53 DALESKI, H. M. *The Forked Flame: A Study of D. H. Lawrence* (London: Faber; Evanston, Ill.: Northwestern UP, 1965).

54 DATALLER, Roger. 'Mr. Lawrence and Mrs. Woolf'. *Essays in Criticism* 8 (Jan. 1958), 48–59. [Traces DHL's revisions in two stories that became 'The Prussian Officer' and 'The Thorn in the Flesh'.]

55 DELANY, Paul. *D. H. Lawrence's Nightmare: The Writer and His Circle in the*

Years of the Great War (NY: Basic Books, 1978; Hassocks: Harvester P, 1979).

56 DELAVENAY, Emile. *D. H. Lawrence and Edward Carpenter: A Study in Edwardian Transition* (London: Heinemann; NY: Taplinger, 1971).

57 DELAVENAY, Emile. 'D. H. Lawrence and Sacher-Masoch'. *D. H. Lawrence Review* 6 (summer 1973): 119–48.

58 DELAVENAY, Emile. *D. H. Lawrence: The Man and His Work: the Formative Years: 1885–1919* (London: Heinemann; Carbondale, Ill.: Southern Illinois UP, 1972). [Translated by Katherine M. Delavenay from longer French version pub. 1969.]

59 DIGAETANI, John Louis. 'Situational Myths: Richard Wagner and D. H. Lawrence'. In his *Richard Wagner and the Modern British Novel* (Rutherford, N.J.: Fairleigh Dickinson UP; London: Associated U Presses, 1978), pp. 58–89.

60 DRAPER, R. P. *D. H. Lawrence* (London: Routledge & Kegan Paul; NY: Humanities P, Profiles in Literature Series, 1969). [Brief biography precedes extracts from DHL's work and commentaries on his style, characterisation, themes, symbolism.]

61 DRAPER, R. P. *D. H. Lawrence* (NY: Twayne, English Authors Series; St Martin's P, The Griffin Authors Series, 1964).

62 DRAPER, R. P. *D. H. Lawrence: The Critical Heritage* (NY: Barnes & Noble; London: Routledge & Kegan Paul, 1970; revd. 1979. [Ninety-seven original reviews and short commentaries on those of DHL's works published before 1930, arranged more or less chronologically.]

63 EISENSTEIN, Samuel A. *Boarding the Ship of Death: D. H. Lawrence's Quester Heroes* (The Hague: Mouton, 1974).

64 ENGEL, Monroe. 'The Continuity of Lawrence's Short Novels'. *Hudson Review* 11 (summer 1958): 201–9; rptd in Spilka, *DHL: A Collection of Critical Essays* **132**, 93–100. [On *Fox, Captain's Doll, Ladybird, St Mawr, Man Who Died*.]

65 FINNEY, Brian H. 'D. H. Lawrence's Progress to Maturity: From Holograph Manuscript to Final Publication of *The Prussian Officer and Other Stories*'. *Studies in Bibliography* 28 (1975): 321–32.

66 FORD, George H. *Double Measure: A Study of the Novels and Stories of D. H. Lawrence* (NY: Holt, Rinehart, & Winston, 1965).

67 FREEMAN, Mary. *D. H. Lawrence: A Basic Study of His Ideas* (Gainesville, Fla.: U of Florida P, 1955).

68 GARCIA, Reloy, and James Karabatsos (eds.). *A Concordance to the Short Fiction of D. H. Lawrence* (Lincoln, Nebr.: U of Nebraska P, 1972). [Word index to DHL's stories, short novels.]

69 GOMME, A. H. (ed.). *D. H. Lawrence: A Critical Study of the Major Novels and Other Writings* (NY: Barnes & Noble; Hassocks: Harvester P, 1978). [Collects ten essays, nine of them previously unpublished, by different writers.]

70 GOODHEART, Eugene. *The Utopian Vision of D. H. Lawrence* (Chicago, Ill.: U of Chicago P, 1963).

71 GREEN, Martin. *The von Richthofen Sisters: The Triumphant and the Tragic Modes of Love* (London: Weidenfield; NY: Basic Books, 1974). [Extensively comments on DHL's life, works, ideas.]

72 GREGORY, Horace. *Pilgrim of the Apocalypse: A Critical Study of D. H.*

Lawrence (NY: Viking, 1933; London: Secker, 1934); rvd. and rptd. with new introduction as *D. H. Lawrence: Pilgrim of the Apocalypse* (NY: Grove, 1957).

73 **HAMALIAN, Leo** (ed.). *D. H. Lawrence: A Collection of Criticism* (NY: McGraw-Hill, 1973). [Includes twelve previously published articles, and DHL's 'Autobiographical Sketch'.]

74 **HARRIS, Janice H.** 'Insight and Experiment in D. H. Lawrence's Early Short Fiction'. *Philological Quarterly* 55 (summer 1976): 418–35.

75 **HOCHMAN, Baruch.** *Another Ego: The Changing View of Self and Society in the Work of D. H. Lawrence* (Columbia, S.C.: U of South Carolina P, 1970).

76 **HOFFMAN, Frederick J., and Harry T. Moore** (eds.). *The Achievement of D. H. Lawrence* (Norman, Okla.: U of Oklahoma P, 1953). [Collection of eighteen articles and excerpts from longer works, on DHL.]

77 **HOLBROOK, David.** *The Quest for Love* (Cambridge: Cambridge University Press, U of Alabama P, 1965), pp. 192–366. [Ch. 4 (pp. 192–333) on *Lady Chatterley*, and Ch. 5 (pp. 334–56) on *Look! We Have Come Through!*]

78 **HOLDERNESS, Graham.** *Who's Who in D. H. Lawrence* (London: Hamish Hamilton; NY: Taplinger, 1976). [Alphabetical list of more than four hundred characters from DHL's fiction, with brief commentaries.]

79 **HOUGH, Graham.** *Image and Experience: Studies in a Literary Revolution* (London: Duckworth; Lincoln, Nebr.: U of Nebraska P, 1960). [Pp. 94–7 discuss DHL's 'Snake'; pp. 133–59 reprint Hough's earlier *Two Exiles: Lord Byron and D. H. Lawrence* (Nottingham: U of Nottingham, 1956).]

80 **HOUGH, Graham.** *The Dark Sun: A Study of D. H. Lawrence* (London: Duckworth, 1956; NY: Macmillan, 1957).

81 **HOWE, Marguerite Beede.** *The Art of the Self in D. H. Lawrence* (Athens, Ohio: Ohio UP, 1977).

82 **INNISS, Kenneth.** *D. H. Lawrence's Bestiary: A Study of His Use of Animal Trope and Symbol* (The Hague & Paris: Mouton, 1971; rptd. NY: Humanities P, 1972).

83 **JOHN, Brian.** 'D. H. Lawrence and the Quickening Word'. In his *Supreme Fictions: Studies in the Work of William Blake, Thomas Carlyle, W. B. Yeats, and D. H. Lawrence* (Montreal & London: McGill-Queen's UP, 1974), pp. 231–309. [Writers in the line of Romantic vitalism.]

84 **JOOST, Nicholas, and Alvin Sullivan.** *D. H. Lawrence and 'The Dial'* (Carbondale & Edwardsville, Ill.: Southern Illinois UP; London & Amsterdam: Feffer & Simons, 1970).

85 **KERMODE, Frank.** *D. H. Lawrence* (London: Fontana; NY: Viking P [Modern Masters Series], 1973).

86 **KERMODE, Frank.** 'Lawrence and the Apocalyptic Types'. *Critical Quarterly* 10 (spring–summer 1968): 14–33; rptd. in his *Continuities* (London: Routledge & Kegan Paul; NY: Random House, 1968), pp. 122–51 and *Modern Essays* (London: Fontana, 1971), pp. 153–81; and rptd. in Clarke, *D. H. Lawrence: 'The Rainbow' and 'Women in Love'* 255, 203–18. [*Women in Love* as DHL's chief attempt to create a fictional art appropriate to what he viewed as an 'apocalyptic' age.]

87 **KINKEAD-WEEKES, Mark.** 'The Marble and the Statue: The Exploratory

Imagination of D. H. Lawrence'. In *Imagined Worlds*, ed. by Maynard Mack and Ian Gregor (London: Methuen, 1968), pp. 371–418; excerpt rptd. in Kinkead-Weekes's *Twentieth Century Interpretations of 'The Rainbow'* **262**, 96–120. [Evolution of *Rainbow* and *Women in Love*.]

88 LEAVIS, F. R. *D. H. Lawrence: Novelist* (London: Chatto & Windus, 1955; NY: Knopf, 1956); rptd. (Harmondsworth: Penguin, 1964; Chicago: U of Chicago P, 1979).

89 LEAVIS, F. R. *Thought, Words and Creativity: Art and Thought in Lawrence* (NY: Oxford UP; London: Chatto & Windus, 1976). [Chapters on *Plumed Serpent, Women in Love*, 'Captain's Doll', *Rainbow*.]

90 LERNER, Laurence. *The Truthtellers: Jane Austen, George Eliot, D. H. Lawrence* (London: Chatto; NY: Schocken, 1967), pp. 66–71, 78–83, 172–235, 289–91.

91 LEVY, Mervyn (ed.). *Paintings of D. H. Lawrence* (NY: Viking; London: Cory, Adams & McKay, 1964). [Includes sixteen colour plates, two of paintings wrongly attributed to DHL, twenty-four pages of monochrome plates, and several articles: Harry T. Moore, 'D. H. Lawrence and His Paintings', 17–34; Jack Lindsay, 'The Impact of Modernism on Lawrence', 35–53; and Herbert Read, 'Lawrence as a Painter', 55–64.]

92 LEWIS, Wyndham. *Paleface: The Philosophy of The 'Melting Pot'* (London: Chatto, 1929) (rptd. NY: Haskell, 1969). [Expanded from article in *The Enemy* 2 (Sept. 1927): 3–112. Attacks DHL's romantic primitivism, particularly as seen in *Mornings in Mexico*.]

93 LITTLEWOOD, J. C. F. 'D. H. Lawrence's Early Tales'. *Cambridge Quarterly* 1 (spring 1966): 107–24. [*Prussian Officer* stories.]

94 LITTLEWOOD, J. C. F. *D. H. Lawrence I: 1885–1914* (London: Longman [No. 254, *Writers and Their Work* Series], 1976). [60-page study.]

95 MACKENZIE, D. Kenneth M. 'Ennui and Energy in *England, My England*'. In Gomme, *DHL: A Critical Study* **69**, 120–41.

96 MAES-JELINEK, Hena. *Criticism of Society in the English Novel Between the Wars* (Paris: Societe d'Editions 'Les Belles Lettres', 1970), pp. 11–100.

97 MERIVALE, Patricia. 'D. H. Lawrence and the Modern Pan Myth'. *Texas Studies in Literature and Language* 6 (autumn 1964): 297–305; rptd. as Ch. 6 in her *Pan the Goat-God: His Myth in Modern Times* (Cambridge, Mass.: Harvard UP, 1969), pp. 194–219. [Pan-tradition in 'Pan in America', 'The Last Laugh', *St Mawr*, and *Plumed Serpent*.]

98 MEYERS, Jeffrey. *Homosexuality and Literature 1890–1930* (London: Athlone, and Montreal: McGill-Queen's UP, 1977). [Ch. 9, 'D. H. Lawrence', pp. 131–61.]

99 MEYERS, Jeffrey. *Painting and the Novel* (Manchester: Manchester UP; NY: Barnes & Noble, 1975), pp. 46–82. [Includes three essays on DHL's references to paintings in *White Peacock, Rainbow, Women in Love*.]

100 MIKO, Stephen J. *Toward 'Women in Love': The Emergence of a Lawrentian Aesthetic* (New Haven, Conn.: Yale UP [Yale Studies in English, vol. 177], 1971).

101 MILES, Kathleen M. *The Hellish Meaning: The Demonic Motif in the Works of D. H. Lawrence* (Carbondale, Ill.: Southern Illinois U Monographs, 1969).

102 MILLER, James E., Jr., Karl Shapiro, and Bernice Slote (eds.). *Start With* *the Sun: Studies in Cosmic Poetry* (Lincoln, Nebr.: U of Nebraska P, 1960; rptd. as *Start With the Sun: Studies in the Whitman Tradition* (Lincoln, Nebr.: U of Nebraska P, Bison Book Edition, 1963). [Part II, 'Whitman and Lawrence', pp. 57–134.]

103 MILLETT, Kate. 'D. H. Lawrence'. In her *Sexual Politics* (Garden City, N.Y.: Doubleday, 1970), pp. 237–93. [Accuses DHL of elevating 'male supremacy' into a mystical religion in novels, of subordinating female characters.]

104 MOORE, Harry T. (ed.). *A D. H. Lawrence Miscellany* (Carbondale, Ill.: Southern Illinois UP, 1959). [Thirty items including critical essays, reminiscences of DHL, and early versions of *The Fox* and 'Hymns in a Man's Life'.]

105 MOORE, Harry T. *The Life and Works of D. H. Lawrence* (NY: Twayne; London: Allen & Unwin, 1951): rvd. as *D. H. Lawrence: His Life and Works* (NY: Twayne, 1964). [Critical biography.]

106 MOYNAHAN, Julian. *The Deed of Life: The Novels and Tales of D. H. Lawrence* (Princeton, N.J.: Princeton UP, 1963).

107 MURFIN, Ross C. *Swinburne, Hardy, Lawrence and the Burden of Belief* (Chicago, Ill.: U of Chicago P, 1978). [DHL: pp. 170–220; pp. 170–86 on DHL's poetry, later passages on *White Peacock, Rainbow.*]

108 MURRY, John Middleton. *Love, Freedom and Society* (London: Cape, 1957), pp. 23–123. [Describes DHL's search for a new religious consciousness.]

109 MURRY. John Middleton. *Son of Woman: The Story of D. H. Lawrence* (London: Cape; NY: Cape & Harrison Smith, 1931). [Psychological portrait of DHL and his work.]

110 NAHAL, Chaman. *D. H. Lawrence: An Eastern View* (South Brunswick: Yoseloff; NY: Barnes, 1970; Delhi: Atma Ram, 1971). [Notes affinities between DHL's thought and Vedantic philosophy, and considers major works.]

111 NIN, Anais. *D. H. Lawrence: An Unprofessional Study* (Paris: Titus, 1932) (rptd. London: Spearman, 1961; Denver: Alan Swallow, 1964).

112 NIVEN, Alastair. *D. H. Lawrence: The Novels* (Cambridge & NY: Cambridge UP, 1978).

113 PANICHAS, George. *Adventure in Consciousness: The Meaning of D. H. Lawrence's Religious Quest* (Studies in English Literature, III) (The Hague: Mouton, 1964).

114 PANICHAS, George. *The Reverent Discipline: Essays in Literary Criticism and Culture* (Knoxville, Tenn.: U of Tennessee P, 1974), pp. 135–69, 205–28, 335–70. [Reprints several of Panichas's previously published articles.]

115 PINION, F. B. *A D. H. Lawrence Companion: Life, Thought, and Works* (London: Macmillan, 1978; NY: Barnes & Noble, 1979).

116 PINTO, Vivian de Sola. 'D. H. Lawrence, Letter-Writer and Craftsman in Verse: Some Hitherto Unpublished Material'. *Renaissance and Modern Studies* 1 (1957): 5–34. [Quotes several unpublished letters, publishes early drafts of several poems.]

117 POTTER, Stephen. *D. H. Lawrence: A First Study* (London: Cape; NY: Cape & Harrison Smith, 1930).

118 PRITCHARD, R. E. *D. H. Lawrence: Body of Darkness* (London: Hutchinson U Library, 1971).

119 **PRITCHARD, William H.** *Seeing Through Everything: English Writers 1918–1940* (Oxford: Oxford UP, 1977), pp. 70–89, 114–33. [Includes long section on DHL's poetry.]

120 **REMSBURY, John.** ' "Real Thinking": Lawrence and Cézanne'. *Cambridge Quarterly* 2 (spring 1967): 117–47. [Appraises DHL's critical theories and philosophy.]

121 **ROSSMAN, Charles.** 'Myth and Misunderstanding D. H. Lawrence'. In *Twentieth-Century Poetry, Fiction, Theory*, ed. by Harry R. Garvin (Cranbury, N.J.: Bucknell UP, 1977), pp. 81–101.

122 **ROSSMAN, Charles.** ' "You are the call and I am the answer": D. H. Lawrence and Women'. *D. H. Lawrence Review* 8 (fall 1975): 255–328. [Examines DHL's major works to discover how his attitudes toward women changed through his career.]

123 **SAGAR, Keith.** *D. H. Lawrence: A Calendar of his Works*, with 'A Checklist of the Manuscripts of D. H. Lawrence', by Lindeth Vasey (Manchester: Manchester UP; Austin, Tex.: U of Texas P, 1979). [Pp. 1–190: detailed 'calendar' of DHL's work, based primarily on his letters. Pp. 191–266: an alphabetical list of 'all known Lawrence manuscripts', which revises and extends Section E of *A Bibliography of D. H. Lawrence* 4 compiled by Warren Roberts.]

124 **SAGAR, Keith.** *The Art of D. H. Lawrence* (Cambridge: Cambridge UP, 1966; rptd. 1975).

125 **SALE, Roger.** *Modern Heroism: Essays on D. H. Lawrence, William Empson, and J. R. R. Tolkein* (Berkeley, Cal.: U of California P, 1973), pp. 16–106.

126 **SANDERS, Scott.** *D. H. Lawrence: The World of the Major Novels* (London: Vision P, 1973); pub. as *D. H. Lawrence: The World of the Five Major Novels* (NY: Viking P, 1974).

127 **SCOTT, James F.** 'D. H. Lawrence's *Germania*: Ethnic Psychology and Cultural Crisis in the Shorter Fiction'. *D. H. Lawrence Review* 10 (summer 1977): 142–64.

128 **SELIGMANN, Herbert J.** *D. H. Lawrence: An American Interpretation* (NY: Seltzer, 1924). [76-page monograph; first published book on DHL.]

129 **SLADE, Tony,** *D. H. Lawrence* (London: Evans, 1969; NY: Arco [Arco Literary Critiques Series], 1970).

130 **SMITH, Anne** (ed.). *Lawrence and Women* (London: Vision P; NY: Barnes & Noble, 1978). [Collection of nine essays of varied interests on DHL, his response to women in his literature and life. Smith contributes 'A New Adam and a New Eve – Lawrence and Women: A Biographical Overview', pp. 9–48.]

131 **SPENDER, Stephen** (ed.). *D. H. Lawrence: Novelist, Poet, Prophet* (London: Weidenfeld & Nicolson; NY: Harper & Row, 1973). [Fifteen essays on various topics related to DHL.]

132 **SPILKA, Mark.** *D. H. Lawrence: A Collection of Critical Essays* (Englewood Cliffs, N.J.: Prentice-Hall, 1963).

133 **SPILKA, Mark.** *The Love Ethic of D. H. Lawrence* (Bloomington, Ind.: Indiana UP, 1955) (rptd. Bloomington, Ind.: Indiana UP; London: Dobson, 1965).

134 **STEWART, J. I. M.** *Eight Modern Writers* (Oxford & NY: Oxford UP, 1963),

pp. 484–593. [Comments on most of DHL's major works.]

135 STOLL, John E. *The Novels of D. H. Lawrence: A Search for Integration* (Columbia, Mo.: U of Missouri P, 1971).

136 SWIGG, Richard. *Lawrence, Hardy and American Literature* (NY: Oxford UP, 1972).

137 TEDLOCK, E. W., Jr. *D. H. Lawrence: Artist and Rebel: A Study of Lawrence's Fiction* (Albuquerque, N. Mex.: U of New Mexico P, 1963).

138 TENENBAUM, Elizabeth Brody. *The Problematic Self: Approaches to Identity in Stendhal, D. H. Lawrence, and Malraux* (Cambridge, Mass.: Harvard UP, 1977). [Ch. 2, 'D. H. Lawrence', pp. 65–112.]

139 TINDALL, William York. *D. H. Lawrence and Susan His Cow* (NY: Columbia UP, 1939). [An unsympathetic examination of DHL's primitivism and mysticism. Praises *The Plumed Serpent* as DHL's best novel.]

140 TIVERTON, Father William [pseud. of Martin Jarrett-Kerr]. *D. H. Lawrence and Human Existence*, with 'Foreword' by T. S. Eliot (London & Rockliff, N.Y.: Philosophical Library, 1951) (2nd ed. rvd. Martin Jarrett-Kerr (London: SCM Press, 1961). [Sympathetic study of DHL's philosophy by Anglican priest.]

141 VICKERY, John B. 'Myth and Ritual in the Shorter Fiction of D. H. Lawrence'. *Modern Fiction Studies* 5 (spring 1959): 65–82; rptd. in rvd. and enlgd. form in Ch. 9: 'D. H. Lawrence: The Mythic Elements', *The Literary Impact of the Golden Bough* (Princeton, N.J.: Princeton UP, 1973), pp. 294–325.

142 VIVAS, Eliseo. *D. H. Lawrence: The Failure and the Triumph of Art* (Evanston, Ill.: Northwestern UP, 1960; London: Allen & Unwin, 1961) (rptd. Bloomington, Ind.: Indiana UP, Midland Book, 1964).

143 WALKER, Ronald G. *Infernal Paradise: Mexico and the Modern English Novel* (Berkeley & Los Angeles, Cal., and London: U of California P, 1978), pp. 28–104.

144 WEISS, Daniel A. *Oedipus in Nottingham: D. H. Lawrence* (Seattle, Wash.: U of Washington P, 1962). [Analyzes the 'Oedipal situation' in *Sons and Lovers*, some *Prussian Officer* stories, and other DHL works.]

145 WEST, Anthony. *D. H. Lawrence* (London: Barker; Denver, Colo.: Alan Swallow, 1950) (rptd. London: Barker, 1957; 2nd ed. London: Barker, 1966).

146 WIDMER, Kingsley. *The Art of Perversity: D. H. Lawrence's Shorter Fictions* (Seattle, Wash.: U of Washington P, 1962).

147 WILLIAMS, Raymond. *The English Novel from Dickens to Lawrence* (London: Chatto, 1970), pp. 169–84.

148 WORTHEN, John. *D. H. Lawrence and the Idea of the Novel* (London: Macmillan; Totowa, N.J.: Rowman, 1979).

149 YUDHISHTAR. *Conflict in the Novels of D. H. Lawrence* (Edinburgh: Oliver and Boyd; NY: Barnes & Noble, 1969).

150 ZYTARUK, George J. *D. H. Lawrence's Response to Russian Literature* (The Hague: Mouton, 1971).

V FICTION

SOME COLLECTIONS WHICH INCLUDE LAWRENCE'S SHORTER FICTIONS (arranged alphabetically)

THE COMPLETE SHORT STORIES OF D. H. LAWRENCE, 3 vols. (London: Heinemann, 1955). Three new editions of the stories were published, using the same 3-volume format, in: 1961 (NY: Viking, Compass); 1974, as *THE COLLECTED SHORT STORIES OF D. H. LAWRENCE* (London: Heinemann, Phoenix); 1976, as *THE COMPLETE SHORT STORIES OF D. H. LAWRENCE* (NY: Penguin).

ENGLAND, MY ENGLAND AND OTHER STORIES (NY: Seltzer, 1922) (new ed. Harmondsworth: Penguin, 1970).

FOUR SHORT NOVELS (NY: Viking, 1965) (new ed. NY: Penguin, 1976).

LOVE AMONG THE HAYSTACKS AND OTHER STORIES (Harmondsworth: Penguin, 1970). Contains also 'The Lovely Lady', 'Rawdon's Roof', 'The Rocking-Horse Winner', 'The Man Who Loved Islands' and 'The Man Who Died'.

THE LOVELY LADY AND OTHER STORIES (London: Secker, 1933) (facsimile ed. Freeport, NY: Books for Libraries P, 1972).

A MODERN LOVER (London: Secker, 1934) (facsimile ed. Freeport, NY: Books for Libraries P, 1972).

THE MORTAL COIL AND OTHER STORIES, ed. by Keith Sagar (Harmondsworth: Penguin, 1971).

PHOENIX: THE POSTHUMOUS PAPERS OF D. H. LAWRENCE, ed by Edward D. McDonald (London: Heinemann; NY: Viking, 1936) (new ed. Heinemann, 1961; new ed. Penguin, 1978).

PHOENIX II: UNCOLLECTED, UNPUBLISHED, AND OTHER PROSE WORKS BY D. H. LAWRENCE, ed. by Warren Roberts & Harry T. Moore (London: Heinemann; NY: Viking, 1968) (new ed. Penguin, 1978).

THE PORTABLE D. H. LAWRENCE, ed. by Diana Trilling (NY: Viking, 1947) (new ed. Penguin, 1977).

THE PRINCESS AND OTHER STORIES, ed. by Keith Sagar (Harmondsworth: Penguin, 1971).

THE PRUSSIAN OFFICER AND OTHER STORIES (London: Duckworth, 1914) (new ed. Harmondsworth: Penguin, 1968).

THE SHORT NOVELS, 2 vols. (London: Heinemann, Phoenix, 1956).

STORIES, ESSAYS AND POEMS, ed. by Desmond Hawkins (London: Dent, 1939); rptd. as *D. H. LAWRENCE'S STORIES, ESSAYS, AND POEMS* (London: Dent [Everyman's Library], 1967).

THE TALES OF D. H. LAWRENCE (London: Secker, 1934); rptd. in 2 vols. (St. Claire Shores, Mich.: Scholarly P, 1972).

THREE NOVELLAS: THE FOX, THE LADYBIRD, THE CAPTAIN'S DOLL (Harmondsworth: Penguin, 1970).

THE WOMAN WHO RODE AWAY AND OTHER STORIES (London: Secker; NY: Knopf, 1928) (new ed. Harmondsworth: Penguin, 1970).

STUDIES OF INDIVIDUAL WORKS OF FICTION

AARON'S ROD

Published: 1st ed.: NY, Seltzer, 14 April 1922; 1st English ed: London, Secker, June 1922.

Recent Printings: Heinemann Phoenix ex. (1954); Penguin (1976).

Criticism: **CAVITCH, 43,** 108–15; **DALESKI, 53,** 188–213; **DRAPER, 62,** 177–83; **EISENSTEIN, 63,** 77–86; **GREGORY, 72,** 51–60; **HOUGH, 80,** 95–103; **HOWE, 81,** 79–91; **LEAVIS, 88,** 23–39, 45–7; **MEYERS, 98,** 149–55; **MILLETT, 103,** 269–80; **MOYNAHAN, 106,** 95–101; **MURRY, 109,** 180–204; **NAHAL, 110,** 173–82; **NIVEN, 112,** 133–42; **PINION, 115,** 182–9; **POTTER, 117,** 71–8; **SAGAR, 124,** 102–14; **VIVAS, 142,** 21–36; **WORTHEN, 148,** 118–35; **YUDHISHTAR, 149,** 210–32.

151 BAKER, Paul G. 'Profile of an Anti-Hero: Aaron Sisson Reconsidered'. *D. H. Lawrence Review* 10 (summer 1977): 182–92.

152 BARR, William R. *'Aaron's Rod* as D. H. Lawrence's Picaresque Novel'. *D. H. Lawrence Review* 9 (summer 1976): 213–25.

153 MYERS, Neil. 'Lawrence and the War'. *Criticism IV* (winter 1962), 44–58. [The effect of the war on the structure of *Aaron's Rod*.]

'ADOLF'

Published: *Dial*, Sept. 1920; also in *The New Keepsake for the Year 1921*.

Collected: *Young Lorenzo* **20** in 1932; also in *Phoenix*, 1936.

Recent printings: *The Mortal Coil and Other Stories*, Penguin (1971); *Stories, Essays, and Poems*, Dent (1967); *Phoenix*, Penguin (1978).

154 MARKS, W. S. 'D. H. Lawrence and his Rabbit Adolph: Three Symbolic Permutations'. *Criticism* 10 (1968): 200–16. [Traces 'rabbit episode' from *Paul Morel* through 'Adolf' sketch and *Women in Love*.]

'THE BLIND MAN'

Published: *English Review*, July 1920; also *Living Age*, 7 Aug. 1920.

Collected: *England, My England*, Oct. 1922.

Recent printings: *England, My England*, Penguin (1970): *Collected Short Stories*, vol. 2, Heinemann Phoenix (1974); *Complete Short Stories*, vol. 2, Penguin (1976); *Portable D. H. Lawrence*, Penguin (1977).

Criticism: **DELAVENAY, 58,** 435–7; **MACKENZIE, 95,** 128–31; **SPILKA, 133,** 25–9, 151–3 (rvd. and rptd. in **132,** 112–16); **TEDLOCK, 137,** 109–11; **WIDMER, 146,** 44–46.

155 ABOLIN, Nancy. 'Lawrence's "The Blind Man": The Reality of Touch'. In Moore, **104,** 215–30.

156 MARKS, W. S. 'The Psychology in D. H. Lawrence's "The Blind Man" '. *Literature and Psychology* 17 (winter 1967): 177–92. [Jungian archetypal pattern in story.]

157 ROSS, Michael L. 'The Mythology of Friendship: D. H. Lawrence, Bertrand Russell, and "The Blind Man" '. In *English Literature and British Philosophy*, ed. by S. P. Rosenbaum (Chicago, Ill.: U of Chicago P, 1971), 285–315.

158 WEST, Ray B., Jr. 'The Use of Point of View and Authority in "The Blind

Man" '. In his *Reading the Short Story* (NY: Crowell, 1968), 105–17; rptd. in his *The Art of Writing Fiction*.
159 WHEELER, Richard P. 'Intimacy and Irony in "The Blind Man" '. *D. H. Lawrence Review* 9 (summer 1976): 236–53.

'THE BLUE MOCCASINS'
Published: *Eve: The Lady's Pictorial*, 22 Nov. 1928; also *Plain Talk*, Feb. 1929.
Collected: *The Lovely Lady*, Jan. 1933.
Recent printings: *The Princess and Other Stories*, Penguin (1971); *Collected Short Stories*, vol. 3, Heinemann, Phoenix (1974); *Complete Short Stories*, vol. 3, Penguin (1976).
Criticism: **TEDLOCK, 6**, 69–71; **137**, 220–1; **WIDMER, 146**, 104–7.

'THE BORDER LINE'
Published: *Hutchinson's Magazine*, Sept. 1924; also *Smart Set*, Sept. 1924.
Collected: *The Woman Who Rode Away*, May 1928.
Recent printings: *The Woman Who Rode Away*, Penguin (1970); *Collected Short Stories*, vol. 3, Heinemann, Phoenix (1974); *Complete Short Stories*, vol. 3, Penguin (1976).
Criticism: **COWAN, 47**, 52–5; **SCOTT, James F., 127**, 159–62; **TEDLOCK, 137**, 173–5; **WEST, 145**, 99–104; **WIDMER, 146**, 53–6.
160 HUDSPETH, Robert N. 'Duality as Theme and Technique in D. H. Lawrence's "The Border Line" '. *Studies in Short Fiction* 4 (1966): 51–6.

THE BOY IN THE BUSH (written with Mollie L. Skinner)
Published: 1st ed.: London, Secker, Aug. 1924; 1st American ed.: NY, Seltzer, 30 Sept. 1924.
Recent printings: Southern Illinois UP (1971); Feffer & Simons (1971); Penguin (1972); Heinemann, Phoenix (1972).
Criticism: **DRAPER, 62**, 232–42; **KERMODE, 85**, 110–12; **MURRY, 109**, 240–7; **SAGAR, 124**, 137–41; **TEDLOCK, 137**, 167–70
161 MOORE, Harry T. 'Preface' to *The Boy in the Bush* by D. H. Lawrence and M. L. Skinner (Carbondale & Edwardsville, Ill.: Southern Illinois UP; London & Amsterdam: Feffer & Simons, 1971), pp. vii–xxviii. [Traces history of DHL's collaboration with Skinner on novel, and offers critical evaluation.]
162 REES, Marjorie. 'Mollie Skinner and D. H. Lawrence'. *Westerly* 1 (March 1964): 41–9. [Quotes Skinner's unpublished autobiography and several letters from DHL to her; background of their co-authorship of this story.]
163 SKINNER, Mollie L. 'D. H. Lawrence and *The Boy in the Bush*', *Meanjin* (Melbourne) 9 (summer 1950): 260–3; rptd. in Nehls, **30**, vol. 21, pp. 271–4. [See also Katherine Susannah Prichard's remarks on the DHL–Skinner collaboration, in *Meanjin* 9 (summer 1950): 256–9; rptd. in Nehls, vol. 2, pp. 274–8.]

THE CAPTAIN'S DOLL
Published and collected: 1st ed.: London, Secker, March 1923, in *The Ladybird, The Fox, The Captain's Doll*; 1st American ed.: NY, Seltzer, Nov. 1923, in *The Captain's Doll: Three Novelettes*
Recent printings: *Short Novels*, vol. 1, Heinemann, Phoenix (1956); *Three Novellas*,

Penguin (1970); *Four Short Novels*, Penguin (1976).
Criticism: **DALESKI, 52**, 156–8; **DRAPER, 62**, 191–6; **HOUGH, 80**, 177–9;
LEAVIS, 88, 242–78; **LEAVIS, 89**, 92–121; **PANICHAS, 113**, 109–11;
STEWART, 134, 571–7; **TEDLOCK, 137**, 124–8; **WIDMER, 146**, 157–65.
164 BORDINAT, Philips. 'The Poetic Image in D. H. Lawrence's *The Captain's
Doll'*. *West Virginia University Bulletin: Philological Papers* 19 (July 1972): 45–9.
165 DAWSON, Eugene W. 'Love Among the Mannikins: *The Captain's Doll.*'
D. H. Lawrence Review 1 (summer 1968): 137–48.
166 MELLOWN, Elgin W. '*The Captain's Doll*: Its Origins and Literary Allusions'.
D. H. Lawrence Review 9 (summer 1976): 226–35.

'THE CHRISTENING'
Published: *Smart Set*, Feb. 1914.
Collected: *The Prussian Officer*, Nov. 1914.
Recent printings: *The Prussian Officer*, Penguin (1968); *Collected Short Stories*, vol. 1,
Heinemann, Phoenix (1974); *Complete Short Stories*, vol. 1, Penguin (1976).
Criticism: **DELAVENAY, 58**, 186–7; **HARRIS, 74**, 423–5; **TEDLOCK, 137**,
29–30; **WEISS, 144**, 77–9.
167 CUSHMAN, Keith. ' "A Bastard Begot": The Origins of D. H. Lawrence's
"The Christening" '. *Modern Philology* 70 (Nov. 1972): 146–8; rptd. in rvd. and
enlgd. form in his *DHL at Work* **50**, 216–23.

'DAUGHTERS OF THE VICAR'
Published: *Time and Tide*, 24 March 1934 (an early version, titled 'Two Marriages').
Collected: *The Prussian Officer*, Nov. 1914.
Recent printings: *The Prussian Officer*, Penguin (1968); *Collected Short Stories*, vol. 1,
Heinemann, Phoenix (1974); *Complete Short Stories*, vol. 1, Penguin (1976).
Criticism: **CUSHMAN, 50**, 77–115; **FINNEY, 65**, 329–32; **GREEN, 71**, 25–7;
LEAVIS, 88, 77–95, 100–7; **LITTLEWOOD, 93**, 108–15; **TEDLOCK, 137**,
30–3; **VIVAS, 142**, 165–7; **WEISS, 144**, 88–92; **WIDMER, 146**, 126–31.
168 EARL, G. A. '**Correspondence**'. *Cambridge Quarterly* 1 (summer 1966):
273–5. [The 'back-washing' scene.]
169 KALNINS, Mara. 'D. H. Lawrence's "Two Marriages" and "Daughters of the
Vicar" '. *Ariel* 7 (Jan. 1976): 32–49. [Compares 'Two Marriages', an early
version, with final version.]

'DELILAH AND MR BIRCUMSHAW'
Published: *Virginia Quarterly Review*, spring 1940.
Collected: *Phoenix II*, 1968.
Recent printings: *The Mortal Coil and Other Stories*, Penguin (1971); *Phoenix II*,
Penguin (1978).

'A DREAM OF LIFE'
Published and collected: *Phoenix*, 1936 (as 'Autobiographical Fragment').
Recent printings: *The Princess and Other Stories*, Penguin (1971); *Phoenix*, Penguin
(1978).
Criticism: **SAGAR, 124**, 214–15.

'ENGLAND, MY ENGLAND'

Published: *English Review*, Oct. 1915, and in slightly rvd. form in *Metropolitan*, April 1917.

Collected: *England, My England*, Oct. 1922.

Recent printings: *Stories, Essays, and Poems*, Dent (1967); *England, My England*, Penguin (1970); *Collected Short Stories*, vol. 2, Heinemann, Phoenix (1974); *Complete Short Stories*, vol. 2, Penguin (1976).

Criticism: **CLARKE, 45**, 116–20; **DELAVENAY, 58**, 431–4; **LEAVIS, 88**, 332–5; **MACKENZIE, 95**, 123–7; **ROSSMAN, 121**, 83–90; **VICKERY, 141**, 71–6; **WIDMER, 146**, 17–22.

170 LODGE, David. *The Modes of Modern Writing* (London, Arnold; Ithaca, N.Y.: Cornell, 1977, 164–76. [Stylistic analysis.]

171 LUCAS, Barbara. 'Apropos of "England, My England" '. *Twentieth Century* 169 (March 1961): 288–93. [Seeks to correct errors in Moore's account **28** of the 'real-life sources'.]

'THE ESCAPED COCK' (see *THE MAN WHO DIED*)

'FANNY AND ANNIE'

Published: *Hutchinson's Magazine*, 21 Nov. 1921.

Collected: *England, My England*, Oct. 1922.

Recent printings: *England, My England*, Penguin (1970); *Collected Short Stories*, vol. 2, Heinemann, Phoenix (1974); *Complete Short Stories*, vol. 2, Penguin (1976).

Criticism: **LEAVIS, 88**, 95–100; **MACKENZIE, 95**, 136–8; **WIDMER, 146**, 124–6.

172 SECOR, Robert. 'Language and Movement in "Fanny and Annie" '. *Studies in Short Fiction* 6 (summer 1969): 395–400.

'THE FLY IN THE OINTMENT'

Published: Early version: *Young Lorenzo* **20**, 1932; also *Phoenix II*, 1968; revised version: *New Statesman*, 16 Aug. 1913.

Collected: Early version: *Young Lorenzo* (see above); revised version: *The Mortal Coil and Other Stories*, Penguin (1971).

Recent printing: Early version: *Phoenix II*, Penguin (1978).

Criticism: **WIDMER, 146**, 244–5.

173 CUSHMAN, Keith. 'A Note on Lawrence's "Fly in the Ointment" '. *English Language Notes* 15 (1977): 47–51.

'THE FLYING FISH' (unfinished story)

Published and collected: *Phoenix*, 1936.

Recent printings: *The Princess and Other Stories*, Penguin (1971); *Phoenix*, Penguin (1978).

Criticism: **CAVITCH, 43**, 189–93; **COWAN, 47**, 128–37; **PINION, 115**, 250–2; **SAGAR, 124**, 206–10.

THE FOX

Versions: DHL wrote the story in late 1918, cut it for magazine publication in July

1919, and rewrote it (with a long new ending) in November 1921.

Published: MS version: *A D. H. Lawrence Miscellany* **104**, 1959; magazine version: *Hutchinson's Story Magazine*, Nov. 1920; long version: *Dial*, May, June, July, Aug. 1922.

Collected: Long version: 1st ed.: London, Secker, March 1923, in *The Ladybird, The Fox, The Captain's Doll*; 1st American ed.: NY, Seltzer, Nov. 1923, in *The Captain's Doll: Three Novelettes*.

Recent printings: Long version: *Short Novels*, vol. 1, Heinemann, Phoenix (1956); *Stories, Essays, and Poems*, Dent (1967); *Three Novellas*, Penguin (1970); *The Fox and The Virgin and the Gipsy*, Heinemann Educational Books (1971); *Four Short Novels*, Penguin (1976); *Portable D. H. Lawrence*, Penguin (1977).

Criticism: **DALESKI, 52**, 151–6; **DRAPER, 62**, 191–6; **GOODHEART, 70**, 51–6; **INNISS, 82**, 159–63; **LEAVIS, 88**, 320–32; **MOYNAHAN, 106**, 196–209; **TEDLOCK, 137**, 116–20; **VICKERY, 141**, 79–82.

174 BERGLER, Edmund. 'D. H. Lawrence's *The Fox* and the Psychoanalytic Theory on Lesbianism'. In Moore, **104**, 49–55. [Rptd. from *The Journal of Nervous and Mental Disease* (1958).]

175 BRAYFIELD, Peg. 'Lawrence's "Male and Female Principles" and the Symbolism of *The Fox*', *Mosaic* 4, No. 3 (1971): 41–65.

176 DAVIS, Patricia C. 'Chicken Queen's Delight: D. H. Lawrence's *The Fox*'. *Modern Fiction Studies* 19 (winter 1973–4): 565–71. [On Henry's 'homoerotic drive'.]

177 DRAPER, R. P. 'The Defeat of Feminism: D. H. Lawrence's *The Fox* and "The Woman Who Rode Away" '. *Studies in Short Fiction* 3 (1966): 186–98.

178 GREGOR, Ian. '*The Fox*: A Caveat'. *Essays in Criticism* 9 (Jan. 1959): 10–21.

179 ROSSI, Patrizio. 'Lawrence's Two Foxes: A Comparison of the Texts'. *Essays in Criticism* 22 (July 1972): 265–78.

180 RUDERMAN, Judith G. '*The Fox* and the "Devouring Mother" '. *D. H. Lawrence Review* 10 (fall 1977): 251–69.

'A FRAGMENT OF STAINED GLASS'

Published: *English Review*, Sept. 1911; also in *Pearson's Magazine*, Mar. 1922.

Collected: *The Prussian Officer*, Nov. 1914.

Recent printings: *The Prussian Officer*, Penguin (1968); *Collected Short Stories*, vol. 1, Heinemann, Phoenix (1974); *Complete Short Stories*, vol. 1, Penguin (1976).

Criticism: **FORD, 66**, 71–2; **WIDMER, 146**, 51–3.

181 BAIM, Joseph. 'Past and Present in D. H. Lawrence's "A Fragment of Stained Glass" '. *Studies in Short Fiction* 8 (spring 1971): 323–6.

'GLAD GHOSTS'

Published: *Dial*, July, Aug. 1926; also as *Glad Ghosts* (London: Benn, Nov. 1926).

Collected: *The Woman Who Rode Away*, May 1928.

Recent printings: *The Woman Who Rode Away*, Penguin (1970); *Collected Short Stories*, vol. 3, Heinemann, Phoenix (1974); *Complete Short Stories*, vol. 3, Penguin (1976).

Criticism: **FORD, 66**, 101–3; **JOOST/SULLIVAN, 84**, 133–6; **MOORE**, (1964) **105**, 220–2; **TEDLOCK, 137**, 204–6; **WIDMER, 146**, 187–91.

'GOOSE FAIR'
Published: *English Review*, Feb. 1910.
Collected: *The Prussian Officer*, Nov. 1914.
Recent printings: *The Prussian Officer*, Penguin (1968); *Collected Short Stories*, vol. 1, Heinemann, Phoenix (1974); *Complete Short Stories*, vol. 1, Penguin (1976).
Criticism: **TEDLOCK, 137**, 22–3.

'HER TURN'
Published: *Saturday Westminster Gazette*, 6 Sept. 1913 (under title 'Strike-Pay I, Her Turn'); also in *Esquire*, Aug. 1934 (as 'Turnabout is Fair').
Collected: *A Modern Lover*, 1934.
Recent printings: *The Mortal Coil and Other Stories*, Penguin (1971); *Collected Short Stories*, vol. 1, Heinemann, Phoenix (1974); *Complete Short Stories*, vol. 1, Penguin (1976).
Criticism: **TEDLOCK, 137**, 28–9.

'THE HORSE-DEALER'S DAUGHTER'
Published: *English Review*, Apr. 1922; also *The Best British Short Stories for 1923*.
Collected: *England, My England*, Oct. 1922.
Recent printings: *England, My England*, Penguin (1970); *Collected Short Stories*, vol. 2, Heinemann, Phoenix (1974); *Complete Short Stories*, vol. 2, Penguin (1976).
Criticism: **FORD, 66**, 91–6; **LEAVIS, 88**, 311–15; **WIDMER, 146**, 172–4.
182 JUNKINS, Donald. 'D. H. Lawrence's "The Horse-Dealer's Daughter" '. *Studies in Short Fiction* 6 (winter 1969): 210–13. [Explores story's 'mythic' themes and motifs.]
183 McCABE. Thomas H. 'Rhythm as Form in Lawrence: "The Horse-Dealer's Daughter" '. *PMLA* 87 (Jan. 1972): 64–8.
184 PHILLIPS, Steven R. 'The Double Pattern of D. H. Lawrence's "The Horse-Dealer's Daughter" '. *Studies in Short Fiction* 10 (winter 1973): 94–7.
185 RYALS, Clyde de L. 'D. H. Lawrence's "The Horse-Dealer's Daughter": An Interpretation'. *Literature and Psychology* 12 (spring 1962): 39–43. [Jungian 'rebirth archetype' dramatised in the story's symbolism.]

'IN LOVE'
Published: *Dial*, Nov. 1927.
Collected: *The Woman Who Rode Away*, May 1928.
Recent printings: *Woman Who Rode Away*, Penguin (1970); *Collected Short Stories*, vol. 3, Heinemann, Phoenix (1974); *Complete Short Stories*, vol. 3, Penguin (1974).
Criticism: **JOOST/SULLIVAN, 84**, 103–5, 129–36; **TEDLOCK, 137**, 212–13; **WIDMER, 146**, 131–2.

'JIMMY AND THE DESPERATE WOMAN'
Published: *Criterion*, Oct. 1924; also *The Best British Short Stories of 1925*.
Collected: *The Woman Who Rode Away*, May 1928.
Recent printings: *The Woman Who Rode Away*, Penguin (1970); *Collected Short Stories*, vol. 3, Heinemann, Phoenix (1974); *Complete Short Stories*, vol. 3, Penguin

(1976).
Criticism: **COWAN, 47**, 55–8; **TEDLOCK, 137**, 172–3; **WIDMER, 146**, 139–44.

KANGAROO
Published: 1st ed.: London, Secker, Sept. 1923; 1st American ed.: NY, Seltzer, Sept. 1923.
Recent printings: Heinemann, Phoenix (1955); Penguin (1960).
Criticism: **DRAPER, 62**, 214–23; **EISENSTEIN, 63**, 87–113; **FREEMAN, 67**, 158–76; **HOUGH, 80**, 103–17; **HOWE, 81**, 92–105; **INNISS, 82**, 163–8; **LEAVIS, 88**, 39–44, 51–5, 66–71; **MAES-JELINEK, 96**, 72–81; **MOYNAHAN, 106**, 101–7; **MURRY, 109**, 218–39; **NIN, 111**, 59–66; 116–29; **NIVEN, 112**, 143–65; **SAGAR, 124**, 131–7; **VIVAS, 142**, 37–63; **WORTHEN, 148**, 136–51; **YUDHISHTAR, 149**, 232–50.

186 ALEXANDER, John. 'D. H. Lawrence's *Kangaroo*: Fantasy, Fact or Fiction?' *Meanjin* (Melbourne) 24 (1965): 179–95. [DHL knew Australian people, politics, better than critics acknowledge.]

187 DRAPER, R. P. 'Authority and the Individual: A Study of D. H. Lawrence's *Kangaroo*'. *Critical Quarterly* 1 (autumn 1959): 208–15; rptd. in shorter form in his *D. H. Lawrence* (1964) **61**, 96–101.

188 FRIEDERICH, Werner P. *Australia in Western Imaginative Prose Writings 1600–1960* (Chapel Hill, N.C.: U of North Carolina P, 1967), pp. 226–33.

189 GURKO, Leo. '*Kangaroo*: D. H. Lawrence in Transit'. *Modern Fiction Studies* 10 (winter 1964–5): 349–58. [In a sort of reverse anthropomorphism, DHL breathes the qualities of the land into the people.]

190 HAEGERT, John W. 'Brothers and Lovers: D. H. Lawrence and the Theme of Friendship'. *Southern Review* (Adelaide) 8 (March 1975): 39–50.

191 HOPE, A. D. 'D. H. Lawrence's *Kangaroo*: How It Looks to an Australian'. In *The Australian Experience: Critical Essays on Australian Novels*, ed. by W. S. Ramson (Canberra: Australian National U, 1974), 157–73.

192 JARVIS, F. P. 'A Textual Comparison of the First British and American Editions of D. H. Lawrence's *Kangaroo*'. *Papers of the Bibliographical Society of America* (fourth quarter 1965): 400–24.

193 SAMUELS, Marilyn Schauer. 'Water, Ships and the Sea: Unifying Symbols in Lawrence's *Kangaroo*'. *University Review* (Kansas City) 37 (Oct. 1970): 46–57.

194 WILDING, Michael. ' "A New Show": The Politics of *Kangaroo*'. *Southerly* 30, No. 1 (1970): 20–40.

LADY CHATTERLEY'S LOVER
Versions: Lawrence wrote the first version of the novel in autumn 1926, completed a second version early in 1927, and wrote the third and final version during Dec. 1927 and early Jan. 1928. All three versions were subsequently published.
Published: 1st version: As *The First Lady Chatterley* (NY: Dial, 1944); 2nd version: As *La Seconda Lady Chatterley*, in *Le Tre 'Lady Chatterley'*, trans. into Italian by Carlo Izzo (Italy: Mondadori, 1954). 1st publication in English, as *John Thomas and Lady Jane* (London: Heinemann; NY: Viking, 1972). 3rd version: As *Lady Chatterley's Lover* (Florence: privately printed, July 1928); authorised

expurgated ed. (London: Secker, Feb. 1932); 1st authorised unexpurgated American ed. (NY: Grove, 1959); 1st authorised unexpurgated English ed. (London: Penguin, 1960).

Recent printings: 1st version: *The First Lady Chatterley*, Heinemann (1972); Penguin (1973); 2nd version: *John Thomas and Lady Jane*, Heinemann (1972); Penguin (1973); 3rd version: *Lady Chatterley's Lover*, Grove (1959); Modern Library (1960); Heinemann, Phoenix (1963); Bantam Modern Classics (1968); Penguin (1969); New American Library [Signet Classics])1972).

Criticism: **BEDIENT, 40,** 172–82; **BLACK, 41,** 169–83; **DALESKI, 53,** 258–311; **DRAPER, 62,** 278–97; **HOLBROOK, 77,** 192–333; **HOUGH, 80,** 148–66; **MILLETT, 103,** 237–45; **MOYNAHAN, 106,** 117–20, 140–72; **MURRY, 109,** 339–49; **ROSSMAN, 122,** 307–17; **SAGAR, 124,** 179–98; **SANDERS, 126,** 172–205; **SPILKA, 133,** 177–204; **TEDLOCK, 6,** 20–7, 277–316; **TIVERTON, 140,** 77–89; **VIVAS, 142,** 119–51; **WORTHEN, 148,** 168–82; **YUDHISHTAR, 149,** 266–87, 298–301.

195 BLANCHARD, Lydia. 'Women Look at Lady Chatterley: Feminine Views of the Novel'. *D. H. Lawrence Review* 11 (fall 1978): 246–59.

196 GREGOR, Ian, and Brian Nicholas. 'The Novel as Prophecy: *Lady Chatterley's Lover*'. In *The Moral and The Story* (London: Faber & Faber, 1962), pp. 217–48.

197 HENRY, G. B. McK. 'Carrying On: *Lady Chatterley's Lover*'. *Critical Review* (Melbourne) 10 (1967): 46–62; rptd. in Andrews, *Critics on DHL* **37,** 89–104.

198 JACKSON, Dennis. 'The "Old Pagan Vision": Myth and Ritual in *Lady Chatterley's Lover*'. *D. H. Lawrence Review* 11 (fall 1978): 260–71.

199 KNIGHT, G. Wilson. 'Lawrence, Joyce and Powys'. *Essays in Criticism* 11 (Oct. 1961): 403–17; included in his *Neglected Powers* (London: Routledge; NY: Barnes & Noble, 1971): 142–55. [Argues (403–5) that anal intercourse occurs in *LCL* and (405–9) that anal penetration similarly occurs during 'Excurse' in *Women in Love*.]

200 LAWRENCE, Frieda. 'Foreword' to *The First Lady Chatterley* by D. H. Lawrence (NY: Dial P, 1944), pp. v–xiii. [See also Esther Forbes's 'A Manuscript Report', pp. xv–xviii.]

201 MOORE, Harry T. 'Afterword: *Lady Chatterley's Lover*: The Novel as Ritual'. In *Lady Chatterley's Lover* by D. H. Lawrence (NY: Signet, 1962), pp. 285–99.

202 MOORE, Harry T. 'Love as a Serious and Sacred Theme'. *New York Times Book Review*. 3 May 1959, Section 7, p. 5; rptd. as '*Lady Chatterley's Lover* as Romance' in Moore, **104,** 262–4. [Reviews 1959 edition.]

203 PORTER, Katherine Anne. 'A Wreath for the Gamekeeper'. *Shenandoah* 11 (autumn 1959): 3–12; rptd. in *Encounter* 14 (Feb. 1960): 69–77.

204 REMBAR, Charles. *The End of Obscenity: The Trials of Lady Chatterley, Tropic of Cancer, and Fanny Hill* (NY: Random House, 1968), pp. 59–160. [Recounts 1959 trial.]

205 ROLPH, C. H. [pseud. of C. R. Hewitt]. *The Trial of Lady Chatterley: Regina V. Penguin Books Limited* (Harmondsworth: Penguin Books, 1961). [Transcript of English trial, 1960.]

206 SCHORER, Mark. 'On *Lady Chatterley's Lover*.' *Evergreen Review* 1, No. 1

(1957): 149–78; rptd. as 'Introduction' to *Lady Chatterley's Lover* by D. H. Lawrence, first authorised unexpurgated American ed. (NY: Grove P, 1959), pp. ix–xxxix; rptd. in his *The World We Imagine* (NY: Farrar, Straus & Giroux, 1968), pp. 122–46.

207 SPARROW, John. 'Regina v. Penguin Books Ltd.: An Undisclosed Element in the Case'. *Encounter* 18 (Feb. 1962): 35–43; rptd. in his *Independent Essays* (London: Faber & Faber, 1963). [Argues that 'buggery' is performed by the lovers on the 'night of sensual passion'. See rebuttal by Colin MacInnes, *Encounter* 18 (March 1962): 63–5.]

208 SQUIRES, Michael. 'Pastoral Patterns and Pastoral Variants in *Lady Chatterley's Lover*'. *English Literary History* 34 (1972): 129–46; rptd. in his *The Pastoral Novel: Studies in George Eliot, Thomas Hardy and D. H. Lawrence* (Charlottesville, Va.: UP of Virginia, 1974), 196–212.

209 STRICKLAND, G. R. 'The First *Lady Chatterley's Lover*'. In Gomme, *DHL: A Critical Study* **69**, 159–74. [Previously pub. in *Encounter* 36 (Jan. 1971): 44–52.]

210 VOELKER, Joseph C. 'The Spirit of No-Place: Elements of the Classical Ironic Utopia in D. H. Lawrence's *Lady Chatterley's Lover*'. *Modern Fiction Studies* 25 (summer 1979): 223–39.

211 WIDMER, Kingsley. 'The Pertinence of Modern Pastoral: The Three Versions of *Lady Chatterley's Lover*'. *Studies in the Novel* 5 (1973): 298–313.

'THE LADYBIRD'

Published and collected: 1st ed.: London, Secker, March 1923, in *The Ladybird, The Fox, The Captain's Doll*; 1st American ed.: NY, Seltzer, Nov. 1923, in *The Captain's Doll: Three Novelettes*.

Recent printings: *Short Novels*, vol. 1, Heinemann, Phoenix (1956); *Three Novellas*, Penguin (1970); *Four Short Novels*, Penguin (1976).

Criticism: **CLARKE, 45,** 113–15; **DALESKI, 52,** 143–50; **LEAVIS, 88,** 55–66; **SCOTT, James F., 127,** 152–6; **TEDLOCK, 137,** 120–4; **WIDMER, 146,** 45–51.

212 COWAN, James C. 'D. H. Lawrence's Dualism: The Apollonian–Dionysian Polarity and *The Ladybird*'. In *Forms of Modern British Fiction*, ed. by Alan Warren Friedman (Austin, Tex., & London: U of Texas P, 1975), pp. 75–99.

213 DENNY, N. V. E. *'The Ladybird'*. *Theoria* (South Africa) 11 (Oct. 1958): 17–28.

214 MASON, R. 'Persephone and the Ladybird: A Note on D. H. Lawrence'. *London Review* 2 (autumn 1967): 42–9.

'THE LAST LAUGH'

Published: *New Decameron IV*, Blackwell, Mar. 1925.

Collected: *The Woman Who Rode Away*, May 1928.

Recent printings: *The Woman Who Rode Away*, Penguin (1970); *Collected Short Stories*, vol. 3, Heinemann, Phoenix (1974); *Complete Short Stories*, vol. 3, Penguin (1976).

Criticism: **COWAN, 47,** 58–61; **MERIVALE, 97,** 207–13; **MOORE, (1964) 105,** 216–18; **TEDLOCK, 137,** 170–2.

215 BAIM, Joseph. 'The Second Coming of Pan: A Note on D. H. Lawrence's "The Last Laugh" '. *Studies in Short Fiction* 6 (fall 1968): 98–100.

'LESSFORD'S RABBITS' and 'A LESSON ON A TORTOISE'
Published and collected: *Phoenix II*, 1968.
Recent printings: *The Mortal Coil and Other Stories*, Penguin (1971); *Phoenix II*, Penguin (1978).

THE LOST GIRL
Published: 1st ed.: London, Secker, Nov. 1920; 1st American ed.: NY, Seltzer, Jan. 1921.
Recent printings: Heinemann, Phoenix (1955); Penguin (1978).
Criticism: **ALBRIGHT, 33,** 62–7; **DRAPER, 62,** 141–54; **EISENSTEIN, 63,** 43–76; **HOUGH, 80,** 90–5; **MOYNAHAN, 106,** 117–20, 121–40; **MURRY, 29,** 214–18; **MURRY, 109,** 125–33; **NIVEN, 112,** 114–32; **PINION, 115,** 177–82; **SAGAR, 124,** 36–8, 114–15; **TEDLOCK, 137,** 132–42; **WORTHEN, 148,** 105–17; **YUDHISHTAR, 149,** 200–10.
216 GURKO, Leo. '*The Lost Girl:* D. H. Lawrence as a "Dickens of the Midlands" '. *PMLA* 78 (Dec. 1963): 601–5.
217 HAFLEY, J. '*The Lost Girl* – Lawrence Really Real'. *Arizona Quarterly* 10 (1954): 312–22.
218 HEYWOOD, Christopher. 'D. H. Lawrence's *The Lost Girl* and Its Antecedents by George Moore and Arnold Bennett'. *English Studies* 47 (1966): 131–4.

LOVE AMONG THE HAYSTACKS
Published and collected: *Love Among the Haystacks and Other Pieces* (London: Nonesuch, Nov. 1930; NY: Viking, Oct. 1933).
Recent printings: *Short Novels*, vol. 1, Heinemann, Phoenix (1956); *Love Among the Haystacks and Other Stories*, Penguin (1970); *Four Short Novels*, Penguin (1976).
Criticism: **DELAVENAY, 58,** 112–14; **FORD, 66,** 98–101; **TEDLOCK, 137,** 33–6; **WIDMER, 146,** 121–3.
219 GROSS, Theodore, and Norman Kelvin. *An Introduction to Literature: Fiction* (NY: Random House, 1967), pp. 205–10.

'THE LOVELY LADY'
Published: *The Black Cap, New Stories of Murder and Mystery Compiled by C. Asquith*, Hutchinson, Oct. 1927.
Collected: *The Lovely Lady*, Jan. 1933.
Recent printings: *Stories, Essays, and Poems*, Dent (1967); *Love Among the Haystacks and Other Stories*, Penguin (1970); *Collected Short Stories*, vol. 3, Heinemann, Phoenix (1974); *Complete Short Stories*, vol. 3, Penguin (1976); *Portable D. H. Lawrence*, Penguin (1977).
Criticism: **FORD, 66,** 45–7; **MOORE, (1964) 105,** 237–40; **NAHAL, 110,** 87–9; **TEDLOCK, 137,** 211–12; **WIDMER, 146,** 95–9.
220 FINNEY, Brian H. 'A Newly Discovered Text of D. H. Lawrence's "The Lovely Lady" '. *Yale University Library Gazette* 49 (Jan. 1975): 245–52.

THE MAN WHO DIED

Published: Part I: *Forum*, 1928, as 'The Escaped Cock'; full story: as *The Escaped Cock*, Paris, Black Sun Press, Sept. 1929; 1st English ed.: as *The Man Who Died*, London, Secker, 1931; 1st American ed.: as *The Man Who Died*, NY, Knopf, 1931.

Collected: *The Tales of D. H. Lawrence*, London, Secker, 1934.

Recent printings: *Short Novels*, vol. 2, Heinemann, Phoenix (1956); *St. Mawr and The Man Who Died*, Random House (1959); *Love Among the Haystacks and Other Stories*, Penguin (1970); as *The Escaped Cock*, ed. by Gerald Lacy, Black Sparrow Press (1976).

Criticism: **ANDREWS, 37**, 109–16; **EISENSTEIN, 63**, 126–48; **FORD, 66**, 88–94, 104–12; **GOODHEART, 70**, 149–60; **HOUGH, 80**, 246–52; **MURRY, 109**, 349–60; **NAHAL, 110**, 216–35; **PANICHAS, 113**, 128–35; **SAGAR, 124**, 216–25; **SPILKA, 133**, 219–31; **WIDMER, 146**, 200–14; **ZYTARUK, 150**, 134–43, 158–68.

221 HINZ, Evelyn J., and John J. Teunissen. 'Savior and Cock: Allusion and Icon in Lawrence's *The Man Who Died*'. *Journal of Modern Literature* 5 (Apr. 1976): 279–96.

222 KROOK, Dorothea. 'Messianic Humanism: D. H. Lawrence's *The Man Who Died*'. In her *Three Traditions of Moral Thought* (Cambridge: Cambridge UP, 1959), pp. 255–92.

223 KUNKEL, Francis L. 'Lawrence's *The Man Who Died*: The Heavenly Cock'. In his *Passion and The Passion: Sex and Religion in Modern Literature* (Philadelphia, Pa.: Westminster P, 1975), pp. 37–57.

224 LACY, Gerald M. 'Commentary' in *The Escaped Cock* by D. H. Lawrence, ed by Gerald M. Lacy (Los Angeles, Cal.: Black Sparrow P, 1973), pp. 121–70. [Remarks on DHL's theme, the story's composition and publication history.]

225 LEDOUX, Larry V. 'Christ and Isis: The Function of The Dying and Reviving God in *The Man Who Died*'. *D. H. Lawrence Review* 5 (summer 1972): 132–48.

226 MacDONALD, Robert H. 'The Union of Fire and Water: An Examination of the Imagery of *The Man Who Died*'. *D. H. Lawrence Review* 10 (spring 1977): 34–51.

'THE MAN WHO LOVED ISLANDS'

Published: *Dial*, July 1927; also *London Mercury*, Aug. 1927.

Collected: *The Woman Who Rode Away* (Knopf American ed. only), May 1928; also in *The Lovely Lady*, London, Secker, Jan. 1933.

Recent printings: *Love Among the Haystacks and Other Stories*, Penguin (1970); *Collected Short Stories*, vol. 3, Heinemann, Phoenix (1974); *Complete Short Stories*, vol. 3, Penguin (1976).

Criticism: **FORD, 66**, 80–90; **JOOST/SULLIVAN, 84**, 124–6, 132–6 *passim*; **TEDLOCK, 137**, 213–16; **WIDMER, 146**, 11–17.

227 KARL, Frederick R. 'Lawrence's "The Man Who Loved Islands": The Crusoe Who Failed'. In Moore, *A DHL Miscellany* **104**, 265–79.

228 MOYNAHAN, Julian. 'Lawrence's "The Man Who Loved Islands": A Modern Fable'. *Modern Fiction Studies* 5 (spring 1959): 57–64; rvd. and rptd. in his *The*

Deed of Life **106**, 185–96.
229 WILLBERN, David. 'Malice in Paradise: Isolation and Projection in "The Man
Who Loved Islands" '. *D. H. Lawrence Review* 10 (fall 1977): 223–41.

'THE MAN WHO WAS THROUGH WITH THE WORLD' (unfinished story)
Published: Essays in Criticism, July 1959.
Collected: The Princess and Other Stories, Penguin (1971).
Criticism: **SAGAR, 124,** 176–7.
230 ELLIOTT, John R. ' "The Man Who Was Through with the World": An
Unfinished Story by D. H. Lawrence'. *Essays in Criticism* 9 (July 1959): 213–21.
[Text of DHL's fragment pub. here with an introduction by Elliott.]

'MERCURY'
Published and collected: Phoenix, 1936.
Recent printings: The Princess and Other Stories, Penguin (1971); *Phoenix*, Penguin
(1978).

'THE MINER AT HOME'
Published: Nation, 16 Mar. 1912.
Collected: Phoenix, 1936.
Recent printings: The Mortal Coil and Other Stories, Penguin (1971); *Phoenix*,
Penguin (1978).

MR NOON (incomplete novel)
Published and collected: A Modern Lover, Oct. 1934; also in *Phoenix II*, 1968.
Recent printing: Phoenix II, Penguin (1978).
Criticism: **PINION**, *DHL Companion* **115**, 249–50.

'A MODERN LOVER'
Published: Life and Letters, Sept.–Nov. 1933.
Collected: A Modern Lover, Oct. 1934.
Recent printings: The Woman Who Rode Away, Penguin (1970); *Collected Short
Stories*, vol. 1, Heinemann, Phoneix (1974); *Complete Short Stories*, vol. 1, Penguin
(1976).
Criticism: **CUSHMAN, 50,** 121–7; **TEDLOCK, 137,** 15–17.
231 SAGAR, Keith. ' "The Best I Have Known": D. H. Lawrence's "A Modern
Lover" and "The Shades of Spring" '. *Studies in Short Fiction* 4 (winter 1967):
143–51. [esp. 144–6.]

'MONKEY NUTS'
Published: Sovereign, 22 Aug. 1922.
Collected: England, My England, Oct. 1922.
Recent printings: England, My England, Penguin (1970); *Collected Short Stories*,
vol 2, Heinemann, Phoenix (1974); *Complete Short Stories*, vol. 2, Penguin
(1976).
Criticism: **SLADE, 129,** 105–6; **TEDLOCK, 137,** 111–12; **WIDMER, 146,** 136–7.

'THE MORTAL COIL'
Published: *Seven Arts*, July 1917.
Collected: *Phoenix II*, 1968.
Recent printings: *The Mortal Coil and Other Stories*, Penguin (1971); *Phoenix II*, Penguin (1978).

'MOTHER AND DAUGHTER'
Published: *New Criterion*, Apr. 1929.
Collected: *The Lovely Lady*, Jan. 1933.
Recent printings: *The Princess and Other Stories*, Penguin (1971); *Collected Short Stories*, vol. 3, Heinemann, Phoenix (1974); *Complete Short Stories*, vol. 3, Penguin (1976).
Criticism: **BLANCHARD, 42**, 95–7; **LEAVIS, 88**, 346–51; **WIDMER, 146**, 99–101.

232 MEYERS, Jeffrey. 'Katherine Mansfield, Gurdjieff, and Lawrence's "Mother and Daughter" '. *Twentieth Century Literature* 22 (Dec. 1976): 444–53. [DHL's story an 'allegory' of Mansfield's 'seduction by the mysticism' of Gurdjieff.]

'NEW EVE AND OLD ADAM'
Published and collected: *A Modern Lover*, Oct. 1934.
Recent printings: *The Mortal Coil and Other Stories*, Penguin (1971); *Collected Short Stories*, vol. 1, Heinemann, Phoenix (1974); *Complete Short Stories*, vol. 1, Penguin (1976).
Criticism: **DELAVENAY, 58**, 151–2, 190–2; **TEDLOCK, 137**, 84–5; **WIDMER, 146**, 102–3.

'NONE OF THAT'
Published and collected: *The Woman Who Rode Away*, May 1928.
Recent printings: *The Woman Who Rode Away*, Penguin (1970); *Collected Short Stories*, vol. 3, Heinemann, Phoenix (1974); *Complete Short Stories*, vol. 3, Penguin (1976).
Criticism: **TEDLOCK, 137**, 201–2; **WIDMER, 146**, 78–81.

'ODOUR OF CHRYSANTHEMUMS'
Published: early version: *Renaissance and Modern Studies*, 1969; later version: *English Review*, June 1911.
Collected: later version: *The Prussian Officer*, Nov. 1914.
Recent printings: (later version): *Stories, Essays, and Poems*, Dent (1967); *Prussian Officer*, Penguin (1968); *Collected Short Stories*, vol. 2, Heinemann, Phoenix (1974); *Complete Short Stories*, vol. 2, Penguin (1976).
Criticism: **AMON, 36**, 223–6; **CUSHMAN, 50**, 47–76; **LITTLEWOOD, 94**, 15–20; **MOYNAHAN, 106**, 181–5; **TEDLOCK, 6**, 33–7.

233 BOULTON, James T. 'D. H. Lawrence's "Odour of Chrysanthemums": An Early Version'. *Renaissance and Modern Studies* 13 (1969): 5–11. [DHL's revisions of story.]

234 FORD, Ford Madox. 'D. H. Lawrence', in *Portraits from Life* (Boston, Mass.: Houghton Mifflin, 1937), 70–89. [Pp. 70–5 discuss 'Odour of Chrysanthemums'; this material rptd. in Nehls, *Composite Biography*, vol. 1, **30**, 106–9.]

235 HUDSPETH, Robert N. 'Lawrence's "Odour of Chyrsanthemums": Isolation and Paradox. *Studies in Short Fiction* 6 (1969): 630–6.

236 KALNINS, Mara. 'D. H. Lawrence's "Odour of Chrysanthemums": The Three Endings'. *Studies in Short Fiction* 13 (1976): 471–9.

'THE OLD ADAM'

Published and collected: *A Modern Lover*, Oct. 1934.

Recent printings: *The Mortal Coil and Other Stories*, Penguin (1971); *Collected Short Stories*, vol. 1, Heinemann, Phoenix (1974); *Complete Short Stories*, vol. 1, Penguin (1976).

Criticism: **TEDLOCK, 137,** 17–19; **WEISS, 144,** 84–8; **WIDMER, 146,** 153–4.

'ONCE'

Published and collected: *Love Among the Haystacks and Other Pieces* (London: Nonesuch, Nov. 1930; NY: Viking, Oct. 1933).

Recent printings: *Phoenix II*, 1968; *The Mortal Coil and Other Stories*, Penguin (1971); *Phoenix II*, Penguin (1978).

Criticism: **TEDLOCK, 6,** 42–4.

'THE OVERTONE'

Published and collected: *The Lovely Lady*, Jan. 1933.

Recent printings: *The Princess and Other Stories*, Penguin (1971); *Collected Short Stories*, vol. 3, Heinemann, Phoenix (1974); *Complete Short Stories*, vol. 3, Penguin (1976).

Criticism: **MERIVALE, 97,** 213–15; **TEDLOCK, 137,** 199–201; **WIDMER, 146,** 152–3.

THE PLUMED SERPENT

Published: 1st ed.: London, Secker, Jan. 1926; 1st American ed.: NY, Knopf, Feb. 1926.

Recent printings: Knopf (1951); Random House (1955); Heinemann, Phoenix (1955); Penguin (1970).

Criticism: **COWAN, 47,** 99–121; **DALESKI, 53,** 213–57; **DRAPER, 62,** 263–71; **FREEMAN, 67,** 177–88; **HOCHMAN, 75,** 230–54; **HOUGH, 80,** 117–38; **HOWE, 81,** 105–32; **INNISS, 82,** 176–88; **JOHN, 83,** 259–75; **LEAVIS, 89,** 34–61; **LERNER, 90,** 172–80; **MURRY, 109,** 282–302; **SAGAR, 124,** 159–68; **SANDERS, 126,** 136–71; **SPILKA, 133,** 205–19; **TINDALL, 139,** 113–18; **VIVAS, 142,** 65–91; **WALKER, 143,** 79–99; **WORTHEN, 148,** 152–67; **YUDHISHTAR, 149,** 250–66.

237 APTER, T. E. 'Let's Hear What the Male Chauvinist is Saying: *The Plumed Serpent*'. In Smith, **130,** 156–78.

238 BALDWIN, Alice. 'The Structure of the Coatl Symbol in *The Plumed Serpent*'. *Style* 5 (spring 1971): 138–50.

239 CLARK, L. D. *Dark Night of the Body: D. H. Lawrence's 'The Plumed Serpent'* (Austin, Tex.: U of Texas P, 1964).

240 CLARK, L. D. 'The Making of a Novel: The Search for the Definitive Text of D. H. Lawrence's *The Plumed Serpent*'. In *Voices from the Southwest*, ed. by Donald C. Dickinson, W. David Laird, and Margaret F. Maxwell (Flagstaff, Ariz.:

Northland, 1976), pp. 113–30.
241 KESSLER, Jascha. 'Descent in Darkness: The Myth of *The Plumed Serpent*'. In Moore, **104**, pp. 239–61.
242 MEYERS, Jeffrey. '*The Plumed Serpent* and the Mexican Revolution'. *Journal of Modern Literature* 4 (Sept. 1974): 55–72.
243 VEITCH, Douglas W. *Lawrence, Greene and Lowry: The Fictional Landscape of Mexico* (Waterloo, Ontario: Wilfred Laurier UP, 1978). [Ch. 2, 'D. H. Lawrence's Elusive Mexico', 14–57, treats *PS* extensively.]
244 VICKERY, John B. '*The Plumed Serpent* and the Reviving God'. *Journal of Modern Literature* 2 (Nov. 1972): 505–32. [Influence of Frazer's *The Golden Bough*.]
245 WATERS, Frank. 'Quetzalcoatl Versus D. H. Lawrence's *Plumed Serpent*'. *Western American Literature*, 3 (1968), 103–13.

'*A PRELUDE*'
Published: *Nottinghamshire Guardian*, 7 Dec. 1907 (also separately as *A Prelude*, Merle Press, 1949).
Collected: *Phoenix II*, 1968.
Recent printings: *The Mortal Coil and Other Stories*, Penguin (1971); *Phoenix II*, Penguin (1978).
Criticism: **WIDMER, 146**, 123–4.

'*THE PRIMROSE PATH*'
Published and collected: *England, My England*, Oct. 1922.
Recent printings: *England, My England*, Penguin (1970); *Collected Short Stories*, vol. 2, Heinemann, Phoenix (1974): *Complete Short Stories*, vol. 2, Penguin (1976).
Criticism: **TEDLOCK, 137**, 106–7; **WIDMER, 146**, 25–6.

'*THE PRINCESS*'
Published: *Calendar of Modern Letters*, Mar., Apr., May 1925.
Collected: *St Mawr Together with The Princess*, Secker, May 1925.
Recent printings: *The Princess and Other Stories*, Penguin (1971); Collected Short Stories, vol. 2, Heinemann, Phoenix (1974); *Complete Short Stories*, vol. 2, Penguin (1976); *Portable D. H. Lawrence*, Penguin (1977).
Criticism: **CAVITCH, 43**, 170–3; **LEAVIS, 88**, 335–42; **MOORE,** (1964) **105**, 199–201; **ROSSMAN, 121**, 93–6; **WIDMER, 146**, 81–6.
246 COWAN, James C. 'D. H. Lawrence's "The Princess" as Ironic Romance'. *Studies in Short Fiction* 4 (spring 1967): 245–51; rptd. in **47**, 64–70.
247 WEINER, S. Ronald. 'Irony and Symbolism in "The Princess"'. In Moore, **104**, 221–38.

'*THE PRUSSIAN OFFICER*'
Published: As 'Honour and Arms' in *English Review*, Aug. 1914; also *Metropolitan*, Nov. 1914.
Collected: As 'The Prussian Officer' in *The Prussian Officer*, Nov. 1914.
Recent printings: *The Prussian Officer*, Penguin (1968); *Collected Short Stories*, vol. 1, Heinemann, Phoenix (1974); *Complete Short Stories*, vol. 1, Penguin (1976);

Portable D. H. Lawrence, Penguin (1977).
Criticism: **AMON, 36,** 226–31; **CUSHMAN, 50,** 167–73, 209–15; **DATALLER, 54,** 50–3; **FORD, 66,** 75–80; **SALE, 125,** 44–7; **WEISS, 144,** 69–97; **WIDMER, 146,** 6–11.
248 ADELMAN, Gary. 'Beyond the Pleasure Principle: An Analysis of D. H. Lawrence's "The Prussian Officer" '. *Studies in Short Fiction*, 1 (fall 1963): 8–15.
249 ENGLANDER, Ann. ' "The Prussian Officer": The Self Divided'. *Sewanee Review* 71 (Oct.–Dec. 1963): 605–19.
250 HUMMA, John B. 'Melville's *Billy Budd* and Lawrence's "The Prussian Officer": Old Adam and New'. *Essays in Literature* (Western Illinois U) 1 (1974): 83–8.

THE RAINBOW
Published: 1st ed.: London, Methuen, 30 Sept. 1915; 1st American ed.: NY, Huebsch, 30 Nov. 1915.
Recent printings: Heinemann, Phoenix (1954); Heinemann Educational Books (1968); Penguin (1976).
Criticism: **ALLDRITT, 35,** 54–69, 73–136; **BLANCHARD, 42,** 75–91; **CAVITCH, 43,** 37–57; **CLARKE, 45,** 45–69 and *passim*; **DAICHES, 51,** 152–66; **DALESKI, 53,** 74–125; **DELAVENAY, 58,** 344–85; **DRAPER, 62,** 84–109; **FORD, 66,** 115–68; **HOWE, 81,** 28–51; **KINKEAD-WEEKES, 87,** 371–418; **LEAVIS, 88,** 108–74; **LEAVIS, 89,** 122–46; **MIKO, 100,** 108–85; **MOORE,** (1974) **28,** 223–52; **MOYNAHAN, 106,** 42–72; **MURRY, 109,** 59–75; **NIVEN, 122,** 59–113; **SAGAR, 124,** 41–72; **SALE, 125,** 52–76; **SANDERS, 126,** 60–93; **SPILKA, 133,** 93–120; **SWIGG, 136,** 81–131, 314–19; **VIVAS, 142,** 201–23; **WORTHEN, 148,** 45–82; **YUDHISHTAR, 149,** 113–57.
251 ADAMOWSKI, T. H. '*The Rainbow* and "Otherness" '. *D. H. Lawrence Review* 7 (spring 1974): 58–77.
252 BALBERT, Peter. *D. H. Lawrence and the Psychology of Rhythm: The Meaning of Form in 'The Rainbow'* (The Hague: Mouton, 1974).
253 BERTHOUD, Jacques. '*The Rainbow* as Experimental Novel'. In Gomme, *DHL: A Critical Study* **69,** 53–69.
254 BRANDABUR, A. M. 'The Ritual Corn Harvest Scene in *The Rainbow*'. *D. H. Lawrence Review* 6 (fall 1973): 284–302.
255 CLARKE, Colin (ed.). *D. H. Lawrence: 'The Rainbow' and 'Women in Love'* (London: Macmillan, 1969; Nashville, Tenn.: Aurora, 1970). [Casebook with pertinent documents and a number of previously published articles.]
256 DRAPER, R. P. '*The Rainbow*'. *Critical Quarterly* 20, No. 3 (autumn 1978): 49–64. [On Ursula's development of a 'distinctly modern consciousness'.]
257 ENGELBERG, Edward. 'Escape from the Circles of Experience: D. H. Lawrence's *The Rainbow* as a Modern *Bildungsroman*'. *PMLA* 78 (March 1963): 103–13; excerpt rptd. in Andrews, **37,** 67–80.
258 GAMACHE, Lawrence B. 'The Making of an Ugly Technocrat: Character and Structure in Lawrence's *The Rainbow*'. *Mosaic* 12 (autumn 1978): 61–78.
259 GOLDBERG, S. L. '*The Rainbow*: Fiddle-Bow and Sand'. *Essays in Criticism* (Oxford) 11 (Oct. 1961): 418–34. [Second half of novel is flawed by DHL's 'over-

certainty'.]
260 HELDT, Lucia Henning. 'Lawrence on Love: The Courtship and Marriage of Tom Brangwen and Lydia Lensky'. *D. H. Lawrence Review* 8 (fall 1975): 358–70.
261 HINZ, Evelyn J. '*The Rainbow*: Ursula's "Liberation"'. *Contemporary Literature* 17 (winter 1976): 24–43.
262 KINKEAD-WEEKES, Mark (ed.). *Twentieth Century Interpretations of 'The Rainbow'* (Englewood Cliffs, N.J.: Prentice-Hall, 1971). [Casebook, with seven previously published pieces on *The Rainbow*.]
263 MUDRICK, Marvin. 'The Originality of *The Rainbow*'. *Spectrum* 3 (winter 1959): 3–28; also pub. in Moore, **104**, 56–82; rptd. in Kinkead-Weekes, **262**, 11–32; rptd. in Spilka, **132**, 29–49.
264 ROSS, Charles L. *The Composition of 'The Rainbow' and 'Women in Love': A History* (Charlottesville, Va.: UP of Virginia, 1979).
265 SAGAR, Keith. 'The Genesis of *The Rainbow* and *Women in Love*'. *D. H. Lawrence Review* 1 (fall 1968): 179–99.
266 SALE, Roger. 'The Narrative Technique of *The Rainbow*'. *Modern Fiction Studies* 5 (spring 1959): 29–38.

'RAWDON'S ROOF'
Published: As *Rawdon's Roof*, No. 7 of the Woburn Books, Matthews & Marrot, Mar. 1929.
Collected: *The Lovely Lady*, Jan. 1933.
Recent printings: *Love Among the Haystacks and Other Stories*, Penguin (1970); *Collected Short Stories*, vol. 3, Heinemann, Phoenix (1974); *Complete Short Stories*, vol. 3, Penguin (1976).
Criticism: **TEDLOCK, 137,** 213; **WIDMER, 146,** 151.

'REX'
Published: *Dial*, Feb. 1921; also *Stories from the Dial*, 1924.
Collected: *Phoenix*, 1936.
Recent printings: *The Mortal Coil and Other Stories*, Penguin (1971); *Phoenix*, Penguin (1978).

'THE ROCKING-HORSE WINNER'
Published: *Harper's Bazaar*, July 1926; also *The Ghost Book, 16 New Stories of the Uncanny Compiled by Lady C Asquith*, Hutchinson, Sept. 1926.
Collected: *The Lovely Lady*, Jan. 1933.
Recent printings: *Love Among the Haystacks and Other Stories*, Penguin (1970); *Collected Short Stories*, vol. 3, Heinemann, Phoenix (1974); *Complete Short Stories*, vol. 3, Penguin (1976); *Portable D. H. Lawrence*, Penguin (1977).
Criticism: **AMON, 36,** 231–3; **WIDMER, 146,** 92–5.
267 BARRETT, Gerald R., and Thomas L. Erskine (eds.). *From Fiction to Film: D. H. Lawrence's 'The Rocking-Horse Winner'* (Encino and Belmont, Calif.: Dickenson, 1974). [Casebook on story and film; reprints three articles on DHL's story and includes useful 'Annotated Bibliography', 236–8, of fifteen other critical pieces.]
268 CONSOLO, Dominic P. (ed.). *D. H. Lawrence: The Rocking-Horse Winner*

(Columbus, Ohio: Charles E. Merrill, 1969). [Casebook with text of story, an 'Introduction' by Consolo (pp. 1–5), fourteen previously published essays on DHL's story, and a new article by Frederick W. Turner, III, 'Prancing in to a Purpose: Myths, Horses, and the True Selfhood in Lawrence's "The Rocking-Horse Winner" ', 95–106.]

269 GOLDBERG, Michael. 'Lawrence's "The Rocking-Horse Winner": A Dickensian Fable?' *Modern Fiction Studies* 15 (winter 1969–70): 525–36.

270 MARKS, W. S. 'The Psychology of the Uncanny in Lawrence's "The Rocking-Horse Winner" '. *Modern Fiction Studies* 11 (winter 1965–6): 381–92.

271 SNODGRASS, W. D. 'A Rocking-Horse: The Symbol, the Pattern, the Way to Live'. *Hudson Review* 11 (summer 1958): 191–200; rptd. in Spilka, **132**, 117–26; rptd. in Barrett/Erskine, **267**, 58–69; rptd. in his *In Radical Pursuit* (NY: Harper & Row, 1975), 128–40.

ST MAWR

Published: 1st ed.: *St. Mawr Together with The Princess*, London, Secker, May 1925; 1st separate ed.: As *St Mawr*, Knopf, June 1925.

Collected: *The Tales of D. H. Lawrence*, Secker, 1934.

Recent printings: *Short Novels*, vol. 2, Heinemann, Phoenix (1956); *St. Mawr and The Man Who Died*, Random House (1959); *St Mawr and The Virgin and the Gipsy*, Penguin (1971).

Criticism: **CAVITCH, 43**, 151–63; **COWAN, 47**, 81–96; **DRAPER, 62**, 250–7; **GOODHEART, 70**, 56–62; **HOUGH, 80**, 180–6; **JOHN, 83**, 278–86; **LEAVIS, 88**, 279–306; **LERNER, 90**, 185–91; **SAGAR, 124**, 151–9; **VIVAS, 142**, 151–65; **WIDMER, 146**, 66–75.

272 CRAIG, David, Mark Roberts, and T. W. Thomas. 'The Critical Forum'. *Essays in Criticism* 5 (Jan. 1955): 64–80. [Critical arguments; each writer replies to Robert Liddell's 'Lawrence and Dr. Leavis: The Case of *St Mawr*'. *Essays in Criticism* 4 (July 1954): 321–7.]

273 GIDLEY, Mick. 'Antipodes: D. H. Lawrence's *St Mawr*'. *Ariel* 5 (Jan. 1974): 25–41. [Story develops through tension of 'antitheses' associated with horse.]

274 RAGUSSIS, Michael. 'The False Myth of *St Mawr*: Lawrence and the Subterfuge of Art'. *Papers on Language and Literature* 11 (spring 1975): 186–96.

275 SMITH, Bob L. 'D. H. Lawrence's *St Mawr*: Transposition of Myth'. *Arizona Quarterly* 24 (autumn 1968): 197–208.

276 WILDE, Alan. 'The Illusion of *St Mawr*: Technique and Vision in D. H. Lawrence's Novel'. *PMLA* 79 (Mar. 1964): 164–70.

'SAMSON AND DELILAH'

Published: *English Review*, Mar. 1917; also *Lantern*, June 1917.

Collected: *England, My England*, Oct. 1922.

Recent printings: *England, My England*, Penguin (1970); *Collected Short Stories*, vol. 2, Heinemann, Phoenix (1974); *Complete Short Stories*, vol. 2, Penguin (1976).

Criticism: **MACKENZIE, 95**, 131–3; **TEDLOCK, 137**, 108–9; **WIDMER, 146**, 148–9.

'SECOND BEST'
Published: *English Review*, Feb. 1912.
Collected: *The Prussian Officer*, Nov. 1914.
Recent printings: *The Prussian Officer*, Penguin (1968); *Collected Short Stories*, vol.
   1, Heinemann, Phoenix (1974); *Complete Short Stories*, vol. 1, Penguin (1976).
Criticism: **HARRIS**, **74**, 431–3; **TEDLOCK**, **137**, 23–4.

'THE SHADES OF SPRING'
Published: *Forum*, Mar. 1913, as 'The Soiled Rose'; also *Blue Review*, May 1913.
Collected: *The Prussian Officer*, Nov. 1914.
Recent printings: *The Prussian Officer*, Penguin (1968); *Collected Short Stories*, vol.
   1, Heinemann, Phoenix (1974); *Complete Short Stories*, vol. 1, Penguin (1976).
Criticism: **CUSHMAN**, **50**, 116–47; **DELAVENAY**, **57**, 131–6, 138–42; **WEISS**,
   144, 80–4.
277 CUSHMAN, Keith. 'Lawrence's Use of Hardy in "The Shades of Spring" ',
   Studies in Short Fiction 9 (fall 1972): 402–4.
278 SAGAR, Keith. ' "The Best I Have Known": D. H. Lawrence's "A Modern
   Lover" and "The Shades of Spring" '. *Studies in Short Fiction* 4 (winter 1967):
   143–51.

'THE SHADOW IN THE ROSE GARDEN'
Published: *Smart Set*, Mar. 1914.
Collected: *The Prussian Officer*, Nov. 1914.
Recent printings: *The Prussian Officer*, Penguin (1968); *Collected Short Stories*, vol.
   1, Heinemann, Phoenix (1974); *Complete Short Stories*, vol. 1, Penguin (1976).
Criticism: **FINNEY**, **65**, 326–9; **TEDLOCK**, **6**, 32–3; **WIDMER**, **146**, 154–6.
279 CUSHMAN, Keith. 'D. H. Lawrence at Work: "The Shadow in the Rose
   Garden" '. *D. H. Lawrence Review* 8 (spring 1975): 31–46. [Traces evolution of
   story.]
280 SEIDL, Frances. 'Lawrence's "The Shadow in the Rose Garden" '. *Explicator*
   32 (Oct. 1973): item 9. [Symbolism of garden in story.]

'A SICK COLLIER'
Published: *New Statesman*, 13 Sept. 1913; also *Pearson's Magazine*, Feb. 1922.
Collected: *The Prussian Officer*, Nov. 1914.
Recent printings: *The Prussian Officer*, Penguin (1968); *Collected Short Stories*, vol.
   1, Heinemann, Phoenix (1974); *Complete Short Stories*, vol. 1, Penguin (1976).
Criticism: **WIDMER**, **146**, 149–51.

'SMILE'
Published: *Nation and Athenaeum*, 19 June 1926; also *New Masses*, June 1926.
Collected: *The Woman Who Rode Away*, May 1928.
Recent printings: *Woman Who Rode Away*, Penguin (1970); *Collected Short Stories*,
   vol. 2, Heinemann, Phoenix (1974); *Complete Short Stories*, vol. 2, Penguin
   (1976).
Criticism: **COWAN**, **47**, 50–2; **MOORE**, **105**, 218–19; **TEDLOCK**, **137**, 198–9.

SONS AND LOVERS

Published: 1st ed.: London, Duckworth, May 1913; 1st American ed.: NY, Kennerley, Sept. 1913.

Recent printings: Heinemann, Phoenix (1953); Modern Library (1962); Heinemann Educational Books (1963); Collins, Gift Classics (1974); Penguin (1976); Viking/Penguin (1977); U of California P (facsimile of the manuscript) (1978).

Criticism: **ALLDRITT, 35**, 16–42; **DALESKI, 53** 42–73; **DELAVENAY, 58**, 4–10, 15–29, 44–54, 115–26, 166–74; **DRAPER, 62**, 58–80; **FORD, 66**, 28–47; **HOUGH, 80**, 35–54; **MIKO, 100**, 59–107; **MILLETT, 103**, 245–57; **MOORE, 105**, 78–90, 285–305; **MOORE, 28**, 36–53; **MOYNAHAN, 106**, 13–31; **NIVEN, 112**, 36–58; **SAGAR, 124**, 19–36; **SALE, 125**, 22–39; **SANDERS, 126**, 21–59; **SPILKA, 133**, 39–89; **STOLL, 135**, 62–150; **TEDLOCK, 137**, 54–69; **VIVAS, 142**, 173–99; **WEISS, 144**, 3–67 and *passim*; **WORTHEN, 148**, 26–44; **YUDHISHTAR, 149**, 82–113.

281 BALBERT, Peter H. 'Forging and Feminism: *Sons and Lovers* and the Phallic Imagination'. *D. H. Lawrence Review* 11 (summer 1978): 93–113.

282 BEARDS, Richard D. '*Sons and Lovers* as Bildungsroman'. *College Literature* 1 (fall 1974): 204–17.

283 BEEBE, Maurice. 'Lawrence's Sacred Fount: The Artist Theme of *Sons and Lovers*'. *Texas Studies in Literature and Language* 4 (winter 1963): 539–52; rptd. in his *Ivory Towers and Sacred Founts* (NY: New York UP, 1964), pp. 101–13; rptd. as 'The Artist Theme', in Salgãdo, **294**, 177–90.

284 BETSKY, Seymour. 'Rhythm and Theme: D. H. Lawrence's *Sons and Lovers*', in Hoffman/Moore, **76**, 131–43.

285 FARR, Judith (ed.). *Twentieth Century Interpretations of 'Sons and Lovers': A Collection of Critical Essays* (Englewood Cliffs, N.J.: Prentice-Hall, 1970). [Casebook with pertinent letters and documents, numerous previously published essays.]

286 GOMME, A. H. 'Jessie Chambers and Miriam Leivers – An Essay on *Sons and Lovers*'. In Gomme, **69**, 30–52.

287 HINZ, Evelyn J. '*Sons and Lovers:* The Archetypal Dimensions of Lawrence's Oedipal Tragedy'. *D. H. Lawrence Review* 5 (spring 1972): 26–53.

288 KAZIN, Alfred. 'Sons, Lovers, and Mothers'. *Partisan Review* 29 (summer 1962): 373–85; rptd. as 'Introduction', *Sons and Lovers* by D. H. Lawrence (NY: Random House, Modern Library, 1962), pp. vii–xix; rptd. in Tedlock, **298**, 238–50.

289 KUTTNER, Alfred Booth. '*Sons and Lovers:* A Freudian Appreciation'. *Psychoanalytic Review* 3 (July 1916): 295–317; rptd. in Tedlock, **298**, 76–100; rptd. in Salgãdo, **294**, 69–94.

290 LITTLEWOOD, J. F. C. 'Son and Lover'. *Cambridge Quarterly*, (aut./winter 1969/70): 323–61.

291 MOYNAHAN, Julian (ed.). *'Sons and Lovers': Text, Background, and Criticism* (NY: Viking P [Viking Critical Library Ed], 1968). [Critical edition with pertinent letters, several DHL essays and poems, and memoirs, early reviews, and a number of previously published essays.]

292 PANKEN, Shirley. 'Some Psychodynamics in *Sons and Lovers*: A New Look at the Oedipal Theme'. *Psychoanalytic Review* 61 (1974–5): 571–89.

293 PULLIN, Faith. 'Lawrence's Treatment of Women in *Sons and Lovers*'. In Smith, **130**, 49–74. [Also discusses *The White Peacock*.]

294 SALGADO, Gāmini (ed.). *D. H. Lawrence: 'Sons and Lovers', A Selection of Critical Essays* (London: Macmillan, 1969); also pub. as *D. H. Lawrence: 'Sons and Lovers', A Casebook* (Nashville, Tenn.: Aurora, 1970). [Casebook with pertinent letters and documents, early reviews and fourteen previously published essays.]

295 SCHORER, Mark. 'Introduction' to *D. H. Lawrence: 'Sons and Lovers': A Facsimile of the Manuscript* (Berkeley, Cal., and London: U of California P, 1977), pp. 1–9. [Precedes facsimiles of parts of *Paul Morel* manuscript and of all the manuscript of *S& L*.]

296 SCHORER, Mark. 'Technique as Discovery'. *Hudson Review* 1 (spring 1948): 67–87 (especially on DHL 75–78); rptd. at least a dozen times, including (in excerpt) Tedlock, **298**, 164–9; (in excerpt) Salgādo, **294**, 106–11; and (in excerpt) Farr, **285**, 97–9.

297 SCHWARZ, Daniel R. 'Speaking of Paul Morel: Voice, Unity, and Meaning in *Sons and Lovers*'. *Studies in the Novel* 8 (fall 1976): 255–77.

298 TEDLOCK, E. W., Jr. (ed.). *D. H. Lawrence and 'Sons and Lovers': Sources and Criticism* (NU: New York UP, 1965; London: U of London P, 1966). [Includes sixteen critical articles or excerpts from previously published materials related to *S& L*.]

299 VAN GHENT, Dorothy. 'On *Sons and Lovers*'. In her *The English Novel: Form and Function* (NY: Holt, Rinehart & Winston, 1953), pp. 245–61 and 454–62; rptd. with minor changes in Spilka, **132**, 15–20; rptd. with alterations in Tedlock, **298**, 170–87; rptd. in Salgādo, **294**, 112–29.

'STRIKE-PAY'

Published: *Saturday Westminster Gazette*, 13 Sept. 1913 as 'Strike-Pay II, Ephraim's Half Sovereign'; also *Esquire*, June 1934; and *Lovat Dickson's Magazine*, Aug. 1934.

Collected: *A Modern Lover*, Oct. 1934.

Recent printings: *The Woman Who Rode Away*, Penguin (1970); *Collected Short Stories*, vol. 1, Heinemann, Phoenix (1974); *Complete Short Stories*, vol. 1, Penguin (1976).

Criticism: **TEDLOCK, 137**, 27–8.

'SUN'

Published: first version: *New Coterie*, autumn 1926; also separately by E. Archer, London, Sept. 1926; second version: Paris, The Black Sun Press, Oct. 1928.

Collected: first version: *The Woman Who Rode Away*, May 1928; second version: *The Princess and Other Stories*, Penguin (1971)

Recent printings: first version: *Woman Who Rode Away*, Penguin (1970); *Collected Short Stories*, vol. 1, Heinemann, Phoenix (1974); *Complete Short Stories*, vol. 1, Penguin (1976); second version: Penguin (1971).

Criticism: **LEAVIS, 88**, 355–7; **SAGAR, 124**, 173–5; **TEDLOCK, 137**, 202–4; **WIDMER, 146**, 195–8.

300 ROSS, Michael L. 'Lawrence's Second "Sun" '. *D. H. Lawrence Review* 8 (1975): 1–18, 373–4. [Ross has since been proved correct by Sagar, **123**, 172.]

'THE THIMBLE'
Published: *Seven Arts*, Mar. 1917.
Collected: *Phoenix II*, 1968; also *The Mortal Coil and Other Stories*, Penguin (1971).
Recent printing: *Phoenix II*, Penguin (1978).
Criticism: **WIDMER, 146**, 230–1.

'THINGS'
Published: *Bookman*, Aug. 1928; also *Fortnightly Review*, Oct. 1928.
Collected: *The Lovely Lady*, Jan. 1933.
Recent printings: *The Princess and Other Stories*, Penguin (1971); *Stories, Essays, and Poems*, Dent (1967); *Collected Short Stories*, vol. 3, Heinemann, Phoenix (1974); *Complete Short Stories*, vol. 3, Penguin (1976).
Criticism: **DRAPER**, (1969) **60**, 25–8; **LEAVIS, 88**, 357–62; **MOORE, 105**, 242–4; **TEDLOCK, 137**, 221–3; **WIDMER, 146**, 89–91.

'THE THORN IN THE FLESH'
Published: *English Review*, June 1914.
Collected: *The Prussian Officer*, Nov. 1914.
Recent printings: *The Prussian Officer*, Penguin (1968); *Collected Short Stories*, vol. 1, Heinemann, Phoenix (1974); *Complete Short Stories*, vol. 1, Penguin (1976).
Criticism: **DATALLER, 54**, 53–8; **LITTLEWOOD, 93**, 115–19; **SCOTT, 127**, 148–51; **WIDMER, 146**, 133–6.
301 CUSHMAN, Keith. 'D. H. Lawrence at Work: "Vin Ordinaire" into "The Thorn in the Flesh" '. *Journal of Modern Literature* 5 (Feb. 1976): 46–58; rvd. and enlgd. **50**, 167–9, 173–89 and *passim*.

'TICKETS, PLEASE'
Published: *Strand*, Apr. 1919 as 'Tickets, Please'; *Metropolitan*, Aug. 1919 as 'The Eleventh Commandment'.
Collected: *England, My England*, Oct. 1922.
Recent printings: *England, My England*, Penguin (1970); *Collected Short Stories*, vol. 2, Heinemann, Phoenix (1974); *Complete Short Stories*, vol. 2, Penguin (1976); *Portable D. H. Lawrence*, Penguin (1977).
Criticism: **SLADE, 129**, 103–5; **WIDMER, 146**, 137–40.
302 KEGEL-BRINKGREVE, E. 'The Dionysian Tramline'. *Dutch Quarterly Review* 5 (1975): 180–94.
303 LAINOFF, Seymour. 'The Wartime Setting of Lawrence's "Tickets, Please" '. *Studies in Short Fiction* 7 (fall 1970): 649–51.
304 WHEELER, Richard P. ' "Cunning in His Overthrow": Give and Take in "Tickets, Please" '. *D. H. Lawrence Review* 10 (fall 1977): 242–50.

THE TRESPASSER
Published: 1st ed.: London, Duckworth, May 1912; 1st American ed.: NY, Kennerley, May 1912.
Recent printings: Heinemann, Phoenix (1935); Penguin (1970).

Criticism: **DIGAETANI, 59**, 66–77; **DRAPER, 62**, 44–50; **EISENSTEIN, 63**, 32–42; **FREEMAN, 67**, 30–5; **MIKO, 100**, 35–58; **NIVEN, 112**, 27–36; **STOLL, 135**, 42–61; **WORTHEN, 148**, 15–25; **YUDHISHTAR, 149**, 73–82.

305 BLISSETT, William. 'D. H. Lawrence, D'Annunzio, Wagner'. *Wisconsin Studies in Contemporary Literature* 7 (winter–spring 1966): 21–46. [D'Annunzio as 'influence and analogue' for *The Trespasser*.]

306 CORKE, Helen. 'The Writing of *The Trespasser*'. *D. H. Lawrence Review* 7 (fall 1974): 227–39.

307 GURKO, Leo. '*The Trespasser:* D. H. Lawrence's Neglected Novel'. *College English* 24 (Oct. 1962): 29–35.

308 HINZ, Evelyn J. '*The Trespasser:* Lawrence's Wagnerian Tragedy and Divine Comedy', *D. H. Lawrence Review* 4 (summer 1971): 122–41.

309 KESTNER, Joseph. 'The Literary Wagnerism of D. H. Lawrence's *The Trespasser*'. *Modern British Literature* 2 (fall 1977): 123–38.

310 MILLETT, Robert. 'Greater Expectations: D. H. Lawrence's *The Trespasser*'. In *Twenty-Seven To One*, ed. by Bradford D. Broughton (Ogdensburg, N.Y.: Ryan P, 1970), pp. 125–32.

311 SHARPE, Michael C. 'The Genesis of D. H. Lawrence's *The Trespasser*'. *Essays in Criticism* 11 (Oct. 1961): 34–9.

312 WRIGHT, Louise. 'Lawrence's *The Trespasser*: Its Debt to Reality'. *Texas Studies in Literature and Language* 20 (summer 1978): 230–48.

'TWO BLUE BIRDS'

Published: *Dial*, Apr. 1927; also *Pall Mall*, June 1928, and *Great Stories of All Nations*, Brentano's, New York, Sept. 1927.

Collected: *The Woman Who Rode Away*, May 1928.

Recent printings: *The Woman Who Rode Away*, Penguin (1970); *Collected Short Stories*, vol. 2, Heinemann, Phoenix (1974); *Complete Short Stories*, vol. 2, Penguin (1976).

Criticism: **JOOST/SULLIVAN, 84**, 126–36 *passim*; **LEAVIS, 88**, 351–5; **TEDLOCK, 137**, 210–11; **WIDMER, 146**, 107–10.

'THE UNDYING MAN' (unfinished story)

Published and collected: *Phoenix*, 1936.

Recent printings: *The Princess and Other Stories*, Penguin (1971); *Phoenix*, Penguin (1978).

313 ZYTARUK, George J. ' "The Undying Man": D. H. Lawrence's Yiddish Story'. *D. H. Lawrence Review* 4 (spring 1971): 20–7.

THE VIRGIN AND THE GIPSY

Published: Separately: G. Orioli, Florence, May 1930; 1st English ed.: London, Secker, Oct. 1930; 1st American ed.: NY, Knopf, Nov. 1930.

Collected: *The Tales of D. H. Lawrence*, Secker, 1934.

Recent printings: *Short Novels*, vol. 2, Heinemann, Phoenix (1956); Bantam (1968); Penguin (1970).

Criticism: **CRAIG, 48**, 21–5; **DRAPER, 61**, 141–4; **LEAVIS, 88**, 362–71; **MOYNAHAN, 106**, 209–18; **TEDLOCK, 137**, 206–8; **WIDMER, 146**, 178–87.

314 GUTIERREZ, Donald. 'Lawrence's *The Virgin and the Gipsy* as Ironic Comedy'. *English Quarterly* (Waterloo, Ontario) 5 (winter 1972–1973): 61–9.
315 MEYERS, Jeffrey. ' "The Voice of Water": Lawrence's *The Virgin and the Gipsy*'. *English Miscellany* 21 (1970): 199–207.
316 PENRITH, Mary. 'Some Structural Patterns in *The Virgin and the Gipsy*'. *University of Cape Town Studies in English* 6 (1976): 46–52.

THE WHITE PEACOCK
Published: 1st ed.: NY, Duffield, 19 Jan. 1911; English impression: London, Heinemann, 20 Jan. 1911.
Recent printings: Penguin (1950); Heinemann, Phoenix (1955); Southern Illinois UP (1966).
Criticism: **ALLDRITT, 35,** 4–15; **CORKE, 16,** 47–55; **DELAVENAY, 58,** 89–97; **DRAPER, 62,** 33–43; **FORD, 66,** 47–55, 57–60; **FREEMAN, 67,** 20–9; **HOUGH, 80,** 23–34; **INNISS, 82,** 108–16; **LITTLEWOOD, 94,** 20–7; **MIKO, 100,** 5–34; **MOYNAHAN, 106,** 5–12; **MURFIN, 107,** 187–98; **MURRY, 109,** 22–30; **NAHAL, 110,** 55–76; **NIVEN, 112,** 10–26; **STOLL, 135,** 16–41; **TEDLOCK, 137,** 40–9; **WORTHEN, 148,** 1–14; **YUDHISHTAR, 149,** 58–73.
317 BEN-EPHRAIM, Gavriel. 'The Pastoral Fallacy: Tale and Teller in D. H. Lawrence's *The White Peacock*'. *Literary Review* 19 (summer 1976): 406–31.
318 GAJDUSEK, Robert E. 'A Reading of "A Poem of Friendship", a Chapter in Lawrence's *The White Peacock*'. *D. H. Lawrence Review* 3 (spring 1970): 47–62.
319 GAJDUSEK, Robert E. 'A Reading of *The White Peacock*'. In Moore, **104,** 188–203.
320 HINZ, Evelyn J. 'Juno and *The White Peacock*: Lawrence's English Epic'. *D. H. Lawrence Review* 3 (summer 1970): 115–35.
321 KEITH, W. J. 'D. H. Lawrence's *The White Peacock*: An Essay in Criticism'. *University of Toronto Quarterly* 37 (Apr. 1968): 230–47.
322 MASON, H. A. 'D. H. Lawrence and *The White Peacock*'. *Cambridge Quarterly* 7, No. 3 (1977): 216–31.
323 MORRISON, Kristin. 'Lawrence, Beardsley, Wilde: *The White Peacock* and Sexual Ambiguity'. *Western Humanities Review* 30 (1976): 241–8.
324 SQUIRES, Michael. 'Lawrence's *The White Peacock*: A Mutation of Pastoral'. *Texas Studies in Literature and Language* 12 (summer 1970): 263–83; rptd. in his *The Pastoral Novel: Studies in George Eliot, Thomas Hardy and D. H. Lawrence* (Charlottesville, Va.: UP of Virginia, 1974), 174–95.

'THE WHITE STOCKING'
Published: *Smart Set*, Oct. 1914.
Collected: *The Prussian Officer*, Nov. 1914.
Recent printings: *The Prussian Officer*, Penguin (1968); *Collected Short Stories*, vol. 1, Heinemann, Phoenix (1974); *Complete Short Stories*, vol. 1, Penguin (1976).
Criticism: **DELAVENAY, 58,** 193–5; **FINNEY, 65,** 322–5; **LEAVIS, 88,** 308–10; **WIDMER, 146,** 145–7.
325 CUSHMAN, Keith. 'The Making of D. H. Lawrence's "The White Stocking" '. *Studies in Short Fiction* 10 (winter 1973): 51–65; rvd. and rptd. in **50,** 148–66.

'THE WILFUL WOMAN'
Published and collected: *The Princess and Other Stories*, Penguin (1971).

'WINTRY PEACOCK'
Published: *Metropolitan*, Aug. 1921; also, in rvd. form, in *The New Decameron III*, Blackwell, June 1922.
Collected: *England, My England*, Oct. 1922 (from the 1921 text).
Recent printings: *England, My England*, Penguin (1970); *Collected Short Stories*, vol. 2, Heinemann, Phoenix (1974); *Complete Short Stories*, vol. 2, Penguin (1976).
Criticism: **TEDLOCK, 137**, 112; **WIDMER, 146**, 110–12.
326 HALL, James B., and Joseph Langland. *The Short Story* (NY: Macmillan, 1956), 250–1.

'THE WITCH À LA MODE'
Published: *Lovat Dickson's Magazine*, June 1934; also *Esquire*, Sept. 1934.
Collected: *A Modern Lover*, Oct. 1934.
Recent printings: *The Mortal Coil and Other Stories*, Penguin (1971); *Collected Short Stories*, vol. 1, Heinemann, Phoenix (1974); *Complete Short Stories*, vol. 1, Penguin (1976).
Criticism: **DIGAETANI, 59**, 64–5; **HARRIS, 74**, 427–30; **TEDLOCK, 137**, 19–21; **WIDMER, 146**, 103–4.

'THE WOMAN WHO RODE AWAY'
Published: *Dial*, July, Aug. 1925; also *New Criterion*, July 1925, Jan. 1926, and *The Best British Short Stories of 1926*.
Collected: *The Woman Who Rode Away*, May 1928.
Recent printings: *Stories, Essays, and Poems*, Dent (1967); *The Woman Who Rode Away*, Penguin (1970); *Collected Short Stories*, vol. 2, Heinemann, Phoenix (1974); *Complete Short Stories*, vol. 2, Penguin (1976).
Criticism: **ALBRIGHT, 33**, 62–9; **CAVITCH, 43**, 163–9; **COWAN, 47**, 70–8; **EISENSTEIN, 63**, 87–113; **HOUGH, 80**, 138–46; **JOOST/SULLIVAN, 84**, 86–9, 122–4, 147–9; **LEAVIS, 88**, 342–6; **MILLETT, 103**, 285–93; **ROSSMAN, 121**, 97–101; **WIDMER, 146**, 29–34.
327 DRAPER, R. P. 'The Defeat of Feminism: D. H. Lawrence's *The Fox* and "The Woman Who Rode Away" ', **177**, 186–98.
328 WASSERSTROM, William. 'Phoenix on Turtle Island: D. H. Lawrence in Henry Adams' America'. *Georgia Review* 32 (spring 1978): 172–97. [Defends DHL's 'good writing' in 'WWRA' against 'ill-intentioned reading' by critics such as Kate Millett and Norman Mailer.]

WOMEN IN LOVE
Published: 1st ed.: NY, privately printed for subscribers only, 9 Nov. 1920; 1st trade, ed: London, Secker, June 1921; 1st ed, English issue: NY, privately, June 1922 [Limited autographed edition].
Recent printings: Heinemann, Phoenix (1954); Viking Compass (1960); Penguin (1976).
Criticism: **ALLDRITT, 35**, 162–218; **CLARKE, 45**, 70–110 and *passim*;

DALESKI, 53, 126–87; **DRAPER, 62,** 157–72; **FORD, 66,** 160–222; **HOWE, 81,** 52–78; **KERMODE, 86,** *passim*; **KINKEAD-WEEKES, 87,** 371–418; **LEAVIS, 88,** 175–241; **LEAVIS, 89,** 62–91; **LERNER, 90,** 191–205; **MIKO, 100,** 215–89; **MOYNAHAN, 106,** 72–91; **MURRY, 29,** 218–27; **NIVEN, 112,** 59–113; **PANICHAS, 113,** 151–79 (rptd. in **114,** 205–28); **SAGAR, 124,** 78–98; **SALE, 125,** 79–105; **SANDERS, 126,** 94–135; **SPILKA, 133,** 121–73; **STOLL, 135,** 151–97; **SWIGG, 136,** 132–86; **VIVAS, 142,** 225–72; **WORTHEN, 148,** 83–104; **YUDHISHTAR, 149,** 160–200.

329 ADAMOWSKI, T. H. 'Being Perfect: Lawrence, Sartre, and *Women in Love*'. *Critical Inquiry* 2 (winter 1975): 345–68.

330 BERTOCCI, Angelo. 'Symbolism in *Women in Love*'. In Moore, **104,** 83–102.

331 CLARKE, Colin (ed.). *D. H. Lawrence: 'The Rainbow' and 'Women in Love'* **255.** [Casebook with pertinent documents and nine previously published articles. Includes new item by Clarke, ' "Living Disintegration": A Scene from *Women in Love* Reinterpreted', 219–34, on 'Moony'.]

332 FORD, George H. 'An Introductory Note to D. H. Lawrence's Prologue to *Women in Love*'. *Texas Quarterly* 4 (spring 1963): 92–7. [Previously unpublished 'Prologue' follows, 98–111.]

333 FORD, George H. ' "The Wedding" Chapter of D. H. Lawrence's *Women in Love*'. *Texas Studies in Literature and Language* 6 (summer 1964): 134–47.

334 HARPER, Howard M., Jr. '*Fantasia* and the Psychodynamics of *Women in Love*'. In *The Classic British Novel,* ed. by Howard M. Harper, Jr. and Charles Edge (Athens, Ga.: U of Georgia P, 1972), 202–19.

335 MIKO, Stephen J. *Twentieth Century Interpretations of 'Women in Love'* (Englewood Cliffs, N.J.: Prentice-Hall, 1969). [Casebook with new essay by David J. Gordon, '*Women in Love* and the Lawrencean Aesthetic', 50–60, and a number of previously published essays.]

336 MILES, Thomas H. 'Birkin's Electro-Mystical Body of Reality: D. H. Lawrence's Use of Kundalini'. *D. H. Lawrence Review* 9 (summer 1976): 194–212. [DHL used his own understanding of Hindu 'kundalini energy' to describe the transcendental experiences between Birkin and Ursula.]

337 OATES, Joyce Carol. 'Lawrence's Götterdämmerung: The Tragic Vision of *Women in Love*'. *Critical Inquiry* 4 (spring 1978): 559–78.

338 RAGUSSIS, Michael. 'D. H. Lawrence: The New Vocabulary of *Women in Love*: Speech and Art Speech'. In his *The Subterfuge of Art: Language and the Romantic Tradition* (Baltimore, Md.: Johns Hopkins UP, 1978), 172–225.

339 REDDICK, Bryan D. 'Point of View and Narrative Tone in *Women in Love*: The Portrayal of Interpsychic Space'. *D. H. Lawrence Review* 7 (summer 1974): 156–71.

340 ROSS, Charles L. *The Composition of 'The Rainbow' and 'Women in Love': A History,* **264.**

341 SAGAR, Keith. 'The Genesis of *The Rainbow* and *Women in Love*', **265,** 179–99.

342 SALGĀDO, Gāmini. 'Taking a Nail for a Walk: On Reading *Women in Love*'. In *The Modern English Novel: The Reader, The Writer, and The Work,* ed. by Gabriel Josipovici (NY: Barnes & Noble, 1977), 95–112.

343 SCHORER, Mark. '*Women in Love* and Death'. *Hudson Review* 6 (spring 1953): 34–47; rptd. as '*Women in Love*', in Hoffman/Moore, **76**, 163–77; rptd. in Spilka, **132**, 50–60; rptd. in Schorer's *The World We Imagine* (NY: Farrar, Straus & Giroux, 1968), 107–21.

344 SPILKA, Mark. 'Lawrence Up-Tight, or the Anal Phase Once Over'. *Novel* 4 (spring 1971): 252–67. [Discussion of the significance of anal sex/genital sex; see also George Ford, Frank Kermode, Colin Clarke, and Mark Spilka, 'Critical Exchange: On "Lawrence Up-Tight": Four Tail-Pieces'. *Novel* 5 (fall 1971): 54–70.]

345 VITOUX, Pierre. 'The Chapter "Excurse" in *Women in Love*: Its Genesis and The Critical Problem'. *Texas Studies in Literature and Language* 17 (winter 1976): 821–36.

346 WILLIAMS, Raymond. 'Tolstoy, Lawrence, and Tragedy'. *Kenyon Review* 25 (autumn 1963): 633–50; rvd. and rptd. as 'Social and Personal Tragedy: Tolstoy and Lawrence', in his *Modern Tragedy* (London: Chatto & Windus; Stanford, Cal.: Stanford UP, 1966), 121–38. [*Anna Karenina* and *W in L*.]

'YOU TOUCHED ME'
Published: *Land and Water*, 29 Apr. 1920.
Collected: *England, My England*, Oct. 1922.
Recent printings: *England, My England*, Penguin (1970); *Collected Short Stories*, vol. 2, Heinemann, Phoenix (1974); *Complete Short Stories*, vol. 2, Penguin (1976).
Criticism: **LEAVIS, 88**, 315–21; **LERNER, 90**, 206–8; **MACKENZIE, 95**, 134–6; **TEDLOCK, 137**, 113–14; **WIDMER, 146**, 57–9.

VI POETRY

COLLECTIONS OF LAWRENCE'S POETRY (in alphabetical order)
AMORES (London: Duckworth, July 1916; NY: Huebsch, 1916).
BAY: A BOOK OF POEMS (London: Beaumont P, Nov. 1919).
BIRDS, BEASTS AND FLOWERS (NY: Seltzer, Oct. 1923; London: Secker, Nov. 1923). [Secker edition, only, includes *Tortoises*.]
THE COLLECTED POEMS OF D. H. LAWRENCE 2 vols. (London: Secker, Sept. 1928; NY: Jonathan Cape & Harrison Smith, 1928).
LAST POEMS, ed. by Richard Aldington and Giuseppi Orioli (Florence: G. Orioli, Oct. 1932; NY: Viking, March 1933; London: Heinemann, 1935). ['Introduction' by Aldington, pp. xi–xxii in 1932 ed. It is rptd. in *The Complete Poems*.]
LOOK! WE HAVE COME THROUGH! (London: Chatto, Dec. 1917; NY: Huebsch, 1918).
LOVE POEMS AND OTHERS (London: Duckworth, Feb. 1913; NY: Kennerly, 1913).
NETTLES (London: Faber & Faber, Mar. 1930).
NEW POEMS (London: Secker, Oct. 1918; NY: Huebsch, 1920).
PANSIES (London: Secker, July 1929 [expurgated ed.]; London: privately printed for subscribers only by P. R. Stephenson, Aug. 1929 [unexpurgated definitive ed.];

NY: Knopf, Sept. 1929 [expurgated American ed.]).

TORTOISES (NY: Seltzer, Dec. 1921). [Included in English ed. of *Birds, Beasts and Flowers*, Nov. 1923.]

UNLESS OTHERWISE NOTED, THE POEMS MENTIONED BELOW ARE PRINTED IN

THE COMPLETE POEMS OF D. H. LAWRENCE, collected and edited by Vivian de Sola Pinto and Warren Roberts, 2 vols. (London: Heinemann, 1964); reissued in 1 vol. with corrections (NY: Viking, Compass, 1971); reissued (NY: Penguin, 1977).

SOME OTHER RECENT PRINTINGS OF LAWRENCE'S VERSE

D. H. LAWRENCE: SELECTED POEMS, with introduction by Kenneth Rexroth (NY: New Directions, 1947) (reissued NY: Viking, Compass, 1972). [Rexroth's 'Introduction', pp. 1–23.]

SELECTED POEMS BY D. H. LAWRENCE, ed. by James Reeves (London: Heinemann, 1951) (reissued London: Heinemann Educational Books, 1967). ['Introduction' by Reeves, pp. 1–9.]

D. H. LAWRENCE: POEMS SELECTED FOR YOUNG PEOPLE, ed. by William Cole (London: Macmillan, 1968).

SELECTED POEMS, ed. by Keith Sagar (Harmondsworth: Penguin, 1972). ['Introduction' by Sagar, pp. 11–17.]

GENERAL CRITICISM ON LAWRENCE'S POETRY

347 ALVAREZ, A. 'D. H. Lawrence: The Single State of Man'. In his *The Shaping Spirit: Studies in Modern English and American Poets* (London: Chatto, 1958), also pub. as *Stewards of Excellence* (NY: Scribner's, 1958), 140–61; rptd. in Moore, **104**, 342–59; rptd. in Spender, **131**, 210–24.

348 BAKER, James R. 'Lawrence as Prophetic Poet'. *Journal of Modern Literature* 3 (July 1974): 1219–38. [Focus on DHL's poetry 1920–30.]

349 BARTLETT, Phyllis. 'Lawrence's *Collected Poems*: The Demon Takes Over'. *PMLA* 66 (Sept. 1951): 583–93. [DHL's 'revision' of certain poems.]

350 BLACKMUR, Richard. 'D. H. Lawrence and Expressive Form'. In his *The Double Agent* (NY: Arrow Editions, 1935), pp. 103–20; rptd. in his *Language as Gesture* (NY: Harcourt, Brace, 1952), 286–300. [An 'attack' on DHL as a poet.]

351 DRAPER, R. P. *D. H. Lawrence: The Critical Heritage*, **62**, 177–83 [*Amores*]; 224–31 [*Birds, Beasts and Flowers*]; 121–31, 137–40 [*Look! We Have Come Through!*] 51–7, 224–7 [*Love Poems*]; 306–14 [*Pansies*]; 299–305 [*Collected Poems*, 1928].

352 EISENSTEIN, Samuel A. *Boarding the Ship of Death*, **63**, 149–58 [*Ship of Death*.]

353 GARCIA, Reloy, and James Karabatsos (eds.). *A Concordance to the Poetry of D. H. Lawrence* (Lincoln, Nebr.: U of Nebraska P, 1970). [Word index keyed to *Complete Poems* (1964).]

354 GILBERT, Sandra M. *Acts of Attention: The Poems of D. H. Lawrence* (Ithaca, N.Y.: Cornell UP, 1972). [*Look! We Have Come Through!*, 73–115; *Birds, Beasts and Flowers*, 119–89; *Pansies*, 207–30, 243–61; *Nettles*, 207–30;

More Pansies, 243–61; *Last Poems*, 265–318.]

355 GREGORY, Horace. *Pilgrim of the Apocalypse* (1957), **72,** 1–16 [*Amores, Love Poems*]; 28–34 [*Look! We Have Come Through!*] 109–18 [*Pansies, Nettles, Last Poems*].

356 HASSALL, Christopher. 'Black Flowers: A New Light on the Poetics of D. H. Lawrence'. In Moore, **104,** 370–7; also pub. in enlgd. form as 'D. H. Lawrence and the Etruscans'. *Essays by Divers Hands*, n.s. 31 (1962): 61–78.

357 HEHNER, Barbara. ' "Kissing and Horrid Strife": Male and Female in the Early Poetry of D. H. Lawrence'. *Four Decades of Poetry, 1890–1930* 1 (Jan. 1976): 3–26.

358 HOLBROOK, David. *The Quest for Love*, **77,** 334–56 [*Look! We Have Come Through!*].

359 HOUGH, Graham. *The Dark Sun*, **80,** 191–216 [Ch. 4, 'The Poems'].

360 INNISS, Kenneth. *D. H. Lawrence's Bestiary*, **82,** 57–65 [*Look! We Have Come Through!*]; 65–90 [*Birds, Beasts and Flowers*]; 90–105 [*Pansies and Last Poems*].

361 JANIK, Del Ivan. 'D. H. Lawrence's "Future Religion": The Unity of *Last Poems*'. *Texas Studies in Literature and Language* 16 (winter 1975): 739–54. [Thematic and formal patterns follows outlines of DHL's 'Future Religion'.]

362 JENNINGS, Elizabeth. 'D. H. Lawrence: A Vision of the Natural World'. In her *Seven Men of Genius* NY: Barnes & Noble, 1976), 45–80. [Discusses many DHL poems, often in some detail.]

363 JONES, R. T. 'D. H. Lawrence's Poetry: Art and the Apprehension of Fact'. In Gomme, **69,** 175–89.

364 JOOST, Nicholas, and Alvin Sullivan. *D. H. Lawrence and 'The Dial'*, **84,** 38–40, 160–3 ['Apostolic Beasts']; 38–41, 156–69, 188–90 [*Birds, Beasts and Flowers*]; 106–13, 156–8, 169–78 [*Pansies*].

365 KENMARE, Dallas. *Fire-bird: A Study of D. H. Lawrence* (London: James Barrie, 1951; NY: Philosophical Library, 1952).

366 KIRKHAM, Michael. 'D. H. Lawrence's *Last Poems*'. *D. H. Lawrence Review* 5 (summer 1972): 97–120.

367 LUCIE-SMITH, Edward. 'The Poetry of D. H. Lawrence – with a Glance at Shelley'. In Spender, **131,** 224–33.

368 MARSHALL, Tom. *The Psychic Mariner: A Reading of the Poems of D. H. Lawrence* (NY: Viking, 1970). [*Look! We Have Come Through!*, 70–93; *Birds, Beasts and Flowers*, 116–59 (*Tortoises*, 144–9); Poems from *The Plumed Serpent*, 159–63; *Pansies*, 164–83 and 191–4; *Last Poems*, 195–225. Includes useful bibliography of critical works on DHL's poems, 262–7.]

369 OATES, Joyce Carol. *The Hostile Sun: The Poetry of D. H. Lawrence* (Los Angeles, Cal.: Black Sparrow P, 1973).

370 PANICHAS, George. *Adventure in Consciousness: The Meaning of D. H. Lawrence's Religious Quest*, **113,** 180–207 [*Last Poems*].

371 PINION, F. B. *A D. H. Lawrence Companion: Life, Thought, and Works*, **115,** 93–126 [102–6, *Look! We Have Come Through!*; 106–14, *Birds, Beasts and Flowers*; 115–18, *Pansies*].

372 PINTO, Vivian de Sola. 'Poet without a Mask'. *Critical Quarterly* 3, No. 1

(spring 1961): 5–18; rptd. in Spilka, **132**, 127–41; and rvd. and enlgd. as 'D. H. Lawrence: Poet without a Mask', as the introduction to *Complete Poems* (1964), 1–21.

373 PINTO, Vivian de Sola. 'The Burning Bush: D. H. Lawrence as a Religious Poet'. *Mansions of the Spirit*, ed. by George A. Panichas (NY: Hawthorne, 1967), pp. 213–35.

374 POTTS, Abbie Findlay. 'Pipings of Pan: D. H. Lawrence'. *The Elegiac Mode* (Ithaca, N.Y.: Cornell UP, 1967), pp. 395–432. [Calls DHL the prime English elegist of this century; 410–17 focus on *Look! We Have Come Through!* poems.]

375 PRITCHARD, William. *Seeing Through Everything: English Writers 1918–1940*, **119**, 114–33.

376 SAGAR, Keith. *The Art of D. H. Lawrence*, **124**, 119–29 [*Birds, Beasts and Flowers*]; 231–3 [*Pansies*]; 236–40 [*More Pansies*]; 239–45 [*Last Poems*].

377 SHAKIR, Evelyn. ' "Secret Sin": Lawrence's Early Verse'. *D. H. Lawrence Review* 8 (summer 1975): 155–75.

378 SLOTE, Bernice. 'The *Leaves* of D. H. Lawrence'. In Miller/Shapiro/Slote, **102**, 71–98. [Notes strong resemblances of DHL's poetry to that of Whitman.]

379 SMAILES, T. A. *Some Comments on the Verse of D. H. Lawrence* (Port Elizabeth, South Africa: U of Port Elizabeth, 1970). [Discusses *Look! We Have Come Through!*, 20–35; *Birds, Beasts and Flowers*, 36–51; *Pansies* and *Last Poems*, 52–72.]

380 SULLIVAN, Alvin. 'D. H. Lawrence and *Poetry*: The Unpublished Manuscripts'. *D. H. Lawrence Review* 9 (summer 1976): 266–77. [Discusses documents in U of Chicago Regenstein Library which concern DHL's relationship with *Poetry*.]

381 VICKERY, John B. 'D. H. Lawrence's Poetry: Myth and Matter'. *D. H. Lawrence Review* 7 (spring 1974): 1–18.

382 YOUNGBLOOD, Sarah. 'Substance and Shadow: The Self in Lawrence's Poetry'. *D. H. Lawrence Review* 1 (summer 1968): 114–28. [Concentrates on *Look! We Have Come Through!* and *Birds, Beasts and Flowers*.]

STUDIES OF INDIVIDUAL POEMS

'BABY TORTOISES' (see Tortoises)

'BALLAD OF A WILFUL WOMAN'
Published and collected: *Look! We Have Come Through!*, 1917.

383 MITCHELL, Judith. 'Lawrence's "Ballad of a Wilful Woman" '. *Explicator* 36, No. 4 (1978): 4–6.

'BAVARIAN GENTIANS'
Published and collected: *Last Poems*, 1932. ['Appendix' to *Last Poems* includes another version of 'Bavarian Gentians'. Both versions are reprinted in *Complete Poems*.]

Criticism: **GILBERT, 354**, 293–9; **JENNINGS, 362**, 76–8; **MARSHALL, 368**, 52–3, 202–5; **SMAILES, 379**, 63–6; **VICKERY, 381**, 16–18.

384 HARVEY, R. W. 'On Lawrence's "Bavarian Gentians" '. *Wascana Review* 1 (1966): 74–86. [Traces the poem's evolution from its original form as 'Glory of

Darkness'.]
385 SAGAR, Keith. 'The Genesis of "Bavarian Gentians"'. *D. H. Lawrence Review* 8 (spring 1975): 47–53. [Contends the version printed in 'Appendix' to *Last Poems* is 'not only the final version . . . but also the best'.]

'THE BRIDE'
Published and collected: *Amores*, 1916. [Included in *Young Lorenzo* **20**, 1932, in different version titled 'The Dead Mother'.]
Criticism: **GILBERT, 354,** 65–9; **MARSHALL, 368,** 49–50.
386 PITTOCK, Malcolm. 'Lawrence the Poet'. *Times Literary Supplement,* 2 Sept. 1965, 755. [Letter to editor about omission of an earlier version of 'The Bride' from Pinto and Roberts's *The Complete Poems of D. H. Lawrence*. Both versions, as 'The Dead Mother' and 'The Bride', are reprinted and briefly compared.]

'ELOI, ELOI, LAMA SABACHTHANI?'
Published: *Egoist*, 1 May 1915; rptd. in *Modern Language Notes*, June 1952, and in *Complete Poems*.
387 SULLIVAN, Alvin, 380, 269–71. [Presents a previously unpublished early version and briefly discusses DHL's revisions.]
388 TEDLOCK, E. W., Jr. 'A Forgotten War Poem by D. H. Lawrence'. *Modern Language Notes* 67 (June 1952): 410–13. [Reprints and offers brief commentary.]

'EMBANKMENT AT NIGHT, BEFORE THE WAR, CHARITY'
Published and collected: *New Poems*, Oct. 1918.
389 SMAILES, T. A. 'The Evolution of a Lawrence Poem'. *Standpunte* 89 (June 1970): 40–2. [Compares three versions of poem.]

'FISH'
Published: *English Review*, June 1922.
Collected: *Birds, Beasts and Flowers*, 1923.
Criticism: **GILBERT, 354,** 169–73; **MARSHALL, 368,** 138–40; **MURFIN, 107,** 217–18.
390 CAVITCH, David. 'Merging – with Fish and Others'. *D. H. Lawrence Review* 7 (summer 1974): 172–8. [Analysis.]
391 LANGBAUM, Robert. *The Modern Spirit: Essays on the Continuity of Nineteenth and Twentieth Century Literature* (NY: Oxford UP, 1970), pp. 114–18.

'HOW BEASTLY THE BOURGEOIS IS'
Published and collected: *Pansies*, 1929.
392 LERNER, Laurence. 'How Beastly the Bourgeois Is'. *Critical Survey* 1 (spring 1963): 87–9; rptd. in **90,** 220–4.

'LIGHTNING'
Published: *Nation*, 4 Nov. 1911.
Collected: *Love Poems and Others*, 1913. [A revised version appears in *The Collected Poems of D. H. Lawrence*. Both versions are reprinted in *Complete Poems*.]
393 GUTIERREZ, Donald. 'The Pressures of Love: Kinesthetic Action in an Early

Lawrence Poem'. *Contemporary Poetry* 1 (winter 1973): 6–20.

'LUI ET ELLE' *(see Tortoises)*

'THE MAN OF TYRE'
Published and collected: *Last Poems*, 1932.
Criticism: **GILBERT, 354,** 278–80; **JONES, 363,** 181–4; **KIRKHAM, 366,** 112–16; **SMAILES, 379,** 59–61.
394 SMAILES, T. A. 'Lawrence's Verse: More Editorial Lapses'. *Notes and Queries* n.s. 17 (Dec. 1970): 465–66. [Notes mistakes in Pinto & Roberts's editing of *Complete Poems*, and refutes an editorial note on 'The Man of Tyre'.]

'PIANO'
Published and collected: *New Poems*, 1918.
Earlier version published: as 'The Piano', in an article by Vivian de Sola Pinto in *Renaissance and Modern Studies* 1957 **116.**
Earlier version collected: as 'The Piano' in Appendix III of *Complete Poems* (1964).
Criticism: **GILBERT, 354,** 47–9; **MARSHALL, 368,** 55–6; **PINTO, 116,** 26–8; **SMAILES, 379.** 30–1.
395 BLEICH, David. 'The Determination of Literary Value'. *Literature and Psychology* 17 (1967): 19–30. [Discusses students' response to 'Piano' reported by I. A. Richards in **397.**]
396 LEAVIS, F. R. ' "Thought" and Emotional Quality'. *The Living Principle* (London: Chatto, 1975), pp. 75–9. [Contrasts 'Piano' with Tennyson's 'Break, break, break'.]
397 RICHARDS, I. A. 'Poem 8'. *Practical Criticism* (London: K. Paul, Trench, Trubner; N.Y.: Harcourt, Brace, 1929; rptd. paperback ed., 1966), 99–112.

'THE RED WOLF'
Published and collected: *Birds, Beasts and Flowers*, 1923.
Criticism: **MARSHALL, 368,** 156–8.
398 SAGAR, Keith. 'D. H. Lawrence'. *Times Literary Supplement*, 10 Sept. 1971, 1086. [Letter to editor on a textual matter.]

'RESURRECTION'
Published: *Poetry*, June 1917; also in *The New Poetry*, May 1923.
Collected: *The Complete Poems of D. H. Lawrence*, 1964.
399 SULLIVAN, Alvin, 380, 271–3. [Discusses two versions of 'Resurrection' which differ from the poem as published in the 1971 ed. of *Complete Poems*, and lists variants.]

'THE SHIP OF DEATH'
Published and collected: *Last Poems*, 1932. [Two other versions of the poem are printed in 'Appendix' here. All three versions are reprinted in *Complete Poems*.]
Criticism: **EISENSTEIN, 63,** 151–8; **GILBERT, 354,** 307–13, 316–18; **JANIK, 361,** 749–52; **MARSHALL, 368,** 51–2, 215–22; **PANICHAS, 113,** 197–207; **SMAILES, 379,** 66–71.
400 HONIG, Edwin. 'Lawrence: The Ship of Death'. In *Master Poems of The English Language*, ed. by Oscar Williams (NY: Washington Square P, 1967), pp.

954–7.

401 ORRELL, Herbert M. 'D. H. Lawrence: Poet of Death and Resurrection'. *The Cresset* 34 (Mar. 1971): 10–13. ['The Ship of Death' compared to Donne's 'Holy Sonnet X'.]

'SNAKE'
Published: *Dial*, July 1921; also in *London Mercury*, Oct. 1921, and *Georgian Poetry 1920–1922*, 1922.
Collected: *Birds, Beasts and Flowers*, Oct. 1923.
Criticism: **GILBERT, 354,** 134–5, 173–5; **HOUGH, 79,** 94–7; **JENNINGS, 362,** 45–50; **JOOST/SULLIVAN, 84,** 162–9; **MARSHALL, 368,** 140–4; **MOORE, 28,** 318–20; **PRITCHARD, William, 119,** 128–30; **SAGAR, 124,** 120–6; **SMAILES, 379,** 39–41.

402 BRASHEAR, Lucy M. 'Lawrence's Companion Poems: "Snake" and *Tortoises'*. *D. H. Lawrence Review* 5 (spring 1972): 54–62.

403 DALTON, Robert O. ' "Snake": A Moment of Consciousness'. *Brigham Young University Studies* 4 (spring–summer 1962): 243–53.

404 SMITH, L. E. W. 'Snake'. *Critical Survey* 1 (spring 1963): 81–6.

405 YOUNG, Archibald M. 'Rhythms and Meaning in Poetry: D. H. Lawrence's "Snake" '. *English* 17 (summer 1968): 41–7.

'SONG OF A MAN WHO HAS COME THROUGH'
Published and collected: *Look! We Have Come Through!*, 1917.
Criticism: **GILBERT, 354,** 104–8; **JENNINGS, 362,** 79–80; **MARSHALL, 368,** 83–6; **SMAILES, 379,** 28–9.

406 STEINBERG, Erwin R. ' "Song of a Man Who Has Come Through" – A Pivotal Poem'. *D. H. Lawrence Review* 11 (spring 1978): 50–62.

407 ZANGER, Jules. 'D. H. Lawrence's Three Strange Angels'. *Papers on English Language and Literature* 1 (spring 1965): 184–7. [Identifies 'three strange angels', says poem celebrates DHL's marriage.]

'SORROW'
Published: *Poetry*, Dec. 1914 (as 'Weariness').
Collected: *Amores*, 1916.
Criticism: **GILBERT, 354,** 64–5; **MARSHALL, 368,** 50–1.

408 ARBUR, Rosemarie. ' "Lilacs" and "Sorrow": Whitman's Effect on the Early Poems of D. H. Lawrence'. *Walt Whitman Review* 24 (Mar. 1978): 17–21.

TORTOISES ('Baby Tortoises', 'Tortoise Shell', 'Tortoise Family Connections', 'Lui et Elle', 'Tortoise Gallantry', 'Tortoise Shout')
Published: *Tortoises*, NY, Seltzer, 1921. [The poems were reprinted in the Nov. 1923 edition of *Birds, Beasts and Flowers* (London: Secker). They were not published separately in England.]
Criticism: **GILBERT, 354,** 186–8 ('Tortoise Shout'); **MARSHALL, 368,** 145–9; **SAGAR, 124,** 127–8.

409 BLOOM, Harold. 'Lawrence, Blackmur, Eliot, and the Tortoise'. In Moore, **104,** 360–9.

410 BRASHEAR, Lucy M. 'Lawrence's Companion Poems: 'Snake' and *Tortoises'*,

402, 54–62.

411 SAGAR, Keith. ' "Little Living Myths": A Note on Lawrence's *Tortoises*'. *D. H. Lawrence Review* 3 (summer 1970): 161–7.

'THE TURNING BACK'
Published: *D. H. Lawrence Review*, summer 1972. [A fragment of the poem appeared as 'We Have Gone Too Far' in *Complete Poems*. It had first appeared in a letter to Lady Cynthia Asquith, 2 Nov. 1915, printed in *The Letters of D. H. Lawrence* (1932).]

412 FARMER, David. 'D. H. Lawrence's "The Turning Back": The Text and Its Genesis in Correspondence'. *D. H. Lawrence Review* 5 (summer 1972): 121–31. [Full poem printed here for first time, with commentary.]

'WE HAVE GONE TOO FAR' (*see* 'THE TURNING BACK')

'WEDDING MORN'
Published and collected: *Love Poems and Others*, 1913.

413 MITRA, A. K. 'Revisions in Lawrence's "Wedding Morn" '. *Notes and Queries* n.s. 16 (July 1969): 260.

VII NON-FICTION PROSE

IN ADDITION TO THE SEPARATE NON-FICTION PUBLICATIONS CITED BELOW, MANY OF LAWRENCE'S SHORTER ESSAYS APPEARED IN THESE COLLECTIONS
PHOENIX: THE POSTHUMOUS PAPERS OF D. H. LAWRENCE, ed. by Edward D. McDonald (London: Heinemann; NY: Viking, 1936) (rptd. Penguin, 1978).

PHOENIX II: UNCOLLECTED, UNPUBLISHED, AND OTHER PROSE WORKS BY D. H. LAWRENCE, ed. by Warren Roberts and Harry T. Moore (London: Heinemann; NY: Viking, 1968) (rptd. Penguin, 1978).

APOCALYPSE
Published: Florence, G. Orioli, June 1931; 1st English ed.: London, May 1932; 1st American ed.: NY, Viking, Nov. 1931.

Recent Printing: Penguin (1977).

Criticism: **CARTER, 14**, 59–62 and *passim*; **CORKE, 16**, 57–132; **GOODHEART, 70**, 42–50; **GREGORY, 72**, 102–8.

414 CLARK, L. D. 'The Apocalypse of Lorenzo'. *D. H. Lawrence Review* 3 (summer 1970): 141–60.

415 GUTIERREZ, Donald. ' "New Heaven and an Old Earth", D. H. Lawrence's *Apocalypse*, Apocalyptic, and the *Book of Revelation*'. *Review of Existential Psychology and Psychiatry* 14, No. 1 (1977): 61–85.

'ART AND THE INDIVIDUAL'
Published: *Young Lorenzo* **20**, 1932.

Recent printing: *Phoenix II*, Penguin (1978).

Criticism: **DELAVENAY, 56**, 170–6.

416 PITTOCK, Malcolm. 'Lawrence's "Art and the Individual" '. *Études Anglaises* 26 (July–Sept. 1973): 312–19.

'THE CROWN'
Published: *Signature*, 4 Oct., 18 Oct., 4 Nov. 1915.
Collected: *Reflections on the Death of a Porcupine* (Philadelphia, Pa.: Centaur P, 1925; London: Secker, 1934).
Recent printing: *Reflections on the Death of a Porcupine*, Indiana UP (1963); also in *Phoenix II*, Penguin (1978).
Criticism: **DELANY, 55,** 146–52; **DELAVENAY, 58,** 327–36 and *passim*; **KINKEAD-WEEKES, 87,** 393–9; **MIKO, 100,** 204–14; **PINION, 115,** 72–5.
417 BEKER, Miroslav. ' "The Crown", "The Reality of Peace", and *Women in Love'. D. H. Lawrence Review* 2 (fall 1969): 254–64. [Uses the essays to interpret the novel.]

'EDUCATION OF THE PEOPLE'
Published: *Phoenix*, 1936.
Recent printing: *Phoenix*, Penguin (1978).
Criticism: **MOORE, 105,** 155–7; **DELAVENAY, 58,** 484–90; **PINION, 115,** 77–80.
418 GATTI, Hilary. 'D. H. Lawrence and the Idea of Education'. *English Miscellany* 21 (1970): 209–31.
419 WALSH, William. 'The Writer as Teacher: The Educational Ideas of D. H. Lawrence'. In his *The Use of Imagination: Educational Thought and the Literary Mind* (London: Chatto & Windus, 1964), 199–228. [Also 'The Writer and The Child', 163–74, discusses Ursula's teaching experience in *The Rainbow*.]

ETRUSCAN PLACES (*see* TRAVEL)

FANTASIA OF THE UNCONSCIOUS (*see* PSYCHOLOGICAL ESSAYS)

'INTRODUCTION TO "MEMOIRS OF THE FOREIGN LEGION" '
Published: In *Memoirs of the Foreign Legion*, by M. M. (London: Secker, 1924).
Collected: *Phoenix II*, 1968.
Recent printing: *Phoenix II*, Penguin (1968).
Criticism: **MOORE, 105; PINION, 115,** 154–6; **PRITCHARD, 118,** 132–4.
420 DOUGLAS, Norman. *D. H. Lawrence and Maurice Magnus: A Plea for Better Manners* (Florence: privately printed, 1924); rptd. in his *Experiments* (London: Chapman & Hall, 1925), 223–64. [Reply to DHL's 'Introduction to Memoirs . . . .' Lawrence's defence in a letter to the *New Statesman* is reprinted in *Phoenix*, 806–7, as 'The Late Mr. Maurice Magnus: A Letter'.]
421 FRASER, Keath. 'Norman Douglas and D. H. Lawrence: A Sideshow in Modern Memoirs'. *D. H. Lawrence Review* 9 (summer 1976): 283–95.

'INTRODUCTION TO THESE PAINTINGS'
Published: as introduction to *The Paintings of D. H. Lawrence*, London, Mandrake P, 1929.
Collected: *Pornography and So On*, London, Faber & Faber, Sept. 1936; also in *Phoenix*, Oct. 1936.

Recent printing: *Phoenix*, Penguin (1978).
Criticism: **GORDON, 433**, 104–6; **REMSBURY, 120**, 122–47.
422 REMSBURY, John and Ann. 'Lawrence and Art'. In Gomme, **69**, 190–218.
423 RICHARDSON, John Adkins, and John I. Ades. 'D. H. Lawrence on Cézanne: A Study in the Psychology of Critical Intuition'. *Journal of Aesthetics and Art Criticism* 28 (summer 1970): 441–53.

LETTERS
(Some Major Collections in chronological order)
THE LETTERS OF D. H. LAWRENCE, ed. by Aldous Huxley (London: Heinemann; NY: Viking, 1932). ['Introduction' by Huxley, pp. ix–xxxiv.]
D. H. LAWRENCE'S LETTERS TO BERTRAND RUSSELL, ed. by Harry T. Moore (NY: Gotham Book Mart, 1948). ['Introduction' by Moore, pp. 1–26.]
THE COLLECTED LETTERS OF D. H. LAWRENCE, 2 vols., ed. by Harry T. Moore (London: Heinemann; NY: Viking, 1962). ['Introduction' by Moore, pp. ix–xxvii.]
LAWRENCE IN LOVE: LETTERS TO LOUIE BURROWS, ed. by James T. Boulton (Nottingham: U of Nottingham, 1968). ['Introduction' by Boulton, pp. vii–xxviii.]
THE QUEST FOR RANANIM, D. H. LAWRENCE'S LETTERS TO S. S. KOTELIANSKY, 1914–1930, ed. by George J. Zytaruk (Montreal: McGill–Queens UP, 1970). ['Introduction' by Zytaruk, pp. xi–xxxvi.]
LETTERS FROM D. H. LAWRENCE TO MARTIN SECKER 1911–1930, ed. by Martin Secker (Bridgefoot, Iver, Bucks, England: privately published, 1970).
THE CENTAUR LETTERS, ed. by F. W. Roberts (Austin, Tex.: Humanities Research Center, U of Texas, 1970). [Thirty DHL letters to Edward D. McDonald and Harold T. Mason.]
LETTERS TO THOMAS AND ADELE SELTZER, ed. by Gerald M. Lacy (Santa Barbara, Calif.: Black Sparrow P, 1976).
THE LETTERS OF D. H. LAWRENCE, VOLUME I: SEPTEMBER 1901–MAY 1913, ed. by James T. Boulton (Cambridge: Cambridge UP, 1979). ['Introduction' by Boulton, pp. 1–20; this Cambridge edition will eventually contain some 5,500 letters and postcards in all, many of them published for the first time.]

COMMENTARIES ON LAWRENCE'S LETTERS
424 CAZAMIAN, Louis. 'D. H. Lawrence and Katherine Mansfield as Letter Writers'. *University of Toronto Quarterly* 3 (Apr. 1934): 286–307.
425 DONOGHUE, Denis. ' "Till the Fight is Finished": D. H. Lawrence in His Letters'. In Spender, **131**, 197–209.
426 GREGORY, Horace, 72, 92–102.
427 LEAVIS, F. R. ' "Lawrence Scholarship" and Lawrence'. *Sewanee Review* (winter 1963); rptd. in his *Anna Karenina and Other Essays* (London: Chatto, 1967), 167–76. [A hostile reaction to Moore's edition of the letters.]
428 MOORE, Harry T. 'Some New Volumes of Lawrence's Letters'. *D. H. Lawrence Review* 4 (spring 1971): 61–71. [Review essay on *Lawrence in Love*; *The Quest for Rananim*; and *Letters from D. H. Lawrence to Martin Secker*.]
429 PANICHAS, George, 113, 62–94.

430 PINTO, Vivian de Sola, 116, 5–10.

LITERARY CRITICISM
(a) **General**; (b) *Studies in Classic American Literature*; (c) **'Study of Thomas Hardy'**

(a) **General**
SOME RECENT EDITIONS OF LAWRENCE'S CRITICAL WRITINGS
D. H. LAWRENCE: SELECTED LITERARY CRITICISM, ed. by Anthony Beal
   (London: Heinemann, 1955; NY: Viking, Compass, 1966; London: Heinemann
   Educational Books, 1967).
STUDIES IN CLASSIC AMERICAN LITERATURE (London: Heinemann,
   Phoenix, 1964; Penguin, 1977).
PHOENIX, Penguin (1978), and *PHOENIX II*, Penguin (1978).

COMMENTARIES ON LAWRENCE'S CRITICAL WRITINGS
431 CURA-SAZDANIC, Ileana. *D. H. Lawrence as Critic* (Delhi: Munshiram
   Manoharlal, 1969).
432 FOSTER, Richard. 'Criticism as Rage: D. H. Lawrence'. In Moore, **104,**
   312–25.
433 GORDON, David J. *D. H. Lawrence as a Literary Critic* (New Haven, Conn.,
   & London: Yale UP [Yale Studies in English, vol. 161], 1966).
434 KLINGOPULOS, G. D. 'L's Criticism'. *Essays in Criticism* 7 (July 1957):
   294–303. [Review article on *D. H. Lawrence: Selected Literary Criticism*, ed. by
   Anthony Beal.]
435 PINION, F. B., 155, 275–84.
436 SALGÃDO, Gãmini. 'D. H. Lawrence as Literary Critic'. *London Magazine* 7
   (Feb. 1960): 49–57.
437 SITESH, Aruna. *D. H. Lawrence: The Crusader as Critic* (Delhi, Bombay,
   Calcutta, Madras: Macmillan, 1975).
438 WHITE, Richard L. 'D. H. Lawrence the Critic: Theories of English and
   American Fiction'. *D. H. Lawrence Review* 11 (summer 1978): 156–74.

(b) *Studies in Classic American Literature*
Published: All but four essays (the two on Melville, the one on Dana, and that on
   Hawthorne's *Blithedale Romance*) were first published in magazines (usually
   English Review) between Nov. 1918 and July 1921; 1st collected ed.: NY, Seltzer,
   Aug. 1923; 1st English ed.: London, Secker, June 1924; 1st ed., early version:
   under title *The Symbolic Meaning: The Uncollected Versions of 'Studies in Classic
   American Literature'*, ed. by Armin Arnold. London, Centaur P. May 1962.
Recent printings: *Studies in Classic American Literature*, Heinemann, Phoenix
   (1964); Penguin (1977).
Criticism: **COWAN, 47,** 24–33; **DRAPER, 62,** 208–13; **GORDON, 433,** 127–9,
   133–40; **PRITCHARD R. E., 118,** 117–25 (on *The Symbolic Meaning*);
   SWIGG, 136, 283–308 (on *The Symbolic Meaning*) and 345–62 (on *Studies . . .*);
   SELIGMANN, 128, 62–73.
439 ARNOLD, Armin. 38, 28–102. [Major study of *SCAL*.]
440 GRANT, Douglas. 'Hands Up, America!' *Review of English Literature* 4, No. iv

(1963).

441 PIERLE, Robert C. 'D. H. Lawrence's *Studies in Classic American Literature*: An Evaluation'. *Southern Quarterly* 6 (Apr. 1966): 333–40.

442 SCHNEIDERMAN, Leo. 'Notes on D. H. Lawrence's *Studies in Classic American Literature*'. *Connecticut Review* 1 (Apr. 1968): 57–71.

443 WEST, Paul. 'D. H. Lawrence: Mystical Critic'. *Southern Review*, n.s. 1 (Jan. 1965): 210–28; rvd. and enlgd. in his *The Wine of Absurdity* (University Park, Pa., and London: Pennsylvania State UP, 1966), pp. 19–38. [Review essay on *The Symbolic Meaning*.]

(c) 'Study of Thomas Hardy'

Published: Chapter 3 in *Book Collector's Quarterly*, Jan.–Mar. 1932 (as 'Six Novels of Thomas Hardy and the Real Tragedy'). The entire essay, *Phoenix*, 1936.

Recent printings: *Phoenix*, Penguin (1978); also in *D. H. Lawrence: Selected Literary Criticism*, Heinemann Educational Books (1967).

Criticism: **ALCORN, 34**, 78–89; **DALESKI, 53**, 24–32; **DELANY, 55**, 30–6; **DELAVENAY, 58**, 296–327; **HOCHMAN, 75**, 4–21; **MIKO, 100**, 186–204; **SWIGG, 136**, 58–80.

444 BEARDS, Richard D. 'D. H. Lawrence and the "Study of Thomas Hardy", His Victorian Predecessor'. *D. H. Lawrence Review* 2 (fall 1969): 210–29.

445 KINKEAD-WEEKES, Mark. 'Lawrence on Hardy'. In *Thomas Hardy after Fifty Years*, ed. by Lance St John Butler (Totowa, N.J.: Rowman & Littlefield, 1977): 90–103.

MORNINGS IN MEXICO (see TRAVEL)

MOVEMENTS IN EUROPEAN HISTORY

Published: London, Oxford UP, Feb. 1921 (under pseudonym 'Lawrence H. Davison').

Recent printing: Oxford UP (1971) [with previously unpublished Epilogue].

Criticism: **COWAN, 47**, 8–11; **DELAVENAY, 58**, 491–3; **MOORE, 105**, 147–9.

446 BOULTON, James T. 'Introduction to the New Edition' of *Movements in European History* by D. H. Lawrence (Oxford: Oxford UP, 1971), pp. vii–xxiv.

447 HINZ, Evelyn J. 'History as Education and Art: D. H. Lawrence's *Movements in European History*'. *Modern British Literature* 2 (fall 1977): 139–52.

PSYCHOLOGICAL ESSAYS

FANTASIA OF THE UNCONSCIOUS published: NY, Seltzer, Oct. 1922; 1st English ed.: London, Secker, Sept. 1923.

PSYCHOANALYSIS AND THE UNCONSCIOUS published: NY, Seltzer, May 1921; 1st English ed.: London, Secker, July 1923.

Recent printing: In *Fantasia of the Unconscious and Psychoanalysis and the Unconscious*, Heinemann, Phoenix (1961); Penguin (1978).

Criticism: **COWAN, 47**, 15–24; **DRAPER, 62**, 184–7 (*Fantasia*); 219–20 (*both*); **GOODHEART, 70**, 103–15; **LEAVIS, 89**, 20–8; **MOORE, 105**, 157–61 (*Fantasia*): **MURRY, 29**, 237–42 (*Fantasia*); **PRITCHARD, 118**, 125–8 (*Psychoanalysis*); 200–5 (*Fantasia*); **PINION, 115**, 82–8.

448 HARPER, Howard M., Jr. '*Fantasia* and the Psychodynamics of *Women in Love*', **334**, 202–19.

449 HINZ, Evelyn J. 'The Beginning and the End: D. H. Lawrence's *Psychoanalysis* and *Fantasia*'. *Dalhousie Review* 52 (summer 1972): 251–65.

450 RIEFF, Philip. 'Introduction' to *Psychoanalysis and the Unconscious and Fantasia of the Unconscious* by D. H. Lawrence (NY: Viking P, 1960), vii–xxiii.

451 RIEFF, Philip. 'The Therapeutic as Mythmaker: Lawrence's True Christian Philosophy'. In his *The Triumph of the Therapeutic: Uses of Faith After Freud* (NY: Harper & Row; London: Chatto & Windus, 1966) (rptd. NY: Harper & Row, Harper Torchbooks, 1968), pp. 189–231.

452 ROBERTS, Mark. 'D. H. Lawrence and the Failure of Energy'. In his *The Tradition of Romantic Morality* (London: Macmillan; NY: Barnes & Noble, 1973), pp. 322–48. [DHL's 'doctrine' as set down in *Fantasia* and *Psychoanalysis*.]

'THE REALITY OF PEACE'

Published: *English Review*, May, June, July, Aug. 1917.
Collected: *Phoenix*, 1936.
Recent printing: *Phoenix*, Penguin (1978).
Criticism: **DELANY, 55**, 284–91; **DELAVENAY, 58**, 452–55; **MOORE, 105**, 151–3.

453 BEKER, Miroslav. ' "The Crown", "The Reality of Peace", and *Women in Love*'. **417**, 254–64.

SEA AND SARDINIA (*see* TRAVEL)

STUDIES IN CLASSIC AMERICAN LITERATURE (*see* LITERARY CRITICISM)

'STUDY OF THOMAS HARDY' (*see* LITERARY CRITICISM)

TRANSLATIONS

TRANSLATIONS BY LAWRENCE

CAVALLERIA RUSTICANA AND OTHER STORIES, by Giovanni Verga (London: Cape; NY: Dial P, 1928).

'THE GENTLEMAN FROM SAN FRANCISCO', in Ivan Bunin's *The Gentleman from San Francisco and Other Stories*, trans. by S. S. Koteliansky and Leonard Woolf (London: Hogarth P, 1922). [DHL collaborated with Koteliansky in translating Bunin's title story.]

LITTLE NOVELS OF SICILY, by Giovanni Verga (NY: Seltzer; Oxford: Blackwell, 1925; Harmondsworth: Penguin, 1973).

MASTRO-DON GESUALDO, by Giovanni Verga (NY: Seltzer, 1923; London, Cape, 1925; Harmondsworth: Penguin, 1970).

THE STORY OF DOCTOR MANENTE: BEING THE TENTH AND LAST STORY FROM THE SUPPERS OF A. F. GRAZZINI CALLED IL LASCA (Florence: G. Orioli, 1929; London: Grey, 1930).

COMMENTARIES ON LAWRENCE'S TRANSLATIONS:

454 ARNOLD, Armin. 'Genius with a Dictionary: Re-evaluating D. H. Lawrence's Translations'. *Comparative Literature Studies* 5 (Dec. 1968): 389–401.

455 CECCHETTI, Giovanni. 'Verga and D. H. Lawrence's Translations'.

Comparative Literature 9 (fall 1957): 333–44.

TRAVEL
(a) **General**; (b) *Etruscan Places*; (c) *Mornings in Mexico*; (d) *Sea and Sardinia*; (e) *Twilight in Italy*

(a) General
SOME RECENT EDITIONS OF LAWRENCE'S TRAVEL BOOKS:
D. H. LAWRENCE AND ITALY: TWILIGHT IN ITALY, SEA AND SARDINIA, ETRUSCAN PLACES (NY: Viking, Compass, 1972; Harmondsworth: Penguin, 1972). ['Introduction', pp. vii–xiii, by Anthony Burgess.]
MORNINGS IN MEXICO AND ETRUSCAN PLACES (London: Heinemann, Phoenix, 1956; Harmondsworth: Penguin, 1971).

COMMENTARIES ON LAWRENCE'S TRAVEL BOOKS:
456 JAMES, Clive. 'D. H. Lawrence in Transit'. In Spender, **131**, 159–69. [On DHL's travels and travel books.]
457 PINION, F. B., 115, 256–64.
458 TRACY, Billy T. 'D. H. Lawrence and the Travel Book Tradition'. *D. H. Lawrence Review* 11 (fall 1978): 272–93.

(b) *Etruscan Places*
Published: London, Secker, Sept. 1932; 1st American ed.: NY, Viking, Nov. 1932.
Recent printings: In *D. H. Lawrence and Italy*, Viking, Compass (1972) and Penguin (1972); also in *Mornings in Mexico and Etruscan Places*, Heinemann, Phoenix (1956) and Penguin (1971).
Criticism: **CAVITCH, 43**, 205–9; **HASSALL, 356**, 370–7 (1959) and 61–78 (1962); **JOHN, 83**, 286–9; **PRITCHARD, R.E., 118**, 200–5; **SAGAR, 124**, 210–13.
459 JANIK, Del Ivan. 'D. H. Lawrence's *Etruscan Places*: The Mystery of Touch'. *Essays in Literature* (Western Illinois U) 3 (1976): 194–205.
460 TRACY, Billy T. ' "Reading up the Ancient Etruscans": Lawrence's Debt to George Dennis'. *Twentieth Century Literature* 23 (Dec. 1977): 437–50. [DHL's debt to Dennis's 1848 *The Cities and Cemeteries of Etruria*.]
461 GUTIERREZ, Donald. 'D. H. Lawrence's Golden Age'. *D. H. Lawrence Review* 9 (fall 1976): 377–408. [Study of *Etruscan Places*.]

(c) *Mornings in Mexico*
Published: London, Secker, June 1927; 1st American ed.: Knopf, Aug. 1927.
Recent printings: In *Mornings in Mexico and Etruscan Places*, Heinemann, Phoenix (1956) and Penguin (1971).
Criticism: **CAVITCH, 43**, 175–8; **PRITCHARD, R.E., 118**, 165–8; **WALKER, 143**, 61–70.
462 AIKEN, Conrad. 'Mr. Lawrence's Prose'. *Dial* 83 (15 Oct. 1927): 343–6; rptd. in his *A Reviewer's ABC* (NY: Meridian, 1958) 263–6. [Reviews *Mornings*.]
463 LEWIS, Wyndham, 92. [Comments extensively on *Mornings*.]
464 WHITAKER, Thomas R. 'Lawrence's Western Path: *Mornings in Mexico*'. *Criticism* 3 (summer 1961): 219–36.

(d) *Sea and Sardinia*

Published: NY, Seltzer, Dec. 1921, 1st English ed.: London, Secker, 1923.

Recent Printings: Heinemann, Phoenix (1956); Heinemann Educational Books (1968); Penguin (1969); also included in *D. H. Lawrence and Italy*, Viking, Compass (1972) and Penguin (1972).

Criticism: **CAVITCH, 43**, 115–20; **DRAPER, 62**, 173–6; **JOOST/SULLIVAN, 84**, 40–9, 141–5.

465 ELLIS, David. 'Reading Lawrence: The Case of *Sea and Sardinia*'. *D. H. Lawrence Review* 10 (spring 1977): 52–63.

466 GERSH, Gabriel. 'In Search of D. H. Lawrence's *Sea and Sardinia*'. *Queen's Quarterly* 80 (1973): 581–8.

467 WEINER, S. Ronald. 'The Rhetoric of Travel: The Example of *Sea and Sardinia*'. *D. H. Lawrence Review* 2 (fall 1969): 230–44.

(e) *Twilight in Italy*

Published: London, Duckworth, June 1916; 1st American ed.: NY, Huebsch, 1916.

Recent printings: Heinemann, Phoenix (1956); Viking (1958); Penguin (1969); also included in *D. H. Lawrence and Italy*, Viking, Compass (1972) and Penguin (1972).

Criticism: **DELANY, 55**, 136–40; **GREEN, 71**, 343–6; **PRITCHARD, R. E., 118**, 55–60; **PINION, 115**, 66–7, 257–60.

468 FAHEY, William A. 'Lawrence's San Gaudenzio Revisited'. *D. H. Lawrence Review* 1 (spring 1968): 51–9.

469 JANIK, Del Ivan. 'The Two Infinites; D. H. Lawrence's *Twilight in Italy*'. *D. H. Lawrence Review* 7 (summer 1974): 179–98.

470 NICHOLS, Ann Eljenholm. 'Syntax and Style: Ambiguities in Lawrence's *Twilight in Italy*'. *College Composition and Communication* 16 (Dec. 1965): 261–6.

'THE TWO PRINCIPLES'

Published: *English Review*, June 1919.

Collected: *The Symbolic Meaning: The Uncollected Versions of 'Studies in Classic American Literature'*, ed. Armin Arnold (London: Centaur P, 1962). [Not included in *Studies in Classic American Literature*.]

Recent printing: *Phoenix II*, Penguin (1978).

Criticism: **DELAVENAY, 56**, 129–31; **ARNOLD, 38**, 74–6.

471 MacDONALD, Robert H. ' "The Two Principles": A Theory of the Sexual and Psychological Symbolism of D. H. Lawrence's Later Fiction'. *D. H. Lawrence Review* 11 (summer 1978): 132–55. [Pp. 132–41 especially.]

VIII DRAMA

SOME COLLECTIONS OF LAWRENCE'S PLAYS (in chronological order):

THE PLAYS OF D. H. LAWRENCE (London: Secker, 1933).

THE COMPLETE PLAYS OF D. H. LAWRENCE (London: Heinemann, 1965; Viking, 1966).

THE WIDOWING OF MRS HOLROYD AND THE DAUGHTER-IN-LAW
(London: Heinemann Educational Books, 1968).
THREE PLAYS BY D. H. LAWRENCE: A COLLIER'S FRIDAY NIGHT, THE DAUGHTER-IN-LAW, THE WIDOWING OF MRS HOLROYD (Harmondsworth: Penguin, 1969).

GENERAL CRITICISM ON LAWRENCE'S PLAYS

472 GRAY, Simon. 'Lawrence the Dramatist'. In Coombes, **46**, 453–7. [First appeared in *New Society*, 21 March 1968.]
473 PINION, F. B., 115, 265–74.
474 SAGAR, Keith. 'D. H. Lawrence: Dramatist'. *D. H. Lawrence Review* 4 (summer 1971): 154–82.
475 SKLAR, Sylvia. *The Plays of D. H. Lawrence: A Biographical and Critical Study* (NY: Barnes & Noble, 1975).
476 WATERMAN, Arthur E. 'The Plays of D. H. Lawrence'. *Modern Drama* 2 (Feb. 1960): 349–57; rptd. in Spilka, **132**, 142–50.

STUDIES OF INDIVIDUAL PLAYS
ALTITUDE (unfinished)
Published: *Laughing Horse*, No. 20 (summer 1938): 121–3. [First scene only.]
Collected: *Complete Plays*, 1965.
Criticism: **SKLAR, 475**, 212–22.

A COLLIER'S FRIDAY NIGHT
Published: London, Secker, June 1934.
Collected: *Complete Plays*, 1965; also in *Three Plays*, 1969.
Criticism: **SAGAR, 474**, 155–9; **SKLAR, 475**, 37–61, 109–11, 254–6.
477 O'CASEY, Sean. 'A Miner's Dream of Home'. *New Statesman and Nation* 8 (28 July 1934): 124; rptd. in his *Blasts and Benedictions*, ed. by Ronald Ayling (London: Macmillan, 1967), pp. 222–5. [Praising review.]

THE DAUGHTER-IN-LAW
Published and collected: *Complete Plays*, 1965; also collected in *The Widowing of Mrs Holroyd* and *The Daughter-in-Law* (1968) and in *Three Plays* (1969).
Criticism: **SAGAR, 474**, 173–7; **SKLAR, 475**, 86–112, 254–7.
478 SAGAR, Keith. 'The Strange History of *The Daughter-in-Law*'. *D. H. Lawrence Review* 11 (summer 1978): 175–84.
479 SKLAR, Sylvia. '*The Daughter-in-Law* and *My Son's My Son*'. *D. H. Lawrence Review* 9 (summer 1976): 254–65.

DAVID
Published: London, Secker, March 1926; 1st American ed.: NY, Knopf, April 1926.
Collected: *The Plays of D. H. Lawrence* (1933) and in *Complete Plays* (1965).
Criticism: **DRAPER, 62**, 261–2; **SAGAR, 474**, 178–80; **SKLAR, 475**, 223–48, 252–4.
480 PANICHAS, George A. 'D. H. Lawrence's Biblical Play *David*'. *Modern Drama* 6 (Sept. 1963): 164–76; rptd. in his *Adventure* **113**, pp. 136–50.
481 ROSTON, Murray. *Biblical Drama in England From the Middle Ages to the*

Present Day (London: Faber & Faber, 1968), pp. 275–9.

THE FIGHT FOR BARBARA
Published: *Argosy* (London), 14, No. 91 (Dec. 1933): 68–90, as 'Keeping Barbara'.
Collected: *Complete Plays*, 1965.
Criticism: **SKLAR, 475**, 113–15, 156–77.
482 KIMPEL, Ben D., and T. C. Duncan Eaves, '*The Fight for Barbara* on Stage'. *D. H. Lawrence Review* 1 (spring 1968): 72–4. [Reviews 1967 Mermaid Theatre production.]

THE MARRIED MAN
Published: *Virginia Quarterly Review* 16 (autumn 1940): 523–47.
Collected: *Complete Plays*, 1965.
Criticism: **SKLAR, 475**, 136–55.

THE MERRY-GO-ROUND
Published: *Virginia Quarterly Review* 17 (winter 1941): 1–44 (of Christmas Supplement).
Collected: *Complete Plays*, 1965.
Criticism: **SKLAR, 475**, 113–35.

NOAH'S FLOOD (unfinished)
Published: *Phoenix*, 1936.
Collected: *Complete Plays*, 1965.
Criticism: **SKLAR, 475**, 212–22.

TOUCH AND GO
Published: London, C. W. Daniel, May 1920; 1st American ed.: NY, Seltzer, June 1920.
Collected: *The Plays of D. H. Lawrence* (1933) and in *Complete Plays* (1965).
Criticism: **DELANY, 55**, 381–3; **PANICHAS, 113**, 33–5; **SAGAR, 474**, 176–8; **SKLAR, 475**, 178–211.
483 LOWELL, Amy. 'A Voice in Our Wilderness: D. H. Lawrence's Unheeded Message "to Blind Reactionaries and Fussy, Discontented Agitators" '. *New York Times Book Review*, 22 Aug. 1920, Section 3, p. 7; rptd. in her *Poetry and Poets: Essays* (Boston & NY: Houghton Mifflin, 1930), pp. 175–86.

THE WIDOWING OF MRS HOLROYD
Published: NY, Kennerly, 1 April 1914; 1st English issue: London, Duckworth, April 1914.
Collected: *The Plays of D. H. Lawrence* (1933); *Complete Plays* (1965); *The Widowing of Mrs Holroyd* and *The Daughter-in-Law* (1968); and *Three Plays* (1969).
Criticism: **CUSHMAN, 50**, 62–7; **DELAVENAY, 58**, 107–9; **SAGAR, 474**, 160–2, 171–2; **SKLAR, 475**, 29–35, 62–85, 108–11.
484 CONIFF, Gerald. 'The Failed Marriage: Dramatization of a Lawrentian Theme in *The Widowing of Mrs Holroyd*'. *D. H. Lawrence Review* 11 (spring 1978): 21–37.
485 WILLIAMS, Raymond. 'D. H. Lawrence: *The Widowing of Mrs Holroyd*'. In

Drama from Ibsen to Brecht (Harmondsworth: Penguin, 1973), 292–6. [Originally pub. London: Chatto & Windus, 1968.]

IX FILMS

FILMS BASED ON LAWRENCE'S WORKS:
THE ROCKING-HORSE WINNER, 1949.
L'AMANT DE LADY CHATTERLEY, 1956.
SONS AND LOVERS, 1960.
THE FOX, 1968.
WOMEN IN LOVE, 1970.
THE VIRGIN AND THE GIPSY, 1970

COMMENTARIES ON LAWRENCE AND FILM:
486 MOORE, Harry T. 'D. H. Lawrence and the Flicks'. *Literature/Film Quarterly* 1 (Jan. 1973): 3–11.

487 PHILLIPS, Gene D. 'Sexual Ideas in the Films of D. H. Lawrence'. *Sexual Behavior* 1, No. 3 (June 1971): 10–16.

488 SOLECKI, Sam. 'D. H. Lawrence's View of Film'. *Literature/Film Quarterly* 1 (Jan. 1973): 12–16. [Based on DHL's comments in *The Lost Girl* and several essays.]

STUDIES OF INDIVIDUAL FILMS BASED ON LAWRENCE'S WORKS

L'AMANT DE LADY CHATTERLEY (French, Columbia 1956. Director: Marc Allégret. From a stage play by Gaston Bonheur and Philippe de Rothchild. Black and white).
489 SCOTT, James F. 'The Emasculation of *Lady Chatterley's Lover*'. *Literature/Film Quarterly* 1 (Jan. 1973): 37–45. [Review.]

THE FOX (Claridge Pictures 1968: Director: Mark Rydell. Screenplay by Lewis John Carlino and Howard Koch. Colour).
490 CRUMP, G. B. '*The Fox* on Film'. *D. H. Lawrence Review* 1 (fall 1968): 238–44.
491 MELLEN, Joan. 'Outfoxing Lawrence: Novella into Film'. *Literature/Film Quarterly* 1 (Jan. 1973): 17–27; rptd. in *Women and Their Sexuality in the New Film* (NY: Horizon P, 1973), pp. 216–28.

THE ROCKING-HORSE WINNER (Two Cities Films 1949. Director and Screenplay: Anthony Pelissier. Black and white).
492 BARRETT and Erskine (eds.). *From Fiction to Film: D. H. Lawrence's 'The Rocking-Horse Winner'* **267**. [Includes three articles on film version.]
493 BECKER, Henry, III. '*The Rocking-Horse Winner*: Film as Parable'. *Literature/Film Quarterly* 1 (Jan. 1973): 55–63; rptd. in Barrett and Erskine, **267**, 204–13.

SONS AND LOVERS (Twentieth Century–Fox 1960. Director: Jack Cardiff. Screenplay by Gavin Lambert and T. E. B. Clarke. Produced by Jerry Wald. Black and white).

494 BALDANZA, Frank. '*Sons and Lovers*: Novel to Film as a Record of Cultural Growth'. *Literature/Film Quarterly* 1 (Jan. 1973): 64–70.

495 GILLETT, John. '*Sons and Lovers*'. *Film Quarterly* 14 (fall 1960): 41–2. [Review.]

THE VIRGIN AND THE GIPSY (London Screenplays 1970. Director: Christopher Miles. Screenplay by Alan Plater. Colour).

496 CRUMP, G. B. 'Gopher Prairie or Papplewick?: *The Virgin and the Gipsy* as Film'. *D. H. Lawrence Review* 4 (summer 1971): 142–53.

497 SMITH, Julian. 'Vision and Revision: *The Virgin and the Gipsy* as Film'. *Literature/Film Quarterly* 1 (Jan. 1973): 28–36.

WOMEN IN LOVE (United Artists 1970. Director: Ken Russell. Produced and Screenplay by Larry Kramer. Colour).

498 CRUMP, G. B. '*Women in Love*: Novel and Film'. *D. H. Lawrence Review* 4 (spring 1971): 28–41.

499 FARBER, Stephen. '*Women in Love*'. *Hudson Review* 23 (summer 1970): 321–6. [Review.]

500 ZAMBRANO, Ann Laura. '*Women in Love*: Counterpoint on Film'. *Literature/Film Quarterly* 1 (Jan. 1973): 46–54. [Review.]

Rose Marie Burwell

2
A checklist of Lawrence's reading

PROCEDURE FOLLOWED IN ASSEMBLING THE INFORMATION

Entries are arranged within each section by month and within each month by
   author. At the end of such monthly tabulations, reading which can be dated
   only by year is arranged alphabetically by author. Finally, most sections
   include items which I cannot identify by either author or title, and these
   have been placed in a sub-category at the end of that section.

Reading from earliest childhood to 1909, the content of the first and
   longest section, has been arranged by year rather than by month because of
   the limited sources for this period. After Lawrence left Nottinghamshire in
   1908, and especially after his departure from England in 1912, his
   correspondence allows one to date rather accurately when a work or an
   author was encountered. But until this steady flow of letters appears, we are
   limited largely by memoirs and biographies which are often vague and
   sometimes inaccurate.

From 1910 on the sections are annual.

Undatable reading has been catalogued after the brief section covering
   1930, the year in which Lawrence died.

SCOPE OF THE STUDY

I have included every book, play, poem, essay, and manuscript which I can establish that Lawrence read. Works which are basically collections of pictures or 'art books' have also been designated as reading since they usually contained introductory material, commentary, and sometimes critical remarks.

Since this is not intended to be a concordance of all of Lawrence's mentions of works and authors, only one source for each item is usually cited. I have tried to cite the source that gives the earliest evidence of his acquaintance with that work or author. In a few instances, I have cited more than one source because I felt that the accumulation of mentions would better establish a fact which might be less convincing from a single mention.

Re-reading is catalogued at the time it occurs and the annotation of that entry indicates, if known, when the original reading was done.

Evidence of reading drawn from the works is catalogued under the year in which that work was written according to Keith Sagar, *D. H. Lawrence: a Calendar of his works* (Manchester University Press, 1979). Where the writing of a work spanned two years or more, the reading evidence is catalogued under the year of that work's completion. The single exception to this method of dating occurs in the case of *Studies in Classic American Literature*, a work with a complex textual history. Both the textual problems and the method of dating for this collection are fully explained in a headnote to Section J where most of the reading is catalogued.

Periodicals and newspapers are listed only if Lawrence's mention indicates that he read some portion of them or if an accumulation of mentions indicates that he habitually read them. An exception to this rule is *The English Review*; since he apparently read it from the time it was founded until his death and since he mentions it frequently, I have simply noted in the original entry of the first period that he continued to read it regularly and have *not* catalogued it for every year. It cannot be assumed that Lawrence read, or even received, all of the periodicals where his work appeared.

Reviews are included only if it is possible to establish which ones they were. Both the periodicals where Lawrence's work originally appeared and those in which it was reviewed are catalogued in the Roberts bibliography.

FORMAT OF INDIVIDUAL ENTRIES

Works are listed alphabetically by author's last name within each chronological section, if the author is known. If, as in a few cases, the author is not known, the work is listed alphabetically by title. Where evidence of reading in a subject area is discernible but no title or author is given, the entry is catalogued alphabetically by subject, and it is usually placed in the 'Unidentifiable' sub-section at the end of a section.

Titles are given in full although Lawrence often made briefer references, sometimes just to the name of a character within the work. If the title is given in a foreign language, it is thus catalogued, although it is not safe to assume that a title given in a foreign language means that the work was read in that language.

Editions are identified only if they can be readily determined from the cited source, or if it was necessary to determine editions for some other reason – for example, in order to tell when the works became available in translation.

Differentiating between books borrowed and owned has not seemed useful because Lawrence's life was essentially a nomadic one and most of it was spent in straitened financial circumstances. He therefore frequently borrowed books or received them as gifts and gave them away when he moved.

The annotation of each entry is intended largely to indicate the extent of Lawrence's acquaintance with that item, not to establish his reaction to it. An exception to this practice has been made when the title of a non-fiction work is either not indicative of the subject treated therein or is misleading. In such instances I have indicated briefly in the annotation the scope of the work. In order to indicate the extent of Lawrence's knowledge of a work, I have used such terms as 'quotes', 'discusses', 'mentions', 'familiar', and 'knows'. The last three of these designations perhaps need some definition. 'Mentions' means simply that Lawrence uses the name of a work or an author in such a way that I cannot determine whether he has read any part of that work or author. 'Familiar' indicates that he refers to the work or author with enough detail to assure me that he has some first-hand acquaintance with it. 'Knows' is used for items which he gives evidence of having read thoroughly. Such distinctions are, at best, subjectively determined; therefore, the user of the catalogue is given the exact source from which each inference was made so that he may weigh the evidence for himself.

If disagreement between authorities exists as to whether Lawrence was familiar with an item, I have so indicated in the annotation – citing both assertions and leaving the decision to the reader.

The final item of each entry is the abbreviation for the source on which it is based. (See the Abbreviation Code for Bibliographical Sources.) It has seemed useful in most cases to identify the frequently cited sources by the initials of the author rather than by an abbreviation of the title. Directories of the people with whom Lawrence was closely associated will be found in both the Moore letter collection and the Nehls biography. Where the source is an unpublished letter, I have indicated the recipient and the current holder as well as the date.

ORGANIZATION OF THE INDEX

With the goal of making the information of this study as readily accessible as possible, I have arranged the index in the following manner. Works which are entered in the text by author – as most works are – are indexed by author. Where the author could not be discovered, the title is indexed. Newspapers and periodicals are indexed by title with (n) or (p) following for further identification. If the quantity of reading on any subject indicated a significant interest in the area, I have set up a subject-matter category for it in the index. A list of these categories precedes the index. Since it seems useful to know which authors of other nations Lawrence read, I have established categories for his reading of American, Australian, French, German, Italian, Russian, Scandinavian, and Spanish authors. If a work or an author was read in a language other than English, an asterisk precedes the entry number or the name of the author. Authors are listed with their first names or initials following the last name only in their individual entries. When they appear under a subject-matter or national author category, they are designated only by last names unless an initial is needed for clarity, as for example in case of Henry and William James.

The original version of this checklist, published in the *D. H. Lawrence Review* in 1970, did not contain any evidence of Lawrence's reading drawn from his fiction, partly because of the doubtful status of such evidence, and partly because the source and influence studies which would have been entailed were beyond the scope of the checklist as then envisaged. However, Lawrence's fiction is now in the process of being edited and annotated for the Cambridge University Press edition of his complete works, and some novels are appearing in the Penguin English Library. This scholarship will be incorporated into editions of the *Handbook* as it becomes available.

Acknowledgements. A number of Lawrence scholars throughout the world have been generous with their time and knowledge. I am particularly grateful to Armin Arnold, McGill University, Montreal; Paul Delany, Columbia; Edward Tedlock, Jr., University of New Mexico and George Zytaruk, Nipissing College, North Bay, Ontario. Robert Scholes, now of Brown University, in whose seminar this catalogue began, provided personal encouragement and scholarly example of an immeasurable nature. My children, Keith, Lyle, Hope, David, Julia and Mary Patricia gave many hours of their free time to obligations rightfully mine in order that this manuscript might be completed. However, my indebtedness to John Gerber and Robert Irwin of the University of Iowa supercedes all others, for without their interest, encouragement and support I would not have had an opportunity to undertake the doctoral programme from which this study resulted.

ABBREVIATION CODE FOR BIBLIOGRAPHICAL SOURCES

AA Arnold, Armin. *D. H. Lawrence and German Literature.* Montreal: Mansfield Book Mart, H. Heinemann, 1963.

AA/DHL Arnold, Armin. *D. H. Lawrence and America.* Linden Press, 1958.

ALC Clarke, Ada Lawrence, and Stuart Gelder. *Young Lorenzo: The Early Life of D. H. Lawrence.* Florence: Orioli, 1931.

APOCALYPSE Lawrence, D. H. *Apocalypse and the Writings on Revelation,* ed. Mara Kalnins. Cambridge: Cambridge University Press, 1980.

BR Lawrence, D. H. *D. H. Lawrence's Letters to Bertrand Russell,* ed. Harry T. Moore. New York: Gotham Book Mart, 1948.

CENTAUR McDonald, Edward, ed. *The Centaur Letters* (by D. H. Lawrence). Austin, Tex: Humanities Research Centre, University of Texas, 1970.

CORKE/INFANCY Corke, Helen. *In Our Infancy.* Cambridge University Press, 1975.

CC Carswell, Catherine. *The Savage Pilgrimage: a Narrative of D. H. Lawrence.* New York: Harcourt, Brace, 1932.

CM Mackenzie, Compton. *My Life and Times: Octave Five.* Chatto & Windus, 1966.

DB Brett, Dorothy. *Lawrence & Brett: a Friendship.* Philadelphia, Pa., J. B. Lippincott Co., 1933.

DG Goldring, Douglas. *Odd Man Out.* Nicholson & Watson, 1945.

DHLR *D. H. Lawrence Review.*

E&AB Brewster, Earl and Achsah, eds. *D. H. Lawrence: Reminiscences and Correspondence.* Martin Secker, 1934.

ED Delavenay, Emile. *D. H. Lawrence and Edward Carpenter.* New York: Taplinger Co., 1971.

EF Fay, Eliot. *Lorenzo in Search of the Sun.* New York: Bookman Associates, 1953.

EN Nehls, Edward., ed. *D. H. Lawrence: a Composite Biography.* 3 vols. Madison, Wis: University of Wisconsin Press, 1957, 1958, 1959.

EP Lawrence, D. H. *Etruscan Places.* New York: Viking, 1966.

EWT Tedlock, E. W., Jr., ed. *The Frieda Lawrence Collection of D. H. Lawrence Manuscripts: a Descriptive*

Bibliography. Albuquerque, N. Mex.: University of New Mexico Press, 1948.

FL Lawrence, Frieda. *'Not I, But the Wind . . .'* New York: Viking, 1934.

FLMC Lawrence, Frieda. *Frieda Lawrence: the Memoirs & Correspondence*, ed. E. W. Tedlock, Jr. New York: Alfred A. Knopf, Inc. 1964.

FU Lawrence, D. H. *Fantasia of the Unconscious & Psychoanalysis and the Unconscious*. Phoenix Edition. W. Heinemann Ltd., 1961.

GL Lacy, Gerald. 'An Analytical Calendar of the Letters of D. H. Lawrence.' Unpublished doctoral dissertation, University of Texas, Austin, Tex.: 2 vols., 1971.

GZ Lawrence, D. H. *The Quest for Rananim: D. H. Lawrence's Letters to S. S. Koteliansky*, ed. George J. Zytaruk. Montreal: McGill–Queen's University Press, 1970.

GRANSDEN Gransden, K. Y. 'Rananim: D. H. Lawrence's Letters to S. S. Koteliansky,' *Twentieth Century* 159 (Jan.–June 1956), 22–32.

HC Corke, Helen. *D. H. Lawrence: the Croydon Years*. Austin, Tex.: University of Texas Press, 1965.

HL Lawrence, D. H. *The Letters of D. H. Lawrence*, ed. Aldous Huxley. W. Heinemann Ltd., 1956.

IL Litvinoff, Ivy. 'A Visit to D. H. Lawrence,' *Harper's Bazaar*, 80 (October 1946) 411–18.

ILA *International Literary Annual*, 1959.

JBH Hobman, J. B., ed. *David Eder: Memoirs of a Modern Pioneer*. V. Gollancz, 1945.

JOOST Joost, Nicholas & Alvin Sullivan. *D. H. Lawrence and the Dial*. Carbondale, Ill.: Southern Illinois University Press, 1970.

JC Chambers, Jessie ('E.T.'). *D. H. Lawrence: a Personal Record*. New York: Barnes & Noble, Inc., 1965.

JF Foster, Joseph. *D. H. Lawrence in Taos*. Alburquerque, N. Mex.: University of New Mexico Press, 1972.

JMM Murry, John Middleton. *Reminiscences of D. H. Lawrence*. New York: Henry Holt, 1933.

JMM/S Murry, John Middleton. *Son of Woman: the Story of D. H. Lawrence*. New York: Cape & Smith, 1931.

KC Cushman, Keith. 'D. H. Lawrence and Nancy Henry', *D. H. Lawrence Review*, 6 (spring 1973), 21–32.

KM Merrild, Knud. *With D. H. Lawrence in New Mexico*. New York: Barnes & Noble, Inc., 1965. (Originally published as *A Poet & Two Painters*.)

KS Sagar, Keith. *D. H. Lawrence: a Calendar of His Works*. Manchester: Manchester University Press, 1979.

LACY/COCK Lacy, Gerald, ed. *The Escaped Cock*. Los Angeles, Calif.: Black Sparrow Press, 1973.

LACY/SELTZER Lacy, Gerald, ed. *D. H. Lawrence Letters to Thomas & Adele Seltzer*. Santa Barbara, Calif.: Black Sparrow Press, 1976.

LDC Clark, L. D. *The Dark Night of the Body*. Austin, Tex.: Texas University Press, 1964.

LLB Boulton, James T. ed. *The Letters of D. H. Lawrence*, vol. I. Cambridge University Press, 1979.

LW Waterfield, Lina. *Castle in Italy*. New York: Thos. Crowell Co., 1961.

MCC Chambers, Maria Cristina. 'Afternoons in Italy with D. H. Lawrence', *Texas Quarterly* 7 (winter, 1964) 114–20.

MDL Luhan, Mabel Dodge. *Lorenzo in Taos*. Martin Secker, 1933.

MEH Lawrence, D. H. *Movements in European History*. Oxford: Oxford University Press, 1922.

MIH Moore, Harry T. *The Intelligent Heart: The Story of D. H. Lawrence*. New York: Grove Press, Black Cat Edition, 1962.

ML Lawrence, D. H. *The Collected Letters of D. H. Lawrence*. 2 vols., ed. Harry T. Moore. New York: Viking, 1962.

MPR Moore, Harry T. *Post Restante: A Lawrence Travel Calendar*. Berkeley, Calif.: University of California Press, 1956.

MS Secker, Martin. *Letters from a Publisher: Martin Secker to D. H. Lawrence and Others*. Enitharmon Press, 1970.

MS/DHL *Letters from D. H. Lawrence to Martin Secker, 1911–1930*. Privately printed, 1970.

PD Lawrence, D. H. 'D. H. Lawrence: Twelve Letters', ed. Paul Delany. *D. H. Lawrence Review*, 2 (fall 1969), 195–209.

PD/NIGHTMARE Delany, Paul. *D. H. Lawrence's Nightmare*. New York: Basic Books, 1978.

PH Lawrence, D. H. *Phoenix: The Posthumous Papers of D. H. Lawrence*, ed. Edward McDonald. W. Heinemann Ltd., 1956.

PH–II Lawrence D. H. *Phoenix II: Uncollected, Unpublished and Other Prose Works by D. H. Lawrence*. ed. Harry T. Moore and Warren Roberts. New York: Viking, 1967.

POL Moore, Harry T. *The Priest of Love*. New York: Farrar, Straus & Giroux, 1974.

PREDILICTIONS Moore, Marianne. *Predilictions*. New York: Viking, 1955.

RA Aldington, Richard. *D. H. Lawrence: Portrait of a Genius, But* . . . New York: Duell, Sloan & Pearce, Inc., 1950.

RA/L Aldington, Richard. *Life for Life's Sake*. New York: Viking, 1941.

RA/LETTERS Richard Aldington, ed. *D. H. Lawrence: Letters Selected by Richard Aldington*. Penguin, 1950.

RGH Gathorne-Hardy, Robert, ed. *Ottoline at Garsington*. Faber & Faber, 1974.

RLD Drain, R. L. 'Formative Influences on the Work of D. H. Lawrence.' Unpublished dissertation, Cambridge University, 1962.

R&MS Pinto, Vivian de Sola. *Renaissance & Modern Studies*, I (1957), 5–39.

SFD Damon, S. Foster. *Amy Lowell: a Chronicle*. New York: Houghton Mifflin, 1935.

SPARROW Skinner, Mollie. *The Fifth Sparrow*. Sydney: Sydney University Press, 1972.

SJD Darroch, Sandra Jobson. *Ottoline*. Chatto & Windus, 1976.

SM Lawrence, D. H. *The Symbolic Meaning*. Arundel: Centaur, 1962.

S&S Lawrence, D. H. *Sea & Sardinia*. New York: Viking Press, 1963.

TWI Lawrence, D. H. *Twilight in Italy*. Penguin Books, 1960.

THROSSELL Throssell, Katharine Prichard. 'Lawrence in Australia', *Meanjin* 9 (summer 1950), 252–9.

WB Bynner, Witter. *Journey with Genius*. New York: John Day Co., 1951.

WR Roberts, Warren. *A Bibliography of D. H. Lawrence*. Rupert Hart-Davis, 1963.

WYT Tindall, William York. *D. H. Lawrence & Susan His Cow*. New York: Columbia University Press, 1939.

ZYTARUK–MALAHAT Zytaruk, George, ed. 'D. H. Lawrence: Letters to Koteliansky', *Malahat Review* 1 (January 1967), 17–40.

ZYTARUK–CHAMBERS Zytaruk, George, ed. *The Collected Letters of Jessie Chambers, D. H. Lawrence Review.* vol. 12 nos. 1–2, 1979.

(SECTION A) 1885–1909

1901

A1 Alcott, Louisa M. *Little Women* (fiction). Gave to Jessie. JC-92.

A2 Barrie, J. M. *The Little Minister, Tommie and Grizel, A Window in Thrums* (fiction). Lawrence and his mother discussed these and other of Barrie's works (see A180) with the Chambers family. EN, I-38.

A3 Hube, Rodolph von. *Griseleia in Snotingscire* (history of Nottinghamshire). Read soon after its publication. MIH-92; R&MS, I, 1957, p. 15.

A4 Longfellow, Henry Wadsworth. 'Hiawatha', 'Evangeline' (poetry). Read to Jessie. JC-94.

A5 Watts-Dunton, W. T. *Aylwin* (fiction). Read by summer. JC-92.

1902

A6 Dickens, Charles. *Bleak House, Dombey and Son* (fiction). Read. JC-96.

A7 Eliot, George (Mary Ann Evans). *Romola* (fiction). Read. JC-98.

A8 Reade, Charles. *The Cloister and the Hearth* (fiction). Read. EN, III-582.

1904

A9 Blackmore, Richard. *Lorna Doone* (fiction). Read. JC-96.

A10 Blake, William. As early as 1904 Lawrence was giving Jessie biographical information about Blake. JC-63. At Christmas 1905 the two exchanged copies of *Songs of*

Innocence and *Songs of Experience.* JC-101.

A11 Cooper, James Fenimore. *The Last of the Mohicans, The Pathfinder* (fiction). Read. JC-96.

A12 Dickens, Charles. *David Copperfield* (fiction). Read. JC-95.

A13 Eliot, George (Mary Ann Evans). *Adam Bede, Mill on the Floss* (fiction). Read by late this year. JC-97.

A14 Farrar, Frederick W. *Darkness and Dawn* (fiction). Recommended to Jessie. She errs regarding author's first name. JC-94.

A15 FitzGerald, Edward. 'The Rubáiyát of Omar Khayyám' (poem). Gave to Jessie at Christmas. JC-101.

A16 Hope, Anthony. *The Prisoner of Zenda, Rupert of Hentzau* (fiction). Read. JC-94.

A17 Stevenson, R. L. *Kidnapped, The Master of Ballantrae, Treasure Island* (fiction). Read. JC-96.

A18 Swift, Jonathan. *Journal to Stella* (letters). Read, along with other writings by and about Swift. JC-99.

A19 Tennyson, Alfred. 'Lady of Shallot', 'Morte d'Arthur', 'Elaine', 'The Lotus Eaters', 'Locksley Hall', 'Maud', 'Ulysses' (poems). Read. JC-95.

1905

A20 Bacon, Francis. *Essays.* Read by December. JC-101.

A21 Darwin, Charles. Read some Darwin by this year. JC-112. Re-reading *The Voyage of the Beagle* in 1927. ML-1020.

A22 De Quincey, Thomas. Quoting by this year. JC-100.

A23 Dickens, Charles. *A Tale of Two Cities* (fiction). Read by spring. JC-102.

A24 Emerson, Ralph Waldo. *Essays.* Read by December. JC-101.

A25 Haggard, H. Rider. Read his romances with Jessie. JC-94.

A26 Hugo, Victor. *Waterloo* (fiction). Read. JC-57.

A27 Lamb, Charles. *Essays*. Knew by this year. Favourites were 'Dissertation on Roast Pig', 'Dream Children', and 'The South Sea House'. JC-64; 101.

A28 Maupassant, Guy de. *Tales*. Familiar. JC-107.

A29 Petrarch, Francesco. Note by Lawrence in A30 indicates familiarity with sonnets to Laura. EN, I-67.

A30 Shakespeare, William. Shows wide knowledge: 'Shakespeare was the product of his age. Everything was somehow concentrated in him'. JC-59.

A31. Shakespeare, William. *Coriolanus*. Read. JC-61.

A32 Textbooks. In a letter to *The Teacher* (March 1905) Lawrence discusses the texts he used in teacher preparation. LLB-26. They are identified as: Evan Daniel, *The Grammar, History and Derivation of the English Language* (1881); John M. D. Meiklejohn, *The English Language* (12th ed., 1895) or possibly Meiklejohn's *English Literature* (1904); Cyril Ransome, *An Advanced History of England* (5th ed. 1901) or possibly Ransome's *A Short History of England* (12th ed., 1901); Samuel R. Gardiner, *Outline of English History* (1881) or possibly Gardiner's *A Student's History of England* (1890). In arithmetic the text was probably Gilbert A. Christian and George Collar's *A New Arithmetic* (3rd ed., 1899); in geography George Gill's *Gill's Imperial Geography* (1886) or *The Oxford and Cambridge Geography* (1886); or Meiklejohn's *A Short*

Geography (1889) or *A New Geography* (22nd ed., 1899).

A33 Shelley, Percy Bysshe. *The Sensitive Plant* (poetry collection). Gave to Jessie at Christmas. JC-135.

A34 Thoreau, Henry David. *Walden*. Read by December. JC-101.

A35 Tolstoy, Leo. *Anna Karenina* (fiction). Read. EN, III-593.

1906

A36 Borrow, George. *Lavengro* (fiction). Read. JC-110.

A37 Brontë, Emily. *Wuthering Heights* (fiction). Read. JC-102.

A38 Carlyle, Thomas. *The French Revolution, Heroes and Hero Worship, Sartor Resartus*. Read by spring. JC-101-2.

A39 Carroll, Lewis (Charles L. Dodgson) *Alice in Wonderland* (fiction). Read. JC-102.

A40 Darwin, Charles. *The Origin of Species*. Took to Haggs Farm. EN, III-609.

A41 Daudet, Alphonse. *Lettres de mon Moulin* (fiction). Read in summer. JC-107. In *Sons and Lovers* Paul reads *Tartarin de Tarascon* (fiction).

A42 Fielding, Henry. By summer Lawrence had read some, perhaps all, of Fielding's novels. JC-105.

A43 Flaubert, Gustave. *Madame Bovary, Salammbô* (fiction). Read. JC-107.

A44 Gaskell, Elizabeth. *Cranford* (fiction). Read. JC-102.

A45 Gissing, George. *The Private Papers of Henry Ryecroft* (fiction). Read by autumn. JC-110.

A46 *The Gong* (Nottingham University Magazine). Read, submitted work to it. LLB-31.

A47 Ibsen, Henrik. *Hedda Gabler, The Lady from the Sea, Rosmersholm*. Read. LLB-113-4.

A48 Loti, Pierre (Julien Vaud). *Pêcheur d'Islande* (fiction). Familiar. JC-105.

A49 Metaphysical poets. Took a metaphysical poetry course at Nottingham University. JC-77.

A50 Rutherford, Mark (William Hale White). *The Autobiography of Mark Rutherford, Clara Hapgood* (fiction). Read. JC-110.

A51 Saintine, Xavier. *Picciola* (fiction). Read. JC-105.

A52 Shakespeare, William. *Hamlet, Macbeth*. Had read by summer. JC-108.

A53 Souvestre, Émile. *Un Philosophie sou les Toits* (fiction). Read. JC-105.

A54 Wilde, Oscar. 'The Ballad of Reading Gaol' (poem); *Intentions* (aesthetic essays); *The Picture of Dorian Gray* (fiction). Read by autumn. JC-110.

1907

A55 Blatchford, Robert. *God and My Neighbour* (theology). Read. LLB-39.

A56 Campbell, R. J. *The New Theology*. Read. JC-84.

A57 Cellini, Benvenuto. *The Memoirs of Benvenuto Cellini* (probably J. A. Symons translation). Read. JC-112.

A58 Huxley, T. H. *Man's Place in Nature* (philosophy). Read. JC-84, 112.

A59 James, William. *Pragmatism*. Read. JC-112.

A60 Locke, John. *Essay Concerning Human Understanding*. Read. JC-112.

A61 Mill, John Stuart. Familiar by late this year. JC-113.

A62 Motley, J. L. *The Rise of the Dutch Republic*. Read. LLB-37.

A63 *Nottinghamshire Guardian* (newspaper). Reading regularly. LLB-38.

A64 Renan, Ernest. *The Life of Jesus*.

Read. JC-112.

A65 Rossetti, D. G. Gave Jessie *The Blessed Damozel* one Christmas and once quoted 'Sister Helen' to her. JC-101, 146; LLB-157, 159–60.

A66 Spencer, Herbert. *First Principles of a New System of Theology*. Read during second year at Nottingham University. LLB-36.

A67 Tolstoy, Leo. Gave Louie Burrows a familiar volume. LLB-42.

A68 Vivian, Philip (Harry V. M. Phelips). *The Churches and Modern Thought* (theology). Read. LLB-36-7.

1908 Arrangement by month begins here.

April

A69 Arnold, Edwin. 'The Light of Asia' (poem). Quotes. LLB-46.

May

A70 Diderot, Denis. *Encyclopédie*. (Completed by D'Alembert). PH-II-224.

A71 Gorky, Maxim. Mentions. PH-II-224.

A72 Hegel, Wilhelm. Mentions. PH-II-223.

A73 Herbart, Johann. Mentions. PH-II-221. The only work in translation was *The Science of Education and the Aesthetic Revelation of the World.*.

A74 Hood, Thomas. 'Song of the Shirt' (poem). Mentions. PH-II-224. In *Sons and Lovers* Lawrence mentions 'Fair Ines' (poem).

A75 Hume, David. Mentions. PH-II-225.

A76 *International Library of Famous Literature* ed. Richard Garnett. Professor Boulton establishes that this was an important and frequent source of Lawrence's early reading. LLB-4-6, 50.

A77 Lund, T. W. *The Religion of Art in*

Three Pictures. Mentions the painting of Luke Filde in 'Art and the Individual'. PH-II-224. Lawrence may have read this book, since it contains a plate of Greiffenhagen's 'The Idyll', which he copied several times.

A78 Meredith, George. *Diana of the Crossways* (fiction). Familiar. LLB-52.

A79 Poe, Edgar Allen. Mentions. PH-II-224. In *Sons and Lovers* Paul knows 'The Raven'.

A80 Pope, Alexander. Mentions. PH-II-224.

A81 Schiller, Friedrich. Mentions. PH-II-223.

A82 Shakespeare, William. *Much Ado About Nothing*. Quotes. LLB-48.

A83 Zola, Emile. Mentions. PH-II-224.

June

A84 Brontë, Charlotte. *Jane Eyre* (fiction). Read. LLB-59.

A85 Coleridge, S. T. 'Rime of the Ancient Mariner' (poem). Quotes. LLB-55.

August

A86 Lessing, Gotthold. 'Läokoon' (critical essay). Mentioned in 'Art and the Individual', Lawrence purchased two gift copies this month. LLB-136.

September

A87 Macaulay, Thomas. *Lays of Ancient Rome*. Quotes 'Horatius', LLB-74.

A88 Nietzsche, Friedrich. Jessie recalls that Lawrence began to talk of Nietzsche's philosophy after going to Croydon in autumn. JC-120. T. E. Callander, Chief Librarian of the Croydon Central Library reported to R. L. Drain that the following works were in that library by the time Lawrence left the school in late 1911:

Beyond Good and Evil; Thus Spake Zarathustra; Twilight of the Gods; The Future of Educational Institutions; Human, All-Too-Human; Will to Power; and *Joyful Wisdom*. RLD.

A89 Maistre, Xavier de. *Le Jeune Sibérienne* (fiction). Quotes. LLB-76. In *Sons and Lovers* Paul recommends *Voyage Autour de ma Chambre* (fiction) to Miriam.

A90 Goethe, J. W. von. Quotes 'Gretchen at the Spinning Wheel'. LLB-73.

A91 Thayer, E. L. 'Casey at the Bat' (poem). Parodies. LLB-74-5.

A92 Verlaine, Paul. 'Kaléidoscope' (poem). Quotes. LLB-75. Jessie recounts that Verlaine and Baudelaire were very important to Lawrence during this period. JC-121.

A93 Spenser, Edmund. *The Faerie Queen* (epic poem). Familiar. LLB-73.

November

A94 Balzac, Honoré de. *Eugénie Grandet* (fiction). Familiar. LLB-89.

A95 Brontë, Charlotte. *Shirley* (fiction). Knows well. LLB-88.

December

A96 Balzac, Honoré de. *The Atheist's Mass, Old Goriot, Shorter Stories* (Walter Scott ed.), *The Wild Ass's Skin*. Knows. LLB-98.

A97 Butler, Samuel. *Erewhon* (fiction). Familiar. LLB-100.

A98 Coleridge, S. T. 'Christabel' (poem). Read about this time. JC-115.

A99 Doughty, Charles. *Adam Cast Forth* (verse play). Read about this time. JC-119.

A100 Haweis, H. R. *Music and Morals*. Knows. LLB-99.

A101 *The English Review* (periodical). Read regularly from the time of its founding this month. JC-156.

A102 Housman, A. E. *A Shropshire Lad* (poetry collection). Received for Christmas. LLB-108.

A103 Newman, Ernest (English music critic 1868–1959). Has some familiarity with his writing. LLB-100.

A104 Shaw, G. B. Familiar. LLB-101.

A105 Thackeray, W. M. Familiar. LLB-98.

A106 Titterton, W. R. *Love Poems.* Familiar. LLB-100.

A107 Young, Edward. *Night Thoughts* (poetry). Familiar. LLB-103.

Undated reading for which evidence appears during 1908

A108 Austen, Jane. *Pride and Prejudice* (fiction). Familiar. MIH-89.

A109 Bennett, Arnold. Lawrence and Jessie read a column in *The New Age* which Bennett wrote under the pseudonym Jacob Tonson during 1908/9. JC-120.

A110 Browning, Robert. Has read much of Browning, including *The Ring and the Book,* 'Paracelsus' and portions of a pocket volume, *Selections.* JC-115.

A111 Cowper. William. Has read at least the Cowper poems in Palgrave (A190). JC-100.

A112 Haeckel, Ernst. *The Riddle of the Universe.* Read. JC-100.

A113 Herbert, George. Knew the selections in Palgrave (A190). JC-100.

A114 Keats, John. Knew the selections in Palgrave (A190). JC-99.

A115 Mahony, Francis. 'Bells of Shandon' (Poem). Knew. MIH-103.

A116 Meredith, George. 'Love in the Valley' (poem). Read. JC-110.

A117 *The New Age* (periodical) ed. A. R. Orage. Read regularly during 1908/9. JC-120.

A118 Ruskin, John. Has read much of Ruskin by this year. The only title remembered by Jessie is *Sesame and Lilies.* JC-107.

A119 Schopenhauer, Arthur. *Essays of Schopenhauer* (trans. Mrs Rudolph Dircks, Walter Scott ed., 1903). Read and discussed with Jessie. JC-98, 111. An article discussing the annotations Lawrence made in his copy is reprinted in EN, I-66-70.

A120 Shakespeare, William. *Sonnets.* Read those in Palgrave (A190). JC-100.

A121 Thackeray, W. M. *The Four Georges and English Humorists* (essays). Read. JC-98.

A122 *The Antiquities of Nottinghamshire* (chronicle, 1677). Lawrence read or had related to him either Robert Thoroton's or J. Throsby's revision of *Thoroton's History of Nottinghamshire* which had been re-issued in 1790. MIH-91.

A123 Tonson, Jacob. See A109.

A124 Turgenev, Ivan. *Fathers and Sons* (fiction). Read. JC-121.

A125 Wood, Ellen (Mrs Henry Wood). *East Lynne* (fiction). Mrs Lawrence discussed with her son and the Chambers family. It is probable they had all read it. EN, I-7.

1909

January

A126 Davies, W. H. *Nature Poems.* Read. LLB-106.

A127 Douglas, Alfred. *The City of the Soul* (poetry collection). Read. LLB-107.

A128 France, Anatole. *L'île des Pinguins* (fiction). Read. LLB-104.

A129 Gaskell, Elizabeth. *The Life of Charlotte Brontë.* Familiar. LLB-105.

A130 Machen, Arthur. *Hieroglyphics: a*

Note upon the Ecstasy of Literature. Familiar. LLB-107.

A131 Meredith, George, 'Where Did You Come From, Baby Dear?' (poem). Quotes. LLB-109.

A132 Pushkin, Alexander. Reading. LLB-104.

A133 Yeats, W. B. Has read 'a lot of Yeats'. LLB-107.

February

A134 Ibsen, Henrik. *Lady Inger, The Pretenders, The Vikings.* Lawrence sent Louie a volume containing these plays. LLB-112.

A135 Wells, H. G. *Kipps* (fiction). Knows. LLB-116.

March

A136 Bjornson, Bjornstjerne (Norwegian dramatist 1832–1910). Read. LLB-118.

A137 Browning, Robert. 'Rabbi Ben Ezra' (poem). Quotes. LLB-119.

A138 Hewlett, Maurice. *The Forest Lovers* (fiction). Familiar. LLB-120.

A139 Wells, H. G. *Tono-Bungay* (fiction). Read. LLB-119.

May

A140 Dostoyevsky, F. M. *Crime and Punishment* (fiction). Read. LLB-126.

A141 Robertson, J. M. *Letters on Reasoning.* Familiar. LLB-126.

A142 Swinburne, Algernon. 'Atalanta in Calydon', 'Ave Atque Vale' (poems). Read by spring. JC-119; HC-9.

A143 Tolstoy, Leo. *War and Peace* (fiction). Has read. LLB-127.

A144 Wells, H. G. *Love and Mr Lewisham, The War of the Worlds* (fiction). Has read. LLB-127.

July

A145 Burrows, Louise. Read mss. of two stories by Louie. Neither was published. LLB-78; 132-3.

A146 Coleridge, S. T. 'Youth and Age' (poem). Quotes. LLB-132.

September

A147 Jefferies, Richard. *The Open Air* (nature sketches). Received. LLB-137.

October

A148 Sedgwick, Anne D. 'The Nest' (fiction). Recommends. LLB-139.

November

A149 Bennett, Arnold. *The Old Wives' Tale* (fiction). Has read. LLB-142.

A150 Ford, Ford Madox. *A Call: The Tale of Two Passions* (fiction). Read as serialised in *English Review.* LLB-142.

A151 Galsworthy, John. *A Country House, The Man of Property* (fiction). Has read. JC-121; LLB-142.

A152 Moore, George. *Evelyn Innes* (fiction). Has read. LLB-142.

A153 Synge, J. M. *The Playboy of the Western World* (drama). Requests. LLB-142.

A154 Taylor, Rachel Annand (Scottish poet 1876–1960). 'The Epilogue of the Dreaming Women', 'The First Time', 'The Mask of Proteus', 'Three Poems'. Read in *English Review.* LLB-141.

A155 Thompson, Francis. 'Absence', 'Hound of Heaven' (poems). Familiar. LLB-145.

December

A156 Moore, T. S. *The Rout of the Amazons* (fiction). Gave to Agnes Holt. LLB-140.

Undated reading for which evidence appears during 1909

A157 Aristophanes. *The Frogs* (drama). Read. JC-121.

A158 Baudelaire, Charles. Jessie recalls that Baudelaire and Verlaine were the two greatest lights in Lawrence's poetic firmament during 1909. JC-121, 122. Among the poems he specifically mentioned were *Les Fleurs du Mal* and 'Sonnet d'Automne'.

A159 Byron, George Gordon. In addition to the Byron selections in Palgrave (A190) Lawrence knew at least 'The Destruction of Sennacherib', which he taught to his Croydon class in 1909. MIH-116.

A160 Carlyle, Thomas. Lawrence had read much by Carlyle. JC-102.

A161 Cervantes, Miguel de. *Don Quixote* (fiction). Knew. JC-122.

A162 Conrad, Joseph. *Lord Jim* (fiction). Read. JC-121.

A163 Davidson, John. Gave a volume of Davidson's poems to Helen Corke shortly after his death in 1909. HC-5.

A164 Euripides (trans. Gilbert Murray). *The Bacchae, Electra, Medea, The Trojan Women, Alcestis.* Read. JC-121; LLB-160, 261; DHLR (fall 1974) 230–1, respectively.

A165 Goethe, J. W. von. Lawrence used German poetry, among it Goethe and Heine, for teaching Helen Corke German in 1909. HC-5.

A166 Grimm, Jacob and Friedrich. *Grimm's Fairy Tales.* Knew. LLB-126.

A167 Heine, Heinrich. See A165.

A168 Hudson, W. H. *South American Sketches* (fiction). Gave to Jessie. JC-122.

A169 James, William. *Varieties of Religious Experience* (philosophy). Read. JC-113. But see K31.

A170 Maeterlinck, Maurice. *Pelléas and Mélisande, The Sightless* (drama). Read. JC-122.

A171 Musset, Alfred de. Familiar with his work. JC-121.

A172 Nietzsche, Friedrich. *The Will to Power* (philosophy). Read. JC-120.

A173 Pound, Ezra. Became acquainted with his work in 1909. MIH-129.

A174 Sand, George. Had read some of her work by this time. JC-121.

A175 Shakespeare, William. *The Tempest.* Taught to his students at Croydon in 1909. EN, I-86.

A176 Turgenev, Ivan, *Rudin* (fiction). Read. JC-121.

A177 Whitman, Walt. *Leaves of Grass* (poetry collection). Knew. JC-122.

A178 Wordsworth, William. Had read the poems in Palgrave (A190). JC-99.

Reading for unidentified dates within the 1885–1909 period

A179 Ballantyne, Robert. *Coral Island* (fiction). Ada Lawrence Clark recalls that this and similar adventure stories were read to the Lawrence children. EN, I-13.

A180 Barrie, J. M. *Margaret Ogilvy* (biography), *When a Man's Single* (fiction). Lawrence's mother knew them well; thus he had probably read them too. EN, III-562.

A181 *Black and White* (periodical). Lawrence frequently brought this illustrated record and review to the Chambers home. EN, I-38.

A182 Burns, Robert. Knew the selections in Palgrave (A190). JC-100.

A183 Burns, Robert. *Letters of Robert Burns* (probably the Walter Scott, 1877, ed. by J. L. Robertson). Read. JC-122.

A184 *The Chatterbox* (later *The Chatterbox and the Prize for Boys and Girls*). The Lawrence children read regularly. EN, I-19.

A185 Defoe, Daniel. *Robinson Crusoe* (fiction). Read. *Zytaruk-Malahat-26.*

A186 de la Mare, Walter (Walter Ramal, pseud.). *The Return* (fiction). Read.

EN, I-142; LLB-348, 370.

A187 Féval, Paul. *A Noble Sacrifice* (fiction). See A202.

A188 Fothergill, Jessie. *The First Violin* (fiction). Read while at Croydon. MIH-112.

A189 Gautier, Théophile. *Jettatura* (fiction). See A202.

A190 *The Golden Treasury of the Best Songs and Lyrical Poems in the English Language*, ed. Francis T. Palgrave. Carried a copy with him frequently and read from it at every opportunity. JC-80-99.

A191 Hogarth, William. Perused a book of prints. JC-99.

A192 Horace. Wrote prose translation of Horatian Odes i, iii, v, vi, vii while studying at Nottingham. R&MS, I, p. 11.

A193 Hughes, Thomas. *Tom Brown's Schooldays* (fiction). Read. HL-601.

A194 Kingsley, Charles. *Yeast* (fiction). Read. MIH-100.

A195 Mann, Mary. Read her novels between 1908 and 1911. MIH-112; LLB-256.

A196 Morris, William. R. L. Drain concludes, in his unpublished dissertation, that Lawrence must have read at least the socialist prose of Morris about the time he read Ruskin and Carlyle.

A197 *Nature* (periodical). Probably the magazine which Lawrence frequently brought to the Chambers home. JC-110.

A198 *The Oxford Song Book*. Emily Lawrence King recalls that her brother knew every song in it. EN, I-21.

A199 Peacock, Thomas Love. Read during the Croydon years. EN, I-90.

A200 *The Prize for Boys and Girls*. See A184.

A201 Querido, Izrael, *The Toils of Men* (fiction). Read during Croydon years. MIH-112.

A202 Sardou, Victorien. *The Black Pearl* (fiction). This French romance was bound with *Jettatura* which Lawrence and Jessie read. It seems likely, therefore, that he knew of it as well as of *A Noble Sacrifice* by Paul Féval, also bound in the volume. JC-105.

A203 Schopenhauer, Arthur. 'The Metaphysics of Love' (essay). Lawrence was interested in the ideas of this essay and in their relation to the marriage of Maggie and Philip in Eliot's *The Mill on the Floss*. JC-98.

A204 Scott, Sir Walter. Discussed Scott's novels with Jessie. JC-94. In *Sons and Lovers* Paul and Miriam are familiar with *The Lady of the Lake*, *The Bride of Lammermoor*, *Ivanhoe*, *Rob Roy*, *Guy Mannering* and 'The Lord of the Isles'.

A205 Shirley, James. Read the poems in Palgrave (A190).

A206 Sterne, Laurence. *A Sentimental Journey* (fiction). Gave a copy to Jessie. JC-122.

A207 Stowe, Harriet Beecher. *Uncle Tom's Cabin* (fiction). Read during childhood. PH-237.

A208 Thompson, Francis. 'Essay on Shelley'. Recommended to Jessie. JC-119.

A209 Verhaeren, Émile. Read works by him during Croydon years. EN, I-90.

A210 Virgil. *The Georgics* (poems). Read while writing *The White Peacock*, 1905-10. JC-107.

A211 Watson, John. *Beside the Bonnie Briar Bush* (fiction collection). Lawrence's mother suggested he read this during the early years of his friendship with Jessie. EN, III-562.

Unidentified Reading 1885–1909

A212 *The Student's Rome*. A childhood

friend, William Hopkin, recalls that during charades he once acted out this title, infuriating Lawrence. EN, I-24.

Addenda

A213 Adams, Sir John. *The Herbartian Psychology Applied to Education* (1897). Read Jessie Chambers' copy while at college. ZYTARUK– CHAMBERS 98.

A214 Dumas, Alexander *fils*. *La Dame aux Camelias*. Lawrence saw Theatre Royal, Nottingham, 15 June 1908. LLB 56, 59.

A215 Ingelow, Jean. *Poems*, 3rd Series, 1885. In *Sons and Lovers* Paul is familiar with her poems.

A216 Merimée, Prosper. 'Colomba' (short story). In *Sons and Lovers* Paul recommends to Miriam.

A217 Rooper, Thomas Godolphin. *School and Home Life (1907)*. Read Jessie Chambers' copy while at college. ZYTARUK-CHAMBERS 98.

(SECTION B) 1910

January

B1 Burrows, Louise. 'The Chimney Sweeper' (fiction). Read in ms. Never published. LLB-152.

B2 Harrison, Austin. 'Puntilla' (fiction). Familiar. Had been published in January *English Review*. LLB-152.

B3 Henley, W. E. 'Invictus' (poem). Quotes. LLB-154.

B4 Jacobs, W. W. Familiar with *The Lady of the Barge* collection. LLB-152-3.

B5 Moore, George. *Esther Waters, Evelyn Innes, Sister Teresa* (fiction). Ordered. LLB-154.

B6 *The Strand* (periodical). Familiar. LLB-152.

B7 Wells, H. G. *Ann Veronica* (fiction). Read. LLB-154.

February

B8 Corke, Helen. Read a portion of the ms. for her novel, *Neutral Ground* which became the germ of *The Trespasser*. POL-134.

B9 Flaubert, Gustave. *A Sentimental Education* (fiction). Familiar. POL-116.

March

B10 Villon, Francois. 'Ballad of the Dead Ladies' (poem). Quotes. LLB-157.

May

B11 Schreiner, Olive. *Story of an African Farm* (fiction). Has read. LLB-161.

June

B12 Beckford, William. *Vathek* (fiction). Familiar with the history of its publication. LLB-166.

B13 Cannan, Gilbert. *Devious Ways* (fiction). Read in proof. LLB-162.

B14 Collins, Wilkie. Familiar with his work. LLB-166.

B15 Shakespeare, William. *As You Like It*. Quotes. LLB-167.

B16 Tennyson, Alfred. 'The Princess' (poem). Quotes. LLB-167.

B17 Wilde, Oscar. *Salome* (fiction). Familiar with the history of its publication. LLB-166.

July

B18 Crowley, Aleister. *Ambergris* (poetry collection). Familiar. LLB-169.

B19 de la Mare, Walter. *Henry Brocken* (fiction). Received from Helen Corke. HCI-184.

B20 Douglas, G. *The House with the Green Shutters* (fiction). Recommends. LLB-172.

B21 Forster, E. M. *Howards End* (fiction). Received from Helen Corke. HCI-184. See C25.

B22 Gissing, George. *The Odd Women*

(fiction). Recommends to Louie. LLB-172.

B23 Hauptmann, Gerhart. *Einsame Menschen, Elga, Versunken Glocke* (drama). Read. LLB-171, 164, 168, respectively.

B24 London, Jack. *White Fang* (fiction). Recommends to Louie. LLB-172.

B25 *A Lute of Jade* (classical Chinese poetry) ed. L. Cranmer-Byng. Has read. LLB-168.

B26 Norris, Frank. *The Octopus, The Pit* (fiction). Recommends to Louie. LLB-172.

B27 Phillpots, Eden. *The Farm of the Dagger* (fiction). Recommends to Louie. LLB-172.

B28 *Red Magazine.* Read first issue, 24 July. LLB-172.

B29 Wilde, Oscar. 'Symphony in Yellow' (poem). Familiar. LLB-169.

August
B30 Barrie, James. *Sentimental Tommy* (fiction). Knows. LLB-175.

B31 Garborg, Arne. Familiar with his work. LLB-174.

September
B32 Taylor, Rachel Annand. *The Hours of Fiammetta: a Sonnet Sequence.* Knows well. LLB-179.

October
B33 Douglas, Alfred. *Sonnets.* Familiar. Quotes 'Silence'. LLB-180.

B34 Taylor, Rachel Annand. *Poems, Rose and Vine.* Read. LLB-180, 185, respectively.

B35 Wilde, Oscar. *The Importance of Being Earnest.* Familiar. LLB-185.

November
B36 Yeats, W. B. *A Pot of Broth* (drama). Read and saw. LLB-186, 246.

December
B37 *Aucassin and Nicolette* (13th-century Provençal legend). Mentions in lecture on Rachel Annand Taylor given in autumn. Gave colleague A. W. McLeod a copy at Christmas. LLB-213.

B38 Browne, Sir Thomas. *Religio Medici.* Bought. LLB-205.

B39 Corneille, Pierre. Acquaintance loaned Lawrence four volumes, suggesting he begin by reading *Cinna.* LLB-217.

B40 Daudet, Léon. *Le Partage de L'Enfant* (fiction). Gave to Jessie. LLB-212.

B41 Dickens, Charles. *The Old Curiosity Shop* (fiction). Gave an inscribed copy to a Croydon student. EN, I-551, note 22.

B42 Egyptian Folk Songs. Translating from the German some songs his uncle, Dr Fritz Krenkow, had translated from Arabic. LLB-196.

B43 Gorky, Maxim, *Tales from Gorky* (fiction collection). Familiar with the volume, which he gave to Louie. LLB-209.

B44 Hardy, Thomas. *Jude the Obscure* (fiction). Recommends to Louie. LLB-205.

B45 Hood, Thomas. 'The Death Bed' (poem). Knows. LLB-192.

B46 Kingsley, Charles. 'A Farewell' (poem). Quotes. LLB-210.

B47 LaMotte-Fouqué, Friedrich. *Undine* (fiction). Read at Christmas. LLB-213.

B48 Lockhart, J. G. *Spanish Ballads.* Bought. LLB-205.

B49 Meredith, George. *The Ordeal of Richard Feverel, Rhoda Fleming* (fiction). Knows. LLB-214, 191, respectively.

B50 Renan, Ernest, and W. R. Thomson. Translation of *The Song of Songs.* Knows. LLB-219.

B51 Richardson, Samuel. *Clarissa*

Harlowe (fiction). Familiar. LLB-217.

B52 Rousseau, Jean Jacques. *La Nouvelle Héloise* (fiction). Familiar. LLB-203.

B53 St Pierre, Bernadin de. *Paul et Virginie* (fiction). Bought. LLB-205.

B54 *The Schoolmaster* (educational association periodical). Intends to read. LLB-204.

B55 Swift, Jonathan. 'On Poetry; a Rhapsody' (Poem). Quotes. LLB-216.

Unidentified reading for which evidence appears during 1910

B56 Latin poems. Received a volume from Croydon colleague A. W. McLeod for Christmas. LLB-213.

(SECTION C) 1911

January

C1 Dehan, Richard (Clotilde Inez Mary Graves). *The Dop Doctor* (fiction). Read some of it. LLB-221.

C2 Reviews of *The White Peacock*. Read in *Times Literary Supplement* of 26 Jan. and in *The Observer* of 29 Jan. LLB-225.

February

C3 Reviews of *The White Peacock*. Read in: *Daily Chronicle* of 10 Feb. LLB-227; *Daily News* of 14 Feb. LLB-231; *Daily Mail* of 3 Feb. LLB-231; *Eastwood and Kimberly Advertiser* of 10 Feb. LLB-233; *Morning Post* of 9 Feb. LLB-229 and *The Standard* of 3 Feb. LLB-228.

March

C4 *The Academy* (periodical). Read review of *The White Peacock* in spring issue. LLB-241.

C5 Maeterlinck, Maurice. *Tresor des Humbles* (essays). Recommends to Louie. LLB-237.

C6 Meredith, George. 'Love in the Valley', 'Modern Love', 'The Woods of Westermain' (poems). Recommends to Louie. LLB-242.

C7 *French Songs and Verse for Children*, ed. Helen Terry. Sent to Louie. LLB-242.

C8 Shakespeare, William. *As You Like It*. Reading with Croydon Class. LLB-245.

C9 Sophocles. *Oedipus Tyrannus*. Read. LLB-235, 261.

C10 Swinburne, Algernon. 'Tristram of Lyonesse' (poem). Reading. LLB-241.

April

C11 *The Bookman* (periodical). Probably read review of *The White Peacock* in April issue. AA-DHL-14.

C12 Chesterton, G. K. 'Ballad of the White Horse' (poem). Discussed with Helen Corke in spring of this year. Manuscript, 'Not in Entire Forgetfulness', University of Texas.

C13 Dowson, Ernest. Discusses in source for C12.

C14 Meredith, George. *The Tragic Comedians* (fiction). Reading. LLB-250.

C15 Middleton, Richard. Discussed in C12 source.

C16 Shelley, Percy Bysshe. 'To Music' (poem). Quotes. LLB-248.

C17 Stendhal. *Le Rouge et le Noir* (fiction). Reading in French. LLB-251, 262.

C18 Synge, J. M. *Riders to the Sea* (drama). Recommends. LLB-260.

C19 Weyman, Stanley. *Under the Red Robe* (fiction). Read. LLB-258.

C20 Zola, Emile. *L'Assommoir* and *La Débâcle*. Offers to Louie. LLB-258.

May

C21 Browning, Robert. 'The Last Ride Together' (poem). Familiar. LLB-271.

C22 Chambers, Jesse. Read ms. of a short story by her. LLB-267.

C23 Hewlett, Maurice. *The Spanish Jade* (fiction). Has read. LLB-271.

C24 Wordsworth, William. 'Ode to Duty' (poem). Knows. LLB-270.

June

C25 Forster, E. M. *Howards End* (fiction). Has read. LLB-278. See B21.

July

C26 Garvice, Charles. Familiar. LLB-294.

C27 Gilbert, W. S. 'The Yarn of the Nancy Bell' (ballad). Quotes. LLB-293.

C28 Moody, D. W. and Sankey, I. D. *Gospel Hymns*. Quotes Annie Herbert's hymn. LLB-228. In writing 'Hymns in a Man's Life' (1928), Lawrence drew heavily on this volume.

C29 Schreiner, Olive. *Women and Labour*. (essays). Familiar. LLB-287.

C30 Whitman, Walt. 'O, Captain, My Captain' (poem). Quotes. LLB-293.

August

C31 Morris, William. *Defence of Guenevere and Other Poems*. Reading. LLB-298.

September

C32 Galsworthy, John. *The Little Dream* (drama). Received. LLB-326.

C33 Moréas, Jean. Asks Louie to purchase a Moréas book for him. LLB-300.

October

C34 Garnett, Edward. *The Breaking Point, The Feud* (drama). Read. LLB-317, 344-45.

C35 Thurston, Katherine. *John Chilcote, M.P.* (fiction). Has read. LLB-312.

November

C36 *Contemporary Belgian Poetry*, ed. Jethro Bithell. Sending to Louie Burrows. LLB-325.

C37 Jacobsen, Jens Peter. *Nihls Lykke* (fiction). Read. LLB-323.

December

C38 Bithell, Jethro. *The Minnesingers* (poetry collection). Reviewed. LLB-331; KS-24.

C39 Hudson, W. H. *Nature in Downland* (Sussex history). Read. LLB-334.

C40 Jefferies, Richard. *The Story of My Heart* (fiction). Knows. LLB-337.

C41 Liliencron, Detlev. Lawrence's review of C42 indicates that he read the essay on Liliencron in the October 1909 *Contemporary Review*. AA-16, 24.

C42 *The Oxford Book of German Verse*, ed. H. G. Fiedler. Reviewed. LLB-324; KS-24.

C43 Prior, James. Familiar. LLB-334.

C44 Quierdo, Israel. *The Toils of Men* (fiction). Received from A. W. McLeod. LLB-341. See also A201.

C45 Turgenev, Ivan. *The Torrents of Spring* (fiction). Has read. LLB-334.

Undated reading for which evidence appears during 1911

C46 Fabre, Jean-Henri. Had some familiarity with the work of Fabre, which was reported in the *English Review*. RLD-210.

C47 Pound, Ezra. *A Lume Spento* (poetry collection). Received proof copy from Pound. EN, I-142.

C48 Verlaine, Paul. Quotes the poem 'Colloque Sentimental' in 'The Soiled Rose'.

(SECTION D) 1912

January

D1 Andreyev, Leonid. Familiar. Possibly *Silence and Other Stories*. LLB-349, 353.

D2 Bone, Gertrude. *Provincial Tales* (fiction collection). Read 'Poverty', and 'The Right Eye'. LLB-353.

D3 *The Century* (periodical). Familiar. LLB-345.

D4 Garnett, Edward (James Byrne, pseud.) *Lords and Masters* (drama). Read. LLB-344.

D5 Gissing, George. *House of Cobwebs* (fiction collection). Read. LLB-354.

February

D6 Abercrombie, Lascelles. *Emblems of Love* (poetry collection). Read. LLB-362.

D7 Ford, Ford Madox. *High Germany* (poetry collection). Requests its return. LLB-359.

D8 *Hibberts Journal* (periodical). Read the October 1911 issue. Mentions the A. J. Balfour essay, 'Creative Evolution and Philosophical Doubt'. LLB-359.

March

D9 de la Mare, Walter (Walter Ramal, pseud.). *Songs of Childhood*. Has read, probably much earlier. See A186. LLB-348, 370.

D10 Lawson, Henry. *Children of the Bush* (fiction). Familiar. LLB-376.

D11 Shaw, George Bernard. *Man and Superman*. Knows. LLB-373, 377.

April

D12 *Athenaeum* (periodical). Read review of Ernest Weekley's *Romance of Words* in 6 April issue. LLB-384.

D13 Chekhov, Anton. *The Seagull, The Cherry Orchard* (drama). Received. LLB-385.

D14 *The Eyewitness* (periodical) Familiar. LLB-379.

D15 *London Daily News*. Read Edward Garnett's review of J. A. T. Lloyd's *A Great Russian Realist: Feodor Dostoieffsky* in 3 April issue. LLB-380.

May

D16 *Morning Post*. Read announcement of Edward Garnett's play, *The Spanish Lovers*, in 24 May issue. LLB-414.

June

D17 *Saturday Westminster Gazette*. Read review of *The Trespasser* in 8 June issue. LLB-419.

July

D18 *Nottinghamshire Guardian*. Read review of *The Trespasser* in 2 July issue. LLB-425.

September

D19 Conrad, Joseph. *Under Western Eyes*. Read recently. LLB-456.

D20 Heine, Heinrich. Sent volume to David Garnett. LLB-450.

October

D21 Bennett, Arnold. *Anna of the Five Towns* (fiction). Read. LLB-459.

D22 Reid, Forrest. *The Bracknels: A Family Chronicle* (fiction). Read. LLB-462.

D23 Strindberg, August. *Miss Julia, There Are Crimes and Crimes, The Stronger* (drama). Read. LLB-464.

November

D24 Browne, Granville. *The Reign of Terror at Tabriz: England's Responsibility*. 'Looked at it'. LLB-469.

D25 Collings, Ernest. *Sappho, the Queen of Song*. Read, along with ms. of poems by Collings. LLB-468, 472–73.

D26 Conrad, Joseph. *Twixt Land and Sea* (fiction collection). Possibly the volume Lawrence read at this time. LLB-465.

D27 Dickens, Charles. *Nicholas Nickleby* (fiction). Familiar. LLB-474.

D28 Garnett, Edward. *The Trial of Jeanne D'Arc* (drama). Read. LLB-469.

D29 Jerrold, Douglas. *Mrs Caudle's Curtain Lectures*. Quotes. LLB-474.

D30 *Manchester Guardian*. Read review of Garnett's *Lords and Masters* in 23 May issue. LLB-469.

D31 Rutherford, Mark. *Revolution in Tanner's Lane* (fiction). Read. LLB-481-82.

D32 Shakespeare, William. *A Midsummer Night's Dream*. Knows. LLB-476.

December

D33 Fielding, Henry. *Tom Jones* (fiction). Received. LLB-487.

D34 Filippi, Rosina. *Bernadine* (fiction). Read. LLB-496.

D35 Lockhart, J. G. *The Life of Robert Burns*. Received. LLB-487.

D36 Moliére. *Georges Dandin* (drama). Quotes. LLB-497.

D37 Reynolds, Stephen. *Alongshore* (fiction). Read. LLB-488.

D38 Yeats, W. B. *Poems*. Probably the volume received. LLB-488.

Undated reading for which evidence appears during 1912

D39 Arnold, Matthew. Familiar with his theories of the effect of industrialism on culture. POL-160.

(SECTION E) 1913

January

E1 Böcklin, Arnold (Swiss painter, 1827–1901). Has biographical knowledge of his experience in Paris during the Revolution of 1848. LLB-503.

E2 *The Poetry of Robert Burns*, ed. W. E. Henley and T. E. Henderson. A. W. McLeod probably sent Lawrence notes on the biographical essay by Henley included here. LLB-504.

E3 Burns, Robert. *Selected Poems of Robert Burns*, ed. Andrew Lang. Received. LLB-504.

E4 Scott, Sir Walter. *The Talisman* (fiction). Quotes the introduction. LLB-504.

E5 Shakespeare, William. *Hamlet*. Quotes. LLB-504.

E6 Tennyson, Alfred. 'Lady Clara Vere de Vere' (poem). Quotes. LLB-506.

February

E7 Dehmel, Richard. Familiar with his work and that of Ricarda Huch, Detlev Liliencron, Stefan George and Else Lasker-Schüler, possibly from reading done for C42. LLB-513.

E8 Burnett, Frances. *Little Lord Fauntleroy*. Knows. LLB-510.

E9 *Georgian Poetry*, ed. Edward Marsh. Finished review. LLB-508; KS-36.

E10 Moore, George. *Salve* (autobiography). Familiar. LLB-512.

E11 *Rhythm* (periodical). Received the January or February issue, probably also the March issue where E9 was published. LLB-512.

E12 Schofield, Lily. *Elizabeth, Betsy and Bess* (fiction). Read. LLB-512.

March

E13 Byron, George Gordon. 'Lara' (poem). Knows. LLB-523.

E14 Gissing, George. *New Grub Street* (fiction). Requests. LLB-524.

E15 Gorky, Maxim. Has read 'all of the $4\frac{1}{2}$ pence' Gorky available. LLB-524.

E16 Greek tragedians. Requests the

Gilbert Murray translations. LLB-525.

E17 London, Jack. *White Fang.* Requests. LLB-524.

E18 Reviews of *Love Poems*. Read reviews in 6 March issues of the *Daily News* and *Morning Post* and the 13 March issue of *Times Literary Supplement*. LLB-528, 530.

E19 Mann, Mary. Read or scanned a volume. LLB-525.

E20 Masefield, John. Familiar with his work. LLB-523.

E21 Merrick, Leonard. Read something recently. LLB-525.

E22 Wells, H. G. *Marriage* (fiction). Familiar. LLB-528.

E23 Wharton, Edith. *The House of Mirth* (fiction). Familiar. Requests other of her works. LLB-524.

E24 Richardson, Samuel. *Clarissa Harlowe* (fiction). Requests. LLB-524.

E25 Zangwill, Israel. Familiar. LLB-524.

April

E26 d'Annunzio, Gabriele. *The Light Under the Bushel*. Familiar. TinI-68.

E27 Bergson, Henri. Read something recently. Available in translation were *Laughter (1911)* and *The Philosophy of Change (1912)*. LLB-544.

E28 Blake, William. 'The Tyger' (poem). Quotes. TinI-43.

E29 Euripides. *Medea*. Re-reading. LLB-543. Probably Gilbert Murray translation, E16.

E30 Pope, Alexander. 'Essay on Man' (poem). Quotes. TWI-46.

E31 Voynich, E. L. *The Gadfly* (fiction). Reading. Mistakenly assumes the author is male. LLB-525, 543.

E32 Wells, H. G. *The New Machiavelli* (fiction). Reading. LLB-543.

May

E33 *The Blue Review* (periodical). Familiar. LLB-546, 548.

E34 Chambers, Jessie. *The Rathe Primrose* (fiction). Read the ms. sent to him by Edward Garnett. LLB-551.

E35 Goethe, J. W. von. *Iphigenie in Tauris* (drama). Knows. LLB-549.

E36 Mann, Thomas. *Buddenbrooks, Der Tod in Venedig, Tonio Kroeger* (fiction) and *Tristan* (fiction collection). Discusses in essay, 'German Books: Thomas Mann'. Completed in May. LLB-546, KS-38-39.

E37 Noguchi, Yone. Familiar with his work on metrics. (Essay on Noguchi included in E39.) HL-135.

E38 Pope, Alexander, 'Epistle to Dr Arbuthnot' (poem). Quotes. LLB-552.

E39 Ransome, Arthur. *Portraits and Speculations* (essay collection). Read this or *The Book of Friendship* or *The Book of Love*. LLB-552.

E40 Wyspianski, Stanislaus. Reading. FLMC-182.

July

E41 Colette. *La Vagabonde* (fiction). Knows this and other of her works. ML-213.

E42 Middleton, Richard. *Monologues* (essay collection). Familiar with his work. ML-214, 251. Letter to Henry Savage, *Yale University Library Gazette* (April 1972, p. 264) indicates he read this work.

E43 *The Nation* (periodical). Read the review of *Sons and Lovers* in the 11 December 1913 issue. ML-215.

E44 *The New Statesman* (periodical). Familiar in May. LLB-551; Requests now. ML-215.

August

E45 Flecker, James E. *Golden Journey*

to *Samarkand* (poetry collection). Has read. ML-220.

E46 Lamartine, Alphonse. Familiar. ML-221.

October

E47 Bjorkman, Edwin. Read his foreword to *The Widowing of Mrs Holroyd.* AA/DHL-15.

E48 Harrison, Jane. *Ancient Art and Ritual* (anthropology). Read. HL-149.

E49 Hodgson, Ralph. Has read something, probably *The Last Blackbird and Other Lines.* ML-236.

E50 *The New York Times.* Read review of *Sons and Lovers* In 21 Sept. issue. HL-144.

E51 Pater, Walter. Read something recently loaned him by Henry Savage. HL-149.

E52 Sterne, Laurence. *Tristram Shandy* (fiction). Read. HL-149.

November

E53 *Eune Ame D'Enfant.* Read in French this octavo published by the Société Saint-Augustin, an extraction from *Plus Haut. Yale University Library Gazette* (April 1972, p. 266).

E54 Eekhoud, Georges. Read. *Yale University Library Gazette* (April 1972, p. 266).

E55 Stephens, James. *The Crock of Gold* (prose fantasy). Reading. ML-249.

December

E56 Dowson, Ernest. *Pierrot of the Minute* (poetry collection). Read. HL-165.

E57 Liberman, H. *Les Fumeurs d'Opium en Chine.* Requests. ML-250.

E58 Tolstoy, Leo. *The Kreutzer Sonata* (fiction). Has read. ML-250.

Undated reading for which evidence appears during 1913

E59 Dostoyevsky, F. M. *The Brothers Karamazov* (fiction). Read. PH-283.

E60 *The Morning Post* (newspaper). A. W. McLeod had this sent to the Lawrences during 1913–14. HL-173.

(SECTION F) 1914

January

F1 Murray, Gilbert. Reading, possibly the *Rhesus* drama of Euripides which he had recently translated. HL-173.

February

F2 Belloc, Hilaire. Familiar. ML-264.

F3 Crosland, T. W. H. *Sonnets.* Read. ML-264.

March

F4 Collings, Ernest. *Outlines* (drawings). Probably the book (dedicated to him) received and perused. HL-182.

F5 Dostoyevsky, F. M. *House of the Dead* (fiction). Received. HL-180.

April

F6 *The Egoist* (periodical). Read 1 April issue. HL-187.

May

F7 Abercrombie, Lascelles. 'End of the World', 'Mary and the Bramble', 'Sale of St Thomas', 'Shrivelled Zeus' (poems). Familiar. ML-278.

F8 *The Bookman* (periodical). Received an unspecified copy. FLMC-191.

F9 Meredith poems. Received a volume from A. W. McLeod. ML-279. Not clear whether this is George Meredith, or Scottish poet, J. O. Meredith.

F10 *New Numbers* (periodical). Read the first two issues. ML-278.

F11 Waterfield, Lina. *Home Life in*

Italy. Using as a cookbook. LW-142.

F12 Wells, H. G. *Country of the Blind*
(fiction). Knows. HL-194.

June

F13 Carswell, Catherine. Read the ms.
of her novel *Open the Door* (1921)
ML-283.

F14 Futurism. Read essays and
'manifestations' by Paolo Buzzi,
Fillippo Marinetti and Ardengo
Soffici as well as a volume of poetry
and one of pictures. ML-279. At least
Marinetti was read in Italian. ML-
281.

F15 Peshkov, Alexei M. (adopted son of
Maxim Gorky). Read ms. of a short
story which Peshkov brought him. IL-
418.

F16 *Poetry* (periodical). Received the
January issue. ALD/LET-69.

July

F17 Abercrombie, Lascelles. *Thomas
Hardy: A Critical Study*. Borrowed.
HL-205.

November

F18 Dudley, Helen. Read two plays in
ms. which were never published. ML-
294.

F19 *Poetry* (periodical). Received
November issue. HL-211.

December

F20 Artzibasheff, Mikail. Some
familiarity. ML-301. Only work in
translation was *Sanine*.

F21 *Book of Job*. Knows. MPL-211.

F22 Dostoyevsky, F. M. *Letters from the
Underworld* (fiction collection).
Reading Everyman edition. ML-301.

F23 Fielding, Henry. *Amelia* (fiction).
Familiar. 'Study of Thomas Hardy'.

F24 Hardy, Thomas. 'Study of Thomas
Hardy', PH 398-516 was completed in
December. KS-55. It reveals
knowledge of these works: *Desperate

Remedies, discusses. *The Dynasts*,
mentions. *Far from the Madding
Crowd*, discusses. *The Hand of
Ethelberta*, mentions. *Jude the
Obscure*, discusses in depth. *A
Laodicean*, mentions. *The Mayor of
Casterbridge*, discusses. *A Pair of
Blue Eyes*, mentions. *The Return of
the Native*, discusses. *Tess of the
D'Urbervilles*, discusses. *The
Trumpet-Major*, mentions. *Two on a
Tower*, mentions. *Under the
Greenwood Tree*, mentions. *The
Well-Beloved*, mentions. *The
Woodlanders*, mentions.

F25 Jenner, Katherine L. *Christian
Symbolism*. Reading. ML-304.

F26 Mackenzie, Compton. *Sinister
Street* (fiction). Has read. HL-212.

F27 Mann, Heinrich. Familiar. ML-301.

F28 Michelangelo. Has detailed
biographical knowledge of him in
'Study of Thomas Hardy'.

F29 Nietzsche, Friedrich. Has
knowledge of *Ewige Wiederkehr*,
Nietzsche's doctrine of eternal return.
'Study of Thomas Hardy'.

F30 Spinoza, Benedict. Quotes. 'Study
of Thomas Hardy'.

F31 Tolstoy, Ilya (trans. George
Calderon). *Reminiscences of Tolstoy*.
Familiar. 'Study of Thomas Hardy'.

F32 Virgil. *Aeneid* (epic poem).
Familiar. 'Study of Thomas Hardy.'

**Undated reading for which evidence
appears during 1914**

F33 Dante. Knows story of Dante and
Beatrice. 'The Shades of Spring'.

F34 Garnett, Edward. *Tolstoy: His Life
and Writings*, 'Tolstoy's Place in
European Literature'. Certain of
Lawrence's statements about Tolstoy
(and other Russian writers) indicate
he read these works. Letter of January
1969 to me from Professor Armin

Arnold.

F35 Plato. Familiar. 'Study of Thomas Hardy.'

(SECTION G) 1915

January

G1 Palmer, John. *A Comedy of Manners* (critical essays). Read. Unpublished letter to A. W. McLeod. University of Texas.

February

G2 Cannan, Gilbert. *Young Ernest and the Rosary* (fiction). Familiar. ML-319.

G3 Forster, E. M. *The Longest Journey* (fiction), *The Celestial Omnibus* (fiction collection). Received. Read 'The Story of a Panic'. Unpublished letter to E. M. Forster. King's College, Cambridge.

G4 Murry, J. M. *Still Life* (fiction). Read in ms. ML-321.

G5 Weekley, Ernest. *Romance of Names* (language study). Familiar. PD/NIGHTMARE-59.

G6 Woolf, Virginia. *The Voyage Out* (fiction). Returned to Forster. PD/NIGHTMARE-51.

March

G7 Dostoyevsky, F. M. *The Idiot* (fiction). Read. RGH-60.

G8 Nietzsche, Friedrich. *Die Fröhliche Wissenschaft* (philosophy). Familiar. ML-324, 327.

G9 Van Gogh, Elizabeth du Quesne. Read something about Van Gogh. ML-325. Possibly Elizabeth du Quesne Van Gogh's *Personal Recollections of Vincent Van Gogh*.

April

G10 Dostoyevsky, Fyodor, *Letters of F. M. Dostoevsky*, ed. E. C. Mayne. Reading. ML-332.

May

G11 Cannan, Gilbert. *Windmills: A Book of Fables*. Mentions. GL-783.

G12 Farjeon, Eleanor. *The Soul of Kol Nikon*. Read, along with some poems in ms. EN, I-298.

G13 Farquhar, John. *The Crown of Hinduism* (philosophy). Familiar. GL-801.

G14 Soloviev, Vladimir, trans. Alexander Bakshy. *War Progress and the End of History: Including a Short History of the Antichrist* (This had also been translated by Stephen Graham as *War and Christianity from the Russian Point of View: Three Conversations*). Reading. ML-344.

G15 *Some Imagist Poets*, ed. Amy Lowell. Sent to Ottoline Morrell. ML-339.

June

G16 Brailsford, Henry. *Shelley, Godwin and their Circle*. Reading. HL-237.

G17 Molière. *Tartuffe, Le Bourgeois Gentilhomme* (drama). Mentions. Unpublished letter of 2 June to E. M. Forster, King's College, Cambridge.

G18 Strachey, Lytton. *Landmarks in French Literature*. Familiar. HL-237.

July

G19 Burnet, John. *Early Greek Philosophy*. Reading. ML-352.

September

G20 Milton, John. *Paradise Lost* (epic). Familiar. MPL-236.

G21 Russell, Bertrand. 'Justice in Wartime'. Knows. PD-144.

October

G22 Poe, Edgar Allan. 'The Fall of the House of Usher', 'Ligeia'. Familiarity shown in 'The Crown', completed this month. KS-66.

November

G23 Chekhov, Anton. *The Bet and Other Stories*, trans. S. S. Koteliansky. Received. GZ-59.

G24 Meredith, J. O. (Scottish poet). Received a volume from E. M. Forster. ML-373.

G25 Nichols, Robert. Discusses his work. ML-387.

December

G26 Carswell, Catherine. Read a poem by her. *Yale University Library Gazette* (Jan. 1975), p. 254.

G27 Frazer, Sir James. *The Golden Bough, Totemism and Exogamy* (anthropology). Reading. ML-393.

G28 *The Whole Works of Homer* (Chapman translation). Requests. GZ-60.

G29 Malory, Thomas. *Morte d'Arthur*. Familiar. EN, I-345.

G30 Russell, Bertrand. Returned a book of his to him. BR-62.

G31 Shelley, Percy Bysshe. Received a book about Shelley from Ottoline Morrell. HL-299.

G32 Cournos, John. *Babel, Miranda Masters* (fiction). Read the first; received a copy of the second. EN, I-327.

Undated reading for which evidence appears during 1915

G33 *John Bull* (newspaper). Familiar. MIH-252.

G34 Radford, Dollie. Read the ms. of a play. EN, I-307.

G35 Shakespeare. *Othello*. Knows. PD/NIGHTMARE-112.

G36 *Signature* (periodical). Collaborated with John M. Murry and Katherine Mansfield on three issues, probably read them. KS-58.

G37 Wickham, Anna. Familiar. Her poetry collection, *The Contemplative Quarry*, was published this year.

HL-258.

(SECTION H) 1916

January

H1 *Beowulf* (epic poem), Familiar. HL-303.

H2 Beresford, J. D. *The House in Demetrius Road* (fiction). Familiar with this and other of his novels. HL-304.

H3 Carswell, Catherine. Read a 'graveyard' poem. HL-308.

H4 Masters, Edgar Lee. *Spoon River Anthology* (poetry collection). Has read. HL-308.

H5 Radford, Dollie. *Poems*. Read. EN, I-356.

H6 Watson, Grant. *Where Bonds are Loosed* (fiction). Read. HL-307.

February

H7 Bunyan, John. *The Pilgrim's Progress* (allegory). Knows. HL-327.

H8 Daudet, Alphonse. *Tartarin of Tarascon* (fiction). Familiar. GZ-68.

H9 Dostoyevsky, F. M. *The Possessed* (fiction). Read. HL-325.

H10 Salimbene. *From St Francis to Dante: Translations from the Chronicle of Franciscan Salimbene.* Reading. HL-322.

H11 Hall, H. R. *The Ancient History of the Near East from Earliest Times to the Battle of Salambis.* Probably the volume he is reading. ML-424.

H12 Hesiod. Reading. ML-421.

H13 Melville, Herman. *Moby Dick* (fiction). Reading. ML-424.

H14 Nietzsche, Friedrich. *Thus Spake Zarathustra*. Knows. GZ-70.

H15 Petrie, W. M. F. *History of Egypt*. Read. HL-322.

H16 Petronius. Reading. HL-313.

H17 Sidgwick poems. May be by Harold Munro, who was affiliated with

Sidgwick and Duckworth publishers. Munro published *Trees* this year. Letter of 25 Feb. GL-1061.

H18 Synge, J. M. *The Tinker's Wedding* (drama). Mentions. ML-438.

H19 Virgil. Re-reading a volume received from Ottoline Morrell. ML-421.

March

H20 Boldrewood, Ralph (T. A. Browne). Suggests to Koteliansky that he along with Frances Hodgson Burnett, W. H. Kingston, Annie Swan, Juliana Ewing, Harry Collingwood and George Henty are writers for children who deserve to be translated into Russian. ZYTARUK/MALAHAT-26.

H21 Curzon, George. Returned a book to Ottoline Morrell on 15 March. DHLR, 8, summer 1975, 200.

H22 Kuprin, Alexander. *The River of Life*, trans. S. S. Koteliansky and J. M. Murry (fiction collection). Reading. GZ-73.

H23 Tylor, E. B. *Primitive Cultures* (anthropology). Knows. HL-344.

April

H24 Murray, Gilbert. *The Four Stages of Greek Religion*. Familiar. HL-344. Probably the book he received from Ottoline Morrell earlier in the year. HL-328.

H25 Rolland, Romain. *Life of Michael Angelo*. Read. ML-445.

H26 Thucydides. Received a volume from Ottoline Morrell. HL-343.

May

H27 *Berliner Tageblatt* (newspaper). Has read several copies recently. HL-351.

H28 Dana, Richard H. *Two Years Before the Mast* (personal narrative). Read. ML-454.

H29 Dickens, Charles. *The Pickwick*

Papers (fiction). Reading. ML-454.

H30 Manucci, Aldo P. *A Pepys of Mogul India 1653–1708*. Read all but the last of the four volumes, which are an abridgment of *Storia do Mogor*. HL-350; ML-447.

H31 O'Shea, Katherine. *Charles Stewart Parnell*. Reading. ML-451.

H32 Revermort, J. A. (J. A. Crambs). *Hester Rainsbrook* (fiction). Read. May have received other novels by same author. SJD-193-4.

H33 *Some Imagist Poets*. Received. SFD-359.

June

H34 Cooper, James Fenimore. *The Deerslayer, The Last of the Mohicans* (fiction). Knows. GZ-80-1.

H35 *Times Literary Supplement*. Read review of *Twilight in Italy* in 15 June issue. ML-455.

July

H36 De Quincey, Thomas. *Reminiscences of the Lake Poets*. Ordered. ML-465.

H37 Olufson, A. F. *Through the Unknown Pamirs: The Second Danish Pamir Expedition*. Familiar. ML-465.

H38 Shakespeare, William. *Henry IV, Henry V, King Lear*. Discussed with J. M. Murry. JMM-58-59.

H39 Shelley, Percy Bysshe. 'The Question' (poem). Quotes. EN, I-388.

H40 St. Bernard. *Some Letters of St Bernard*, trans. Samuel J. Eales. Reading. HL-360.

H41 Trelawny, Edward. *Recollections of the Last Days of Shelley and Byron*. Probably the book requested from Dollie Radford. EN, I-389.

August

H42 Crèvecoeur, Hector. *Letters from an American Farmer*. Discussed.

SFD-371.

H43 Murry, J. M. *Fyodor Dostoevsky*. Read. ML-469.

H44 Quiller-Couch, Arthur. Disparages his and Compton Mackenzie's portraits of gamekeepers. Unpublished letter to Barbara Low, Southern Illinois University.

September

H45 Burnet, John. *Early Greek Philosophy*. Requests. ML-473.

H46 Herodotus. Received. ML-474.

H47 Kouyoumdjian, Dikran (Michael Arlen). Familiar. Unpublished letter (dated only by month) to Philip Heseltine. University of Texas.

H48 *Daily Mirror*. Read the 27 Sept. issue. HL-367.

H49 *Psychoanalytic Review* (periodical). Sent a copy to Barbara Low. Probably the issue in which *Sons and Lovers* was discussed. GL-1126.

November

H50 D'Annunzio, Gabriele. *Il Fuoco, Il Trionfo della Morte, Vergine delle Rocche, L'Innocente* (fiction). Has read first three. ML-489. Requests last title. ML-486.

H51 Asquith, Herbert. Read ms. of poems, perhaps those he added to his volume *The Volunteer* for the 1917 edition. HL-380.

H52 Baedeker travel guidebook. Received. ML-484.

H53 Brooke, Rupert. Familiar with 'a sonnet'. HL-378.

H54 Cannan, Gilbert. *Mendel* (fiction). Read *some* of it. ML-485.

H55 Marryat, Frederick. *Jacob Faithful, Peter Simple, Poor Jack* (fiction). Requests. Frieda later comments on reading the first. ML-485.

H56 Melville, Herman. *Omoo, Typee* (fiction). Requests. ML-485.

H57 Stendhal. *De L'Amour, La Chartreuse de Parme* (fiction). Familiar. Unpublished letter to E. M. Forster, 11 Nov. King's College, Cambridge.

H58 Turgenev, Ivan. *Sportsman's Sketches* (fiction collection). Read. ML-488.

H59 Zola, Emile. *L'Assommoir, Nana* (fiction). Requests. ML-485.

December

H60 Deledda, Grazia. Requests works by this author or by Matilde Serao. ML-485.

H61 Dostoyevsky, F. M. *Pages from the Journal of an Author*, trans. S. S. Koteliansky and J. M. Murry. Read *parts* of it. ML-492.

H62 Mallock, W. H. *The New Republic* (fiction). Borrowed. ML-495.

H63 Melville, Herman. *Typee* (fiction). Read. PD-280.

H64 Trotter, Wilfred. *Instincts of the Herd in Peace and War* (psychology). Read. EN, I-408.

H65 Verga, Giovanni. 'Cavalleria Rusticana' (fiction). Read in Italian. ML-492.

Undated reading for which evidence appears during 1916

H66 Bürger, G. A. Quotes his poem 'Lenore' in 'The Mortal Coil'.

H67 Maspero, Gaston. *Egypt: Ancient Sights and Modern Scenes, New Light on Ancient Egypt*. Read one of these, loaned by Mrs Julian Huxley. WYT-98.

H68 Petrie, W. M. F. *The Religions of Egypt*. Familiar. WYT-98.

H69 Proust, Marcel. Catherine Carswell remembers that Lawrence hated Proust by this year. CC-41.

Unidentified reading 1916

H70 an 'Egyptian book' received from Ottoline Morrell. HL-314.

H71 Atlases. Received. Unpublished letter of 8 Sept. to Barbara Low. Southern Illinois University.

(SECTION I) 1917

January

I1 H. D. (Hilda Doolittle). Familiar. Unpublished letter of 29 January.

February

I2 Peabody, Josephine. *Harvest Moon* (poetry collection). Requests. HL-399.

I3 *Poetry* (periodical). Received the February issue. HL-399.

March

I4 Angell, Sir Norman. *The Great Illusion* (anti-war tract). Read. PD/NIGHTMARE-290.

I5 Sutton, A. W. and M. H. *The Culture of Profitable Vegetables in Small Gardens*. Requests. ML-507.

April

I6 *Metropolitan* (periodical). Received April issue. Unpublished letter of 3 April to J. B. Pinker.

I7 *Seven Arts* (periodical). Received March issue. Unpublished letter of 3 April to J. B. Pinker.

May

I8 Russian grammar book. Requests. ML-513.

July

I9 Frost, Robert; Sandburg, Carl; Untermeyer, Louis. Mentions their poetry, along with that of Edgar Lee Masters which he read in 1916. ILA-204.

I10 Tietjens, Eunice. *Profiles from China* (free verse sketches). Read. HL-412.

August

I11 Blavatsky, Madame Helena. *The Secret Doctorine* (theosophy). Knows. JBH-119.

I12 Pryse, James M. *The Apocalypse Unsealed* (theosophy). Knows. JBH-119.

I13 *Strand* (periodical). Familiar. HL-414.

September

I14 Carswell, Catherine. Read a 'Hardyesque' poem of hers. *Yale University Library Gazette* (Jan., 1965) p. 257.

I15 Frank, Waldo (founder of *Seven Arts*). Received a book, probably his 1917 novel, *The Unwelcome Man*. ML-524.

October

I16 *Yale Review* (periodical). Reads occasionally. ML-527.

November

I17 Barrie, J. M. *Margaret Ogilvy* (biography). Received. Probably read earlier. See A180. ML-530.

I18 Carswell, Catherine. Continuing to read her work in progress, probably the ms. of her novel, *Open the Door* (1920). ML-530.

Undated reading for which evidence appears during 1917

I19 Chekhov, Anton. *The House with the Mezzanine and Other Stories*, trans. S. S. Koteliansky and Gilbert Cannan. Koteliansky habitually sent Lawrence his translations.

I20 *Geography of the World*. Gave Stanley Hocking, this six-volume work. Possibly the *Penny Geography and Gazeteer*. EN, I-427.

I21 Garnett, Edward. *Turgenev: a Study*. Professor Armin Arnold feels that Lawrence's criticisms of Turgenev indicate he read this. Letter to me, 13 Jan., 1969.

Unidentified reading 1917

I22 American authors and statesmen. Ordered books on and by Melville, Cooper, Whitman, Hawthorne, Emerson, Franklin, Poe, Hamilton and Lincoln. Unpublished letter of 4 Jan. to Robert Mountsier. University of Texas.

I23 A collection of Hebridean songs. Received in October. EN, I-423.

I24 Some 'Italian Books' which contained a wearisome quantity of 'passion, eroticism and sex'. Read in March. GZ-110.

I25 A parcel of unidentified books from Montague Sherman. Received in March. GZ-111.

(SECTION J) 1918

February

J1 Poe, Edgar Allan. *Tales of Mystery and Imagination* (fiction collection). Requests a replacement for his lost copy of the Everyman edition. ML-542. This contains 46 stories, including all those discussed in SM.

April

J2 Frobenius, Leo. *The Voice of Africa*, trans. Rudolf Blind (history). Read in two volumes. ML-550.

J3 Gibbon, Edward. *The Decline and Fall of the Roman Empire*. Reading. ML-551.

June

J4 Revelation, Book of. Gives his first evidence of familiarity with this in SM In his posthumously published work he indicates that he has known it since childhood.

J5 Chateaubriand, François. Familiar with his concept of the noble savage. SM. 'Crèvecoeur' and 'Typee/Omoo'. Probably read *Les Natchez* and *Voyage en Amerique*, since he was later to draw on these in *The Lost Girl*.

J6 Cooper, James Fenimore. *Studies in Classic American Literature* was completed in June. KS-86. It reveals knowledge of the following Cooper novels. *Eve Effingham*, discusses, 'Anglo-american'. *Homeward Bound*, discusses 'Anglo-american'. *The Last of the Mohicans*, discusses, 'Leatherstocking'. *The Oak Openings*, briefly discusses 'Leatherstocking'. *The Pathfinder*, discusses, 'Leatherstocking'. *The Pilot*, discusses, 'Anglo-american'. *The Pioneers*, discusses, 'Leatherstocking'. *The Prairie*, discusses at length, 'Leatherstocking'. *The Spy*, discusses, 'Anglo-american'.

J7 Franklin, Benjamin. *Autobiography of Ben Franklin*. Discusses in SM, 'Franklin'. May also have read a diary in which Franklin records having been at a drunken Indian pow-wow.

J8 Gauguin, Paul. Has some biographical knowledge of him. 'Typee/Omoo'.

J9 Hawthorne, Nathaniel. SM reveals knowledge of the following Hawthorne fiction. *The Blithedale Romance*, discusses, 'Blithedale'. *The House of Seven Gables*, discusses briefly, 'Blithedale'. *The Scarlet Letter*, discusses in depth, 'Scarlet Letter'. *Twice Told Tales*, familiar, 'Blithedale'.

J10 Holmes, Oliver Wendell. Included on Lawrence's list of Transcendentalists in the unpublished second version of the Whitman essay. SM-255.

J11 Melville, Herman. *Pierre, White Jacket* (fiction). Mentions both in the 'Typee/Omoo' section of SM. Armin Arnold relates that J. M. Murry told him Lawrence had not read either novel by the time the essay was written for the first time and quite possibly did not read them at all, but derived his knowledge from Raymond Weaver's book, *Herman Melville, Poet and Mystic (N20)*. AA/DHL-28-29.

J12 Pascal, Blaise. *Pensées*. Quotes, SM, 'Typee/Omoo'.

J13 Rousseau, Jean-Jacques. Refers to his child of nature concept. SM, 'Crèvecoeur', and 'Typee/Omoo'.

J14 St Pierre, Bernardin de. Familiar. SM, 'Crèvecoeur'.

J15 Shelley, Mary. *Frankenstein* (fiction). Familiar. SM, 'Franklin'.

J16 Vaillant, François le. *Voyage to the Interior of Africa*. Professor Tindall feels there is evidence that Lawrence read this work while SM was in progress. WYT-95.

J17 West, Benjamin. Has read somewhere of West's introduction to the *Apollo Belvedere* during his visit to the Vatican. This is recounted in the West biography by John Galt, *The Life, Studies and Works of Benjamin West* (1820) as well as in other writings.

J18 Whitman, Walt. *Leaves of Grass*. SM – 'Whitman'.

July

J19 Henry, Leigh. *Poems of a Prisoner*. Lawrence gives this title to the ms. by Nancy Henry's husband which he read. KC-23.

J20 *New Paths*, ed. C. W. Beaumont and M. T. H. Sadler. Familiar. ML-561.

September

J21 Henry, Nancy. Read the ms. of a short story. KC-29.

November

J22 Lowell, Amy. *Can Grande's Castle* (essays). Familiar. SFD-484.

J23 *Poetry* (periodical). Received the November issue. HL-457.

December

J24 Bulfinch, Thomas. *The Legends of Charlemagne*. Borrowed. December. ML-567.

J25 Jung, Carl. Borrowed a book, with which he was familiar. Perhaps *Psychology of the Unconscious*. EN, I-480; WYT-98.

Undated reading for which evidence appears during 1918

J26 De Quincey, Thomas. Gave the Carswells a 'complete set' of De Quincey when he moved this year. CC-113.

Unidentified reading 1918

J27 Reading a book on the occult in April. ML-551. Asks Mark Gertler for the names of others interested in occult, astrology, magic.

J28 In response to Lawrence's request for a book on the human nervous system, Edith Eder sent him some pages from a medical book which he read and returned in May. JBH-120.

(SECTION K) 1919

January

K1 Bates, H. W. *The Naturalist on the River Amazons* (natural history). Received. ML-575.

K2 Scheffel, Joseph. *Ekkehard: A Tale of the 10th Century* (fiction). Received. ML-575.

February

K3 Boccaccio, Giovanni. *The Decameron*. Familar. MEH-196.

K4 Comnena, Anna. Familar with her memoirs of the Crusaders, MEH-144.

K5 Dante. Chapter 13 of MEH reveals extensive biographical knowledge of both Dante and Petrarch.

K6 Erasmus. *Handbook for the Christian Soldier*. Familiar. MEH-208.

K7 Gladstone, William. *Letters to Lord Aberdeen*. Familiar. MEH-285.

K8 Joachim of Flora. *Introduction to the Everlasting Gospel*. Mentions. MEH-172.

K9 Manzoni, Alessandro. *I Promessi Sposi* (fiction). Knows. Gave to Katherine Mansfield. ML-578.

K10 Mazzini, Giuseppe. *Young Italy Manifesto*. Mentions. MEH-276.

K11 Montesquieu, C. *The Spirit of Laws* (political philosophy). Indicates knowledge of its content and its widespread effect on French thought. MEH-237.

K12 Pellico, Silvio. *My Prisons* (memoir). Familiar. MEH-273.

K13 Pliny the Elder. Familiar with his accounts of the deaths of Christians under Nero. MEH-35-41.

K14 *Poetry* (periodical). Asks that it continue to be sent. HL-468.

K15 Prescott, W. H. *The History of the Conquest of Peru*. Has read. ML-578.

K16 Reade, W. W. *The Martyrdom of Man* (history). ML-581.

K17 Rousseau, Jean-Jacques. *The Social Contract* (political philosophy). Quotes. MEH-237.

K18 Sand, George. *Les Maîtres Sonneurs, Le Marquis de Villemer, François le Champi* (fiction). Has read. Requests other of her works. ML-578.

K19 Tacitus. Familiar with his accounts of Nero's treatment of the early Christians. MEH-35-41.

March

K20 *Athenaeum* (periodical). Familiar. ML-579.

K21 Ballantyne, Robert. *Ungava* (fiction). Recommends. GZ-166.

K22 Belt, Thomas. *Naturalist in Nicaragua* (natural history). Ordered. GZ-166-67. See M20.

K23 Blavatsky, Madame Helena. *Isis Unveiled* (theosophy). Has some familiarity. Requests. HL-476.

K24 Collodi, Carlo. *Pinocchio* (fiction). Recommends. GZ-166.

K25 Deledda, Grazia. Has read something sent by Katherine Mansfield. HL-472.

K26 France, Anatole. *Le Petit Pierre*. (fiction collection).

K27 Gibbon, Edward. *Autobiography of Edward Gibbon*. Ordered. GZ-166-67.

K28 Tunnicliff, H. G. *The Story of the Pilgrim Fathers*. Ordered. GZ-166-67.

K29 Sheppard, Elizabeth. *Charles Auchester: A Memorial* (3 vols.). Ordered. GZ-166-67.

K30 Spyri, Johanna. *Heidi* (fiction). Recommends. GZ-166.

May

K31 James, William. *The Varieties of Religious Experience* (philosophy). Orders, saying he has not read it. ML-587. This casts doubt on Jessie Chambers's recollection, A169.

K32 Francis of Assisi, St. *Fioretti of Saint Francis of Assisi* (life, devotions, etc.). Reading. RA-244.

K33 *Occult Review* (periodical). Familiar. HL-476.

July

K34 Rostand, Edmund. *Cyrano de Bergerac* (drama). Familiar. Preface to *Touch and Go*, completed July. WR-42.

August

K35 Shestov, Leo. *All Things Are Possible* (philosophy). Polishing the translation. ML-591.

September
K36 Burr, Jane. *The Glorious Hope* (fiction). Read. ML-595.

October
K37 De Quincey, Thomas. Gave the Carswells a volume before leaving for Italy. ML-597. Possibly part of J26.
K38 Goethe, J. W. von. Re-read some of his work. ML-597.
K39 Anderson, Sherwood. *Winesburg, Ohio* (fiction). Read. ML-599.
K40 Hippius, Zinaida. *The Green Ring* (drama). Offers Koteliansky's translation of this to a publisher. ML-599.

Undated reading for which evidence appears during 1919
K41 Dulac, Edmund. Requests an unspecified volume, possibly *Sleeping Beauty and Other Tales*. EN, II-8.
K42 Hesse, Hermann. *Demian* (fiction). Read in German. MDL-133.

Unidentified reading for 1919
K43 A poem by a Chinese princess who was given to a Tartar chief as tribute. MEH-71.
K44 Art books received from Mark Gertler on 31 March. GZ-170.

(SECTION L) 1920

January
L1 Burrow, Trigant. In *Psychoanalysis and the Unconscious*, completed this month, Lawrence reveals that he knows of Burrow's theories. In a letter of June 1944, to Mary Freeman, author of *D. H. Lawrence: a Basic Study of his Ideas*, Burrow lists his publications which Lawrence could have read. That letter is reproduced in EN, III-147-48.

L2 Carswell, Catherine. *Open the Door* (fiction). Has read. ML-606. Read the ms. at various times since 1914.
L3 Douglas, Norman. Quotes in Chapter Six of *Psychoanalysis and the Unconscious*.
L4 Freud, Sigmund. Although *Psychoanalysis and the Unconscious* is partially a refutation of certain Freudian theories *as Lawrence understood them*, it is difficult to determine which of Freud's writings he read and which objections are based upon discussions that he may have had with David Eder and Barbara Low, both Freudian analysts. Dr Low published *Psycho-Analysis: a Brief Outline of the Freudian Theory* in 1920.
L5 James, William. Displays knowledge of James's stream of consciousness theory in *Psychoanalysis and the Unconscious*. This is discussed in at least two books to which Lawrence would have had access while at Nottingham, a period when Jessie Chambers reports he was very interested in James: *A Pluralistic Universe* (1907) and *The Principles of Psychology* (1890).

February
L6 Magnus, Maurice. *Memoirs of the Foreign Legion*. Read the ms. when he visited Magnus at Montecassino in February. Later wrote an introduction, *Phoenix II*, 303-61.

March
L7 Goldring, Douglas. *The Fight For Freedom* (drama). Received a copy from the author. Offers to help in getting it reviewed. EN, II-37.
L8 Mackenzie, Compton. *Poor Relations* (fiction). Has read. FLMC-216.
L9 Marks, H. K. *Peter Middleton* (fiction). Received. ML-624.

May

L10 Andreyev, Leonid. *To the Stars* (drama). Read. EN, II-38.

L11 *The Freeman* (periodical). Read the April 7th issue. ML-627.

L12 Goldring, Douglas. *The Black Curtain* (fiction). Read. EN, II-38.

L13 Hamsun, Knut. *Love's Tragedy* (drama) also titled *The Gamble of Life*. Read. EN, II-38.

L14 Hofmannsthal, Hugo von. *The White Fan* (drama). Read. EN, II-38.

L15 Bierbaum, Julius. *The Snake Charmer* (drama). Read. EN, II-38.

L16 Mackenzie, Compton. *The Early Life and Adventures of Sylvia Scarlett* (fiction). Has read. CM-178.

L17 Omptide, George von. *Lady Sofia* (drama). Read. EN, II-38.

June

L18 *Century* (periodical). Familiar. Lacy/Seltzer-10.

July

L19 Gauguin, Paul. *Noa Noa*. Reading. CM-185. Either *Extracts from Noa Noa*, trans. Walter Kuhn, (1913) or *Noa Noa*, trans. O. F. Theis (1919).

L20 Goldring, Douglas. *Reputations* (critical essays). Read. EN, II-39.

L21 *The Metropolitan* (periodical). Familiar. LACY/SELTZER-12.

L22 O'Brien, Fredrick. *White Shadows on the South Seas*. Reading. CM-185.

L23 Stevenson, R. L. Reading or re-reading. See entries in Section A. CM-183.

September

L24 Keate. *An Account of the Pelew Islands*. Purchased this 'old travel book'. CM-190.

October

L25 Hansard, René Juta. *Cape Currey* (fiction) also titled *The Tavern*.

Mentions. EN, II-50.

November

L26 Dickens, Charles. *Martin Chuzzlewit* (fiction). Has read. Letter to Catherine Carswell, *Yale University Library Gazette* (January 1975), p. 259.

Undated reading for which evidence appears during 1920

L27 Galsworthy, John. *Strife* (drama). Has read. MIH-319.

L28 In *The Lost Girl*, written in 1920, Lawrence mentions the following authors and works: Edward George Bulwer-Lytton, George Macdonald, Hans Christian Andersen, Emanuel Swedenborg, *L'Aiglon* by Edmond Rostand.

L29 *Cent Nouvelles Nouvelles, Les* (tales). Familiar with at least the nineteenth tale. *The Lost Girl.*

(SECTION M) 1921

January

M1 Herbert, Agnes. *The Moose*. Familiar. ML-640.

M2 Lagerlof, Selma. Familiar with her work. LACY/SELTZER-30.

M3 Robinson, Edwin Arlington. 'Launcelot' (poem). Familiar. LACY/SELTZER-17.

February

M4 France, Anatole. *Thaïs* (fiction). Has read. ML-643.

M5 Mansfield, Katherine. *Bliss and Other Stories*. Mentions. ML-640.

M6 Scott, Evelyn. *Precipitations* (poetry collection). Received. LACY/SELTZER-19.

March

M7 *The Living Age* (periodical). Read the 7 August 1920 issue. Unpublished letter to J. B. Pinker, 23 March.

University of Texas.

M8 Shakespeare, William. *Richard III.* Familiar. *S&S*-Chap. 4.

April

M9 Young, Francis Brett. *The Black Diamond* (fiction). Discusses. MS-12.

May

M10 Chekhov, Anton. *Notebooks of Anton Chekhov*, trans. S. S. Koteliansky. Received, browsed. ML-654.

M11 Wells, H. G. *The Invisible Man* (fiction). Knows. ML-652.

June

M12 Bunin, Ivan. *The Gentleman from San Francisco and Other Stories*, trans. S. S. Koteliansky. Polished the translation. ML-656.

M13 Einstein, Albert. Requested and received a book on Einstein. GZ-221, 223. Probably either *The Theory of Relativity: An Introductory Sketch* (1920) or *The Special and the General Theory* (1920). The former carried a biographical note.

M14 Marx, Magdeline. *Woman* (fiction). Read. PD-200.

M15 Scott, Cyril. *Blind Mice* (fiction). Read. PD-200.

M16 Scott, Evelyn. *The Narrow House* (fiction). Read. PD-200.

July

M17 Lowell, Amy. *Legends* (poetry collection). Received. MIH-352.

September

M18 Casanova de Seingalt, Giacomo. Read parts of a 'battered' multi-volume work on or by him. ML-662.

M19 *John Bull* (newspaper). Read its criticism of *Women in Love*. EWT-93.

M20 Belt, Thomas. *The Naturalist in Nicaragua* (natural history). Familiar. Foreword to *FU*. See K22.

October

M21 *The Dial* (periodical). Read the October issue. EWT-93.

M22 Haldane, Lord (Probably Richard Burdon, 1st Viscount Haldane, 1856–1928). Quotes his theory of knowledge. *FU-209.*

M23 Heliogabalus (Roman emperor, 218–222 A.D.). Has biographical knowledge. Familiar with the corruption of his reign. *FU-132.*

M24 Lucka, Emil. *Grenzen der Seele* (metaphysicis). Read. ML-663.

M25 Shaw, G. B. *Back to Methuselah* (drama). Familiar. *FU-103.*

November

M26 Verga, Giovanni. *I Malvoglia, Mastro-Don Gesualdo* (fiction). *Cavalleria Rusticana, Novelle Rusticane, Vagabondaggio* (fiction collections). Reading. ML-674.

December

M27 Bjerre, Poul Carl. Received a book by him from Mabel Dodge. MDL-25. Probably *History and Practice of Psychoanalysis* (1920).

Undated reading for which evidence appears during 1921

M28 Fabre, Jean-Henri. *Souvenirs entomologiques*. Shows detailed knowledge in 'The Ladybird'.

M29 Hauptmann, Gerhart. *Hanneles Himmelfahrt* (play). Familiar in 'The Captain's Doll'. See DHLR, 9, 1976, 230-1.

M30 Reid, Thomas Mayne. Mentions in 'The Fox'.

Unidentified reading 1921

M31 A book on Africa by a 'learned German'. RA-271.

M32 Aphrodite. Reading something he refers to as 'Epaphroditus', wishing for a Greek dictionary. E&AB-25.

(SECTION N) 1922

January

N1 Brill, A. A. Comments vigorously on his theories. ML-690. By this time Brill had translated Freud's *The Interpretation of Dreams, Three Contributions to the Theory of Sex, Totem and Taboo.*

N2 Dos Passos, John. *Three Soldiers* (fiction). Mentions in Intro. to *Memoirs of the Foreign Legion.*

N3 Flaubert, Gustave. *The Temptation of St Anthony* (fiction). Familiar. Intro. to *Memoirs of the Foreign Legion.*

N4 Nylander, J. W. *Seevolk* (fiction collection). Read in German. ML-688.

May

N5 A history of Darlington, Australia from the time of its founding until it became a state. William Siebenhaar gave this to him while he was staying with Mollie Skinner. SPARROW-112-3.

N6 Siebenhaar, William. 'Dorothea' (poem). Read. EN, II-133.

N7 Skinner, Mollie. *The House of Ellis* (fiction). Read ms. which under his revision later became *The Boy in the Bush.* WR-72.

June

N8 Carswell, Catherine. *Camomile* (fiction). Read. HL-549.

July

N9 Tolstoy, Ilya. *The Autobiography of Countess Tolstoy*, trans. S. S. Koteliansky. It has been sent to him. ML-712.

N10 Skinner, Mollie. *Letters of a V.A.D.* (fiction) originally published under R. E. Leake. Read. SPARROW-111.

August

N11 Esson, Louis. Read something of his. EN, II-154 and note 78.

N12 Maurice, Furnley. *Eyes of Vigilance* (poetry collection). Read. EN, II-154.

N13 Prichard, Katharine. *The Black Opal* (fiction). Received copy from the author. THROSSELL-254.

N14 Tate, Henry. *Songs of Reverie.* Received. EN, II-154.

October

N15 Aimard, Gustave. Familiar with his novels of the American Indian. EN, III-109.

N16 Balzac, Honoré de. 'Seraphita' (fiction). Read. EN, II-198.

N17 Hecht, Ben. *Fantazius Mallare* (fiction). Read. WB-11.

N18 Multatuli (E. D. Dekker) *Max Havelaar.* Read the first six chapters of William Siebenhaar's translation-in-progress. HL-553. Later wrote an introduction for it.

N19 Spanish grammar text, dictionary. Requested and received. LACY/SELTZER-42-43.

N20 Weaver, Raymond. *Herman Melville, Poet and Mystic.* Received. LACY/SELTZER-43.

November

N21 Bonsels, Waldemar. *The Adventures of Maya, the Bee* (fiction). Familiar. LACY/SELTZER-45.

N22 Joyce, James. *Ulysses* (fiction). Knows. LACY/SELTZER-48.

N23 Maran, René. *Batouala* (fiction). Familiar. LACY/SELTZER-45.

December

N24 *Denver Post* (newspaper). Reading occasionally. GZ249.

N25 Milton, John. 'Il Penseroso' (poem). Gave a copy to Adele Seltzer. LACY/SELTZER-51.

N26 *The Occult Review, The*

Theosophical Review (periodicals). Recommends to Frederick Carter. Unpublished letter of 31 Dec. University of Texas. Michael Ballin suggests that Lawrence had read the articles on Atlantis by Lewis Spence in the February and June issues of *The Occult Review*. DHLR (Spring 1980) pp. 63–78.

Undated reading for which evidence appears during 1922

N27 Frazer, Sir James. *The Golden Bough* (anthropology). Re-reading. EN, II-345.

N28 Lummis, Charles. *The Land of Poco Tiempo.* Received from Mabel Dodge Luhan. AA/DHL-130.

N29 MacFarlane, Gordon. *The Natural Man* (fiction). Probably received this year of its publication. EN, III-112.

N30 MacLaurin, Charles. *Post-Mortem: Essays, Historical and Medical.* Probably read the essay on Henry VIII. EN, III-302 and note 76.

N31 Siebenhaar, William. 'Eduard Douwes Dekker, His Life and Works'. Read. EN, III-106.

N32 Steiner, Rudolf. Frieda Lawrence is alleged to have said that her husband read several books by Steiner. WYT-134.

N33 *The Sydney Bulletin* (newspaper). Frieda says Lawrence read this regularly. If this statement applies only to the period when they were in Australia, as it probably does, it would be April – August.

N34 'One one of the first visits [i.e. Dec. 1922] he made to our cabin, we talked about literature. We asked him what he thought of Scandinavian writers, and Danish writers in particular. I don't remember his words, but he was not enthusiastic and criticized them strongly. He had some respect for Kirkegaard, and of Hamsun he liked 'Pan' the best, and J. P. Jacobsen he only knew slightly, but wanted to read more of him. We talked about Ibsen, Strindberg, Lagerlöf, Nexö, and many others.' KM-88.

N35 Lindsay, Vachel. Familiar. PH-II-238.

Unidentified reading 1922

N36 Received an 'Eros book' from Else Jaffe in September. FL-155.

N37 Received a 'Glands' book from Earl Brewster in June. E&AB-55. Possibly Louis Berman, *Glands Regulating the Personality.*

(SECTION O) 1923

January

O1 *Oxford Song Book.* Asks Adele Seltzer to send a copy. LACY/SELTZER-61.

O2 *Punch, Vanity Fair* (periodicals). Received an issue of each. Later published in VF. LACY/SELTZER-60.

O3 Verga, Giovanni. Polishing the translations of what were titled in Italian *Novelle rusticane.* LACY/SELTZER-54.

February

O4 Chambers, Robert. Mentions in 'Surgery for the Novel . . .'.

O5 Grey, Zane. Mentions in 'Surgery for the Novel . . .' and 'St Mawr'.

O6 Gutierrez de Lara, L. and E. Pinchon. *The Mexican People: Their Struggle for Freedom.* Has read. LACY/SELTZER-73.

O7 Hawthorne, Nathaniel. *The Marble Faun* (fiction). Familiar. Review of *Americans.*

O8 Lewis, Sinclair. *Babbitt* (fiction). Mentions in 'Surgery for the Novel . . .'.

O9 Richardson, Dorothy. *Pointed Roofs* (fiction). Familiar. 'Surgery for the Novel . . .'.

O10 Sherman, Stuart P. *Americans* (criticism). Reviewed. KS-127.

O11 Terry, Thomas P. *Terry's Guide to Mexico*. Received. LACY/SELTZER-101.

March

O12 *The Dial* (periodical). Reading and having sent to his sister. ALC-125.

O13 Prescott, W. H. *The History of the Conquest of Mexico*. Read. EN, II-225.

O14 Schnitzler, Arthur. *Casanova's Homecoming: A Young Girl's Diary* (fiction). Received. LACY/SELTZER-83.

O15 *Tempo* (periodical). The editor solicited a poem from Lawrence. Correspondence suggests he may have sent him a copy. LACY/SELTZER-77.

April

O16 Calderòn de la Barca, Frances. *Life in Mexico* (letters). Familiar. EN, II-225.

O17 Flandrau, Charles. *Viva Mexico!* (memoir). Quoted frequently. WB-118.

O18 Forster, E. M. *Alexandria: A History and a Guide*. Received. GL-2218.

O19 Johnson, Willard. *Horizontal Yellow* (poetry collection). Read in ms. WB-147.

May

O20 Baroja, Pio. *César ó Nada* (fiction). Reading. Orders another unspecified Baroja novel. LACY/SELTZER-101.

June

O21 Boehme, Jacob. Familiar. ML-745.

O22 Brewster, Earl and Achsah. Received a book of pictures by them.

E&AB-72.

O23 Díaz, Bernal. *The True History of the Conquest of New Spain*. Requests this five-volume work. Unpublished letter to Ida Purnell, 1 June. University of Texas.

O24 Dostoyevsky, Fyodor. *Dostoevsky: Letters and Remembrances*, trans. S. S. Koteliansky. Read. ML-747.

O25 Goldenweizer, A. B. *Talks with Tolstoy* (memoir), trans. S. S. Koteliansky; *Tolstoy's Love Letters* also translated by Koteliansky. Received either or both. ML-747.

O26 Goncourt, E. L. and J. A. *Soeur Philomène* (fiction). Ordered. Unpublished letter of 1 June, University of Texas.

August

O27 Bynner, Witter. *Beloved Stranger* (poetry collection). Received, along with a collection of Bynner's plays. HL-575.

O28 Carswell, Catherine. 'Duse' (essay). Familiar. HL-576.

O29 Gorky, Maxim. *Reminiscences of Andreyev*, trans. S. S. Koteliansky. Polished the translation. KS-130.

O30 *The Laughing Horse* (periodical). Received a copy from Editor Willard Johnson. Lawrence began contributing to it in 1922 and received it regularly thereafter. HL-575.

September

O31 *Adelphi* (periodical). Read September issue. HL-578.

O32 Carter, Frederick. *The Dragon of the Alchemists* (astrology). Read an early ms. version. KS-131.

O33 Comfort, Will. Sent a novel of his to Frieda. ML-752.

O34 Mansfield, Katherine. *The Dove's Nest* (fiction collection). Read. LACY/SELTZER-111.

O35 *A Second Contemporary Verse*

Anthology. Reviewed. KS-130.

O36 Skinner, Mollie. *The House of Ellis* (fiction). Read ms., apparently for the second time. SPARROW-122.

October

O37 'Fritz Schnitz Thomas and D. H. Lawrence' (essay). Received from Adele Seltzer. Perhaps a humorous sketch by her, as the name Fritz Schnitz Thomas is one which Lawrence had given to the Seltzers' cat. LACY/SELTZER-111.

O38 Jacobsen, Jens Peter. *Mogens* (fiction collection). Returns to Knud Merrild. ML-755.

O39 Longfellow, Henry Wadsworth. 'A Psalm of Life' (poem). Quotes. HL-583.

O40 Review of *Mastro-Don Gesualdo*. Read. Unspecified LACY/SELTZER-115.

O41 Review of *Studies in Classic American Literature*. Read one by John Macy, 'The American Spirit', in *The Nation* of 10 Oct. 1923. LACY/SELTZER-115.

December

O42 Conrad, Joseph. *Almayer's Folly, The Rover, Typhoon* (fiction). Has read. EN, II-291.

O43 Scott, Sir Walter. 'The Lay of the Last Minstrel'. Quotes in 'On Coming Home'.

Undated reading for which evidence appears in 1923

O44 *Anales del Museo Nacional de Mexico*. According to Tindall Lawrence read several volumes. WYT-114.

O45 *El Informador* (newspaper). Read on at least one occasion. WB-151.

O46 Humboldt, Alexander von. *Vues des Cordillerès*. Read. WYT-114.

O47 Luhan, Mabel Dodge. Sent Lawrence several short stories and poems, some of which were later published in MDL.

O48 Nuttall, Zelia. *Fundamental Principles of Old and New World Civilizations* (anthropology). Frieda Lawrence verified that Lawrence had read this, but denied that he had borrowed any other books from Mrs. Nuttall. WYT-115; FLMC-357.

O49 Ouspensky, P. D. *Tertium Organum: A Key to the Enigmas of the World*, trans. N. Bessaraboff and C. Brangdon. Read and annotated extensively. See Richard O. Young in *D. H. Lawrence Review* (spring 1980), p. 44.

O50 *Palms: A Magazine of Poetry*. Familiar during this and the following year. EN, II-268.

O51 Wetherell, Elizabeth. *The Wide, Wide World* (fiction). Familiar.

Unidentified reading 1923

O52 A book or article on the history of bullfighting, read about Easter. WB-55.

O53 A novel in Spanish read on the train to Mexico in March. WB-35.

(SECTION P) 1924

January

P1 Carter, Frederick. 'The Ancient Science of Astrology'. Made stylistic revisions for this. KS-133.

P2 Luhan, Mabel Dodge. 'Fairytale' (poem). Received along with ms. of poems. Read. ML-772.

P3 Schiff, Sidney (pseud. Stephen Hudson). Offers to return 'Schiff book'. Probably *Tony*. ML-774.

P4 *Times Literary Supplement*. Read review of *Kangaroo* by Raymond Mortimer in 20 Sept. issue. ML-771.

February

P5 Doughty, C. M. *Travels in Arabia Deserta.* Received. Plans to read. New edition with foreword by T. E. Lawrence had been issued in 1921; this probably accounts for Q35. ML-780.

P6 Forster, E. M. *Pharos and Pharillon.* Received. Unpublished letter to author, 19 February. King's College, Cambridge.

P7 Oman, Dr John. *The Book of Revelation.* Reviewed under pseud. L. H. Davidson. KS-134-35.

P8 Ossendowski, Ferdinand Antoni. *Men, Beasts and Gods* (oriental history). Read. MDL-143.

March

P9 Bandelier, Adolph. *The Delight Makers* (fiction). Read. MDL-185.

April

P10 Seligmann, Herbert. *D. H. Lawrence, An American Interpretation.* Read. LACY/SELTZER-133, note 93.

May

P11 Gamio, Manuel. Sent Lawrence one of his books. LACY/SELTZER-135. L. D. Clark identifies it as either *Forjando Patria* (1916) or *La Poblacion del Valle de Teotihucán,* 3 vols. (1922).

June

P12 *Bystander, Hutchinson's, Strand* (periodicals). Asks for one of these to be ordered for him. HL-603.

P13 Machen, Arthur. *Far Off Things, Things Near and Far* (autobiographical novels). Received. MS-26.

P14 *New Decameron, Smart Set, Theatre Arts Monthly.* Mentions that each has bought a piece from him. LACY/SELTZER-138.

P15 Onions, Oliver. *In Accordance with the Evidence.* Received. MS-26. This was a long novel which incorporated an earlier short work, *Whom God Hath Sundered.*

July

P16 Forster, E. M. *A Passage to India* (fiction). Reading. ML-799.

P17 Hargrave, John. *Harbottle* (fiction). Familiar. ML-796.

P18 Meikhopãdhyaya, Dhana-Gopàla. *Caste and Outcaste* (autobiography). Read. GL-2544.

P19 Skinner, Mollie. *Lettie* (fiction). Read the ms. of what became *The Black Swans.* SPARROW-139.

August

P20 Garnett, David. *Lady into Fox* (fiction). Read. ML-800.

P21 Rimski-Korsakov, Nikolai. *My Musical Life* (memoir). Received. MS/DHL 60.

September

P22 *Times Literary Supplement.* Read review of *The Boy in the Bush* in 28 Aug. issue. SPARROW-143.

October

P23 Tolstoy, Leo. *Resurrection* (fiction). Read. KS-140, EWT-137.

November

P24 Luhan, Tony. Read the ms. of a story by Mrs Luhan's husband. MDL-144.

P25 Swift, Jonathan. *Gulliver's Travels* (fiction). Familiar. ML-768.

Undated reading for which evidence appears during 1924

P26 *Adventure* (periodical). Reading regularly during the winter of 1924–5. DB-81, 253.

P27 Quintanilla, Luis. The text of Lawrence's 'See Mexico After, by Luis Q.' indicates he has read something, probably in ms. EWT-190.

P28 In a January 1924 letter to Willard Johnson (ML 767) Lawrence shows some knowledge of the Turquoise Horse of the Navajo, which may derive from Washington Matthews, *Navaho Legends* or 'Navaho Myths, Prayers and Songs', or from Natalie Curtis, *The Indians' Book*. LDC-103.

Unidentified reading 1924

P29 Reading a book on 'Old Mexico'. DB-155.

P30 Chose a book on Mexico from the library of Oaxaca neighbour as a gift. DB-186.

Addendum 1924

P31 Burton, Richard, trans. *The Arabian Nights' Entertainments*. Knows the story of Barmecide. 'St Mawr'.

P32 Coué, Emile. (French psychologist). Mentions. 'St Mawr.'

P33 Euripides. *Hippolytus*. Mentions. 'St Mawr.'

P34 Gautier, Theophile. *Mademoiselle de Maupin*. Familiar. 'St Mawr.'

P35 Gray, Thomas. 'Elegy Written in a Country Churchyard'. Quotes in 'St Mawr.'

P36 Kipling, Rudyard. Knows some work in which Kipling speaks of men being 'pithed'. 'St Mawr.'

P37 *Nibelungenlied*. Mentions. 'The Princess.'

P38 Twain, Mark. *A Connecticut Yankee in King Arthur's Court*. Familiar. 'St Mawr.'

P39 Wells, H. G. *An Outline of History*. Familiar. 'St Mawr.'

(SECTION Q) 1925

January

Q1 *Contemporary* (periodical). Familiar. HL-625.

Q2 *Corriere Della Sera* (newspaper). Read an issue which carried an article about him by Carlo Linati. ML-826.

Q3 Quintanilla, Luis. Working on a ms. by him. See also P28. ML-825.

Q4 Spence, Lewis. *The Gods of Mexico* (anthropology). Reading. DB-203.

Q5 *Theatre Arts* (periodical). Received December 1924 issue. HL-626.

March

Q6 Ellis, Havelock. Received a book by him from his own bibliographer, Dr McDonald. Unpublished letter of 6 March, University of Texas.

April

Q7 Arlen, Michael (Dikran Kouyoumdjian). *The Green Hat* (fiction). Mentions in 'Accumulated Mail', and 'The Novel'.

Q8 *The Nation* (periodical). Has read the 11 February issue; 'Accumulated Mail' is an answer to Edwin Muir's article there. WR-209.

Q9 Gorki, Maxim. *Reminiscences of Leo Nicolayevitch Tolstoi* (trans. Koteliansky and Woolf). Knew by this time. 'The Novel'.

June

Q10 Burrow, Trigant. Received and read reprints of two recent articles. ML-842. Probably 'Psychoanalysis in Theory and in Life', and 'Social Images Versus Reality'. See also L1.

Q11 Dante. *The Divine Comedy*. Discusses in 'The Novel'.

Q12 France, Anatole. *The Crime of Sylvestre Bonnard*. (fiction). Familiar. 'The Novel'.

Q13 Hamsun, Knut. *Pan* (fiction). Mentions. 'The Novel'. Had told Knud Merrild this was the best of Hamsun's novels. KM-88.

Q14 Hutchinson, A. S. *If Winter Comes* (fiction). Mentions. 'The Novel'.

Q15 Kennedy, Margaret. *The Constant Nymph* (fiction). Mentions. 'The Novel'.

Q16 Lewis, Sinclair. *Main Street* (fiction). Mentions. 'The Novel'.

Q17 Plato. *The Dialogues, Timaeus.* Mentions. 'The Novel'.

Q18 Santayana, George. Familiar. 'The Novel'.

Q19 Sherman, Stuart P. Read his review of *St Mawr* in the *New York Herald Tribune*, 14 June. WB-254.

Q20 Tolstoy, Leo. *Anna Karenina, Resurrection, War and Peace* (fiction). May have re-read. Discusses in 'The Novel'.

Q21 Swinnerton, Frank. Received an unspecified novel by him. JF-240.

Q22 Tridon, André. Received an unspecified book by him. JF-240.

Q23 Crichton, Kyle. Read ms. of unpublished story. EN, II-422.

Q24 Fergusson, Harvey, *Women and Wives* (fiction). Familiar. EN, II-411.

July

Q25 Gerhardi, William. *Polyglots* (fiction). Has read. EN, III-10.

August

Q26 'America Loca' (poem). Translated and sent to Lawrence by R. Conway, a British engineer he had met in Mexico City. Author unknown. ML-849.

Q27 *Time* (periodical). Read for the first time. ML-860.

September

Q28 Barnes Foundation publication. Has received twice. Not otherwise identified. CENTAUR-22.

Q29 Leslie, Shane. Requests monograph on Frederick Rolfe by Leslie. MS/DHL-65.

October

Q30 Barbey d'Aurevilly, Jules. *Les Diaboliques* (fiction). Offers to

review. ML-860.

Q31 Burton, Richard, trans. *The Arabian Nights' Entertainments* (fiction collection). Familiar. Review of *Saïd the Fisherman*.

Q32 Corvo, Baron (Frederick Rolfe). *Hadrian VII* (fiction). Reviewed.

Q33 Huysmans, Joris-Karl. Familiar. Review of *Hadrian VII*.

Q34 Kippis, A., ed. *Captain Cook's Voyages.* Offers to review. ML-860.

Q35 Lawrence, T. E. Has biographical knowledge of him. Review of *Saïd the Fisherman*. See P5.

Q36 MacFall, Haldane. *The Wooings of Jezebel Pettyfer* (fiction). Read. ML-860.

Q37 Pickthall, Marmaduke. *Saïd the Fisherman* (fiction). Reviewed.

Q38 Stendhal. *The Life of Henri Brulard* (fiction). Offers to review this new translation by C. A. Phillips. ML-860.

Q39 *The Yellow Book* (periodical). Mentions. Review of *Hadrian VII*.

November

Q40 *Adelphi* (periodical). Received a number of copies. E & AB-86. Mentions reading the November issue. JMM-195.

Q41 Krout, John A. *The Origins of Prohibition.* Reviewed.

Q42 Murry, J. M. *Keats and Shakespeare.* Discusses. ML-863.

December

Q43 Branford, F. V. *Titans and Gods, The White Stallion* (poetry collection). Read. ML-872.

Q44 Crosby, Caresse. Reading some translations by her. Unclear whether they are of Lawrence's work. DHLR (spring 1976), p. 58.

Q45 Huxley, Aldous. *Along the Road* (essays). Read. ML-873.

Q46 Shipley, Joseph. *King John*

(fiction). Read. GL-2848.

Q47 Skinner, Mollie. *Black Swans* (fiction), 'The Hand' (essay). Read mss. ML-869.

Undated reading for which evidence appears during 1925

Q48 *Adventure* (periodical). Reading. EN, II-416.

Q49 Cather, Willa. *The Song of the Lark* (fiction). Received from the author. EN, II-414.

Q50 Hunt, Violet; Sinclair, May. Compared their work in discussion with Kyle Crichton. EN, II.

Q51 Keyserling, Count Herman Graf. Quotes in 'Aristocracy'. His *Travel Diary of a Philosopher* had been translated this year.

Q52 Lowell, Amy. *John Keats*. Plans to order. POL-402.

Q53 Luhan, Mabel Dodge. Continued to receive mss. from her.

Q54 Rilke, Rainer Maria. The fragment which E. W. Tedlock dates from this year, 'Man is essentially a soul . . .', may be a translation from Rilke. EWT-138.

(SECTION R) 1926

January

R1 Bynner, Witter. *Caravan* (poetry collection). Read. ML-885.

R2 Dostoyevsky, F. M. Planning to read him again. ML-881.

R3 Dufferin, Lord (F. T. Hamilton). *Letters from High Latitudes*. Read. HL-648.

R4 Farbman, Michael. *After Lenin: the New Phase in Russia*. Probably the book read. ML-876.

R5 Graves, Robert. *My Head! My Head!* (fiction). Received from Martin Secker on 26 January. MS/DHL 68.

R6 Luhan, Mabel Dodge, 'Southwest'

(fiction). Read. JOOST-93.

R7 *New York Times Book Review*. Read 27 Dec. 1925 issue. HL-647.

R8 Russian grammar text. Asks Koteliansky to send him one. ML-876.

R9 *Times Literary Supplement*. Read review of *The Plumed Serpent* in 21 Jan. issue. HL-649.

R10 *Word: Love* (periodical). Ordered for Edward McDonald. Unpublished card, University of Texas.

February

R11 Douglas, Norman. *Experiments* (essay collection). Read. POL-331.

R12 *The New Statesman* (periodical). Read 13 Feb. issue which carried Norman Douglas's attack on him. ML-889.

March

R13 Dostoyevsky, Madame. *Dostoevsky Portrayed by his Wife: the Diary and Reminiscences of Madame Dostoevsky*, trans. S. S. Koteliansky. Received. FLMC-224.

R14 *Insel Verlag Almanac*. Familar. FL-184.

April

R15 Bandelier, Adolf. *The Gilded Man* (history). Familar. Review of *In the American Grain*.

R16 Dennis, George. *Cities and Cemeteries of Etruria*. Has read. MS-72. But may have read as early as 1920.

R17 Glenn, Isa. *Heat* (fiction). Reviewed.

R18 Keats, John. 'Ode on a Grecian Urn' (poem). Quotes in review of *Heat*.

R19 Loos, Anita. *Gentlemen Prefer Blondes* (fiction). Read. EN, III-23.

R20 Williams, William Carlos. *In the American Grain* (historical sketches).

Reviewed.

May

R21 Couperus, Louis. *Old People and Things that Pass* (fiction). Discusses in introduction to *Max Havelaar*.

R22 Gogol, Nikolai. Familiar with the misanthropic tone of the writings of Gogol, Mark Twain and Jean Paul Richter. Introduction to *Max Havelaar*.

R23 Mommsen, Theodore. Familiar. FL-209, KS-151. Probably a book on the Etruscans, perhaps *The Earliest Inhabitants of Italy*.

R24 Multatuli (E. D. Dekker). *Max Havelaar* (fiction). Read final translation and wrote introduction. WR-211, KS-150.

June

R25 *The Laughing Horse* (periodical). Read the April issue. ML-919.

R26 Shestov, Leo. Still reading Koteliansky's translations of Shestov. ML-923.

R27 *Adelphi* (periodical). Read an issue which contained part of J. M. Murry's 'Life of Christ'. HL-668.

August

R28 Wells, H. G. *God the Invisible King* (philosophy, theology), *The World of William Clissold* (fiction). Familiar with the first title, reviewed the second. WR-272.

R29 Ducati, Pericle. *Etruria Antica*. Reading. RA-370.

September

R30 Klatt, Fritz. *Schöperferische Pause* (educational theory). Read, probably in German. HL-669.

October

R31 Bacchelli, Riccardo. *Lo Sa il Tonno* (fiction). Read. GL-3081.

R32 Brewster, Earl. *The Life of Gotama the Buddha*. Received from the author. Unpublished letter of 25 Oct. University of Texas.

R33 Huxley, Aldous. *Two or Three Graces* (fiction collection). Familiar. MS/DHL-78.

R34 Memoirs of the Duc de Lauzun. Two fragmentary essays which appear in PH-745-54 are identified by Richard Aldington as an introduction to a volume of Lauzun's memoirs translated by him, which Lawrence read in ms. EWT-246.

R35 Restif de la Bretonne. Familiar, 'The Good Man'. PH-750.

R36 Warner, Sylvia T. *Lolly Willowes* (fiction). Read. ML-940.

November

R37 Conrad, Joseph. *The Nigger of the Narcissus* (fiction). Familiar. Review of *Gifts of Fortune*, R38.

R38 Tomlinson, H. M. *Gifts of Fortune* (travel). Reviewed.

R39 Voltaire. Received Voltaire book from Mabel Luhan, probably S. G. Tallentyre's *Life of Voltaire*. ML-947.

December

R40 Cunninghame Graham, R. B. *Pedro de Valdivia: Conqueror of Chile* (biography). Reviewed.

Undated reading for which evidence appears during 1926

R41 Etruscans. Richard Aldington recalls that he had a dozen or so standard works on the Etruscans sent to him in preparation for a visit from Lawrence during the summer. RA/L-302-3.

R42 Knopf, Alfred A. *The Borzoi Almanac*. Familiar. FL-184.

R43 Luhan, Mabel Dodge. *Background* (memoir). Read ms. EN, III-23.

R44 Onions, Oliver. *Widdershins Stories* (fiction collection). Recommends to

Cynthia Asquith. Unpublished letter dated only 1926. University of Texas.

(SECTION S) 1927

February

S1 Austen, Jane. Indicates a more complete knowledge of her work than the early reading (A108) alone would justify. 'John Galsworthy'. PH-540.

S2 Balzac, Honoré de. Took ten paperback volumes of Balzac from Mabel Luhan's in Florence. MDL-292.

S3 Brett, Dorothy. 'Adolescence' (fiction). Read ms. MDL-293.

S4 Burrow, Trigant. 'The Reabsorbed Affect and Its Elimination' (psychological essay). Received. EN, III-681.

S5 Cocteau, Jean. Familiar. Review of *Nigger Heaven*. PH-361.

S6 Dos Passos, John. *Manhattan Transfer* (fiction). Reviewed. PH-363-65.

S7 Euripides. *Hippolytus*. Mentions. 'John Galsworthy'. PH-541.

S8 Galsworthy, John. In the essay, 'John Galsworthy', PH-539-50, Lawrence reveals knowledge of the following fiction: *Five Tales*, discusses in early ms. EWT-170. *Fraternity*, mentions. *The Island Pharisees*, mentions. 'The Stoic', discusses in early ms. EWT-170.

S9 Hemingway, Ernest. *In Our Time* (fiction collection). Reviewed. PH-365-66.

S10 Kasson, Charles le Baron. The Byron Kasson whose psychological theories Lawrence mentions in his review of *Flight* (S17) is probably Baron Kasson, who had recently published *Speculations on Human Life*.

S11 Macaulay, Thomas. Discusses his critical statements in 'John Galsworthy'. PH-539.

S12 Meredith, George. *The Egoist* (fiction). Familiar. 'John Galsworthy'. PH-540.

S13 Morand, Paul. Familiar with his novels. Review of *Nigger Heaven*. PH-361.

S14 Pater, Walter. Discusses his critical theories in 'John Galsworthy'. PH-539.

S15 Sainte-Beuve, Charles. Discusses his critical theories in 'John Galsworthy'. PH-539.

S16 Van Vechten, Carl. *Nigger Heaven* (fiction). Reviewed. PH-361.

S17 White, W. H. *Flight* (fiction). Reviewed. PH-326.

April

S18 Chekhov, Anton. *Anton Tchekhov: Literary and Theatrical Reminiscences*, trans. S. S. Koteliansky. Received. ML-972; GRANDSEN-31.

S19 Dobrée, Louisa Emily. Recommends to Koteliansky for translation. GRANDSEN-31.

S20 Douglas, Norman. *Siren Land* (essays). Received, reading. MS/DHL-87.

S21 *The Great American Ass* (autobiography) anonymous. Received, plans to read. CENTAUR-29.

S22 *Illustrated London News*. Receiving. MS-86.

S23 Rozanov, V. V. *The Apocalypse of our Times* (philosophy), *Solitaria* (fiction). Reviewed the latter title which contained a 20-page abstract from the former. KS-160. PH-367.

S24 Ouïda. Took copies of one or two of her works from the Luhan villa in Florence. MDL-295.

May

S25 Aldington, Richard. *D. H. Lawrence: An Indiscretion*. Read. ML-978.

S26 Balzac, Honoré de. *Lys dans la Vallée* (fiction). Mentions. Introduction to *Mastro-Don Gesualdo*. PH-223.

S27 Bourget, Paul. Mentions in Introduction to *Mastro-Don Gesualdo*. PH-223.

S28 Dickens, Charles. *A Christmas Carol* (fiction). Mentions in Introduction to *Mastro-Don Gesualdo*. PH-223.

S29 Feuillet, Octave. Mentions in Introduction to *Mastro-Don Gesualdo*. PH-223.

S30 Goethe, J. W. von. *The Sorrows of Young Werther* (fiction), Mentions in Introduction to *Mastro-Don Gesualdo*. PH-223.

S31 Gyp (Comtesse de Mirabeau de Martel). Mentions in Introduction to *Mastro-Don Gesualdo*.

S32 Maupassant, Guy de. Displays biographical knowledge of him in Introduction to *Mastro-Don Gesualdo*. PH-223.

S33 Morris, William. *News from Nowhere* (fiction). Familiar. Review of *The Peep Show*. PH-372.

S34 Pirandello, Luigi. Mentions in Intro. to *Mastro-Don Gesualdo*. PH-223.

S35 Roberts, Elizabeth M. *The Time of Man* (fiction). Ordered. PD-206.

S36 Scott, Sir Walter. *Ivanhoe* (fiction). Mentions in Introduction to *Mastro-Don Gesualdo*. PH-223.

S37 Vigny, Alfred de. Indicates biographical knowledge of him. Intro. to *Mastro-Don Gesualdo*.

S38 Wilkinson, Walter. *The Peep Show* (fiction). Reviewed. PH-372-76.

June

S39 Homer. Familiar with Pope's translations. EP-'Volterra'.

S40 Keats, John. 'Ode on a Grecian Urn' (poem). Familiar. EP-'Volterra'.

S41 Shakespeare, William. *Timon of Athens*. Knows. EP-'Volterra'.

S42 Theopompus. Familiar. EP-'Painted Tombs . . .'.

July

S43 Burrow, Trigant. 'The Genesis and Meaning of Homosexuality'. Plans to read. RA/LETTERS-164-65.

S44 Gide, André. *Faux Monnayeurs* (fiction). Read. ML-991.

S45 Proust, Marcel. Tried again — unsuccessfully — to read him. ML-991.

S46 Sinclair, Upton. *Oil!* (fiction). Read. ML-991.

S47 Weege, Fritz. *Etruskische Malerei* (archeology). Borrowed. FL-229.

August

S48 Ainsley. *Views of Etruria*, vol. I. Possibly Sir Robert Ainslie's 1801 drawings of scriptural scenes, published in 1862 as *Views of Egypt*. Familar. MS/DHL-91.

S49 Burrow, Trigant. *The Social Basis of Consciousness*. Reviewed. PH-377-82.

S50 Storm, Theodor. Has been reading his work. MS/DHL-93.

September

S51 James, Henry. Discussed. EN, III-168.

S52 *Jugend* (German periodical). Familiar when the editor, Franz Schoenberner, visited him. EN, III-155.

S53 Verga, Giovanni. *Eros, Eva, Il marito di Elena, Tigre Reale* (fiction). Familiar. Introduction to *Cavalleria Rusticana*. PH-241; 'Note on Giovanni Verga'. PH-277-78.

October

S54 Feuchtwanger, Lion. *Jud Süss* (fiction). Read in German. ML-1006.

S55 Koteliansky, Biela. *Two Jewish Stories*. Polished the translation for *London Mercury*. GZ-322.

S56 Mohr, Max. *Improvisationem im Juni, Tulpen* (drama). Read in German. ML-1010.

S57 Richter, Jean Paul. Received a book on him. ML-1010. Probably *Jean Paul* by Walther Harich. AA-35.

S58 Stein, Gertrude. Familiar with her writing. ML-1011.

November

S59 Beethovan, Ludwig van. *Letters of Beethoven*, ed. A. C. Calisher. Reading. ML-1020.

S60 Carswell, Donald. *Brother Scots* (biography collection). Read. CC-261.

S61 Darwin, Charles. *The Voyage of the Beagle*. Re-read. ML-1024.

S62 Forster, E. M. 'The Celestial Omnibus' (fiction). Re-read. ML-1024.

S63 Huxley, Aldous. *Proper Studies* (essays). Has read. ML-1024.

S64 *Literary Digest* (periodical). Requests the 24 Sept. issue. ML-1019.

S65 Lockhart, John. *The Life of Robert Burns*. Re-reading. HL-695.

S66 Marshall, Sir John. *The Bagh Caves in the Gwalior State*. Probably the 'Bagh cave book' which Lawrence was reading this month. E&AB-153.

December

S67 *Querschnitt* (German periodical). Receiving. ML-1025.

S68 Sinclair, Upton. *Money Writes* (fiction). Recommends. Unpublished letter of 5 Dec. to Mabel Luhan. University of Texas.

Undated reading for which evidence appears during 1927

S69 Bynner, Witter. *The Pamphlet Poets*. Received an issue of this series. WB-332.

S70 Collins, Vere. *Lord Byron in his Letters*. Read. EN, I-472.

S71 Coppard, A. E. Sent A. W. McLeod a volume of Coppard's poems. MIH-446.

S72 Randall-Macivers, D. *Villanovans and Early Etruscans*. Read. Richard Aldington in Introduction to *Etruscan Places* (Heinemann, 1956), vi.

Unidentified reading for 1927

S73 A 'marriage book' received from Brett in February. ML-965.

S74 A parcel of unspecified books received from Mabel Luhan in January. MDL-290.

S75 Tauchnitz books, several of which were among the volumes he got from the Luhan villa. MDL-292. Very possibly English translations of German authors.

(SECTION T) 1928

January

T1 Deledda, Grazia. *The Mother* (fiction). Wrote introduction. PH-263.

T2 Fogazzaro, Antonio. Familiar. Introduction to *The Mother*. PH-263.

T3 Hargrave, John. *Confessions of the Kibbo Kift*. Read. EN, III-79.

February

T4 Chambers, Maria Cristina. Read a story by her in an issue of *Century*. ML-1039.

T5 Gide, André. *Corydon* (fiction). Knows. ML-1036.

T6 *Travel* (periodical). Saw October,

November, December 1927 and January 1928 issues. DHLR (spring 1976), p. 82.

March

T7 Aretino, Pietro, *I Ragionamenti* (fiction). Reading. ML-1050.

T8 Goethe, J. W. von. *Wilhelm Meister* (fiction). Has read, probably much earlier. HL-716.

T9 Massingham, H. J. *Downland Man* (prehistoric anthropology). Received. HL-704.

T10 Mohr, Max. *Venus in den Fischen* (fiction). Read, probably in German. ML-1047.

T11 Randall-Macivers, D. *The Iron Age in Italy*. Ordered. HL-704.

T12 Rickword, Edgell, ed. *Scrutinies by Various Writers*. Read. Contained his John Galsworthy essay. HL-716.

T13 Wilder, Thornton. *The Bridge of San Luis Rey* (fiction). Read. ML-1042.

April

T14 Bynner, Witter. *Cake, an Indulgence* (drama). Read. ML-1054.

T15 Crosby, Harry. *The Chariot of the Sun.* (poetry collection). Wrote the introduction. PH-255.

T16 Dante. *The Divine Comedy*. Mentions in Introduction to *Chariot of the Sun*. PH-255.

T17 *Forum* (periodical). Reading occasionally. HL-726.

T18 *Theatre Essays* (periodical). Read. HL-719.

May

T19 Douglas, Norman. *In the Beginning* (fiction). Read. CENTAUR-33.

June

T20 St Augustine. *City of God*. Gerald Lacy sees *The Escaped Cock* as a response to the enormous philosophical influence of Augustine.

LACY/COCK-126, 132.

T21 Frazer, Sir James. *Adonis, Attis and Osiris* (anthropology). Evidence of this reading obvious in ms. versions of *The Escaped Cock*. LACY/COCK-125-26.

T22 Mohr, Max. *Die Heiden* (fiction). This is the published title (1929) of Mohr's novel in progress of which Lawrence read the ms. this month, and refers to as 'Jungfrau Max'. ML-1048.

July

T23 Baring, Maurice. *Comfortless Memory* (fiction). Reviewed. PH-386.

T24 Byron, Robert. *The Station: Athos, Treasure and Men* (Balkan history). Reviewed. PH-383.

T25 Hardy, Thomas. Re-reading 'Hardy's stories'. HL-738.

T26 Maugham, Somerset. *Ashenden or the British Agent* (fiction). Reviewed. PH-386.

T27 Shaw, George Bernard. *The Intelligent Woman's Guide to Socialism and Capitalism*. Tried, unsuccessfully, to read. ML-1069.

T28 Williams-Ellis, Clough. *England and the Octopus* (a plea for city planning). Reviewed. PH-384.

August

T29 *The Bristol Tune Book*. Familiar. 'Hymns in a Man's Life'. PHII-597-601.

T30 Davies, Rhys. *The Withered Root* (fiction). Read. ML-1083.

T31 *The False Prince*. Read, but declined the task of translating. MS/DHL 110.

T32 Moody, D. W. and I. D. Sankey, *Gospel Hymns*. Quotes in 'Hymns in a Man's Life'. PHII-597-601.

T33 *Transition* (Paris-published literary magazine). Read the August issue, 'the American number'. HL-742.

T34 Verlaine, Paul. 'Après Trois Ans'. Lists among 'poems which have meant most to me' in 'Hymns in a Man's Life'. PHII-597.

T35 Wordsworth, William. 'Intimations of Immortality' (poem). Discusses in 'Hymns in a Man's Life'. PHII-597.

T36 Yorke, Dorothy. Requested mss. of her poems. ML-1078.

September

T37 Gordon, Jan. *Modern French Painters*. Read. ML-1087. Misquotes the title as *Modern French Painting*, which was the title of a later edition.

T38 Milton, John. Familiar with the pastorals. 'Nottingham and the Mining Countryside'. PH-135.

T39 Romain, Jules. *The Body's Rapture, Psyché* (fiction). Read. ML-1092. Also translated as *The Lord God of the Flesh*.

T40 Schmalhausen, S. D. *Why we Misbehave* (psychology). Read some of it. ML-1092.

October

T41 Ernst, Morris. *To the Pure* (study of obscenity and censorship). Read. EN, III-254.

T42 Grazzini, A. F. (Il Lasca). *The Story of Dr Manente* (fiction). Translating. Familiar with Lasca's other stories. EN, III-256, POL-456.

T43 Huxley, Aldous. *Point Counter Point* (fiction). Read. KS-178.

T44 de Medici, Lorenzo. Familiar. Discusses in Introduction to *Story of Dr Manente*. PH-274-78.

November

T45 Bandello, Matteo. Familiar, asks Pino Orioli if Aldous Huxley might translate some stories. Unpublished letter of 22 Nov. UCLA.

T46 Davies, Rhys. *A Bed of Feathers* (fiction). Reading. GL 3766.

T47 Brion, Marcel. *La Vie d'Attila* (biography). Probably the book which Richard Aldington was reading late this year in French. EN, III-254, RA-395.

December

T48 Dahlberg, Edward. *Bottom Dogs* (fiction). Read ms. ML-1108.

T49 Harington, Sir John. *Metamorphosis of Ajax*. Read. MS/DHL-113. This was a reproduction of the 1596 *Anatomie of the Metamorphosis of Ajax*.

T50 Lindsay, Jack. *Dionysus: Nietzsche contra Nietzsche* (philosophy). Received. ML-1109.

T51 Skinner, Mollie. *Eve in the Land of Nod* (fiction). Read and annotated the ms. EN, II-277 and note 208.

T52 Theocritus. Familiar. 'New Mexico'. PH-145.

T53 Tolstoy, Leo. 'What is Art?' (essay). Requests. GZ-370.

Undated reading for which evidence appears during 1928

T54 Aldington, Richard. *Death of a Hero* (fiction). Read the ms. EN, III-254.

T55 Brewster, Earl. 'The Hand of Man' (essay). Read, offered revisional suggestions. EN, III-246.

T56 Chatterji, J. C. *Kashmir Shaivism: Being a Brief Introduction to the History, Literature and Doctorines of the Advaita Trinka System*. Read. EN, III-230 and note 403.

T57 Collins, Vere. *Talks with Thomas Hardy* (memoir). Read. EN, I-472.

T58 Coomaraswamy, Ananda K. *The Dance of Shiva* (essays on Buddhism). Read. EN, III-230.

T59 *The London Aphrodite* (periodical). Read occasionally. EN, III-303. 26 Nov., received No. 2 from Rhys Davies.

Unidentified reading for 1928

T60 Reading a French book about Egypt in February. E&AB-163.

T61 Received a guide book to Spain from Aldous Huxley in December. HL-768.

T62 Chose *Joy go with You* by Norman Kranzler for a false cover to *Lady Chatterley's Lover*. I have not identified the work, but it may not be spurious. Unpublished letter of 27 Aug. to Pino Orioli. Harvard University.

T63 Received and read a 'Northumbrian report' from Rolf Gardiner in January. HL-697.

T64 A 'Rasputin book' which Frieda had received from the Huxleys in December aroused Lawrence's ire. HL-768.

T65 Received 'seven massive Fanfrolico [Press] books' in December. HL-768. One of these was T49.

(SECTION U) 1929

January

U1 Aeschylus, *Orestia* (drama trilogy). Familiar. 'Intro. to these Paintings'. PH-551, ML-1119.

U2 *The American Caravan: A Yearbook of American Literature*, ed. Brooks, Kreymborg, Mumford and Rosenfield. Received the volume covering 1927–28. MOHR-34.

U3 Austin, Mary. Familiar with her work. EN, III-287; WR-286.

U4 Douglas, Norman. *Venus in the Kitchen* (fiction). Painted frontispiece. May have read. KS-181-82.

U5 Bell, Clive. *Art*. Uses the term 'significant form', coined by Bell, in 'Intro. to these Paintings'. PH-551.

U6 Bruyère, Jean de la. *Caractères* (fiction collection). Familiar. Intro. to *Pansies*. PH-279.

U7 Chaucer, Geoffrey. Familiar, 'Intro. to these Paintings'. PH-551.

U8 Donne, John. Familiar, 'Intro. to these Paintings'. PH-552.

U9 Edgeworth, Maria. *Tales of Fashionable Life*. Familiar, 'Intro. to these Paintings'. PH-559.

U10 English history. Has a rather thorough knowledge of the venereal disease which ran through the Tudor and Stuart lines. 'Intro. to these Paintings'. PH-552-53. May be related to N30.

U11 Fry, Roger. *Cézanne: A Study of his Development*. Read. ML-1118.

U12 Hall, Radclyffe. *The Well of Loneliness*. Familiar with at least the conditions of its publication. HL-776.

U13 Jeffers, Robinson. *Cawdor* (poetry collection). Read the shorter poems. EN, III-291.

U14 D'Orbigny, Charles. *Dictionnaire Universal d'Histoire Naturelle*. (3 vols. Paris, 1861). Purchased. Letter of 27 Jan. to Pino Orioli. UCLA.

U15 Restoration dramatists. Familiar, 'Intro. to these Paintings'. PH-553. Perhaps related to G1.

U16 Richardson, Samuel. *Pamela* (fiction). Familiar, 'Intro. to these Paintings'. PH-552.

U17 Swift, Jonathan. 'The Lady's Dressing Room' (poem). Quotes. Introduction to *Pansies*. PH-281-82.

U18 Davies, Rhys. Read 'Interlude' (short story). Unpub. letter to Davies, 26 Jan.

February

U19 *Adelphi* (periodical). Reading. ML-1122.

U20 Dreiser, Theodore. Familiar, 'Intro. to *Bottom Dogs*'. PH-271-72.

U21 Lewis, P. Wyndham. *Paleface*. Familiar. 'Intro. to *Bottom Dogs*'.

PH-271-72.

U22 Powys, T. F. Familiar with his poetry. Unpublished letter to Charles Lahr, 1 February.

U23 Viani, Lorenzo. *Parigi*. Familiar. Intro. to *Bottom Dogs*. PH-270. Although Lawrence calls this a novel, Italian bibliographies list it as a factual narrative.

U24 Zweig, Arnold, *The Case of Sergeant Grischa* (fiction). Read. ML-1125.

April

U25 Brentford, Viscount. 'The Censorship of Books' (essay). Familiar. 'Pornography and Obscenity.' PH-186.

U26 Douglas, Norman. *Nerinda* (fiction). Requests. ML-1142.

U27 Rabelais, François. Familiar. 'Pornography and Obscenity'. PH-174.

U28 Stopes, Marie. Familiar with her work. 'Pornography and Obscenity'. PH-182.

May

U29 Eliot, T. S. 'Le Roman Anglais Contemporain' (essay). Familiar. HL-801.

July

U30 'The Fat Carpenter'. Familiar with this Italian tale. Introduction to *The Story of Dr Manente*. PH-277.

U31 *London Mercury* (periodical). Reading occasionally. ML-1168-69.

August

U32 Biagi, Guido. Received a book by him from Pino Orioli. ML-1176. Perhaps *The Private Life of the Renaissance Florentines* (1896).

U33 Cournos, John. *O'Flaherty the Great* (fiction). Read. ML-1187.

U34 Grazzini, A. F. *Scritti Scelti di A. F. Grazzini in Prosa e in Poesia*, ed.

Raffaello Fornaciari with intro. and critical footnotes. Probably the book he received from Orioli. ML-1176.

October

U35 Carter, Frederick. *Apocalyptic Images, The Dragon of the Alchemists, The Visionary Way* (astrology). Read first two titles, and ms. of the third. Unpublished letter of 29 Oct.

U36 Charles, Robert H. *A Critical and Exegetical Commentary on the Revelation of Saint John* (2 vols.) Borrowed. ML-1208.

U37 *Everyman* (periodical). Read the 3 Oct. issue. ALC-200.

U38 Huxley, Aldous. *Do what you Will*, (essays). Reading. ML-1209.

U39 Loisy, A. F. Ordered a book recommended by Frederick Carter. ML-1208. Probably *L'Apocalypse de Jean* (1923).

U40 Moret, Alexandre. Probably the author whose work Lawrence ordered with U39.

U41 Murry, J. M. *God: An Introduction to the Science of Metabiology*. Slightly familiar. ML-1209.

November

U42 Mann, Thomas. *Buddenbrooks* (fiction). Received. MS/DHL-124.

U43 Inge, W. R. *The Philosophy of Plotinus*. Reading. EN, III-403.

U44 Artzibashev, Mikail. Mentions in review of *Fallen Leaves*. PH-388.

U45 Merejkovski, Dimitry. Mentions in review of *Fallen Leaves*. PH-388.

U46 Rozanov, V. V. *Fallen Leaves*, trans. S. S. Koteliansky (fiction). Reviewed. PH-388-92.

December

U47 Davies, Rhys. Read a short story in *This Quarter*. ML-1226.

U48 Dostoyevsky, F. M. *The Grand*

Inquisitor (fiction). Re-read when he wrote the introduction for translation. WR-215.

U49 Douglas, Norman. *What about Europe?* (essays). Read. ML-1214.

U50 Enoch the Patriarch. Received a book on him from Frederick Carter. ML-1222. Possibly *The Hebrew Book of Enoch* (1928).

U51 Hesiod. *Works and Days, Homeric Hymns and Fragments.* Requested from Charles Lahr along with Plutarch in November. LACY/COCK-89. Received Plutarch this month, ML-1220; may have received Hesiod too. APOCALYPSE-96. Lawrence had also read the *Theogony.* APOCALYPSE-229.

U52 Maillol, Aristide. Received a book of his reproductions. ML-1227.

U53 Moffat, James. Using the Moffat translation of the Bible. EN, III-403.

U54 Plutarch. Received a requested volume. ML-1220.

U55 Tellar, Mark (Vere Collins). *A Young Man's Passage* (fiction). Read a part of the ms. EN, I-472 and note 494.

Undated reading for which evidence appears during 1929

U56 Bynner, Witter. *Indian Earth* (poetry collection). This was dedicated to Lawrence: in all likelihood he received a copy. WB-182.

U57 *The Dial* (periodical). Receiving regularly this year. MM-107.

U58 *New Dostoevsky Letters.* Translated this year by Koteliansky, who habitually sent him translations.

U59 Hastings, James. *Encyclopedia of Religion and Ethics.* Cites Bousset's article in this volume in *Apocalypse* which was being written late this year. KS-188.

U60 Murray, Gilbert. *Five Stages of Greek Religion.* Reading. EN, III-403.

U61 *The New Statesman* (periodical). Seems to be reading regularly. ML-1181, 1219.

U62 Petrie, W. M. F. *Egyptian Tales Translated from the Papyri.* W. Y. Tindall feels that the references to Egyptian tales in *Apocalypse* refer to this volume. WYT-98

Unidentified reading for 1929

U63 *Dickensian Gentleman.* Probably a ms. returned with comments to Aldous Huxley. February, HL-787.

U64 A poem sent by Catherine Carswell in August. HL-817. Called 'a love dialogue by Dunbar', it may have been by William Dunbar, since Lawrence comments that he can't understand all the words.

U65 An Etruscan book received along with other unspecified books from Max Mohr in November. ML-1215.

U66 Technical information on the olive tree and the vine, requested from Maria Huxley in October. HL-832.

Addenda 1929

U67 Adler, Alfred (Austrian psychiatrist). Familiar. APOCALYPSE-208.

U68 Apuleius. *The Golden Ass.* Familiar. APOCALYPSE-137.

U69 Compte, Auguste. Familiar with his 'Law of three stages'. APOCALYPSE-237.

U70 Dryden, John. 'Alexander's Feast' (poem). Quotes. APOCALYPSE-143.

U71 Dupuis. *Religion Universelle.* Read a synopsis by Frederick Carter. APOCALYPSE-210-11.

U72 Eisler, Robert. *Orpheus the Fisher: Comparative studies in Orphic and early Christian cult symbolism.* In October 1929 Lawrence wrote to

Carter 'I agree with Eisler', possibly referring to this book. APOCALYPSE-217.

U73 Jung, Carl. *Psychology of the Unconscious.* Familiar. APOCALYPSE-225.

U74 Kelvin, Lord (Sir William Thomson). Familiar. APOCALYPSE-192.

U75 Plato. *Dialogues.* Familiar with Benjamin Jowett's translation. Also with the *Laws.* APOCALYPSE-96, 113.

(SECTION V) 1930

January

V1 Carter, Frederick. Read a chapter of ms. on 'the antique heavens'. Unpublished letter to Carter, 15 Jan.

V2 Chambers, Maria Cristina. Read ms. of her poems. MCC-119.

V3 Heyward, DuBose. *Mamba's Daughters* (fiction). Read. MIH-522.

V4 Morrell, Philip. *Leaves from the Grenville Diary* (history). Received. ML-1234.

February

V5 Burdett, Osbert. *The Brownings* (biography). Probably the book received from Maria Huxley. MIH-523.

V6 Gill, Eric. *Art Nonsense and other Essays.* Reviewed. PH-393-97.

V7 Whitehead, Alfred North. Familiar. Review of *Art Nonsense* . . .. PH-395.

V8 Lowell, Joan. *Cradle of the Deep.* Read. MIH-523. Presented as a biographical narrative, it was later proved a hoax. In England it was titled *Child of the Deep.*

V9 Staël, Madame de. *Corinne* (fiction). Probably the volume received. MIH-523.

V10 Wolfe, Thomas. *Look Homeward,*

Angel (fiction). May be the book which elicited Lawrence's disgust with 'self-conscious young Americans posing before their own cameras'. MIH-523.

Unidentified reading for 1930

V11 Received a Chinese book from Laurence Pollinger. MIH-522.

V12 Reading a biography of Columbus just before his death. RA-413. If this was from the library of Ad Astra, it may have been Washington Irving's *Life and Voyages of Columbus.* Earl Brewster recalls that Lawrence entered Ad Astra without any reading material and he helped him choose something from the institution's library.

(SECTION W) UNDATABLE

W1 Bushmen stories. In January 1929 Lawrence spoke to Brewster Ghiselin of some translations of stories by 'Bushmen' which he had read in the past in which the qualities of things seemed to be continually changing. EN, III-296.

W2 Butler, Samuel. *The Way of All Flesh* (fiction). Discussed with Else Jaffe. EN, III-426.

W3 Miron, Diaz. A note in the *Ida Purnell Stone: Palms Collection* at the University of Texas says that Lawrence 'edited' something written by Augustin Basave about Miron.

W4 Schiffler, Karl. *Zeit und Stunde.* In an unpublished and untitled essay at the University of Texas Lawrence says he read this work while approaching England on a ship.

W5 Russo, Luigi. Professor Armin Arnold says in 'DHL, the Russians, and Giovanni Verga' (*Comparative Literature Studies,* II (1965), 249-57, that Lawrence read a book on Verga written by Luigi Russo. This was probably *Giovanni Verga*.

INDEX

The following subject matter categories are included in the index: American Authors, Anthropology, Apocalypse, Art: Theory and Criticism, Australian Authors, Bullfighting, Children's Literature, Egypt, English Romantics, Etruscans, French Authors, Futurism, German Authors, Greek Tragedy, History, Italian Authors, India, Mexico, Natural History, Occult, Oriental Thought and Religion, Philosophy, Psychology, Russian Authors, Scandanavian Authors, Spanish Authors, Theology. Entries preceded by an asterisk indicate works which Lawrence read in a foreign language.

Collins, Vere, S70, T57, U55
Collins, Wilkie, B14
Collodi, Carlo, K24
Columbus, Christopher, V12
Comfort, Will, O33
Comnena, Anna, K4
Compte, Auguste, U69
Conrad, Joseph, A162, D19, D26, O42, R37
CONTEMPORARY (p), Q1
CONTEMPORARY BELGIAN POETRY, C36
CONTEMPORARY REVIEW (p), C41
Cook, Capt. James, Q34
Coomaraswamy, Ananda K., T58
Cooper, James Fenimore, A11, H34, I22, J6
Coppard, A. E. S71
Corke, Helen, B8
Corneille, Pierre, B39
*CORRIERE DELLA SERA (n), Q2
Corvo, Baron (Frederick Rolfe), Q29, Q32
Coué, Émile, P32
Couperus, Louis, R21
Cournos, John, G32, U33
Cowper, William, A111
Crèvecoeur, Hector, H42
Crichton, Kyle, Q23
Crosby, Caresse, Q44
Crosby, Harry, T15
Crosland, T. W. H., F3
Crowley, Aleister, B18
Curtis, Natalie, P29
Curzon, George, H21

Dahlberg, Edward, T48
DAILY CHRONICLE, C3
DAILY MAIL, C3
DAILY NEWS, C3, E18
Dana, Richard H., H28
Daniel, Evan, A32
Dante Alighieri, F33, K5, Q11, T16
Darwin, Charles, A21, A40, S61
Daudet, Alphonse, A41, H8
Daudet, Léon, B40
Davidson, John, A163

Davies, Rhys, T30, T46, U18, U47
Davies, W. H., A126
Defoe, Daniel, A185
Dehan, Richard, (Clotilde Inez Mary Graves), C1
Dehmel, Richard, E7
Dekker, E. D. N18, N31
de la Mare, Walter, A186, B19, D9
Deledda, Grazia, H60, K25, T1
Dennis, George, R16
DENVER POST (n), N24
De Quincey, Thomas, A22, H36, J26, K37
DIAL, THE (p), M21, O12, U57
Díaz, Bernal, O23
Dickens, Charles, A6, A12, A23, B41, D27, H29, L26, S28
DICKENSIAN GENTLEMAN, U63
Diderot, Denis, A70
Dircks, Mrs. Rudolph, A30
Dobrée, Louisa Emily, S19
Donne, John, U8
Doolittle, Hilda (H. D.), I1
Dos Passos, John, N2, S6
Dostoyevsky, F. M., A140, D15, E59, F5, F22, G7, G10, H9, H43, H61, O24, R2, R13, U48, U58
Dostoyevsky, Madame, R13
Doughty, Charles, A99, P5
Douglas, Alfred, A127, B33
Douglas, G., B20
Douglas, Norman, L3, R11, R12, S20, T19, U4, U26, U49
Dowson, Ernest, C13, E56
Dreiser, Theodore, U20
Dryden, John, U70
Ducati, Pericle, R29
Dudley, Helen, F18
Dufferin, Lord, (F. T. Hamilton), R3
Dulac, Edmund, K41
Dumas, Alexander *fils* A214
Dunbar, William, U64
Dupuis, U71

EASTWOOD & KIMBERLY ADVERTISER, C3
Eder, Dr David, L4

A. R. and C. P. Griffin

3

A social and economic history of Eastwood and the Nottinghamshire mining country

1. INTRODUCTION

Eastwood is a small market town at the centre of the Erewash Valley, an old coalfield straddling the Nottinghamshire–Derbyshire border which extends from Wollaton, near the river Trent in the south, to Alfreton in the north. Before the building of the canals in the late eighteenth century, the typical Erewash Valley coalmine was very small, because transport difficulties restricted the market area and the local demand for coal was limited. Indeed, coalmining did not achieve dominance as the staple industry of the Eastwood area until well into the nineteenth century: before then hosiery and agriculture absorbed a considerably larger proportion of the labour force than coalmining. Between 1803 and 1848 the quantity of coal shipped by canal from Erewash Valley mines increased from 254,268 tons to 427,670 tons. Then, an even more potent force for change, the main-line railway, was introduced into the district, and by 1869 railway sales totalled 1,709,061 tons whilst canal sales had fallen to 192,902 tons. Taking the two outlets together, sales increased by 169 per cent between 1803 and 1849, and by a further 442 per cent between 1849 and 1869.[1]

The inevitable concomitant of this growth in the size of the market was a considerable increase in the size of the typical coalmine. The typical late-eighteenth or early-nineteenth-century coalmine in the district was, let it be said, nothing like so small as Lawrence himself imagined it: 'foot-rill mines with an opening in the hillside into which the miners walked, or windlass mines, where the men were wound up one at a time in a bucket by a donkey.'[2] There were certainly a few like that, but most local coal pits employed thirty to fifty men and had low-powered steam winding engines. The fixed capital at such a pit was provided by the colliery owner, who sank the shafts, installed the pumps and winding gear and designed the ventilation system. The circulating capital was supplied, in most cases, by contractors (usually called *butties*) who undertook to produce the coal at so much per ton; who hired, paid and supervised the labour; who provided the ropes, ponies or donkeys, pit props and things of that kind; and who virtually controlled the day-to-day running of the pits.

Between 1840 and 1860 there was, however, a profound change. Technological innovations at the coalface, on the road-ways and in the shafts greatly increased the scale of capital investment and the number of men employed at a typical coalmine, and necessitated a concomitant alteration in the management system. Now, the owners had so much capital at risk that they could not leave unlettered butties to manage the pits. Instead, they employed salaried officials. True, there were still sub-contractors commonly called butties, but under this attenuated form of the butty system, a pair of butties merely had control of a section of a long-wall coalface (a 'stall') and they usually had not more than three or four day-wage men working under them, and they provided very little of the circulating capital. Whereas under the 'big' butty system, the butties were effectively the employers of the men, now the 'little' butties were clearly workmen; and in many cases were little better off than their day-wage assistants, who were often their sons or nephews, or sons of their friends.

D. H. Lawrence's father, Arthur, referred to himself as a 'mining contractor' and this has misled some writers[3] into thinking of him as a 'big' butty, and thus ascribing to him a middle-class role, whereas he was clearly a 'little' butty. It is understandable that in paying court to a school teacher, he should have adopted a more impressive style than 'collier', but a collier is what he was.

The 'big' butty in the coalmining industry of the first half of the nineteenth century had his counterpart in the 'bag hosier' of the framework knitting trade. Most framework knitters worked in their own houses on frames usually rented from either a hosiery firm or a bag hosier who was a middle-man putting out work from one or more firms to the knitters. Bag hosiers provided some of the circulating capital, and they saved the knitters the trouble of collecting material from, and returning finished articles to, the hosiers' warehouses. However, they were on the whole bad employers who relied for their living on forcing piece-work wages down, on 'truck' (paying wages in kind rather than in cash, as did many 'big' butties), and on collecting frame rents.

In the second half of the nineteenth century, the framework knitting trade declined rapidly and the bag hosier, like the 'big' butty, was eliminated. Increasingly, the hosiery trade was carried on in factories employing powered machinery rather than in the knitters' houses on manually operated frames. Many hosiery workers, and their sons as they reached working age, entered the mining industry, whose voracious appetite for labour drew males, not just from hosiery, but also from agriculture and other competing occupations.

The wages of piece-work colliers in the Eastwood district more than doubled between the 1850s and 1914 when they averaged 9s 10½d a shift. Over the same period, the weekly earnings of farm labourers advanced by little more than 50 per cent, from around 13s–14s to little more than £1; and skilled craftsmen in surface occupations, whose earnings were higher than those of piecework colliers in the 1850s, averaged only 5s 11d in 1914 in comparison with the collier's 9s 10½d.[4]

In Great Britain, the numbers employed in coalmining rose from about 214,000 in 1854 to 1,248,224 in 1920[5] and this increase is reflected in the Eastwood district. In 1851, 19.8 per cent of males aged over 10 in Eastwood Parish worked in coalmining whilst in 1921 the proportion of gainfully employed males aged over 12 working in coalmining in Eastwood Urban District was 43.2 per cent. The corresponding figures for Agriculture were 5.4 and 1.7 per cent respectively; and the figures for Manufacturing (mainly textiles of one sort or another) were 41.7 and 18.3 per cent respectively. The only category besides coalmining which expanded to any extent over the period was that of Professional and Industrial Services where the corresponding figures were 1.6 and 10.5 per cent respectively, marking the growth of office work particularly.[6]

The increase in the size of the mining industry's labour force was also fed by natural population growth, most colliers' sons following their fathers into the pits; and by immigration. The excess of births over deaths in sample years in the Basford Registration District (of which Eastwood formed part) is shown in Table 1.[7] Many miners had large families (as can be seen from Table 5 below) and it was not uncommon for a middle-aged miner to have three or four sons working underground. Where the father was a butty, his adult sons might well be his day-wage men, or if his stall was full, then they could expect to be taken on by one of his relatives or friends.

The scale of immigration into the area may be gauged from Table 2.[8] Leicestershire, Staffordshire and West Yorkshire had many old coalmines

where wages were lower and working conditions poorer than in the
Eastwood district. In the fifty years 1870–1920, however, new collieries
working virgin top hard coal further to the east, in South Yorkshire, and the
Leen Valley and Mansfield areas of Nottinghamshire, were to prove far
more attractive to immigrant labour than the reconstructed mines around
Eastwood.[9]

Table 1: Births and deaths in Basford Registration District

	Births	Deaths
1860–69 (annual average)	3050	1714
1884	5759	2622
1898	6087	3041

Table 2: Principal birthplaces of population in Basford Registration District in 1861

Nottinghamshire	49,140
Derbyshire	13,705
Leics. & Rutland	2,494
Lincolnshire	629
Yorkshire	425
Staffordshire	310
Ireland	276
London	177
Lancashire	107
Others	6,022
Total population	73,285

Eastwood Parish itself experienced a steady population growth from 1120 in
1811 to 1720 in 1851. The pace then quickened, and by 1901 Eastwood
Urban District (not exactly co-terminous with the Parish) had a population
of 4815. There was considerable movement from the older mining areas of
the Erewash Valley (e.g. Strelley) to the new and reconstructed pits around
Eastwood.

2. MINERS AND COLLIERY OWNERS

In the early nineteenth century there were two large colliery firms in the
Erewash Valley, the Butterley Company and Barber, Walker. In contrast

with the older type of colliery undertaking – like the Wollaton and Radford Collieries of Lord Middleton, which formed part of a landed estate unconcerned with expansion, but providing their owners with current income – these were owned by capitalist entrepreneurs building for the future. Nevertheless, they were both dominated by a few (in the case of Barber, Walker two) families who inherited from the older type of undertaking a paternalistic attitude towards their labour force.

The founders of Barber, Walker were seventeenth century yeomen working shallow seams of coal along with their farming operations, although with the passage of time coalmining became increasingly important. In the early eighteenth century, the partnership's operations were concentrated mainly in the area around Strelley where they leased coal from landowners like Squire Edge, Lord of the Manor of Strelley. When their Strelley leases expired in 1811–38, they concentrated more on their mines in the Eastwood area to the north of Strelley where considerable capital sums were invested in deepening the shafts and expanding operations.[10] D. H. Lawrence was wrong in supposing that these mines were opened only sixty years before he was born (i.e. about 1825). Some were certainly producing in the late eighteenth century, though they were then quite small.[11]

It was in the middle years of the nineteenth century that the widening of the market area by the opening of the railways (which made Erewash Valley coal competitive in London with sea-borne coal from Durham and Northumberland) provided the incentive for modernising the old mines around Eastwood and for sinking new ones to the Top Hard seam one or two miles to the east, as at High Park and Watnall. The output of Barber, Walker's collieries expanded from about 150,000 tons a year in the 1850s to just over a million tons a year in the early 1890s.[12]

D. H. Lawrence's father, Arthur, worked at Brinsley Colliery which was expanded in 1855–6 and again in 1872–6. Prior to 1855 Brinsley had been worked on the 'big' butty system, and it was in the same technologically backward state as most other collieries in the Erewash Valley. In 1855 a shaft was sunk to the Deep Soft Seam, and a ventilation furnace built to provide a more reliable flow of air than the natural convection on which reliance had previously been placed. Presumably, cages held steady in the shaft by guide rails were also installed at this time in place of baskets swinging on a loose rope in which coal had previously been wound out of the mine. In 1872, the ventilation furnace was replaced by a fan, a new shaft was sunk alongside the old one and new headgear and winding engine were installed. The colliery was then much as it remained throughout Arthur

Lawrence's working life and beyond. This reorganisation was started during the boom of 1871–3 when coal sold at famine prices, but was completed during the slump of 1874–9 so that, despite the considerable capital sums invested in the major work of sinking and re-equipping the mine, some of the relatively minor development work which followed was skimped. Thus, Brinsley in the 1870s still had road-ways which were too low to take ponies, so donkeys had to be used instead; as they had been prior to 1855.[13]

Following reorganisation, there was room for about three hundred men and boys at Brinsley Colliery, compared with eighty to a hundred prior to 1855 though the build-up to the higher figure would doubtless have taken a few years to achieve. In 1910 the Barber, Walker collieries in the Eastwood District employed 3123 men and boys as detailed in Table 3. At the same date, collieries owned by other firms were operating in the vicinity of Eastwood (Table 4). Also, some Eastwood miners travelled to collieries at a little distance, e.g. Selston, Alfreton, Cinderhill and Heanor. Men living in houses provided by Barber, Walker (or one of the other firms) had a strong incentive to stay put, however, since leaving the company involved vacating the house.

Table 3: Labour employed at Barber, Walker's collieries in Eastwood District in 1910

Colliery	Underground	Surface	Total
Brinsley	257	52	309
High Park	356	65	421
Moorgreen	644	88	732
Selston	735	92	827
Watnall	700	134	834
Total	2692	431	3123

Table 4: Labour employed at other collieries in Eastwood District in 1910

Colliery	Firm	Underground	Surface	Total
Brookhill	Brookhill Colly. & Pottery Co.	–	1	1 (standing)
Plumtre	Butterley Co.	305	50	355
Digby	Digby Colly. Co.	226	106	332
New London	Digby Colly. Co.	554	59	613
Total		1085	216	1301

Besides building houses, Barber, Walker made other provisions for the social welfare of their employees. From mid-century, they contributed financially to various religious denominations and later helped to finance a Mechanics' Institute (now the Eastwood Miners' Welfare) whose library was used by D. H. Lawrence; built a Welfare Institute at Underwood, and encouraged various sporting activities, particularly cricket and hockey. They also fostered the ambulance brigades which did invaluable work in the mines and the community from about the beginning of the twentieth century.[14] Even so, Barber, Walker were nothing like as philanthropic as some colliery owners, and they were largely motivated by self-interest.

The idyllic picture of the work situation presented by D. H. Lawrence is well drawn:

> And the pit did not mechanize men. On the contrary. Under the butty system, the miners worked underground as a sort of intimate community, they knew each other practically naked, and with curious close intimacy, and the darkness and the underground remoteness of the pit 'stall', and the continual presence of danger, made the physical, instinctive, and intuitional contact between men very highly developed, a contact almost as close as touch, very real and very powerful. This physical awareness and intimate *togetherness* was at its strongest down pit . . . My father loved the pit. He was hurt badly, more than once, but he would never stay away.[15]

This sense of intimacy was reinforced by the fact that there were comparatively few officials, and they usually stayed in the same posts for years; and that the owners were themselves well known to the men. Whether a man liked them or not, at least he knew them; there was a personal relationship between master and man.

3 LIVING IN EASTWOOD

In Eastwood as elsewhere, most people were married at some time in their lives though an excess of females over males in the adult population produced examples of the spinster 'aunt' immortalised in so many of the novels of the period.[16] On average, miners in Eastwood had larger families than others, as Table 5 shows.[17] The mining community included many young immigrants, so miners were, on average, younger than others, and there were fewer of them widowed. Some indication of this can be gathered from the higher average of wives per household among miners than among workers in general or, more particularly, among the professional and business class.

Table 5: *Family composition (arithmetic means)*

| | 1861 | | Miners' families only | |
	Professional and business class	Working classes	1861	1871
Household heads	1.00	1.00	1.00	1.00
Wives per family	0.62	0.77	0.95	0.96
Children	1.40	2.20	2.80	3.20
Family size	3.02	3.97	4.75	5.06

Note: 'Professional' includes professional persons, large businessmen, managers, farmers employing labourers, and people living on investments. 'Working classes' includes skilled, semi- and un-skilled labour (including miners), servants, shopkeepers and tradesmen in a small way of business.

Another important feature of Eastwood family life was that 50 per cent of its families were part of a larger household which might include lodgers, relatives or domestic servants. This situation produced the household composition in Table 6 (excluding the small number of visitors). Upper-class households were generally larger than working-class ones because they contained domestic servants and occupied larger houses. For example, the rector, Henry Plumptre, had a family of six, plus four grandchildren, serviced by seven female and one male domestic servants making a total household of eighteen.[19] Miners' households were large on average because they tended to have more children than others, some 36 per cent of miners' families having four or more children in 1871. More surprising, perhaps, is the fact that four miners each employed a living-in general domestic servant in 1871. These servants were all girls of between eleven and fourteen years of age living with families who occupied some of the most substantial working-class housing in Eastwood.[20] There was a wide range of family incomes in Eastwood not only between professional and business families like the Walkers, colliery proprietors of Eastwood Hall, and the working class; but also between one working-class family and another. A butty in a good stall might earn £5 or £6 a week in the boom years of the Boer War period or the period immediately preceding World War I, some four or five times more than the poorest male manual workers. Where a miner had three or four sons working in the pit his wife was certainly kept busy washing and cooking, preparing baths and drying clothes, but the family income was comparatively high. Some of these families rented, and some others bought, substantial houses stuffed with expensive furniture including, in a fair number of cases, a piano. It was the working-class households, with only one breadwinner and several growing children, which felt the pinch of poverty: the 'endless struggle for bread'; the handing down of clothes; the living in rooms over lock-up shops, or the older miners' hovels.[21]

Table 6: *Household composition (arithmetic means)*

	1861		Miners' households only	
	Professional and business class	*Working classes*	*1861*	*1871*
Family size	3.02	3.97	4.75	5.06
Domestics per household	2.01	0.02	0.00	0.03
Lodgers per household	0.50	0.43	0.14	0.10
Relatives per household	0.28	0.35	0.18	0.12
Household size	5.82	4.77	5.07	5.39

Note: Visitors excluded from household size.

The growth of Eastwood's population was accompanied by an increase in its housing stock from 339 in 1851 to 532 in 1871 and 974 in 1901.[22] On the whole, too, the quality of the housing stock was improving. The main housing for miners before the 1870s was Daykin's Rows, 'two rows of little back-to-back housing' which had a small colliery working between them until the 1870s. Miners and other workers also lived in the several small thatched cottages known as Hell's Row which was appropriately burned down, and in their place were the superior miners' houses known as The Breach, where D. H. Lawrence lived.[23] The improvement in the quality of housing was largely due to the Barber, Walker Company who erected several hundred houses in Eastwood in the 1870s and 1880s, most notably The Buildings or Squares and The Breach. The general character of The Buildings can be gathered from this description by W. E. Hopkin:

It consists of two long streets and three short ones running at right angles. They are mostly five roomed houses, with very few breaks between them, and all inhabited by miners. With the exception of the north side of Princes Street, where the backs look out over the Nethergreen brook valley, all the house backs are enclosed in tiny yards, with high walls, and several houses to each yard. The outlook is to the coal-house, ash-bin and out-offices.

The ground falls away sharply from the Nottingham Road and in one street there are cellar kitchens. The streets being cut across at right angles, there are two inner squares, used for the drying of clothes, gossiping and as playgrounds for the children after school hours.[24]

D. H. Lawrence describes The Breach housing accurately as 'six blocks of rather more pretentious dwellings erected by the company in the valley below, two rows of three blocks, with an alley between', and another of its occupants further described its houses as 'substantial, roomy and decent. They had neat front gardens filled with flowers . . . back gardens leading to Ashpit alley between the blocks'.[25] Construction of the first long row of the The Buildings, Princes Street, was under way at the time of the 1871 census when the first forty dwellings were occupied, and from this evidence it is possible to evaluate the adequacy of the housing provision at that time. The first section of the street consists of a row of thirteen houses, eleven smaller dwellings sandwiched between two larger ones. The internal layout of the two types is shown in the accompanying plan of the last two houses in the row.[26] The actual living space in the two houses is 570 and 754 square feet respectively, which compared favourably with other colliery housing built in the Nottinghamshire coal-field in the third quarter of the nineteenth century as Table 7 indicates.[27] The Eastwood houses considered in detail here were clearly also superior to those at Annesley (built 1870) and Cinderhill (built 1858) in having three bedrooms, and the larger Eastwood type also had the added privacy and convenience of a passage and landing of 90 square feet in total.[28] In terms of living space per person the houses were on the whole generous, and if we take up to two persons per bedroom as an acceptable level for comfortable living then the occupants of the larger houses were fortunate indeed, as Table 8 shows.[29] Two of the small houses were badly overcrowded, though at Annesley, where 43 per cent of the households lived in overcrowded conditions (i.e. with more than two persons per bedroom), the position was far worse. The main cause of overcrowding was the presence of large numbers of children, though in two cases the situation was exacerbated by the presence of relatives living with the family. Three families employed a resident domestic servant and in one case the servant girl brought the household size to the overcrowding level (seven people in three bedrooms).

The houses built by Barber, Walker from the 1870s were representative of the better-quality working-class houses in Eastwood. The general adequacy of houses in Eastwood in relation to occupants in the early twentieth century is indicated in Table 9.[30] Since houses with five or more rooms were not

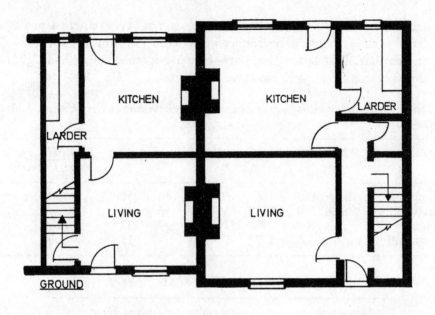

GROUND

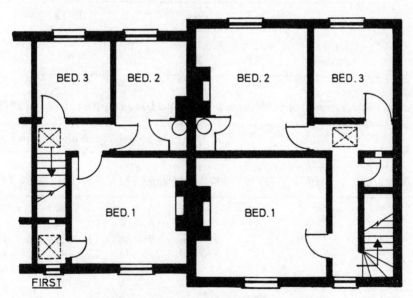

FIRST

PLAN OF HOUSES BUILT BY BARBER WALKER
IN PRINCES ST. EASTWOOD IN 1871

SCALE ⊢⊣⊣⊣ ⊢ ⊣ ⊣ ⊣
0 1 2 3 4 FEET

detailed on the 1901 Census Returns one cannot say whether there was a decrease in the degree of overcrowding between 1901 and 1911, but it will be seen that at the latter date, sixty-three five-roomed houses had eight or more persons sleeping in the three bedrooms.

Table 7: Living space in three examples of Nottinghamshire colliery housing built c. 1850–75

Location	Kitchen	Living room	Bedrooms 1	2	3	Larder	Total living space (square feet)
Eastwood	(large) 160	160	160	144	80	50	*754*
Eastwood	(small) 130	135	135	78	52	40	*570*
Annesley	202	99	174	135	–	32	*642*
Cinderhill	66	177	177	84	–	15	*519*

Table 8: Distribution of household size: Princes Street, 1871

House type	Number of persons in household			
	1–3	4–6	7–9	10–12
Large	1	5	1	–
Small	4	21	6	2

Table 9: The occuptants of habitations in Eastwood Urban District 1901 and 1911

Number of rooms per habitation	Number of habitations 1901	1911	Number of persons 1 1901	1911	2 1901	1911	3 1901	1911	4 1901	1911
1	1	1	1	1	–	–	–	–	–	–
2	37	11	7	1	10	4	10	4	9	1
3	59	77	5	4	9	16	14	28	11	10
4	130	187	3	10	21	45	23	40	31	35
5		471		9		54		101		80
6		150		2		9		23		23
7		54		–		6		11		8
8		27		–		3		4		2
9		11		–		1		1		4
10 or more		20		–		1		1		2

Overcrowded or not, most working-class houses in Eastwood in the early twentieth century were to some degree deficient in terms of essential services. The better houses such as The Buildings enjoyed gas illumination from the Eastwood gas works erected and run by the Barber, Walker Company, but even these houses relied for water on one stand pipe in the backyard per three or four houses, and earth closets and ashpits for the disposal of excrement and rubbish.[31] Even when cleaned out regularly these were a source of nuisance especially in hot weather, and were an actual health hazard in some parts of the town where they were emptied irregularly.[32] A sewerage system was started in the 1880s and was extended in the 1890s but much of the existing housing remained unconnected until the inter-war period.[33] Epidemics of measles, diphtheria, diarrhoea and particularly scarlet fever and whooping cough were common in the late Victorian period and between them accounted for about ten per cent of all deaths in the Basford Rural District (of which Eastwood was a part) in 1898, though as usual the largest single killers were respiratory diseases (tuberculosis and bronchitis), which contributed a further 17 per cent. A serious epidemic of measles in Eastwood in 1912 produced three deaths. In 1914 whooping cough, scarlet fever and diphtheria killed fourteen persons between them, 14 per cent of all deaths in that year (compared with 25 per cent for respiratory diseases).[34] The spread of these epidemics was powerfully assisted, according to the medical officers of health, who were always pressing for sanitary improvements, by overcrowding and

per habitation

	5		6		7		8		9		10 or over	
	1901	*1911*	*1901*	*1911*	*1901*	*1911*	*1901*	*1911*	*1901*	*1911*	*1901*	*1911*
	–	–	–	–	–	–	–	–	–	–	–	–
	1	–	–	–	–	–	–	–	–	–	–	–
	11	6	4	8	3	2	1	2	1	1	–	–
	23	26	11	11	10	7	3	7	3	5	–	1
		70		66		38		23		17		13
		33		16		15		11		11		7
		9		8		5		2		1		4
		4		2		5		3		2		2
		–		–		2		1		1		
		2		7		4		2		1		

Note: Habitations with more than four rooms not shown in 1901.

inadequate disposal of sewage in certain districts of the town. The medical officer of Basford Rural District in the late nineteenth century also blamed parental ignorance and incompetent child rearing for the spread of these epidemics, which hit children in particular (44 per cent of all deaths were of children under 5 in the 1880s).[35] On one occasion he commented: 'While the miner is in his pit, his wife perchance drinks and gossips and his poor children, what becomes of them? At best they imbibe milk made poisonous by gin or beer; or they are left to starve or die from the effects of patent medicines or other narcotics'; and a serious epidemic of whooping cough in 1889 produced the alarming allegation: 'Whooping cough is thought by most people to be caused by something in the air, in the winds; Fallacy No. 1; Fallacy No. 2 is that all children MUST have it. This leads to Fallacy No. 3 which is that if the season is mild, they had better have it at once and get it over with.'[36] There were large demonstrations against the introduction of compulsory vaccination against smallpox in Eastwood in 1898, which also suggests that there was widespread ignorance concerning the best medical practice.[37] Oral evidence taken by C. P. Griffin suggests too that there was before 1914 a heavy reliance on intuition and herbal remedies in the treatment of disease, but those interviewed deny that child neglect was common, though it was not unknown. On this issue J. C. P. Taylor commented fairly of a school photograph of 1893 reproduced in the local newspaper some seventy years later: 'note first the physiognomy of those boys in this group . . . Their appearance is a tribute to the efficiency of the domestic economy of the day, based on the practical application of the three Arts, namely, Washing, Needlework and Cooking.'[38] On balance it would seem that it was environmental factors (particularly perhaps 'the occurrence of decaying matters so constantly existing' on Eastwood's ashpits),[39] combined with a certain degree of ill-advised treatment in an age of private medicine, that boosted the death-rate, particularly of children, rather than deliberate parental neglect.

Few working-class houses were provided with bathrooms or running hot water and there were no pit head baths; and so many miners, on arriving home from work, ate their meals without washing their hands (coal dust was 'clean dirt'), and only then would bathe or 'strip wash' in a galvanised bath or bowl in front of the kitchen fire range.[40]

Indeed the kitchen was the key room in the family life of the miner for, as K. D. Poynter explains, 'It was in this room that most of our daily life was spent . . . The front parlour on the other hand, was of a different order of things. This room was more 'sacred' being reserved for use on Sundays or when guests arrived.' And central to the functioning of the living room/kitchen was the blacklead fireplace consisting of a central fire-grate with an oven on one side, and a boiler on the other. Here the family meals were prepared, and great pride was taken by each household in maintaining this unit.[41] Fortunately the miners' supply of concessionary coal ensured that the fire was always stoked up, and G. A. Tomlinson recollected 'The picture of a miner's house is never complete without a big fire. It is the one real blessing of a miner's life. Getting cheap coal as the miners do they do not stint the fire ever. One can stand hunger much better if one is warm and can sit looking at a big fire.'[42] Cheap coal meant warmth and comfort, hot water and freshly cooked meals and so it is perhaps not to be wondered at that 'one household was ever in competition with its neighbour to see who could produce and keep the best shine'[43] on the fireplace, or that Tomlinson should remark: 'My home, for all its hardships, was a wonderful place . . . The miner is not, and never has been, the miserable object that writers would have the general public believe.'[44]

4 EDUCATION

By 1900 there were four schools in Eastwood: the National, opened in 1863, the British, situated in two buildings opened in 1868 and 1876 respectively, the Undenominational, which had just opened, and Beauvale Board School, opened in the late 1870s. In 1908–9 the county council took over the three independent schools and reorganised them into the Albert Street school for boys, Devonshire Drive school for girls and infants, and the New Eastwood school for mixed infants and juniors.[45]

All the schools taught the basic curriculum of reading, writing and arithmetic, and scripture. Object lessons and topics, including those of a scientific nature, were also considered of value, as was the study of history, geography and music. Yard drill was the usual form of physical training; there was also football for the boys in the winter months.[46] At the National School (boys) nature rambles in the surrounding countryside were introduced in 1906. Violin lessons were introduced in addition to solo and choral singing, and the variety and quality of the latter was much improved by new music books and enthusiastic teaching. General knowledge and reading skills were stimulated by the 'Introduction of an *Observation Book* in which the boys gum interesting newspaper cuttings. These are afterwards taken in a reading lesson and the contents discussed. The boys are very keen on it.' The boys also had gardening added to their practical subjects, and girls were taught cooking in addition to needlework. The headmaster, Mr Darrington, remembered by Poynter as very strict but fair, not only introduced child-centred methods but attempted to increase the level of parental involvement in their children's educational progress by starting 'open afternoons' and providing evening 'lantern shows' for parents and children on such diverse topics as 'the showpieces of Yorkshire' and 'bison hunting'.[47]

By the late nineteenth century, Eastwood children were certainly receiving much more education than those of previous generations. In 1871, for instance, only 82 per cent of sons and 77 per cent of daughters, aged 5 to 9, of Eastwood miners attended school; and for the 10 to 14 age group there were only 49 per cent and 50 per cent respectively. Some 45 per cent of boys were already at work, practically all of them in the mines.[48] By the 1890s not only were most of the children in these age groups at school but attendance was high compared to the 1860s when in the National school average attendance of children on the books was about 50 per cent compared to about 90 per cent in the 1890s.[49] Attendance was frequently disrupted by adverse weather conditions, heavy falls of rain or snow preventing poorly clad and shod children coming to school. Also, attendance could be substantially reduced by epidemics of influenza, measles, whooping cough and scarlet fever. The arrival of a circus, theatre company, menagerie or a troop of soldiers in town was guaranteed to cut attendance, as was the start of a nearby wakes at Heanor, for example. Children would also take time off to go stone-picking in the spring or harvesting in autumn, and mothers 'kept girls at home from bad domestic arrangements'. Warnings or fines for persistent offenders were not always effective, especially in the case of boys who were already working and earning.[50] To some extent the schools made a virtue out of necessity by giving half-day holidays for the Moorgreen flower show, Eastwood and Beggarlee wakes and Empire Day. Holidays were given on special occasions, such as to celebrate the lifting of the siege of Ladysmith or to mark 'the burial of the late Thomas Barber Esq., a gentleman of note in the neighbourhood'. Poor maintenance and cleaning of the heating stove at the British school between 1893 and 1895 caused the staff to send the children home on a number of occasions 'on account of smoke from the stove filling the room'.[51]

When attendance was average or above, the British and National schools were certainly overcrowded and could be so stifling on a hot summer day that the pupils became very apathetic.[52] Effective teaching was very difficult under these conditions. Experienced teachers had their own individual methods of coping with this problem, though in the last resort corporal punishment was used. Some teachers used it too readily, as at the British school in 1901 when Mr Parry had to be asked by the head 'to be more gentle and patient because the bigger boys object to their being driven', and at the National school when the school managers resolved in 1905 that 'we wish it to be clearly understood that no corporal punishment is to be inflicted in the schools except by the Head Teacher, the term "corporal punishment" includes any hitting or rapping of fingers, any boxing of the ears, however slight'.[53] But the problem of maintaining discipline was a very real one, and an inability to control an overcrowded class broke the nerve of some student teachers and led to such incidents as the setting on fire of a classroom cupboard.[54]

The schools tried not only to instil some sense of discipline into their pupils but to control what were considered other undesirable habits. Stone throwing became such a problem in 1899 that the headmaster of the British school gave lectures 'on the dangers of stone throwing' though evidently to little effect since a pupil lost an eye in a stone fight shortly afterwards, though after the damage was done 'several boys expressed a wish to start a subscription on Buxton's behalf to buy him an artificial eye as his parents are very poor'. The growing habit of cigarette smoking was singled out for attention by 'gaffer' Darrington who 'lectured the boys on why they should not smoke . . . pointing out to them the effects of tobacco on the heart, nervous system and quickness of thought'.[55]

The quality of the education being given in the schools was considered by the inspectorate to vary between 'satisfactory' and 'very good'; the passes in the elementary subjects in the various standards of the National school in 1900 of between 80 and 95 per cent being not untypical.[56] The National and British school buildings were, however, frequently condemned as insalubrious and overcrowded from the 1890s; and the National school (boys) fell from grace altogether in 1904 when the inspector reported 'The school has suffered from changes in the teaching staff during the year, and satisfactory instruction is rendered more difficult by the fact that so many classes are taken in a single, large undivided room. Some of the work is very fair, but it is planned on old-fashioned and mechanical lines. Considerable improvement should be made, especially in the object teaching and composition.' The headmaster, Mr Sheldon, was frequently absent through illness, and the pupil teachers were generally demoralised, and it was fortunate for the school that the head retired at the end of 1905 to be

1 Nottingham Road, Eastwood, 1912

2 'Holing under' (i.e. undercutting the coal) at Brinsley Colliery

3 Pony haulage underground, Brinsley Colliery

4 Miners queuing for their pay at the colliery offices

5 'Butties' paying their daymen

At the kitchen fire: (*below* 6) An Eastwood collier 'strip washing'; and (*facing* 7) a collier's wife drying pit-clothes

8 A typical Eastwood collier taking his children for a walk

replaced by Mr Darrington, who was 'both zealous and capable and may be relied upon to remedy before long the various defects observed last year. The general tone of the work is distinctly good, the boys are interested in their work and are smart and orderly in their movements.'[57] This remark suggests that most pupils found school a reasonably enjoyable experience on the whole and this is certainly how they remember it now, though Poynter's description of his schooldays as 'an idyllic period' seems to be an extreme viewpoint which neglects 'the harsh discipline needed to tame the uncouth colliery lads'.[58]

From 1893 onwards, formal education did not necessarily cease on leaving school, for in that November an evening 'continuation school' was started at the British school to provide a practical and commercial education for larger numbers than the elite of scholars who either went on to take technical training in the mining industry at college, or – like Lawrence – became pupil teachers in local schools. The classes started with a group of thirty-five which had grown to 103 within a month. At the end of 1896 attendance was still ninety-three though after the turn of the century numbers attending dropped so that they averaged forty in 1904 and twenty in 1906. The subjects taught included French, Short-hand and Technical Drawing as well as more advanced Mathematics and Grammar than was taught at elementary school. The classes appear to have had some impact in improving the level of educational attainment of Eastwood adults, since inspectors frequently made such comments as 'everyone is trying to learn and not there simply to pass up the time easily and pleasantly', though attendance could be badly affected by such competition as 'two entertainments in the parish' or 'a fine moonlight night and good skating conditions'. However, poor attendance was more usually produced by bad weather conditions such as 'a very wet and stormy night'. Enthusiasm for the school, however, was drying up in the early years of the century and it appears to have ceased functioning during 1906.[59]

5 RELIGION

Religious institutions were one of the prominent features of Eastwood community life and they offered a mixture of religious, social and educational services to their members. There was a wide variety of churches and chapels to cater for the needs of all sections of the population, though some sects, such as the Mormons who had been active in the early 1870s, had never recruited sufficient support to produce an official place of worship.[60]

All denominations had Sunday services, but the free churches extended their religious activities far beyond this. The Primitive Methodists, for instance, held prayer meetings in the private houses of potential converts, held regular outdoor services in the 'Squares', and at the turn of the century adopted a policy of regular 'torch-light processions round the streets, especially at the time when the public houses were closing'. George Purdy, a key figure in the Primitive Methodist chapel from the 1840s to the 1890s, was a fine singer of religious songs and hymns and was 'fetched at all hours to pray and sing with the sick and the dying and was invited to most funerals to sing over the dead at their doors'.[61] The Baptists, too, held outdoor revival services during the 1890s when their membership was flagging, such as one in May 1895 when 'George Hill, a prominent local Baptist layman, conducted a special evangelistic service which took the form of a camp meeting opened by a procession of the Sunday School from the chapel to a field at the top of Lynn Croft. Meetings continued for the rest of the day with a succession of speakers, Sankey's hymns being sung.'[62]

The various religious bodies not only were concerned to bring 'the true principles of religion and sobriety to the populace'[63], but often provided a wide range of social activities such as concerts, entertainments, lectures, lantern slide shows, teas, suppers and bazaars, as well as the more regular meetings of such groups as the Ladies Guild of the Primitive Methodists which offered 'Bright Meetings, a nice room, a warm fire, cheerful companionship, and a cup of tea'.[64] The free churches also warmly embraced the Band of Hope movement and held regular meetings and public demonstrations to expound the cause of temperance.[65] A central feature of Primitive Methodist activity was the choir accompanied by the harmonium, or less frequently a string consort whose players and instruments were considered 'less reliable' than the harmonium. It was a mixed choir of all age groups and entered competitions in the region like one at the Nottingham Mechanics' Institute in 1886. Its repertoire was ambitious and included an annual performance of *Messiah*.[66]

The chief educational endeavour of the religious institutions was the provision of Sunday schools where children were taught to read the Bible, to write, to listen to biblical stories read by their teachers, and to sing religious songs. Attendance by Eastwood children at Sunday school was extremely high, far in excess of their parents' attendance at church or chapel. Many non-religious parents sent their children to Sunday school to keep them off the streets, and playing truant was often punished by a good hiding or loss of Sunday dinner.[67] The educational value of the Sunday schools was probably rather limited given the brief period of attendance and inept or inexperienced teaching. William Purdy noted in 1913 of his experiences of Sunday school in the mid-Victorian period for instance, that his

> recollection of some of the teachers is not very creditable. It was a usual thing for most teachers to have a stick, a cane, or a strap in their hands, and failing these a Bible. It was not at all uncommon to see a boy knocked across the school with a Bible (including myself), and very often never knew what it was for. Neither was it unusual to see the boys armed with stones waiting for some of the teachers coming out of school ... Half an hour was devoted each Sunday morning for writing ... with boys writing with cross-legged and one-legged pens [and this] was not a very desirable subject.[68]

There was a more relaxed atmosphere in the Sunday schools of Edwardian Eastwood, where the singing in particular was enjoyed by the children along with the annual treat such as a garden party at the Vicarage or a picnic at the Codnor monument a few miles away.[69]

There was, finally, during these years a continuation of the link between free church membership and political radicalism. The Methodist chapels in particular still provided both a training ground in public speaking and organisation, and a source of ideological inspiration for leaders of the labour movement.[70] William Purdy of the Primitive Methodists for instance saw nothing incongruous in arguing in his 'Practical Remarks on Sunday School Work' that

> organised Christianity is absolutely useless to the toiling population without organised labour ... Our Sunday Schools must be the nurturing ground for future reform in our religious churches, and justice in our commercial enterprise ... A closer unity between the living and the dying must be maintained, and things for the body as well as the soul ... All subjects relative to Thy Kingdom come, Thy will be done on earth as it is in heaven, must be the theme of discussions, labour and wages, food and clothing, homes and health, laws and liberty ... In our Christian country there are twelve millions of people on the verge of starvation, and five millions living on absolute charity ... Need we wonder at the people refusing to listen to the echoes from the pulpits ... It would be equally ridiculous to be continually saying, Give us this day our daily bread, and make no effort to obtain it, as to be continually saying Thy Kingdom come, Thy will be done on earth as it is in heaven, and fold our arms until some agency bring it.[71]

In Purdy's mind the activities of chapel members should be directed as much to achieving social reform as building a pathway to heaven, and this vision was a constant inspiration to many leaders of the labour movement in the area, as it was in the country at large.[72]

6 LEISURE

J. C. P. Taylor remembered in 1960 that during his boyhood, some seventy years earlier, 'there were six public houses and two beer-offs in one and a quarter miles along Hill Top', and directory evidence indicates that there were some fourteen public houses and beer shops in Eastwood in the mid-1890s, or one to every three hundred or so of its inhabitants.[73] There seems little doubt that drinking was one of the most popular leisure pursuits of Eastwood men and perhaps of their womenfolk too, though they tended perhaps to drink in different places: the man in the 'pub' and the woman at home. K. D. Poynter recalls that 'My father was a collier and like other colliers, enjoyed his pint of beer', and even the father of one of the poorer families endeavoured to 'drink when he had the money'.[74]

Some miners may have seen the public house, as Lawrence suggests, as a refuge from a nagging wife, though Hopkin believed that much more important was the fact that 'having spent the day in the gloom of the mine, they could not stand the awful gloom of their own back yards on the top of it, and so fled to where there was some brightness'.[75] The public house provided comfort, company and cheerful lighting: as G. A. Tomlinson mused in his autobiography,

> I loved those odd hours spent in the tap-room, the gleam of the pots and the tankards in the fire-light, and what a fire-light! . . . A fire that made you happy and comfortable so that you leaned back against the polished panelling and took in everything without effort . . . Then the bursts of laughter as somebody relates an amusing story of some happening in the pit. The tremendous, but quite good-tempered, arguments on all kinds of subjects, who was Prime Minister at the outbreak of the War, what peas grow best on the local soil . . . Each man had a wonderful story to tell of how he had kidney beans of prodigious length. The lengths of the beans grow as the number of pints consumed grow, but that doesn't matter for everybody else has the same chance to tell his story.[76]

As Tomlinson suggests, an equally important leisure pursuit of Eastwood men was the cultivation of gardens and allotments on which every type of vegetable was grown and where the real enthusiasts kept pigs and poultry or grew 'chrysants'. In part this horticultural interest was perhaps a reflection of 'the deep love of the land that generations of pit work has not destroyed'[77], though the contribution which garden produce made to the family budget was also important. Typical of some of Eastwood's poorer families was one where the men maintained two gardens on which they cultivated fruit and vegetables, flowers for sale at the cemetery and kept pigs and chickens for meat and eggs.[78]

Other popular outdoor pursuits included family walks at the weekends in the surrounding countryside, and further afield after the Nottingham to Ripley tramway opened in 1913. Before then, 'a trip to the county capital eight miles away was a major undertaking, and looked upon as something very special – a real occasion'.[79] The periodic wakes held in the neighbourhood attracted much support from the populace, particularly Hill Top Wakes and the annual Eastwood statute fair, or 'statis' as it was popularly known, with its rock and gingerbread stalls, punch and judy and side-shows, and roundabouts at 1d a time.[80] There was also the occasional brief visit of a circus, menagerie or musical entertainment, while there were travelling theatres that sometimes stopped for a few months at a time, and penny readings held in the British school during the winter months.[81] In the early years of the century 'moving picture' shows became increasingly popular: a travelling cinema held regular sessions in the Mechanics' Institute and was replaced by a permanent picture palace, the Empire, in 1913. Travelling street entertainers also regularly passed through Eastwood during the summer months: the ever popular barrel-organ and monkey and the two blind entertainers, a singer accompanied by an accordian player. Regular dances were held in the Mechanics' Institute, including the annual, if rather exclusive, 'Barbers' Hunt Ball'. There were three cricket teams, the best of which was the 'Black Diamonds' (under the patronage of 'Squire Walker'), who played on the cricket ground provided by Barber, Walker adjacent to the Breach. Football, too, was a popular participatory sport, as was ice skating during the winter.[82]

Music and literature provided a valued source of relaxation for many members of the community. According to Hopkin 'The miner has an instinct for beauty of form, sound, colour and speech. No part of the community has a keener ear and love of music than the miner . . . the keen love of beauty in its various forms is their reaction to their gloomy work, and too often gloomy environment'.[83] Choirs, which were encouraged by the churches and chapels, were popular and gave regular concerts, and miners 'would gather together in the squares and sing songs, hymns and part-songs in the evening'. Many miners also enjoyed reading literature and poetry and in the mid-1890s the Mechanics' Institute library contained over three thousand volumes, which were extensively used.[84] Some men joined one of the brass bands which were in great demand for Union Demonstrations, Band of Hope rallies and so on. A few had pianos and 'American Organs' at home. For the more seriously minded inhabitants there were also the educational and recreational activities of the Co-operative movement, which organised debates, discussion groups and visits to places of interest such as Matlock;[85] or active participation in religious, trade union or political affairs.

It seems likely that the married woman's leisure pursuits were more closely confined to the home than her husband's, but there were compensations. It was the usual practice for house doors to be left unlocked so that neighbours could visit and have a chat as they pleased, while the central avenue of the Breach or the back yards of the Square were ideal places for gossiping neighbours – though there were some cases where the husband discouraged gossiping, having 'no time' for the neighbours.[86]

Children had a leisure pattern which was partly related to the adult world, as when they weeded father's garden, did mother's errands, or went for a family walk on Sunday, and partly an enclosed one of their own in which they played such games as snobs, marbles, diabolo, shuttlecock and battledore, whip and top, skipping, leapfrog, lurky, bat and ball, and football. The more adventurous children also undertook such anti-adult activities as 'scrumping' fruit, spirit knocking, tying neighbours' door knobs together with rope and then knocking on the doors, or booby-trapping doors with bricks connected to the knobs. A majority of children went to Sunday school where in addition to lessons there was an annual presentation of prizes and a treat of tea, nuts and sweets. There was also a tradition that 'on Boxing Day each year, the miners' children from miles around were invited to Lamb Close House ... and were given one new penny and one large orange each'.[87]

Another important institutional leisure provision for the boys was the Boys' Brigade where they not only learned the skills required for future empire builders, including boxing instruction, but where they also played games and 'on Sunday evenings the Captain would give us readings from "The Green Eye of the Little Yellow God" or "The Monkey's Paw"', along with distributing amongst us the usual bag of sweets which he had always brought with him'. Many children also went regularly to the 'pictures', particularly after the Empire opened in 1913 with a special children's show on Saturday afternoon for 1d admittance (the 'penny rush') which included a free ticket for an early show on Sunday.[88]

Finally, Eastwood inhabitants shared in the great national celebrations like the Diamond Jubilee of 1897 with its

gala festivities which included representations of local industry and country pursuits, with sports and treats and new Jubilee mugs for the children ... We celebrated in the newly opened recreation field between the lane and the mineral line ... Bottles of herb beer for a ha'penny with enough fizz to blow your head off . . . The mining industry well to the fore . . . Quite a few pits paraded their biggest and heaviest lump of coal for competition. Moorgreen pit was the local winner . . . it tipped the scales at 30½ cwt.[89]

CONCLUSION

The miner's family in the late nineteenth and early twentieth century was an economic unit. A housewife in her forties could well have a husband and two or more sons working underground, daughters in domestic service, or, increasingly, in factory, office or shop, and possibly children still at school. The black-leaded oven at the side of the fire was in requisition for cooking dinner for herself and any children not at work at mid-day, for cooking meals for the others when they came home, and for baking bread, cakes and pastries. The boiler at the other side of the fire, provided the hot water for washing pots, and for the men when they came home with their pit-dirt on them. Winter and summer alike the fire had to be well stoked. Shift work, increasingly common in this period, meant a succession of baths or 'strip washes' in front of the fire. Shift work or not, pit clothes took a deal of washing and mending, so the dolly tub, the scrubbing board, the 'ponch' and the mangle saw prolonged use.

Substantial or not, colliers' homes took a great deal of keeping clean with what today's housewives would consider primitive equipment. The collier's wife was up early to see her husband and other working members of the household off to work, and she worked late. She was the pivot of the family as economic unit, her life largely one of drudgery. Her horizons were necessarily limited, so it is small wonder that she had a reputation for nagging: 'The collier fled out of the house as soon as he could, away from the nagging materialism of the woman. With the women it was always: This is broken, now you've got to mend it! or else: We want this, that, and the other, and where is the money coming from? The collier didn't know and didn't care very deeply – his life was otherwise. So he escaped'.[90] For his wife, there was no escape, except occasionally to visit a relative, or to go to chapel if she was religiously inclined. He had the comradeship of the pit and the public house. She stayed within the narrow confines of the house. Few miners' wives in this locality worked: only two per cent of them did so at the time of the 1871 Census.[91] This was not the pattern for the wives of manual workers in other trades; between a quarter and a third of local housewives were gainfully employed in the 1860s and 1870s.

By the time that Lawrence wrote his famous essay on 'Nottingham and the Mining Countryside' in 1929, conditions in the Erewash Valley were changing considerably. On average, miners' families were smaller, education was improving, horizons were widening, the chapel was no longer so well supported and the coal mining industry was suffering its worst ever depression.

Depression. This was something D. H. Lawrence had not experienced. In his youth, whilst there were cyclical variations in the demand for coal, the long-term trend in demand was upward, and the standard of living of mining folk was rising, not just absolutely, but relatively to other workers. That ended in 1921. Thereafter many miners were unemployed, and those in work were under-employed. No wonder that the idyllic industrial relations which Lawrence remembered were ruptured. No need to postulate, as he did, that colliers pitied themselves because of 'agitators and sentimentalists'. By 1929, 'Robin Hood and his merry men' must have seemed very far away to the unemployed collier applying to the Poor Law Guardians for relief.[92]

APPENDIX A

Table 10: Social class structure of Eastwood household heads 1851–71

Class[1]	Proportion in each class (nearest %)		
	1851	1861	1871
1,2	17	17	12
3	55	63	64
4,5	28	20	24

Note
[1] based on the 1950 Registrar-General's status groups as used by W. A. Armstrong, 'The use of Information About Occupation' in E. A. Wrigley ed., *Nineteenth Century Society*, 1972, 191–310; *Census Enumerators' Books*, Eastwood, 1851–71. *Source:* PRO HO167/2125 (1851), RG9/243 (1861), RG10/3417

Table 11: Occupational structure of Eastwood Parish, 1851–71 and Urban District, 1921[1]

Industrial group[2]	Proportion in each group (%)			
	1851	*1861*	*1871*	*1921*
Agriculture	5.4	4.5	1.4	1.7
Mining	19.8	29.2	36.2	43.2
Building	5.0	3.3	3.8	3.5
Manufacture	41.7	36.1	16.8	18.3
Transport	3.0	3.0	3.8	4.9
Dealing	7.4	8.4	5.1	9.1
Professional and industrial service	1.6	1.2	2.2	10.5
Domestic service	10.7	11.3	16.8	6.9
Property owning and others	3.1	1.4	1.4	3.4
Indefinite[3]	1.3	1.7	6.3	
Labourer[4]			6.2	

Notes

[1] All persons over 10 in 1851–71; only persons over 12 gainfully employed in 1921.

[2] Based on Armstrong, pp. 191–310. .

[3] Mainly scholars.

[4] In the 1851 and 1861 returns the industries in which labourers worked are recorded, but not in 1871, so they have had to be alloted to a category of their own.

Source: Census Enumerators' Books 1851–71, printed volume 1921, Nottinghamshire, p. 48.

Table 12: Eastwood retailers c. 1890 (includes tradesmen who had shops e.g. bootmakers, printers).

Type of retailer	Number
General Store (Langley Mill Co-operative Society)	1
Clothing and footwear	28
Groceries and provisions	16
Publicans and beer sellers	14
Bakers and confectioners	9
Furniture and household goods	6
Hardware	2
Butchers	8
Chemists and druggists	5
Printers and stationers	4
Hairdressers and tobacconists	5
Other shopkeepers	10

Source: F. White, *History, Gazetteer and Directory of Nottinghamshire*, 1894 edition, pp. 124–6.

APPENDIX B

Plans of Work at some Eastwood Schools c. 1890–1910

1. National School (boys) 1895–6

Elementary subjects	basic reading, writing, arithmetic
Scripture	bible readings etc.
Poetry	learning, for example *The Lady of the Lake*
History	The House of Hanover etc.
Geography	for example, the British coastline
Science	for example, the properties and uses of carbon dioxide gas
Music	new song, 'The Flag of England'
Object lessons	for example, the mineral kingdom (coal etc.), the animal kingdom (lions etc.)

2. National School (girls) 1896–7

Elementary subjects	scripture and needlework
Poetry	the trial scene from *The Merchant of Venice* for example
History	biography, for instance Raleigh; narratives, for example The Wars of the Roses
Object lessons	for example, wool, corn, houses
Music	new songs, including 'The Emigrants' Farewell'

3. *Undenominational School 1899–1900*

Elementary subjects	scripture and grammar
History	for example Nelson, the Romans
Geography	for example, high tides on the Lincolnshire coast, plans and siting of school, houses and prominent buildings
Science	things that dissolve, the clouds and rainfall for instance
Object lessons	the materials and animals to be found in agriculture, means of locomotion, properties and uses of coal and timber etc.

Source: School Log Books, Nottinghamshire, C.R.O. SL.58 4/1, 1/2, 2/1.

Notes

1 *Royal Commission on Coal,* 1871, III App. No. 20 p.16 and App. 90, p.91 cited A. R. Griffin, *Mining in the East Midlands 1550–1947* (London, 1971), p. 121 (subsequently *East Mids*).

2 D. H. Lawrence 'Nottingham and the Mining Countryside', *Phoenix,* 133. In the Penguin edition of *Selected Essays* (Harmondsworth, 1950, p. 114) foot-rill is misprinted as 'foot-hill'. Foot-rill is the local term for a drift mine.

3 E.g. the compliers of the catalogue *Young Bert: an exhibition of the early years of D. H. Lawrence* (Nottingham, 1972) p. 11 quoting out of context a passage from A. R. Griffin's *The Miners of Nottinghamshire 1881–1914.*

4 A. R. Griffin, *East Mids*, pp. 113–14; also A. R. Griffin, *The British Coalmining Industry, Retrospect and Prospect* (Buxton, 1977) pp. 78–9 (subsequently *Brit. Coalmining Industry*) and E. H. Hunt, *Regional Wage Variations in Britain 1850–1914* (London, 1973), pp. 62, 70 and 72.

5 A. R. Griffin, *Brit. Coalmining Industry*, p. 73.

6 See Table 11. Eastwood Urban District was not coterminous with Eastwood Parish, but the township of Eastwood formed the core of both.

7 Registrar-General's *Reports.* Henceforth referred to as RG.

8 *1861 Census Report* (only counties with over 100 are shown).

9 A. R. Griffin, *East Mids*, pp. 167–71; *Brit. Coalmining Industry*, pp. 162–7.

10 A. R. Griffin, *East Mids*, pp. 23–4.

11 J. Farey *General View of the Agriculture and Minerals of Derbyshire*, I (London, 1811), p. 182 shows Barber, Walker as working collieries at Greasley, Beggarlee, Brinsley, Eastwood and Newthorpe Common, besides those in the Strelley area, in 1807.

12 C. P. Griffin, 'Robert Harrison and the Barber, Walker Company', *Thoroton Society's Transactions*, 1978, p. 56.

13 A. R. Griffin, 'Brinsley Colliery, a Conflict of Evidence', *Industrial Archaeology*, Feb. 1972, pp. 28–47 and 'Industrial Archaeology as an Aid to the Study of Mining History', *ibid.*, Feb. 1974, p. 27.

14 G. C. H. Whitelock, *250 Years in Coal* (Derby, n.d.), pp. 71–3.

15 D. H. Lawrence, 'Nottingham and the Mining Countryside', *Phoenix,* 135–6.

16 John A. Dolan, *The Economic and Social Background to the works of D. H. Lawrence* (unpublished B.A. dissertation, Nottingham, 1971), pp. 19–20.

17 P.R.O., Census Enumerators' Books, Eastwood parish, RG9/243 (1861), RG 10/3417 (1871).

18 *Ibid.*

19 RG 9/243 (1861).

20 RG 10/3417 (1871).

21 E. Nehls, ed., *D. H. Lawrence: a Composite Biography* (Madison, Wis., 1959), I, 77; J. C. P. Taylor, 'Boys of the Beauvale Breed', printed in the *Eastwood and Kimberley Advertiser* in fifty parts from 30 December 1960 to 17 August 1962. Ada Lawrence Clarke says that 'I don't remember him [Arthur Lawrence] giving Mother more than 35s a week' (Nehls, I, p. 16) while K. D. Poynter remembers his father about 1910–14 giving his mother £6 – 'my best week's money for you yet' K. D. Poynter, 'Reflections on Life in Eastwood since 1900, 1 – 1904–1914', *Transactions of the Lawrence Society*, 1978, p. 16). Both Lawrence and Poynter were butties whose earnings were generally higher than those of the day-wage men. Taylor (Part 16) notes that fifteen out of the thirty-five houses on Walker Street were owner-occupied by miners, and the situation was similar on Lynn Croft according to W. E. Hopkin, *The D. H. Lawrence Country* (unpublished mss., Eastwood Public Library, *c.* 1935, p. 33); also interviews with Eastwood residents born in the 1890s, Hopkin Centre, Eastwood, 26 July 1979.

22 *Census of G.B. 1851, 1871, 1901.*

23 Hopkin, pp. 33–4.

24 *Ibid.*

25 D. H. Lawrence, 'Nottingham and the Mining Countryside), *Phoenix*, 134; Taylor, part 50.

26 Scale drawing reproduced from Broxtowe Borough Council: *The Buildings, Eastwood*, a detailed description of the Eastwood conservation and redevelopment scheme undertaken by the council in 1974.

27 C. P. Griffin, 'The Making of an Industrial Colony, New Annesley in 1871', *Bulletin of Local History, East Midland Region*, XII, 1977, p. 19. (Calculations for the Eastwood housing based on the plan.)

28 Though some of the houses built in the Squares only had two bedrooms and a large cupboard upstairs, others had an additional storey containing scullery and store rooms.

29 RG 10/3417 (1871).

30 Census of Great Britain, 1901, 1911, Nottinghamshire section.

31 Dolan, *op. cit*, p. 27, and interview with retired residents of Princes Street, 19 July 1979.

32 In his autobiography Tomlinson remembers that 'when it was hot in the summer the stench from the ash pits would make me sick and I didn't want to go out'. G. W. A. Tomlinson, *Coal Miner* (1937), p. 13. Tomlinson lived in a 'company house in a small mining town in Nottinghamshire adjacent to Sherwood forest . . . The house was one of a long row, all exactly alike.' We have been unable to trace in which colliery village Tomlinson lived, but it was obviously not unlike Eastwood in terms of housing and environment.

33 Taylor, part 4.
34 Registrar-General's *Annual Report*, 1898, 1912, 1914.
35 Dolan, p. 29.
36 *Ibid.*
37 *Ibid.*, p. 30.
38 Interviews, 26 July 1979; Taylor, part 3.
39 Dolan, quoting M.O.H., p. 29.
40 Nehls, I, p. 22.
41 Poynter, pp. 16–17; Hopkin, p. 29, observed too: 'miners are kitchen dwellers, preferring the big fire and warmth of that room before the prim tidiness of the parlour'.
42 Tomlinson, p. 25. Hopkin, p. 29, also remarks: 'The kitchen fire is always warm and stoked up. This is necessary if the men are to get a breakfast before leaving home for work.'
43 Poynter, p. 16.
44 Tomlinson, p. 25. For a description of furnishings and fittings of colliery houses see Poynter, pp. 16–17, Tomlinson, pp. 22–5, Taylor, part 3.
45 Nottinghamshire County Records Office (Notts. C.R.O.), introduction to Eastwood school log books.
46 See the Plans of Work; Poynter, p. 17.
47 Notts. C.R.O. *SL58 2/1*; Poynter, *loc. cit.*
48 J. Gibbs, *Education and Social Class in Two Nottinghamshire Communities* (unpublished B.Ed. dissertation, Trent Polytechnic, 1976), p. 11.
49 *Ibid.*, pp. 13–14. Notts. C.R.O., Eastwood Schools Attendance Registers, SBX 178/1–7.
50 Notts. C.R.O. *SL58 1/1, 1/2, 2/1, 4/1*.
51 *Loc. cit.*
52 *SL58 2/1.*
53 *SL1/1, 1/2, 2/1.*
54 *Ibid.*
55 *Ibid.*
56 *SL58 1/2.*
57 *SL58 2/1.*
58 Interview 26 July 1979; Poynter, p. 17; Taylor, part 4.
59 Notts. C.R.O. *SL58 1/3.*
60 *White's Directory and Gazetteer of Nottinghamshire* for 1894, for example, lists on page 124 the following places of worship: St Mary's Church (C. of E.), Congregational Church, Wesleyan Methodist Chapel, Baptist Church, Primitive Methodist Chapel; and there was a Roman Catholic chapel and United Methodist Free Chapel in adjacent Langley Mill. George Noble, a Mormon elder of Utah, U.S.A., was staying with a miner, Samuel Robinson, at a house in the Breach at the time of the 1871 census.
61 William Purdy, *The History of the Primitive Methodists of Langley, Heanor, Derbyshire and District* (Eastwood, 1913), p. 14; J. R. Purdy, et al., *Eastwood Pentecostal Methodist Church*, Souvenir Handbook of Jubilee Celebrations 1897–1947 (Langley Mill, 1947), pp. 8–9.

62 F. M. W. Harrison, *The Eastwood Baptist Church 1876–1976* (Eastwood, 1976), pp. 6–8. Membership was twenty-eight in 1877 when the church was erected, forty-eight in 1885, sixty-five in 1890, thirty-one in 1895, thirty-one in 1900 and twenty-six in 1913.

63 W. Purdy, p. 20.

64 *Ibid.*, 10, 15; J. R. Purdy, pp. 44, 47.

65 W. Purdy, pp, 14, 18; D. H. Lawrence, *Apocalypse* (Cambridge U.P., 1980), p. 54; Nehls, I, p. 558. There were, for instance, sixty Primitive Methodist members of the Band of Hope in 1913.

66 W. Purdy, p. 15; J. R. Purdy, p. 10.

67 Interview, 26 July 1979. Lawrence (*op. cit.*) recalled 'always having the Bible read at me or to me' at Sunday school. In 1913, the Primitive Methodist Chapel had 100 adult members and 250 scholars (W. Purdy, p. 18). The Baptists had 43 scholars in 1877, 234 in 1884, 260 in 1890, 183 in 1895, 120 in 1900 and 125 in 1910. Cf. adult membership figures in note 62 above.

68 W. Purdy, pp. 9–11.

69 Interview, 26 July 1979.

70 For a full discussion see A. R. Griffin's 'Methodism and Trade Unionism in the Nottinghamshire Coalfield, 1844–90', *Proceedings of the Wesley Historical Society*, 1969, pp. 1–8.

71 W. Purdy, pp. 23–4.

72 Paul Thompson, *The Edwardians: the Remaking of British Society* (London, 1975), pp. 207–8.

73 Taylor, part 13; White, p. 124; Thompson, p. 202, notes 'In Edwardian Britain there was one public house for every three hundred people'.

74 Poynter, p. 17; interview, 26 July 1979.

75 Lawrence, p. 136; Hopkin, p. 29.

76 Tomlinson, p. 81.

77 *Ibid.*, p. 139. On this point see also Lawrence, pp. 136–7.

78 Interview 26 July 1979.

79 *Loc. cit.*; Poynter, p. 16.

80 Interview, 26 July 1979, p. 38.

81 The 'penny readings' and the activity of the 'strolling theatrical troupes' are described in Moore, *The Priest of Love*, Penguin 1976 p. 34. G. Holderness, the headmaster of the British School, regarded the readings as a mixed blessing, as he said on 1 November 1894, 'The destructive season has come again in the shape of the Saturday evening Penny Readings. On Monday found the bottom torn off a new map and a desk top loose.' Notts. C.T.O. *SL58 1/1*.

82 Interviews with local people, 26 July 1979, Poynter, p. 17; Hopkin, p. 36.

83 Hopkin, pp. 29–30.

84 *Ibid.*, p. 35; Taylor, part 22; Nehls, I, p. 558; Lawrence, p. 138. Taylor says 'Many men indulged a taste for music instrumental and choral, in which they encouraged their children'. The Mechanics' Institute might be fittingly described as Eastwood's social centre. Built in 1863–4 for about £1,000 it contained in the 1890s a library of over three thousand volumes, news, billiard and recreation rooms, and a lecture hall capable of holding 350 people. White, p. 124; Nehls

I, p. 9.
85 Nehls, I, pp. 9, 54; Moore, p. 67.
86 Interview 26 July 1979; Hopkin, p. 25; Taylor, part 22.
87 Poynter, p. 17; Nehls, I, p. 3; Taylor, part 31.
88 Poynter, p. 17.
89 Taylor, part 36.
90 Lawrence, 'Nottingham and the Mining Countryside', *Phoenix*, p. 136.
91 *Census Enumerators' Book*, RG10/3417 (1871).
92 Lawrence, 133, 136. See also A. R. Griffin, *East Mids*, pp. 225–6, 232, 269–70 and *The Miners of Nottinghamshire 1914–1944* (London, 1962), pp. 105 ff.

The photographs of Eastwood are from the National Coal Board, and (with the exception of the first) were taken *c.* 1910–13 by the Reverend F. W. Cobb.

David Gerard

4

A glossary of Nottinghamshire dialect and mining terms

The words listed here are the dialect words and phrases which Lawrence would have heard every day in Eastwood. In the streets and shops of Eastwood, colliers and their families were, and still are, natural dialect speakers, and for anyone with so acute an ear as Lawrence the communication of the words and sound to the printed page would be an easy transition. And speech habits were yet one more manifestation of the conflicts in his own home, for his father invariably spoke the local dialect while his mother, and the children enjoined by the mother, spoke standard English.

The list includes colliery terms as well as dialect words, and most of them are drawn from the plays he wrote which had a mining background more intensely realised than anything in the fiction apart from a few short stories. Finally several words are included which are merely spelt as spoken – quite ordinary English words distorted by accent which is itself a potent feature of any regional speech (e.g. *do not* becomes *dunna*).

The following editions of Lawrence's works are quoted in examples: Poetry: *The Complete Poems of D. H. Lawrence*, ed. Vivian de Sola Pinto and F. Warren Roberts (London: Heinemann; New York: Viking, 1964), cited by line number. Drama: *The Complete Plays of D. H. Lawrence* (London: Heinemann; New York: Viking, 1965), usually cited by act, scene, and page number. Novels: *Aaron's Rod* (London: Heinemann, Phoenix ed., 1954; New York: Viking, 1961); *The First Lady Chatterley* (Penguin, 1973); *Lady Chatterley's Lover* (Penguin, 1960); *The Rainbow* (London: Heinemann, Phoenix ed., 1955; New York: Viking, 1961); *Sons and Lovers* (Penguin English Library, 1981); *The White Peacock* (London: Heinemann, Phoenix ed., 1955), all usually cited by chapter and page number. Short stories: *The Complete Short Stories of D. H. Lawrence*, 3 vols. (London: Heinemann, Phoenix ed., 1955; New York: Viking, 1961), usually cited by page number.

abear Bear. ('I canna abear to think o' leavin' 'er. *The White Peacock*.)

abed In bed. ('Er's non abed yit.' *WP*.)

addle Earn, acquire by one's labour. ' "Get thy money, Sam, tha's addled it." ' 'Strike Pay', p. 46.)

a'e na Have not.

'affle *See* **haffle** *and* **caffle**.

a-gait or **agate** Going on, 'happening' ('What's a-gait now?' 'Nothing.' *The Daughter-in-Law*, III, p. 251.)

allers Always. ('No later than they allers do.' *Sons and Lovers*.)

'am-pat *See* **pat**.

anigh Near. ('Dunna venture anigh me.' *WP*.)

argy-bargyin' Arguing. ('Come – no argy-bargyin' ' *WP*.)

axin' Asking. ('Now, lad, I'm axin' thee summat.' 'The Drained Cup', line 16.)

b'r But a.

bacca Tobacco.

bantle A number of men who ride in the pit cage at any one time. A safety maximum is imposed as a rule. ('An' did 'e come up i' th' same bantle wi' you?' *The Widowing of Mrs Holroyd*, III, p. 50.)

barkle (Of dirt): to adhere, cake, encrust. ('When he comes home barkled up from the pit.' *S and L*.)

barm-man Peddler of barm or yeast. ('Suddenly one morning as she was looking down the alley of the Bottoms for the barm-man, she heard a voice calling her.' *S and L*, III, p. 86.)

batchy Silly, stupid. ('Soft, batchy, sawney.' *The Merry-go-Round*, III, p. 444.)

battle-twig Earwig.

beas'es Beasts, cows. ('His young beas'es 'as broke that bottom fence.' *S and L*.)

beck A brook.

beguy An exclamation. ('Has he, beguy!' *S and L*.)

behint Behind.

Bertie-Willie Dandy, man-about-town. ('Thinks I to myself, she's after a town johnny, a Bertie-Willie an' a yard o' cuffs.' *D-in-L*, I, i, p. 216.)

besom A woman of loose or slovenly habits. ('To think of that brazen besom telling us to go home and go to bed.' *MR*, II, ii, p. 421.)

bezzle Drink immoderately. ('There's money to bezzle with if there's money for nothin' else.' *S and L*, I, p. 58.)

billin' and cooin' Courtship, behaving like lovebirds. ('It's the wrong place for billin' and cooin'.' *WP*.)

bi-out or **be-out** Without. ('Not bi-out I'm theer.' *D-in-L*, I, i, p. 217. ' "Isn't it done?' he cried, 'Then I'm goin' be-out it." ' *S and L*, I, p. 37.)

bitted and bobbed Trifled with. ('. . . for am I to sit an' see my own lad bitted an' bobbed, tasted an' spit out by a madam i' service?' *D-in-L*, I, i, p. 216.)

blackleg Workman who refuses to join a strike. ('Dunna thee play blackleg i' this establishment.' *D-in-L*, III, p. 253.)

bletherin' Talkative. ('Am I goin' bletherin' up street an' down street, think yer?' *D-in-L*, I, ii, p. 233.)

blort Talk nonsense. ('Tha wor blortin' an' bletherin' down at th' office a bit sin', an' a mighty fool tha made o' thysen.' *D-in-L*, I, i, p. 220.)

bobble off Go off. ('I thought tha'd bobbled off ter Manchester ter be i' safety.' *D-in-L*, III, p. 250.)

bobby Cheeky, impertinent. ('See what thy bobby interferin' has done?' *D-in-L*.)

bobby-dazzler Finery; person dressed in finery, attractive woman. (' "Oh, my stars!' he exclaimed. 'What a bobby-dazzler!'. . . . 'It's not a bobby-dazzler at all!' she replied. 'It's very quiet!" ' *S and L*, VI, p. 166.)

bods Birds. ('Ah'm gettin' the coops ready for the young bods.' *Lady C*.)

boss-eyed Cross-eyed.

bottfly Larva of the gadfly found under the skin of cattle. ('It must be a bottfly.' *S and L*.)

brakes Carriages. ('and the brakes from Matlock pulling up at the inn.' *S and L*.)

britch Take the strain, from 'breeching' or 'britching', the harness round the hind parts of a shaft-horse, enabling it to push backwards when going downhill.

browt Brought. (' "I browt yer that there key, my lady!" ' *The First Lady Chatterley*, IV, p. 49.)

bug Conceited, vain.

bully-ragging Blustering, abuse. ('An they would ha' believed it, but for Hewett bully-raggin' Bettesworth 'cos he knowed he was a chappil man.' *D-in-L*, I, i, p. 209.)

butty n. 1. A fellow workman, partner, mate. ('The butty in front shouted to them all to lie down quick; there were four of them.' *Lady C*, VII, p. 83.) 2. Contractor who has a few men working for him. (See Chapter 3.) v. To work alongside, be close friends with.

by Before. ('By I was your age.' *WP*.)

cadin' Tame, accustomed to being petted. (' "Then he slives up an' shoves 'is 'ead on yer, that cadin'." ' *S and L*, IV, p. 104.)

caffle To cavil, quarrel, wrangle. ('To think I should 'ave ter 'affle an' caffle.' 'Whether or Not', line 173.)

carfle An underground wagon filled with coal.

carneyin' Whining, wheedling. ('You see what carneyin' 'll do for you, Rachel.' *MR*, IV, p. 455.)

cavil Quarrel. ('The butties cavilled over the dayman's earnings'. *S and L*.)

chalked off a line Reproved of a fault.

chavel Chew slowly; to mumble, gnaw, nibble.

cheer Chair.

chelp Impudent talk. ('Tha has a bit too much chelp an' chunter.' *D-in-L*, I, i, p. 220.)

childers Children. ('The childers not been long up.' *WP*.)

chittered Shook, vibrated.

choking Screeching.

chomp Chew, eat noisily. ('So it was taters–you had to chomp 'em like raw turnip.' *MR*, III, ii, p. 439.)

chuck Chicken, young bird. ('After all–she wasn't just 'his chuckie'. . .' *The First Lady Chatterley*, XIII, p. 139. 'Shut up, you old chuck! Shoo!' *MR*, II, ii, p. 423.)

chunter Grumble, mutter, murmur. ('Tha goes chunterin' i' th' pantry when somebody's at th' door.' *D-in-L*, I, i, p. 210.)

clammed Starved for want of food. (' "Let's ha'e a bit o' dinner, then–I'm about clammed." ' 'A Sick Collier', p. 268.)

clamp Scallop. ('Spread out like a convex. . .clamp-shell'. *S and L*.)

clap Put. ('to clap thysen into britches'.' *S and L*.)

clat-fart Gossip. ('I believe 'er's a clat-fart.' *D-in-L*, I, ii, p. 230.)

clatch (Clutch): a brood of chickens.

claver Chatter. ('Shut thy claver.' *WMH*, I, ii, p. 21.)

clawk Tear or snatch with nails or claws. ('An' if 'er clawkin' eyes / went through me as the light went out . . .' 'Whether or Not', lines 114–15. ' "Nab 'im, Poll–can ter see 'im–clawk 'im!" ' *WP*, Part II, Chapter IV, p. 181.)

clay-bind or **bind** (Pit term): a type of shale.

clinker 1. Small hard bricks used for paving. 2. Hard cinder. 3. Convincing argument. 4. A sounding blow, knock. 5. Anything large or impressive.

clommaxed Moved awkwardly. ('He 'clommaxed in, in his heavy boots.' 'A Sick Collier', p. 268.)

clout 1. Rag, shred of cloth. ('It's as wet as a clout with sweat.' *S and L*.) 2. Cloth for domestic purposes.

club Friendly society subscription. ('An' his club this week.' *S and L*.)

clunch n. Stiff clay, shale found in mines. (' "Tha'd better stan on a bit o' clunch, then, an' hold it up wi' thy 'ead." ' *S and L*, I, p. 52.) adj. Gruff, sulky, surly.

cluttering Working awkwardly or messily. (' "She's not clutterin' at the nipple." ' *The Rainbow*, I, p. 36.)

cobbler Horse chestnut (used in children's game). ('I'd got a cobbler as 'ad licked seventeen.' *S and L*.)

cod Penis. ('Twit me for havin' a cod between my legs.' *Lady C*.)

colleyfogle Deceive, cheat, ('Then what art colleyfoglin' for?' 'Whether or Not', line 166.)

cop out Surpass, exceed, outdo.

coss Curse. ('They say how he did but coss an' swear about them American Cutters.' *D-in-L*, I, i, p. 212.)

co'tin' Courting. ('Tha mun 'a patience when tu't co'tin' a lass.' *WP*.)

cotter 1. Iron pin, peg used to fasten. 2. Iron belt–(thus, to bolt). 3. Catch up in contact with.

cratch The standard. ('He-he's *never* up to the cratch.' *D-in-L*, I, ii, p. 222.)

crowflower Common buttercup. ('–Ah, an' yaller as a crowflower.' 'Whether or Not', line 11.)

crozzled Shrivelled up with heat. (' "If it's crozzled up to a cinder I don't see why I should care." ' 'Odour of Chrysanthemums', p. 288.)

crozzly Crisp, well-done. ('a nice crozzly bit [of bacon].' *S and L*.)

cut Canal.

dag 1. Sharp, sudden play, thrust with a stick. 2. A shot at something. 3. Boys' game with tops.

daggeroso Inclined to use a dagger. (A Lawrentian coinage) ('I'm not a daggeroso.' *S and L*.)

dayman Day-labourer, one who works and is paid by the day. ('. . . and the butties cavilled for a minute over the dayman's earnings.' *S and L*, VIII, p. 254.)

dern Down. (' 'Ow'll be dern in a minnit'. *WP*.)

dingin' Strike violently. ('dingin' away at a coalface'. *S and L*.)

doesna Don't. ('Tha likes me, doesna ter?' *WP*.)

doited Stupefied. ('An' I'm thinkin', th' childt'll set 'er up again when it comes, for 'er's gone that wezzel-brained an' doited, I'm sure!' *D-in-L*, I, ii, p. 234.)

dolly-tub Wash-tub.

dool-owl or **doolie** Spectre, hobgoblin.

dossn't Dare not.

dosy-baked Stupid, dull. (' 'E never wor but dosy-baked.' *MR*, III, p. 444.)

dot Hit. ('Get out or I'll dot thee.' *S and L*.)

draggletail An untidy, dirty person, a feeble, ill-conditioned person. ('Tha'rt well rid o' such a draggletail.' *MR*, I, i, p. 400.)

dree Long, slow, tedious.

druv Drove, past tense (preterite) of 'drive'.

duffer Person without practical abilities.

dunna Do not. ('dunna thee tell me it's his'n, mother.' 'Whether or Not', line 1.)

dursn't Dare not.

eddish Stubble, aftermath or second crop of grass, clover, etc.

'eered Heard.

'er She. ('An' 'er lays it on ter me.' 'Fanny and Annie.')

fad Take care of. ('I wish I'd somebody to fad after me a bit.' *MR*.)

fairly Well. ('And she's kept fairly?' *S and L*.)

fawce 1. Sharp, shrewd, clever. (' "My word, she's a fawce little thing,' the landlady would say to Brangwen." ' *The Rainbow*, III, p. 81.) 2. Deceitful, cunning, sly.

fend Provide for. (' " 'Appen yer'd better 'ave this key, an' Ah mun fend for t'bods some other road." ' *Lady C*, VIII, p. 97.)

fettle n. Condition, state, order, repair. v. 1. Clean, tidy up. 2. Repair, mend. ('Nay, I can fettle for myself–an' does so.' *MR*, III, ii, p. 438.)

finicky Fastidious. ('Perhaps one does get a bit finicky after a certain time.' *MR*, IV, p. 449.)

flig Eager to fly, originally of birds ready to leave the nest. (' "Tha arena very flig ter go." ' 'The Drained Cup', line 30.)

foisty Fusty, mouldy. ('. . . it's had a foisty cork.' *WMH*, I, ii, p. 22.)

fow Dirty *or* ugly *or* angry, ill-tempered *or* awkward. ('As fow as a jackass.' *WMH*.)

fridging Fraying. ('The town spread upwards fridging the crest with spires.' *S and L*.)

frit Frightened. ('Tha wert frit o' summat.' 'The Drained Cup', line 23.)

frowsty Rough, untidy, dirty. ('And he gives me a frowsty twenty-eight . . .' *A Collier's Friday Night*, II, p. 490.)

fruments Wheat boiled in milk with sweetening spice.

fudge Talk nonsense; deceive by 'cramming' a person. ('If I'd ha' *bin* for marryin' 'er, I'd ha' gone wholesale, not ha' fudged and haffled.' *D-in-L*, I, i, p. 215.)

full-butt With speed or violence; suddenly.

fust First.

gaby A fool, a stupid person. ('It's not many as can find in their heart to love a gaby like that.' *MR*, I, i, p. 398.)

gaffer Master, person in charge. ('I'll show you who's gaffer, though.' *WMH*, I, ii, p. 28.)

gallivant Jaunt, go about, pleasure seeking. (' "... after she's done gallivantin round wherever she's a mind." ' 'Fanny and Annie', p. 463.)

gammy Deformed. ('Here, hutch up, gammy-leg–gammy-arm.' *D-in-L*, I, i, p. 208.)

gassin' Talking idly. ('What a' yer stand gassin' on the causeway for?' 'The Primrose Path.')

gen Gave, given. ('You see, it come on 'im as close as a trap on a mouse, an' gen him no air, an' what wi' th' gas, it smothered him' *WMH*, III, pp. 53–54.)

gie Give. ('Dun gie 't 'im.' *WP*.)

gin-pits Early coal pits using hoists worked by donkeys to draw up the coal. ('There lived the colliers who worked in the little gin-pits.' *S and L*.)

glassie Marble.

gleamy (Of weather): hot, sultry with bright intervals. (' "I'm non walkin' that far of a gleamy day like this." ' 'Strike Pay', p. 47.)

gleg Look asquint furtively, peep shyly. ('An' I'm not goin' ter ha'e none on 'em gleggin' at it.' *MR*, I, i, p. 396.)

goos Goes.

gorp Gaze, stare at. (' "You may back your life Lena an' Mrs Severn'll be gorping, and that clat-fartin' Mrs. Allsop." ' 'A Sick Collier', p. 273.)

grip Shallow furrow.

grizzle Grumble or complain in a whining tone. ('What's 'er grizzlin' about?' *D-in-L*.)

gumption Common sense. ('... they've a sight too much gumption.' *D-in-L*, I, ii, p. 235.)

guttle Eat or drink greedily.

Guy or **Guyney** Disguised form of 'God', used in exclamations. ('By Guy, but 'e 'ings heavy.' *WMH*, III, p. 54.)

guysers Mummers in plays performed at Christmas time.

ha'e or **a'e** Have. ('I s'll ha'e none' and 'Yo'll a'e a drop?.' *WP*.)

haffle Shilly-shally. (*See quotation for* **caffle**.)

haporth Halfpennyworth, a negligible quantity ('Three haporth o' pap.' *S and L*.)

Hanover, what the 'Hanover' became a euphemism for 'Hell' in the eighteenth century due to the unpopularity of the Hanoverian royal family.

happen Perhaps. (' " 'Appen Sir Clifford 'ud know." ' *Lady C*, VIII, p. 93.)

hash Cut into small pieces. ('Hash some cold meat up.' *S and L*.)

hawkse Take out or take. ('I should ha' done, if tha hadna hawksed me out.' *D-in-L*, I, ii, p. 227. ' "... then we shouldna' ha' had to hawkse 'im upstairs ..." ' 'A Sick Collier', p. 269.)

hissen Himself. ('But ta'es twelve hundred a year for hissen.' *D-in-L*, I, i, p. 212.)

hob Back of the grate. ('On the hob a large saucepan steamed.' *S and L*.)

hole (a stint) Undercut a length of coal face to release the coal. ('I hole a stint as well as any man.' *D-in-L*, I, ii, p. 226.)

holled Hurled. ('I should ha' it holled at me.' *S and L*.)

hollin' Hauling.

hook, takes its Makes off.

hurtle Crouch. ('If he didn't hurtle himself up.' *S and L*.)

hutch-up Move nearer, get closer in little jerks. (*See quotation for* **gammy**.)

ikey Proud, conceited. ('So look ikey.' *S and L*.)

'ing Hang. ('Yo' can 'ing it in the back yard.' *The Lost Girl*.)

iron-men Coal-cutting machines. ('A mangy bachelor wi' 'is iron-men.' *D-in-L*, I, i, p. 212.)

'issen *See* **hissen**.

ivry Every.

Jack-gnat A creature never still.

Jew-jaws Gew-gaws, toys, trinkets.

jockey Half contemptuous, half affectionate form of address, like 'cove'. ('I'll stop your whistle, my jockey.' *S and L*.)

jowl Knock.

kest Forestall, get ahead of.

knivey Miserly, mean. ('Another o' Macintyre's dirty knivey dodges, I s'd think.' *D-in-L*, I, i, p. 208.)

lap Flap or fold.

lardy-da Affectedly superior. ('In a bob-tailed evening suit, on the lardy-da.' *S and L*.)

larropin' Rushing. ('Larropin' neck an' crop / I' th' snow! ...' 'Whether or Not', lines 66–7.)

lashins Spending money. ('If you share nivver a drop o' the lashins.' *The Lost Girl*.)

latts Metal strips or wires which form the bedframe beneath the mattress ('that wor th' bed latts goin' bang'. *WP*.)

leading Charge for carting. ('Because Morel's coals had come and the leading was stopped', *S and L*.)

lerky Child's game played in Notts.

let on Light on, come upon unexpectedly, catch someone unawares or unready.

lief As soon ... as; rather. (' "I'd as lief be neighbours with a vixen." ' *S and L*, VIII, p. 258.)

light-o'-love Flighty woman.

linkin' Idling, wasting time, sly, roguish.

linty Idle, lazy.

loose-all End of a working shift. (' "Loose-all 'ad bin gone about ten minutes when we com'n away ..." ' 'Odour of Chrysanthemums', p. 292.)

ma'e Make. (' "Ah know nob'dy as ma'es keys round 'ere." ' *Lady C*, VIII, p. 93.)

mangy Cowardly, mean.

mantled Suffused. ('The blood still mantled below her ears.' *S and L*.)

mard Spoiled, soft, petted. ('That's what your mother did for you—mardin' you up till you were mard-soft.' *D-in-L*, I, i, p. 211.)

mard-arse A namby-pamby, spoiled child. ('–Eh, tha'rt a mard-arsed kid ...' 'The Collier's Wife', line 7.)

mash Make tea. (' "I've mashed th' tea." ' *The First Lady C*, XIX, p. 188.)

maun Must. ('Go then, sin' tha maun.' 'The Drained Cup', line 74.)

May-blobs Marsh marigolds.

measly Mean, miserly. ('A measly twenty five shillings.' *S and L*.)

menagerie Varied assortment.

mester Master, husband, variant of 'Mister'. (' "Mornin', missis! Mester in?" ' *S and L*, I, p. 55.)

middlin' Fair, moderate. ('She keeps pretty middlin'.' *S and L*.)

mind Move over. ('Mind, I want to sit next to you.' *S and L*.)

mingy Contemptible, mean. ('the mingiest set of ladylike snipe.' *Lady C*.)

mizzling Disappearing ('Mizzling away into nothing'. *The Rainbow*.)

moiled Hot and weary with work.

mormin' or **mornin'** Pottering, filling time with trivial activity. ('They stop mormin' about, bletherin' and boomin' an' meals, bless yer, they don't count.' *D-in-L*, III, p. 249.)

mosh Crushed. ('. . . an' one was shot till 'is shoulder was all of a mosh, an' they brought 'em 'ome to me.' *WMH*, III, p. 50.)

moudiwarp Mole. (' "Yi, an' there's some chaps as does go round like moudiwarps." ' *S and L*, I, p. 45.)

mulligurles Stomach ache, fit of sulks. ('Summat's gen im mulligurles.' *MR*, I, i, p. 392.)

mun See **maun**.

mysen Myself. (' "I didna know mysen." ' 'Strike Pay', p. 51.)

nag-nails Long finger nails.

naggles Annoys. ('She naggles thy heart out, maybe.' *D-in-L*, I, ii, p. 235.)

naight. Night.

nedna Need not. ('Tha nedna gi'e me none.' *WP*.)

nesh Tender, sensitive.

nippy Keen, biting cold. ('It's a bit nippy.' *S and L*.)

nobbut Only, nothing but.

nog Wooden ball used in the game of 'shinny'.

noggin Small portion

nowt Nothing.

nubbly Rough, uneven, lumpy. (' "Ma, don't wear that nubbly little bonnet." ' *S and L*.)

nuss Nurse.

oppen Open.

'ormin' Clumsy, shambling. ('Now, Maggie Pearson, don't pretend to be 'ormin'.' *A Collier's Friday Night*, II, p. 502.)

'orry Hurry.

orts Leavings, scraps; fragments. ('I'm not 'avin' your orts an' slarts.' 'Whether or Not', line 167.)

otchel A humpback person. ('A glum old otchel, wi' long / Witch teeth . . .'

'Whether or Not', lines 26–7.)

ow She. ('Ow's puttin' t'owd lady t'bed.' *WP*.)

owd Old.

ower Over.

owt Anything. (' "What, Walter? Is owt amiss?" ' *S and L*, VI, p. 181.)

panchion Large earthenware bowl or vessel (used for washing or for milk). ('Arena' ter goin' ter wesh thee? Go an' get th' panchion.' *D-in-L*, I, ii, p. 321.)

pap Baby food. ('Cunna yer gi'e a man summat better nor this 'ere pap?' *The Lost Girl*.)

parish oven Communal bakehouse used by villagers. ('Did you iver see such a parish oven?' *S and L*.)

pea-bug Wood-louse.

pedgill 1. Bargain, like a pedlar. 2. Pick over and examine, work minutely.

peens Pains.

pee-whip Peewit, lapwing. ('Nay, yo' blessed pee-whips, / Yo' nedna scraight at me!' 'Whether or Not', lines 61–2.)

pent-house Shed, outhouse. ('In the little pent-house under the tiles.' 'Odour'.)

pick-heft or **-haft** Handle of a pick-axe. ('I wor foolin' wi' a wringer an' a pick-heft–ta's it as ter's a mind.' *D-in-L*, I, i, p. 208.)

pod Walk softly ('he podded in his stocking feet.' *S and L*.)

puddin' (Of stones in the pit): conglomerate–pieces of various different kinds of rock converted into a mass.

pulamiting Whining, whimpering. ('You are a base, malingering, pulamiting wretch.' *MR*, V, iii, p. 465.)

puller-off The man who attends to the trams or trucks at the pithead. ('The puller-off swung the small truck.' *S* *and L.*)

raight Right.

rake Stroll about idly

riding A green track or lane cut through a wood. (' "Come to the top of the riding." ' *WP*, Part II, Chapter III, p. 164.)

rip 1. Work speedily, with energy. ('You can rip along wi' 'em.' *S and L*.) 2. Knock out the roof of an underground road in a mine to make more room. ('To get some rippin' done.' Odour of Chrysanthemums'.)

road Way.

ronk Rank, libidinous. ('She's a bit of a ronk 'un.' *MR*, I, ii, p. 403.)

rool Curl up. ('–an' he was always funny-tempered, would rool up like a pea-bug, at a word.' *MR*, IV, p. 447.)

rowdy Streaky (bacon). ('I'd ma'e *his* sides o' bacon rowdy.' *D-in-L*, I, i, p. 211.)

rummage Ransack, search thoroughly.

rusties Buttocks.

sawney Foolish, weak person. ('She was the sort of sawney you ought to have had.' *D-in-L*, II, p. 246.)

scraight Scream, cry. ('–an I've said I should on'y be happy if I was scraightin' at 'er funeral' *D-in-L*, I, i, p. 213.)

scrat' Scratch. (' "Tha looks a man, doesn't ter, at thy age, goin' an' openin' to her when ter hears her scrat' at th' gate ..." 'Fanny and Annie', p. 463.)

scrattlin' Paltry, mean.

screen Type of fork used for grading coal, separating the slack from the larger coal.

screet Screech, make a shrill sound.

scroddy Puny, meagre. ('on'y leave a scroddy bit.' *MR*.)

scullery Small kitchen. ('in a heap into the scullery.' 'The Horse Dealer's Daughter'.)

seed past tense (preterite) of 'see'. ('Tha niver seed such a way.' *S and L*.)

settler A blow. ('It's a settler, it is.' 'Odour of Chrysanthemums'.)

shale Loose substance in a mine, loose ore. ('... and he read with care the latest things on mining and the chemistry of coal and shale which were written in German.' *Lady C*, IX, p. 111.)

shanna, or **shonna** I shall not. ('Tell us what B is, Sam.' 'Shonna.' *WP*.)

sharp-shins An intelligent child. (' "She means you're a sharp-shins." ' *The Rainbow*, III, p. 81.)

shift (make shift of) Manage with difficulty. ('I'm non goin' to be made shift of.' *MR*, II, i, p. 417.)

shift(l)y Unstable person; not quite compos mentis.

shindy Row. ('You thought a father-in-law that kicked up a shindy was enough to scare him off, did you?' *A Collier's Friday Night*, III, p. 528.)

shinny A children's game popular in working-class districts (and would certainly be played in colliery regions). Two rivals stand face to face, placing hands on each other's shoulders. Each may swerve and dodge as he pleases provided the hands are kept on the other's shoulders. They usually push hard against each other as they sway violently about because the object is to stamp as hard and as often as possible on the opponent's feet.

shollt Shall you. ('What shollt a'e, Walter?' *S and L*.)

shonna Shall not.

sile n. Strainer, sieve.

v. 1. Strain, skim. 2. (Of rain): pour heavily, continuously.

sithee See thee, i.e. look here!

skedaddle Disappear. ('He'd got a game on somewhere–toffed himself up to the nines, and skedaddled off as brisk as a turkey-cock.' *WMH*, I, i, p. 12.)

skilk Idler, impostor.

skin-and-grief Mean, irritable person.

skinch Stint, limit, to be parsimonious. (' "Tha'rt skinchin'!" "I arena!" ' 'A Sick Collier', p. 270.)

skirr 1. Scurry with a whirring sound. ('Birds skirred off from the bushes'. *WP*.) 2. Slide, slip. ('The brakes skirr with a shriek.' 'Odour of Chrysanthemums'.)

skivvy A menial, a servant. ('Go as a skivvy.' 'The Horse Dealer's Daughter'.)

slart Splash, of rain or mud. ('You left her with just the slarts of a man.' *D-in-L*, III, p. 256.)

slaver Talk nonsense, drivel. ('But he's mushy–he slavers like a slobbering spaniel' *MR*, V, i, p. 459.)

sleer Sneer.

slikey 1. Cunning, clever. 2. Flattering, smooth-tongued. ('He thinks himself slikey.' *A Collier's Friday Night*, I, p. 477.)

slither Waste, spend idly.

slive Sneak about, creep in a stealthy way. ('Tha's been slivin' somewhere like a tomcat, ever sin breakfast.' *MR*, I, i, p. 394.)

slobber n. Mud, cold rain mixed with snow.
v. To drool. ('An' now tha'lt snap my head off 'cos I slobber, shanna tha?' *D-in-L*, I, ii, p. 224.)

slobbering Sloppy, wet.

slormed Slushy, sloppy. ('Slormed! Thee slorm but one fiftieth part to any lass thee likes, an' see if 'er's not all over thee afore tha's said six words. Slormed!' *D-in-L*, I, i, p. 215.)

sludge Work or walk in a slovenly way so as to bemire oneself with mud. ('A widow of forty-five / As 'as sludged like a horse all 'er life . . .' 'Whether or Not', lines 21–2.)

sludge bump Dirty drudge.

sluthe, sluther Slip, slide, hurry. (' "Sluther up now," said Brangwen . . .' *The Rainbow*, I, p. 30.)

slutherers Slipshod persons; wastrels. ('Strike's 'a they're fit for-a-pack o' slutherers.' *D-in-L*.)

smarmy Ingratiating.

smirkin' Simpering. ('to dirty themselves with smirkin' devilry.' *WP*.)

smite A small portion. (' "I'd rather ha'e a smite o' cheese than this meat." ' 'Her Turn', p. 41.)

smock-ravel Puzzle, perplex. ('Tha *art* smock-ravelled, bunny . . .' 'Whether or Not', line 65.)

snag Tease, quarrel, chide. ('I'm comin' in, you two, so stop snaggin' an snarlin'.' *D-in-L*, I, ii, p. 227.)

snap Food, miner's lunch. ('I' th' stall, at snap time.' *D-in-L*, I, i, p. 208.)

snied Infested with. (' "The place is fair snied wi' 'em." ' *S and L*, IV, p. 104.)

snipey 1. Long-nosed; nosey. (' "You're so ready to side with any snipey vixen who likes to come telling tales against your own children." ' *S and L*.) 2. (Of weather): sharp, frosty.

snirt Noise made through the nose when trying to suppress laughter.

sod Term of abuse, perhaps an abbreviation of 'sodomite'. ('that's the little sod as started it.' *S and L*.)

sorry or **surry** Term of familiar address (corruption of 'Sirrah'). (' "Shall ter finish, Sorry?" cried Barker, his fellow butty.' *S and L*, II, p. 67.)

sot Sat. ('It ma'es no diff'rence to me who's sot on 'em an' who 'asna.' *D-in-L*, I, ii, p. 232.)

spink Chaffinch.

spooney Flirtatious.

sprits (Of potatoes): early sets of potato plants when sprouting.

sprottle Sprawl, kick about helplessly.

spunk, spunky Mettlesome, spirited. ('Nay–I reckon he niver showed the spunk of a sprat-herring to 'er.' *D-in-L*, I, i, p. 215.)

squark Squawk, row. ('There'd be a squark i' th' sky then!' *D-in-L*, I, i, p. 211.)

stall Length of coal face worked by a number of men. ('Well–good night–we've worked i' the same stall ower four years now' *WMH*, III, p. 56.)

stinkpot A disgusting person.

stint Section of coal face of given length; allotted task. ('Here's a man, holin' a stint, just finishin' . . .' *WMH*, III, p. 55.)

stir thysen Move yourself.

stirk Cow between two and three years old.

stool-arsed or **-harsed** Having an office job. ('What ailed him was, he wor in collier's britches, i'stead o' a stool-arsed Jack's.' *D-in-L*, III, p. 255.)

strap Credit. ('Tha could ha' had what things ter wanted on strap.' *D-in-L*, III, p. 259.)

strappin' Lusty, strong. (' 'S a strappin' anuff feller.' *The Lost Girl*.)

strick that road Made that way.

stunts Stumps, tails. (' "Are we to let t'other side run off wi' th' bone, then, while we ait on our stunts an' yowl for it?" ' *Aaron's Rod*, II, p. 17.)

summat Something. ('Tha might be scared o' summat.' *WP*.)

sward Layer of hay just cut. ('The gold sward seemed liquid.' 'Love Among The Haystacks'.)

swarf Make dirty. ('I shall swarf it up.' *WMH*, I, i, p. 12.)

sweal Reduce, melt away. ('they can sweal a tumour away.' *S and L*.)

swelted From **swelt**: faint, swoon. ('. . . melted right into me, Lizzie, till I was verily swelted.' 'Whether or Not', lines 111–12.)

tabs Ears. ('. . . an' a company as 'ud like yer ter scrape yer tabs afore you went home, for fear you took a grain o' coal.' *D-in-L*, I, i, p. 210.)

tack Basic food and drink, used in a depreciatory sense. ('It's thin tack.' *S and L*.)

tan-tafflins Small tarts, apple dumplings; sweet delicacies (as opposed to substantial food). (' "Yi, Missis, them tan-tafflins 'll go down very nicely." ' 'Her Turn', p. 41.)

team Pour. ('If you team it in your saucer.' *S and L*.)

ter You.

termorrer Tomorrow.

tha, or **thai** You (i.e. Thou).

throng Busy, occupied. ('Tha *art* throng!' *D-in-L*, I, ii, p. 223.)

throw-in A pooling of the wages earned by several contractors for doing an allotted piece of work on the coal face.

thysen Yourself. (' "Tha can please thysen," ' *WP*, Part III, Chapter I, p. 238.)

tickle Touchy, critical. (' 'Er's that tickle o' choosin'.' *WP*.)

tidy In tolerably good health. ('Yes, tidy.' *S and L*.)

tilts Encounters, combats.

tip callin' Gossiping. ('Serve her right for tip callin' wi'm all those years.' *D-in-L*.)

tonnup Turnip.

too-in' Fussing. ('Twistin' and too-in' at that painting of yours.' *S and L*.)

top-sawyer One who holds a superior position.

towsled Tousled.

traipse, Trapse Tramp; trudge; go on foot; plod along.

tressing Falling in tresses.

truck-end Buttocks, originally wooden bumpers on coal-trucks.

tweedle Whistle.

twig To understand. ('I thought tha'd twigged, else bin telled.' *D-in-L*, II, p. 243.)

twittermiss Girl chatterbox.

twitchel A narrow passage. ('He caught her hand impulsively, and they went along the narrow twitchel.' *S and L*, XII, p. 383.)

us Our. ('We're expectin' us third just now.' *S and L*.)

'ussy A pert, disreputable girl. ('Tha ungrateful 'ussy!' *WP*.)

wafflin' Floating. (' "She keeps wafflin' it about so's to make 'er slow." ' 'Odour of Chrysanthemums', p. 287.)

waggin' Going. ('Do you keep on waggin' then?' *S and L*.)

waggin' (on) Chattering continuously.

wake Celebration, fair.

wallit A left-handed person, perhaps awkward. ('Yes, that's me, bein' wallit.' *D-in-L*, I, ii, p. 232.)

wambling Staggering.

water blob Yellow water lily.

wench Girl. ('That's the word, my wench.' *WP*.)

werritt Worry. ('Well, I've werritted an' werritted till I'm soul-sick–' *D-in-L*, I, i, p. 212.)

weshin' Washing. ('If tha oppens it again while weshin' me.' *S and L*.)

wezzel-brained Giddy, thoughtless. (*See quotation for* **doited**.)

wheer's Where is.

whipperty-snappin' Being smart, cheeky. ('Think I'm going to have you whipperty-snappin' around?' *S and L*.)

whit-leather Horse skin cured white and not tanned, used for whip thongs. ('Till 'er's tough as whit-leather ...' 'Whether or Not', line 23.)

whittle 1. Pare off, trim wood. 2. Fidget, worry, fret. (' "It means drudging and dragging and whittling and worrying and bein' worn out wi' doin' things–an' being *under*." ' *The First Lady C*, XVIII, p. 180.)

whoam Home. (' "Tha s'lt go whoam, Willy, tha s'lt go whoam." ' 'A Sick Collier', p. 269.)

wift For **whift**–a whiff.

wik Week. ('We s'll be out on strike in a wik or a fortnit–' *D-in-L*, I, i, p. 210.)

winder An oddity. ('Well, that's a winder!' *D-in-L*.)

wizzened Shrivelled, wrinkled. (' "A mean, wizzen-hearted stick." ' *S and L*, I, p. 55.)

wor Were. ('Ah know'd tha wor as spunky as ony.' *WP*.)

worna Were not. (' "How, trouble! It worna no trouble." ' *The First Lady C*, IV, p. 49.)

wringer Crowbar for prising coal off the coal face.

wunna Will not. ('No, I'm afraid 'e wunna.' *MR*, I, ii, p. 402.)

yersen Yourself. ('Seems yer doin' yersen a bit o' weshin'.' *The Lost Girl*.)

yi Yes. ('Yi, an' it felt like it.' *D-in-L*, I, ii, p. 227.)

yit Yet.

Gerald Lacy

5

Lawrence's life in the context of world events: a chronological table

WORLD EVENTS	CULTURE	D.H. LAWRENCE	GENERAL
1885			
26 Jan. Mahdi takes Khartoum; Gordon killed **5 Feb.** Congo State under Leopold established **25 Feb.** Germany annexes Tanganyika and Zanzibar **9 June** Gladstone resigns **25 June** Salisbury Prime Minister **14 Aug.** Irish Land Bill passed	**Literature** Burton: *The Arabian Nights* Maupassant: *Bel Ami* Meredith: *Diana of the Crossways* Pater: *Marius the Epicurean* Zola: *Germinal* **Art** Cézanne: *Mont Sainte-Victoire* Degas: *Woman Bathing* Van Gogh: *The Potato Eaters* **Music** Brahms: *Symphony No. 4* Franck: *Symphonic Variations* Gilbert & Sullivan: *The Mikado*	**11 Sept.** Birth at Eastwood, Nottinghamshire, England	**Deaths/births** Victor Hugo (1802) Alban Berg (1935) Ring Lardner (1933) Sinclair Lewis (1951) André Maurois (1967) Anna Pavlova (1931) Ezra Pound (1972) **Inventions** Single-cylinder auto engine (Benz) Photographic paper (Eastman) Internal combustion engine (Daimler) Gas mantle
1886			
1 Jan. U.K. annexes Upper Burma; Royal Charter for	**Literature** Haggard: *King Solomon's Mines*	(George Arthur Lawrence leaves home permanently and lives in Nottingham.)	**Deaths/births** Emily Dickinson (1830) Franz Liszt (1811)

Niger Co.
27 Jan.
Salisbury resigns
1 Feb.
Liberal Ministry (Gladstone's third)
7 June
Government defeated on Home Rule Bill for Ireland
26 July
Conservative Government: Salisbury

Hardy: *The Mayor of Casterbridge*
Ibsen: *Rosmersholm*
James: *The Bostonians*
Rimbaud: *Les Illuminations*
Stevenson: *Dr Jekyll and Mr Hyde*
Art
Millais: *Bubbles*
Seurat: *Sunday Afternoon on the Grande Jatte*
Last Impressionist Exhibition

Hilda Doolittle (1961)
Siegfried Sassoon (1967)

Marx: *Capital*
Nietzsche: *Beyond Good and Evil*

1887

11 Jan.
Bismarck urges larger German army
20 Feb.
Triple Alliance renewed
4 Apr.
First Colonial Conference
21 June
U.K. annexes Zululand
Queen Victoria's Golden Jubilee
13 Nov.
Irish 'Bloody Sunday' in London

Literature
Doyle: *A Study in Scarlet* (first Sherlock Holmes)
Hardy: *The Woodlanders*
Strindberg: *The Father*
Art
Van Gogh: *A Wheat Field*
Music
Brahms: *Concerto in A Minor*
Paderewski gives first recitals
Verdi: *Otello*

29 Jan. Birth of Jessie Chambers
16 June Birth of Ada Lawrence
11 Sept. Second birthday; moves to new home, The Breach

Deaths/births
Rupert Brooke (1915)
Marc Chagall (1978)
Julian Huxley (1975)
Robinson Jeffers (1962)
Edwin Muir (1959)
Edith Sitwell (1964)

Inventions
Linotype machine
'Esperanto' language

WORLD EVENTS	CULTURE	D. H. LAWRENCE	GENERAL
1888			
12 May U.K. protectorate over North Borneo, Brunei and Sarawak	**Literature** Doughty: *Travels in Arabia Deserta* Kipling: *Plain Tales from the Hills*	**13 Feb.** Birth of Louie Burrows	**Deaths/births** Matthew Arnold (1822) Edward Lear (1812) T. S. Eliot (1965) T. E. Lawrence (1935) Katherine Mansfield (1923) Eugene O'Neill (1953)
15 June William II becomes Emperor of Germany	Rutherford: *The Revolution in Tanner's Lane*		
29 Oct. Suez Canal Convention of Constantinople declares canal open to all nations	Strindberg: *Miss Julie* Zola: *La Terre* **Art** Toulouse-Lautrec: *Place Clichy* Van Gogh: *The Yellow Chair; Sunflowers; The Night Cafe* **Music** Gilbert & Sullivan: *The Yeomen of the Guard* Rimsky-Korsakov: *Scheherazade* Strauss: *Don Juan*		**Inventions** Pneumatic bicycle tyre Kodak box camera A.C. electric motor Motion picture camera Football league founded 'Jack the Ripper' murders six women in London Cecil Rhodes amalgamates Kimberley diamond companies

1889

30 Jan.
Archduke Rudolf commits suicide at Mayerling
31 Mar.
Naval Defence Act enlarges U.K. Navy
8 Apr.
End of Boulanger crisis
19 Aug.–14 Sept.
London Dock Strike (Cardinal Manning mediates)
29 Oct.
Cecil Rhodes's British South Africa Company granted Royal charter

Literature
Pater: *Appreciations*
Stevenson: *The Master of Ballantrae*
Tennyson: *Demeter and Other Poems*
Twain: *A Connecticut Yankee in King Arthur's Court*
Yeats: *The Wanderings of Oisin*
Art
Van Gogh: *Landscape with Olive Trees; Starry Night*
Music
Franck: *Symphony in D Minor*
Gilbert & Sullivan: *The Gondoliers*
Tchaikovsky: *Symphony No. 5*

Deaths/births
Robert Browning (1812)
Gerard Manley Hopkins (1844)
Charles Chaplin (1976)
Adolf Hitler (1945)
Ludwig Wittgenstein (1951)

Eiffel designs 1,056 foot high tower for Paris World Exhibition

Huxley: *Agnosticism*
Shaw: *Fabian Essays*

1890

20 Mar.
Bismarck leaves office
2 July
Brussels Act forbids slave

Literature
France: *Thaïs*
Ibsen: *Hedda Gabler*
Kipling: *The Light That*

Death of Kenneth Forbes Barber in shooting accident (*Women in Love*)

Deaths/births
Sir Richard F. Burton (1821)
Cardinal Newman

WORLD EVENTS	CULTURE	D. H. LAWRENCE	GENERAL
trade and liquor to primitive peoples	*Failed*		(1801)
17 July	C. Rossetti: *Poems*		Vincent Van Gogh (1853)
Cecil Rhodes, Premier of Cape Colony	Tolstoy: *The Kreutzer Sonata*		Dwight D. Eisenhower (1969)
17 Nov.	**Art**		Charles de Gaulle (1970)
O'Shea granted a decree against Parnell	Leighton: *The Bath of Psyche*		Boris L. Pasternak (1960)
12 Dec.	William Morris founds Kelmscott Press		**Inventions**
Parnell resigns leadership of Irish Nationalists	Van Gogh: *Crows Over the Wheat Field*		Sprocketed motion picture film (Edison)
	Music		Free elementary education established in England
	Mascagni: *Cavalleria Rusticana*		Forth Bridge completed
	Tchaikovsky: *Queen of Spades*		Frazer: *The Golden Bough*
			James: *Principles of Psychology*

1891

WORLD EVENTS	CULTURE	D. H. LAWRENCE	GENERAL
6 May	**Literature**	Move to No. 3 Walker Street	**Deaths/births**
Triple alliance renewed for twelve years	Doyle: *The Adventures of Sherlock Holmes*	Attends Beauvale Board School, Eastwood (to 1898)	Herman Melville (1819)
15 May	Gissing: *New Grub Street*		Charles Stewart Parnell (1846)
Pope Leo XIII's encyclical on condition of working	Hardy: *Tess of the D'Urbervilles*		Arthur Rimbaud (1854)
			George Seurat (1859)

Sergei Prokofiev (1953)

Trans-Siberian Railroad construction begins (to 1917)
Dubois discovers Java Man
Population: U.K. 33 million; U.S. 65 million

classes

4 July William II visits London

Oct. 'Newcastle Programme' adopted by British Liberal Party

Dec. Joseph Chamberlain leader of Liberal Unionists

Shaw: *The Quintessence of Ibsenism*
Thompson: *The Hound of Heaven*
Wilde: *The Picture of Dorian Gray*

Art
Gauguin settles in Tahiti
Henri Toulouse-Lautrec produces his first music hall posters

Music
Mahler: *Symphony No. 1*
Rachmaninoff: *Piano Concerto No. 1*

1892

July General Election, Liberal victory; Kier Hardie first Labour M.P.

18 Aug. Gladstone's fourth ministry

10 Nov. Panama Canal scandal in France

Literature
Hauptmann: *The Weavers*
Ibsen: *The Master Builder*
Kipling: *Barrack-Room Ballads*
Shaw: *Mrs Warren's Profession*

Art
Monet begins series on Rouen Cathedral
Toulouse-Lautrec: *At the Moulin Rouge*

(Beauvale Board School)
Death of Cecily Barber by drowning (*Women in Love*)

Deaths/births
Alfred Tennyson (1809)
Walt Whitman (1819)
Richard Aldington (1962)
Osbert Sitwell (1969)
J. R. R. Tolkien (1974)

Inventions
First automatic switchboard
First cans of pineapple
Diesel's engine patented

WORLD EVENTS	CULTURE	D.H. LAWRENCE	GENERAL
	Music Leoncavallo: *I Pagliacci* Tchaikovsky: *The Nutcracker*		Corbett defeats Sullivan for heavy-weight boxing title
1893			
13 Jan. Independent Labour Party founded in U.K. by Kier Hardie **1 Sept.** Gladstone's second Irish Home Rule Bill passes Commons **8 Sept.** Gladstone's second Irish Home Rule Bill rejected by Lords **Nov.** Jameson crushes Matabele revolt and occupies Bulawayo **4 Dec.** Anglo-French agreement over Siam	**Literature** Hofmannsthal: *Der Tor und der Tod* Meynell: *Poems* Wilde: *Salome; Lady Windermere's Fan* Yeats: *Celtic Twilight* **Art** Art Nouveau appears in Europe Aubrey Beardsley's drawings Munch: *The Cry* **Music** Dvořák: *Symphony No. 5* Puccini: *Manon Lescaut* Tchaikovsky: *Symphony No. 6* Verdi: *Falstaff*	(Beauvale Board School) Death of Thomas Barber Friendship with George Neville begins	**Deaths/births** Fanny Kemble (1809) Guy de Maupassant (1850) Tchaikovsky (1840) George Grosz (1959) Wilfred Owen (1918) Cole Porter (1964) Mao Tse-tung (1975) **Inventions** Four-wheel car (Benz) Ford builds his first car Zip fastener (Judson) Carburettor Manchester ship canal completed Bradley: *Appearance and Reality*

1894

3 Mar
Liberal Party split over Irish Home Rule Bill; Gladstone resigns; Earl of Roseberry, P.M.

11 Apr.
Uganda a U.K. Protectorate

1 Aug.
Japan declares war on China

15 Oct.–22 Dec.
Dreyfus arrested on treason charges; condemned and imprisoned on Devil's Island

(Beauvale Board School)

Literature
Hope: *The Prisoner of Zenda*
Kipling: *The Jungle Book*
Moore: *Esther Waters*
Shaw: *Arms and the Man*
Wilde: *A Woman of No Importance*
Art
Beardsley: Oscar Wilde's *Salome*
Degas: *Femme a sa toilette*
Music
Debussy: *L'Après-midi d'un Faune*

Deaths/births
Walter Pater (1839)
Christina Rossetti (1830)
Robert Louis Stevenson (1850)
Philip Heseltine (1930)
Aldous Huxley (1963)

Anti-diphtheria serum used
Horizontal gramophone disc for sound reproduction
Death duties (inheritance tax) imposed

1895

11–25 June
Liberals defeated in Parliament; Conservative–Unionist government (Salisbury)

1 Oct.
Massacre of Armenians in Constantinople

(Beauvale Board School)

Literature
Conrad: *Almayer's Folly*
Crane: *Red Badge of Courage*
Wells: *The Time Machine*
Wilde: *Importance of Being Earnest*
Yeats: *Poems*

Deaths/births
Friedrich Engels (1820)
T. H. Huxley (1825)
Louis Pasteur (1822)
Michael Arlen (1956)
King George VI (1952)
Inventions
Safety razor (Gillette)

WORLD EVENTS	CULTURE	D.H. LAWRENCE	GENERAL
17 Oct. U.K. squadron to Dardanelles **16 Dec.** Cleveland hints at war with U.K. over Guiana **29 Dec.** Jameson raid into Transvaal	**Art** Art Nouveau style predominates **Music** Mahler: *Symphony No. 2* Strauss: *Till Eulenspiegel's Merry Pranks* Promenade Concerts, Queen's Hall **Film** First public film show, Lumière Brothers, Paris		X-rays (Roentgen) Wireless telegraph (Marconi) Oscar Wilde's two trials; convicted in May Freud: *Studies in Hysteria* begins psychoanalysis
1896			
2 Jan. Jameson surrenders at Doornkop **3 Jan.** 'Kruger telegram' of William II **6 Jan.** Rhodes resigns Premiership of Cape Colony **1 Mar.** Italian defeat at Adowa	**Literature** Chekhov: *The Seagull* Hardy: *Jude the Obscure* Housman: *A Shropshire Lad* Jarry: *Ubu Roi* The Kelmscott Chaucer Rutherford: *Clara Hapgood* **Art** *Die Jugend* and *Simplicissimus* appear in	(Beauvale Board School)	**Deaths/births** John Millais (1829) William Morris (1834) Alfred Nobel (1833) Coventry Patmore (1823) Harriet Beecher Stowe (1811) Paul Verlaine (1844) John Dos Passos (1970) F. Scott Fitzgerald (1940) Buster Keaton (1966) Federico García Lorca

12 Mar.
U.K. decides on reconquest of Sudan
July
Irish Land Act furthers tenants' rights
6 Oct.
Severe economic recession in the U.S.

Munich
Music
Last Gilbert & Sullivan comic operetta, *The Grand Duke*
Puccini: *La Bohème*

(1936)

Klondike gold rush begins
London *Daily Mail* founded

1897

4 Mar.
McKinley becomes President
6 Apr.
Slavery abolished in Zanzibar
22 June
Queen Victoria celebrates her Diamond Jubilee
June–July
Second Colonial Conference in London
Nov.
Government inquires into Dreyfus case

(Beauvale Board School)
Poem for Mabel Thurlby

Literature
Conrad: *The Nigger of the 'Narcissus'*
James: *The Spoils of Poynton*
Kipling: *Captains Courageous*
Rostand: *Cyrano de Bergerac*
Wells: *The Invisible Man*

Art
Gauguin: *Noa Noa*
Matisse: *Dinner Table*
Rodin: *Victor Hugo*; *Balzac*
Rousseau: *Sleeping Gypsy*
Sir Henry Tate donates Tate Gallery

World Exhibition at Brussels
Zionist Congress in Basel
Katzenjammer Kids, first American comic strip, appears

Sidney and Beatrice Webb: *Industrial Democracy*
Ellis: *Studies in the Psychology of Sex*

Deaths/births
Johannes Brahms (1833)
William Faulkner (1962)

WORLD EVENTS	CULTURE	D. H. LAWRENCE	GENERAL
1898			
11 Jan. Zola publishes *J'accuse*	**Literature** Hardy: *Wessex Poems*	(Beauvale Board School) Wins County Council Scholarship	**Deaths/births** Aubrey Beardsley (1873)
25 Apr. U.S. declares war on Spain	James: *The Turn of the Screw*	Attends Congregational Chapel; the Rev. Robert Reid	Otto von Bismarck (1815) E. Burne-Jones (1833)
12 Aug. Irish Local Government Act	Pinero: *Trelawny of the Wells*	Mrs Chambers and Mrs Lawrence meet;	Lewis Carroll (1832) W. E. Gladstone (1809)
30 Aug. Col. Henry admits forgery in Dreyfus case	Shaw: *Caesar and Cleopatra* Wells: *The War of the Worlds*	Chambers family moves to Haggs Farm	Stéphane Mallarmé (1842) Bertolt Brecht (1956)
2 Sept. Kitchener defeats Dervishes at Omdurman	Wilde: *The Ballad of Reading Gaol*	**14 Sept.** Enters Nottingham High School (to 1901) with George Neville; daily train trip	Ernest Hemingway (1961) Henry Moore (–)
10 Dec. Treaty of Paris: Spain cedes Philippine Islands to U.S.	**Art** Rodin: *The Kiss* **Music** Toscanini at La Scala		**Inventions** Airship (Zeppelin) Boxer Society formed in China
1899			
4 Feb. Philippine insurrection	**Literature** Ibsen: *When We Dead Awaken*	(Nottingham High School) William Ernest Lawrence begins work in London with John Holroyd & Co.	**Deaths/births** Johann Strauss (1825) Hart Crane (1932)
19 Sept. Dreyfus pardoned	Symons: *The Symbolist Movement in Literature*	Friendship with Miss Wright, George and Florence Cullen	**Inventions** Magnetic recording
12 Oct. Boer War (to 1902)	Tolstoy: *Resurrection*		Aspirin

1 Nov.
Boers take Ladysmith

Dec.
International economic crisis

10–15 Dec.
U.K. suffers 'Black Week' in Boer War

Yeats: *The Wind Among the Reeds*

Art
Munch: *The Dance of Life*

Music
Elgar: *Enigma Variations*
Sibelius: *Symphony No. 1*

Board of Education established for England and Wales
C h a m b e r l a i n , *The Foundations of the XIXth Century*

1900

27 Feb.
Workers Party formed; Ramsay MacDonald, first Secretary (renamed Labour Party)

13 June–14 Aug.
Boxer uprising in China

2 July
Zeppelin trial flight

17 Sept.
Australia Commonwealth created

17 Oct.
Bulow, German Chancellor

6 Nov.
William McKinley re-elected President of the U.S.

(Nottingham High School)
Easter (15 Apr.)
Prizes – Upper Modern 4th Form

July
10th in 21 (5th Form); English 13th; German 13th; French 19th; Mathematics Prize, set 4

Literature
Chekhov: *Uncle Vanya*
Conrad: *Lord Jim*
Dreiser: *Sister Carrie*
Hudson: *Nature in Downland*
Shaw: *Three Plays for Puritans*

Art
Renoir: *Nude in the Sun*
Toulouse-Lautrec: *La Modiste*

Music
Elgar: *Dream of Gerontius*
Puccini: *Tosca*
Sibelius: *Finlandia*

Deaths/births
Stephen Crane (1871)
Ernest Dowson (1867)
Friedrich Nietzsche (1844)
John Ruskin (1819)
Arthur Sullivan (1842)
Oscar Wilde (1856)
Louis Armstrong (1971)

Evans discovers Minoan culture on Crete (to 1910)
Planck's Quantum Theory
Cake Walk – fashionable dance
World Exhibition in Paris
Daily Express founded
W. C. Grace retires

WORLD EVENTS	CULTURE	D. H. LAWRENCE	GENERAL
			Freud: *Interpretation of Dreams*

1901

WORLD EVENTS	CULTURE	D. H. LAWRENCE	GENERAL
Jan. Kitchener's scorched earth policy against Boers	**Literature** Chekhov: *The Three Sisters* Kipling: *Kim* Mann: *Buddenbrooks* Strindberg: *Dance of Death*	**Summer** Visits to Eastwood by Gypsy Dennis	**Deaths/births** Henri Toulouse-Lautrec (1864) Giuseppe Verdi (1813) Alberto Giacometti (1966) André Malraux (—)
22 Jan. Death of Queen Victoria; succeeded by Edward VII	**Art** Gauguin *The Gold in Their Bodies* Munch: *Girls on the Bridge* Picasso's Blue Period (to 1905)	**July** Leaves Nottingham High School; meets Jessie Chambers	Nobel Prizes first given Boxing legalized in England
7 Sept. End of Boxer uprising	**Music** Ravel: *Jeux d'eau* Rachmaninoff: *Piano Concerto No. 2* Ragtime develops in the U.S.	**Sept.** Applies for position as clerk at J. H. Haywood, surgical appliance manufacturer, Nottingham	
8 Sept. Social Revolutionary Party founded in Russia	**Film** Funeral of Queen Victoria	**11 Oct.** Death of Ernest Lawrence	
14 Sept. McKinley assassinated; succeeded by Roosevelt		**Winter** Begins work in Nottingham; stays three months	
13 Dec. First wireless communication between America and Europe		**Dec.** Serious illness	

1902

		Deaths/births
31 May Treaty of Vereeniging ends Boer War; Orange Free State becomes British Crown Colony	(Illness and recovery) **c. 4 Apr.** Convalescence at Skegness, Lincolnshire, boarding house of Mrs Berry, Mrs Lawrence's sister	Samuel Butler (1835) Richard von Krafft-Ebing (1840) Cecil Rhodes (1853) Émile Zola (1840) John Steinbeck (1968)
28 June Triple Alliance renewed	**Oct.** Becomes pupil-teacher at British School, Eastwood; formation of 'The Pagans'	Discovery of hormones
12 July Salisbury retires; Balfour Conservative P.M.	Close friendship with Alan Chambers	Casualties in Boer War: 5,774 British and 4,000 Boers killed.
18 Dec. Education Act extends primary education in England and Wales		*Times Literary Supplement* founded

Literature
Barrie: *The Admirable Crichton*
Bennett: *Anna of the Five Towns*
Doyle: *The Hound of the Baskervilles*
Conrad: *Typhoon*
Gide: *The Immoralist*
James: *The Wings of the Dove*
Masefield: *Salt Water Ballads*
Potter: *Peter Rabbit*

Art
Gauguin: *Riders on the Beach*
Monet: *Waterloo Bridge*

Music
Debussy: *Pelléas et Mélisande*
German: *Merrie England*
Caruso's first recordings

Film
Méliès: *Voyage to the Moon* (extensive special effects)

Croce: *Philosophy of the Spirit*
James: *The Varieties of Religious Experience*

WORLD EVENTS	CULTURE	D. H. LAWRENCE	GENERAL
1903		(Continues as pupil-teacher) Easter Monday: Trip to Wingfield Manor	**Deaths/births** Paul Gauguin (1848) George Gissing (1857) W. E. Henley (1849) Herbert Spencer (1820) James Whistler (1834) George Orwell (1950) Evelyn Waugh (1966)
15 Mar. British occupation of Northern Nigeria completed	**Literature** Butler: *Way of All Flesh* Gorki: *The Lower Depths* Hofmannsthal: *Electra* James: *The Ambassadors* London: *Call of the Wild* Shaw: *Man and Superman*		
21 July Irish Land Purchase Act	**Art** Steer: *Richmond Castle*		Ford Motors and Krupp Works established London taxi cabs appear 'Teddy bears' designed
20 Oct. Alaskan frontier dispute settled	**Music** Bruckner: *Symphony No. 9* Delius: *Sea Drift*		Motor car speed limit set at 20 m.p.h. in U.K.
Nov. Russian Labour Party split: Menshevists and Bolshevists	**Film** *The Great Train Robbery* (First western and, at 12 minutes, longest to date)		Moore: *Principia Ethica*
17 Dec. First powered aircraft flown by Wright brothers			
18 Dec. U.S.–Panama Treaty: Canal Zone in perpetuity created			
1904		(Continues as pupil-teacher) **Mar.** Part time at Pupil-	**Deaths/births** Anton Chekhov (1860) Anton Dvorak (1841)
4 Feb. Russo–Japanese War begins	**Literature** Barrie: *Peter Pan* Chekhov: *The Cherry*		

Historical Events	Lawrence's Life	Literature / Art / Music	Deaths/Births & Science
8 Apr. Entente Cordiale between U.K. and France	Teacher Centre, Ilkeston	*Orchard*	Samuel Smiles (1812)
4 May Panama Canal begun	**Aug.** Trip to Matlock	Conrad: *Nostromo*	Leslie Stephen (1832)
21 Oct. Dogger Bank incident between U.K. and Russia	**5 Nov.** Gives two paintings to sister Emily on her wedding day	Hardy: *The Dynasts*	Salvador Dali (–)
8 Nov. T. Roosevelt elected U.S. President	**Dec.** King's Scholarship	James: *The Golden Bowl*	Graham Greene (–)
	Late 1904 or early 1905, moves to 97 Lynn Croft	Synge: *Riders to the Sea*	Christopher Isherwood (–)
		Art	Pablo Neruda (1973)
		Beerbohm: *Poets' Corner*	Gorgas eradicates yellow fever
		Rousseau: *The Wedding*	*Daily Mirror* founded
		Music	Abbey Theatre founded
		Puccini: *Madame Butterfly*	Rutherford & Soddy: *General Theory of Radioactivity*

1905

Historical Events	Lawrence's Life	Literature / Art	Deaths/births
22 Jan. Workers' Revolt in St Petersburg ('Bloody Sunday')	(Continues as pupil-teacher)	**Literature**	**Deaths/births**
3 Mar. Tsar Nicholas II promises reform	**25 Mar.** Letter to the *Teacher*	Forster: *Where Angels Fear to Tread*	Henry Irving (1838)
27 May Japanese destroy Russian fleet	**23 Apr.** Easter trip to Wingfield Manor and Crich Stand	Wells: *Kipps*	Jules Verne (1828)
28 June Mutiny on Russian battleship *Potemkin*	**Spring** Writes first poems: 'To Guelder Roses', and 'To Campions'	Wilde: *De Profundis*	Arthur Koestler (–)
	June Trip to Great Yarmouth	**Art**	C. P. Snow (1980)
		Cézanne: *Les Grandes Baigneuses*	Motor buses in London
		Picasso's 'Pink Period': *Boy With Pipe*	Bakerloo and Piccadilly underground lines opened
		Rousseau: *The Hungry Lion*	Neon signs displayed
			Einstein's Special Theory of Relativity

WORLD EVENTS	CULTURE	D. H. LAWRENCE	GENERAL
5 Sept. End of Russo-Japanese War **30 Oct.** Tsar's 'October Manifesto' **28 Nov.** Sinn Fein Party founded	**Music** Debussy: *La Mer* Delius: *A Mass of Life* Lehár: *The Merry Widow* Strauss: *Salome*	**July** London matriculation exam **Aug.** Uncertified assistant teacher, Eastwood (Begins attending meetings at home of Willie and Sallie Hopkin)	Freud: *Three Treatises on the Theory of Sex* Santayana: *The Life of Reason*

1906

WORLD EVENTS	CULTURE	D. H. LAWRENCE	GENERAL
12 Jan. Campbell-Bannerman, P.M.; Liberal programme of social reform **May** U.K. forces Turkey to cede Sinai to Egypt **6 May** Russian Constitution promulgated **12 July** Dreyfus now found innocent **22 July** Duma dissolved	**Literature** Galsworthy: *The Man of Property* London: *White Fang* de la Mare: *Poems* Sinclair: *The Jungle* Everyman's Library established in London **Art** Rouault: *At the Mirror* Sickert: *The Lady in the Gondola* Matisse and Fauvism **Music** Elgar: *The Kingdom*	(Continues as assistant teacher) **15 Apr.** Begins work on *The White Peacock* Friendship with Jessie Chambers most intense (1906–8) **Aug.** Holiday at Mablethrope, Lincolnshire with Mrs Lawrence and Jessie Chambers **Sept.** Student – University	**Deaths/births** Paul Cézanne (1839) Henrik Ibsen (1828) Samuel Beckett (–) Dmitry Shostakovich (1975) San Francisco earthquake kills 700; property losses at $400 million London population: 4.5 million Simplon Tunnel opened

	College, Nottingham
Dec. Trades Disputes Act (peaceful picketing)	**1 Nov.** Marriage of May Chambers

1907

		Literature / Art / Music	Deaths/births
Feb.–Apr. Edward VII visits Paris, Rome and Madrid	(Student at University College, Nottingham)	**Literature** Conrad: *The Secret Agent* Gorki: *Mother* Shaw: *Major Barbara* Strindberg: *The Ghost Sonata* Synge: *The Playboy of the Western World*	**Deaths/births** Edvard Grieg (1843) J. K. Huysmans (1848) Francis Thompson (1860) W. H. Auden (1973) Louis MacNeice (1963)
June Stalin steals 200,000 rubles from State Bank	**June** Completes first draft of *The White Peacock*	**Art** First Cubist exhibition, Paris Picasso: *Les Demoiselles d'Avignon* Rousseau: *The Snake Charmer*	First daily comic strip in U.S.: *Mr Mutt* Rasputin gains influence in Russian court
10 June China 'Open Door' agreement	**Aug.** Holiday at Robin Hood's Bay, Yorkshire, with Mrs Lawrence and Jessie Chambers	**Music** Elgar: *Pomp and Circumstance No. 4* Mahler: *Symphony No. 8* Strauss: *Elektra*	Baden-Powell founds Boy Scouts *Lusitania* and *Mauritania* launched
31 Aug. Russia joins the *Entente*	**Oct.** Enters contest offered by *Nottinghamshire Guardian*		Pavlov studies conditioned reflexes
14 Nov. Third Duma meets	**winter** Meets Blanche Jennings at home of Alice Dax		Bergson: *L'Evolution Creatrice*
	7 Dec. Publishes 'A Prelude'		James' Pragmatism

WORLD EVENTS	CULTURE	D.H. LAWRENCE	GENERAL
1908			
8 Apr. Asquith Ministry	**Literature** Bennett: *The Old Wives' Tale*	(Student at University College, Nottingham)	**Deaths/births** Henry Campbell-Bannerman (1836)
14 June Fourth German Navy Bill	Chesterton: *The Man Who Was Thursday*	**spring** Presents 'Art and the Individual'	Rimsky-Korsakov (1844)
20 Aug. Leopold II transfers Congo to Belgium	Davies: *Autobiography of a Supertramp*	**15 June** Sees Sarah Bernhardt in *La Dame aux Camélias*	Donald Bradman (–) Theodore Roethke (1963)
28 Oct. *Daily Telegraph* interview with Kaiser	Forster: *A Room with a View*	**4 July** Completes exam for Teacher's Certificate	London hosts Olympic Games
3 Nov. Taft elected U.S. President	Grahame: *Wind in the Willows*	**July** Works in hayfields	Isadora Duncan popular
10–11 Nov. Reichstag debate on *Daily Telegraph* interview	**Art** Brancusi: *The Kiss*	**Aug.** Holiday at Flamborough, Yorkshire with Mrs Lawrence and Jessie Chambers	Children's Act Ford Madox Hueffer founds *English Review*
	Chagall: *Nu Rouge* Monet: *The Ducal Palace*	**11 Oct.** Teaches at Davidson Road School, Croydon	Union of South Africa established
	Utrillo begins 'White Period'	**winter** Meets Helen Corke	General Motors Corporation founded
	Music Bartók: *String Quartet No. 1*		
	Elgar: *Symphony No. 1*		
	Film *The Last Days of Pompeii* Pathé: First regular newsreel		

1909

29 Apr.
Lloyd George presents 'People's Budget'
25 July
Airplane crossing of Channel
5 Nov.
Commons pass Lloyd George's Finance Bill
30 Nov.
Lords reject Bill
2 Dec.
Asquith denounces Lords; Parliament dissolved

(At Croydon)
6 Feb.
Visits Royal Academy winter exhibition
Mar.
Attends political rally; suffragettes very active
June
Jessie Chambers sends poems to *English Review*
31 July/14 Aug.
Holiday at Shanklin, Isle of Wight
c. 11 Sept.
Meets Hueffer
autumn
Helen Corke returns from traumatic holiday
Nov.
Meets Grace Crawford, Rachel Annand Taylor, Violet Hunt, Ezra Pound, and H. G. Wells

Literature
Meredith: *Last Poems*
Pound: *Personae*
Synge: *Deirdre of the Sorrows*
Wells: *Ann Veronica; Tono-Bungay*

Art
Bonnard: *Standing Nude*
John: *Robin*
Kandinsky founds Absolute Painting
Marinetti coins term 'Futurism'
Matisse: *The Dance*

Music
Diaghilev founds Ballet Russe
Mahler: *Symphony No. 9*
Schoenberg: *Three Piano Pieces*
Vaughan Williams: *Fantasia on a Theme by Tallis*

Film
Cinematograph Licensing Act in U.K.

Deaths/births
George Meredith (1828)
Algernon Swinburne (1837)
J. M. Synge (1871)
Stephen Spender (–)
Simone Weil (1943)
First permanent waves
Selfridge's opens in London
Ford's Model T

WORLD EVENTS	CULTURE	D. H. LAWRENCE	GENERAL
1910			
15 Jan. Liberals return to power in Britain **28 Apr.** British Finance Bill passes **6 May** Edward VII dies; succeeded by George V **5 Oct.** Portugal proclaimed a Republic	**Literature** Forster: *Howards End* Galsworthy: *Justice* Yeats: *The Green Helmet* **Art** Roger Fry arranges first London Post-Impressionist Exhibition Modigliani: *The Cellist* **Music** Puccini: *The Girl of the Golden West* Stravinsky: *The Firebird* Vaughan Williams: *Sea Symphony* **Film** Beginnings of the 'star' system, the feature-length film, and modern film distribution methods	**Apr.–4 Aug.** Croydon; completes *The White Peacock*; begins *The Trespasser* **8–15 Aug.** Holiday with George Neville at Blackpool, Fleetwood and Barrow-in-Furness **Oct.** Begins *Sons and Lovers* **15 Nov** Breaks six-year bethrothal with Jessie Chambers **4 Dec.** Engaged to Louie Burrows **9 Dec.** Death of Mrs Lawrence **24–31 Dec.** Holiday in Brighton with Ada and Frances Cooper	**Deaths/births** Holman Hunt (1827) William James (1842) Florence Nightingale (1820) Henri Rousseau (1844) Leo Tolstoy (1828) Mark Twain (1835) Jean Anouilh (–) Excavation of Knossos, Crete Halley's Comet observed Frazer: *Totemism and Exogamy* Russell: *Philosophical Essays*

1911

	Literature / Art / Music / Film	Jan.–Dec. (Lawrence's Life)	Deaths/births
22 June Coronation of George V	**Literature** Brooke: *Poems*	**Jan.–Dec.** Croydon; a sick year; only antidote is work; writes most of *Amores, Love Poems* and *New Poems*	W. S. Gilbert (1836)
1 Aug. London dockers strike	Chesterton: *Innocence of Father Brown*	**19 Jan.** Publication of *The White Peacock*	Gustav Mahler (1860)
10 Aug. Parliament Bill ends Lords' power to veto legislation	Conrad: *Under Western Eyes*	**Mar.–July** Formulates creed of impersonal God	Tennessee Williams (–)
15 Aug. Rail workers strike	Forster: *The Celestial Omnibus*	**29 July–12 Aug.** Holiday in North Wales with Ada and Louie	U.K. Copyright Act
29 Sept. Tripolitan War (Italy and Turkey)	Mann: *Death in Venice*	**Oct.** Jessie reads *Sons and Lovers* manuscript	9 Aug.: London temperature reaches 100°F
21 Nov. Suffragette riots in Whitehall	Masefield: *The Everlasting Mercy*	**4 Oct.** Meets Edward Garnett	National Health Insurance Act
11 Dec. Settlement of railway dispute	Rilke: *Duino Elegies*	**18–19 Nov.** Has 'ripping time' at the Cearne	Boas: *Primitive Mythology*
	Wells: *The New Machiavelli*	**19 Nov.–4 Jan.** Serious illness	
	Art Braque: *Man With a Guitar*	**11 Dec.** Shaves first beard	
	Renoir L.: *Gabrielle With A Rose*		
	Music Berlin: *Alexander's Rag-Time Band*		
	Ravel: *Daphnis and Chloë*		
	Schoenberg: *Manual of Harmony*		
	Strauss: *Der Rosenkavalier*		
	Film Mack Sennett's Keystone Comedies		

WORLD EVENTS	CULTURE	D. H. LAWRENCE	GENERAL
1912			
26 Feb. Coal miners strike	**Literature** Kafka: *Metamorphosis*	**6 Jan.–3 Feb.** Convalescence at Bournemouth	**Deaths/births** August Strindberg (1849)
28 Mar. Commons reject Women's Franchise	Marsh: *Georgian Poetry* Monroe: *Poetry: A Magazine of Verse*	**Feb.** Last meeting with Helen Corke and Louie Burrows; resigns at Croydon	Eugène Ionesco (–)
23 May London dockers strike	Monro: *Poetry Review* Pound: *Ripostes* (First reference to Imagism)	**Mar.** Meets Frieda Weekley	**Inventions** Cellophane (Brandenberger)
11 June Transport workers strike	Shaw: *Pygmalion* Futurist Poetry anthology published	**Apr.** Last meeting with Jessie Chambers	Stainless steel (Brearley)
25 June Lansbury protests forcible feeding of Suffragettes	**Art** Frampton: *Peter Pan* (Kensington Gardens)	**3 May** Leaves England with Frieda for Germany	Scott reaches South Pole on 18 Jan.
24 July Riots in London	Marc: *Tower of Blue Horses* Modigliani: *Stone Head*	**23 May** *The Trespasser* published	*Titanic* disaster on 15 Apr. 1,513 drowned
18 Oct. Tripolitan War between Italy and Turkey ends	Orpen: *Café Royal* Picasso: *The Violins* Futurist art exhibit in Paris	**25 May–1 June** Beuerberg honeymoon	Minimum Wage Act passed 'Piltdown Man' discovered; proved hoax in 1953
17 Oct.–2 Dec. First Balkan War	**Music** Stravinsky: *Petrushka*	**June** At Icking; *Look!* poems	Lenin establishes connection with Stalin and edits *Pravda*
5 Nov. Wilson elected U.S. President	**Film** Bernhardt: *Queen Elizabeth*	**July** Garnett reads *Sons and Lovers*	Jung: *The Theory of Psychoanalysis*
		5 Aug.–7 Sept. Walking trip with Frieda over Alps to Riva	

1913			Deaths/births
16 Jan. Commons for Home Rule; Lords reject 30 Jan.		**Literature** Flecker: *Golden Journey to Samarkand*	J. Pierpont Morgan (1837)
28 Jan. Suffragettes demonstrate		Meynell: *Poems*	Albert Camus (1961)
3 Feb.–23 Apr. Second Balkan War		Proust: *Du coté de chez Swann*	Bohr's theory of atomic structure
6 May Commons reject Women's Franchise for the second time		Robert Bridges named Poet Laureate	Foxtrot popular dance
30 June Germany's Army and Finance Bills		**Art** Apollinaire: *The Cubist Painters*	Webbs found *New Statesman*
7 July Commons pass Irish Home Rule for second time; Lords reject on 15 July		Epstein: *Rock Drill*	Freud: *Totem and Taboo*
12 July Massive anti-Home Rule demonstration in Ulster		Gilman, Sickert and Lewis form London Group	Russell and Whitehead: *Principia Mathematica*
24 Sept. Ulster Unionists form provisional government		Marc: *Deer in Forest*	Husserl: *Phenomenology*
		Sickert: *Ennui*	

Lawrence's life:

18 Sept. Moves in Villa Igea on Lago di Garda

Jan. Blood knowledge letter to Ernest Collins

Feb. *Love Poems* published

Mar. Begins *The Sisters*; last letter to Jessie; served divorce papers

30 Mar.–11 Apr. Moves to San Gaudenzio

19 Apr.–17 June Irschenhausen

29 May *Sons and Lovers* published

June Returns to England

July Meets the Murrys, Asquiths, Gordon Campbell and Edward Marsh

9 Aug.–18 Sept. Returns to Irschenhausen

Music

Stravinsky: *Le Sacre du Printemps* (riots in Paris)

Film

Quo Vadis?

DeMille: *The Squaw Man*

Pontirz's coverage of Scott's Antarctic

WORLD EVENTS	CULTURE	D.H. LAWRENCE	GENERAL
	Expedition (first documentary) First Chaplin films	**30 Sept.** Lerici, per Fiascherino	

1914

WORLD EVENTS	CULTURE	D.H. LAWRENCE	GENERAL
10 Mar. Suffragettes riot in London **28 June** Archduke Franz Ferdinand assassinated at Sarajevo **26 July** Uprising in Dublin **28 July–4 Aug.** Outbreak of general European War **5–12 Sept.** Battle of the Marne **18 Sept.** Home Rule Bill becomes law; war postpones enactment **16 Dec.** Germans bombard the Yorkshire coast	**Literature** Hardy: *The Dynasts* James: *The Golden Bowl* Joyce: *Dubliners* Moore: *Hail and Farewell* Yeats: *Responsibilities* **Art** Braque: *The Guitarist* John: *George Bernard Shaw* Kandinsky: *Winter* Matisse: *The Red Studio* **Music** Broughton: *The Immortal Hour* Vaughan Williams: *A London Symphony* **Film** Newsreel coverage of World War I (1914—18)	**Jan.** Begins *The Sisters* again **May** Completes *The Sisters;* Pinker offers £300 **28 May** Frieda Weekley divorce **2 June** Reads Futurist works; Garnett dislikes *The Sisters* **27 June** Arrives in London **July** Meets Catherine Jackson (Carswell), Viola Meynell, the Eders, Barbara Low, Amy Lowell, Richard Aldington and H. D.; Pinker becomes agent; breaks with Garnett and Duckworth	**Deaths/births** Dylan Thomas (1953) Panama Canal opened in August Russell: *Our Knowledge of the External World*

		Lawrence's life	Deaths/births
		13 July Marriage at Kensington Register Office	
		5 Aug. Walking in Westmorland with Koteliansky	
		Aug.–Dec. The Triangle: meets Gilbert and Mary Cannan, Mark Gertler and Compton Mackenzie	
		Sept. Study of Hardy	
		Oct. Grows a beard	

World events	Literature / Art	Lawrence's life	Deaths/births
1915			
Jan.–Dec. Trench warfare stabilises Western Front. Poison gas used	**Literature** Conrad: *Victory*	**Jan.** Move to Greatham; Rananim; splits *The Sisters*	Rupert Brooke (1887)
19 Jan. First German airship raid on England	Ford: *The Good Soldier*		James Elroy Flecker (1884)
9 Mar. Defence of Realm Act	Frost: *North of Boston*	**Feb.** Meets Ottoline Morrell, Bertrand Russell, Duncan Grant and E. M. Forster; social revolution necessary; adopts phoenix symbol	Saul Bellow (–)
25–9 Apr. Allied landings at Gallipoli	Masters: *A Spoon River Anthology*		Arthur Miller (–)
	Maugham: *Of Human Bondage*		Beaverbrook buys *Daily Express*
	Pound: *Cathay*		Albert Einstein's General Theory of Relativity
	Art Duchamp: *The Bride Stripped Bare*		U.K. shipping losses are over

WORLD EVENTS	CULTURE	D. H. LAWRENCE	GENERAL
7 May *Lusitania* sunk off Irish Coast **26 May** Asquith coalition government **1 June** First Zeppelin attack on London **14 July** National Registration Act **19–20 Dec.** Allies evacuate Gallipoli	(first Dada painting) Chagall: *The Birthday* Picasso: *Harlequin* **Music** Holst: *The Planets* Novello: *Keep the Home Fires Burning* Powell and Asaf: *Pack up Your Troubles in Your Old Kit Bag* **Film** DeMille: *Carmen* Griffith: *Birth of a Nation*	**Mar.** Finishes *The Rainbow*; rewriting revolutionary philosophy; Cambridge: meets Maynard Keynes **29 Apr.** Divorce costs may cause bankruptcy **9 Sept.** Views Zeppelin raid **30 Sept.** *The Rainbow* published **Oct.–Nov.** *The Signature*: Florida travel plans; meets Dorothy Brett, Philip Heseltine, and Dikran Kouyoumdjian **3 Nov.** Suppression of *The Rainbow* **Dec.** Meets Aldous Huxley; seeks military exemption **30 Dec.** Cornwall: Porthcothan	one million tons Junkers constructs first fighter airplane Motorised taxis appear Sanger: *Family Limitation* (first book on birth control)

1916

21 Feb.–16 Dec.
Battle of Verdun; French hold with heavy casualties

24 Apr.
Easter Monday uprising in Dublin

24 May
Conscription in U.K.

1 July–18 Nov.
Anglo-French offensive on Somme; heavy casualties with slight gains

3 Aug.
Sir Roger Casement executed for treason

7 Nov.
Wilson re-elected President

7 Dec.
Lloyd George replaces Asquith as Prime Minister; institutes War Cabinet

12 Dec.
Peace offer of Central Powers

Literature
D'Annunzio: *La Leda senza cigno*
Joyce: *Portrait of the Artist as a Young Man*
Lowell: *Some Imagist Poets*
Moore: *The Brook Kerith*
Sandburg: *Chicago Poems*

Art
Dada flourishes in Zurich
Gertler: *The Merry-Go-Round*
Monet: *Water Lilies*
Frank Lloyd Wright designs the Imperial Hotel, Tokyo

Music
Bax: *The Garden of Fand*
Jazz sweeps the U.S.

Film
Griffith: *Intolerance*
Ince: *Civilisation*
Battle of Somme (British documentary)

Jan.
Convalescence; Heseltine, Puma and Kouyoumdjian visit

Feb.
The Rainbow Books and Music; Higher Tregerthen; breaks with Russell; invites Murrys to come; Blutbrüderschaft; completes destructive half of philosophy

May
Begins *Women in Love*

19 June
Murrys leave

28 June
Bodmin conscription exam

Sept.
Relationship with William Henry Hocking; breaks with Heseltine

Nov.
Robert Mountsier and Esther Andrews visit: breaks with Ottoline and the Murrys

Deaths/births
Horatio, Lord Kitchener (1850)
Henry James (1843)
Jack London (1876)
Franz Marc (1880)
H. H. Munro (1870)
Grigor Rasputin (1871)
T. E. Lawrence officer to Faisal's army
'Summertime' (Daylight Savings Time) introduced
Severe rationing of food in Germany
War casualties leads to plastic surgery and theories of shell-shock
Jung: *Psychology of the Unconscious*

WORLD EVENTS	CULTURE	D. H. LAWRENCE	GENERAL
		21 Nov. Completes *Women in Love*	
1917			
31 Jan. German unrestricted naval warfare **2 Feb.** Bread rationing in U.K. **8–15 Mar.** February Revolution in Russia; Tsar abdicates **6 Apr.** U.S. declares war on Germany **9 Apr.–4 May** Battle of Arras **16 Apr.–20 May** French disaster on Aisne leads to army mutiny **26 June** U.S. troops in France **29 Sept.–1 Oct.** German aircraft attack London **24 Oct.–26 Dec.** Italian front collapses	**Literature** Douglas: *South Wind* Eliot: *Prufrock and Other Observations* Feuchtwanger: *Jew Süss* Yeats: *Wild Swans at Coole* **Art** Bonnard: *Nude at the Fireplace* Braque: *Woman with Mandolin* Modigliani: *Crouching Female Nude* **Music** Chicago is world's jazz centre Cohan: *Over There* Prokofiev: *Classical Symphony* Respighi: *Fontane di Roma*	**Jan.** Seeks passports to America; Duckworth and Methuen refuse novel **Feb.** Passports refused; Ottoline threatens libel; finishes *Look!* poems **Mar.** Writes *Reality of Peace* articles; *Women in Love* manuscript circulates **June** Bodmin military service rejection **Aug.** Meets Cecil Grey; *At the Gates*, pure metaphysics **Sept.** Writing on Transcendental Element in Classic American Literature	**Deaths/births** Edgar Degas (1834) T. E. Hulme (1883) Auguste Rodin (1840) John Fitzgerald Kennedy (1963) Bobbed hair popular in U.K. and U.S. (short hair a safety precaution in munitions factories) Companion of Honour and Order of British Empire established Freud: *Introduction to Psychoanalysis*

	World events	Lawrence's life	Film / Literature / Art	Deaths/births
	7 Nov. October Revolution in Russia **20 Nov.** Battle of Cambrai; first use of tanks	**12 Oct.** Eviction notice **29 Oct.** London: Montague Shearman assists; plans South American trip with Eders; meets Dorothy Yorke **Dec.** Moves to Dollie Radford's Chapel Farm Cottage	**Film** Pickford: *Poor Little Rich Girl* Buster Keaton makes his film debut *Fritz the Cat* cartoons begin Chaplin's yearly salary reaches $1 million	
1918	**Jan.** Suffrage granted in U.K. for women over thirty **4 Apr.–17 July** German offensives nearly achieve breakthrough **20 July–11 Nov.** Allied offensives begin along Western Front **4 Oct.** Germany requests armistice **Oct.** U.K. flu epidemic most severe	**Jan.** DHL and Frieda ill **Feb.** Money difficulties **Apr.** Seeks assistance from Royal Literary Fund **June** Writes Whitman essay; living on sister's money **July** Oxford University Press asks for book of European history	**Literature** Brooke: *Collected Poems* Hopkins: *Poems* Joyce: *Exiles* Lewis: *Tarr* Lowell: *Can Grande's Castle* Pirandello: *Six Characters in Search of an Author* Strachey: *Eminent Victorians* **Art** Klee: *Gartenplan* Léger: *Discs* Low's cartoons in *The*	**Deaths/births** Henry Adams (1838) Guillaume Apollinaire (1880) Claude Debussy (1862) Wilfred Owen (1893) Alexander Solzhenitsyn (–) U.S. Post Office burns instalments of *Ulysses* U.K. food shortage leads to national food kitchens and rationing World-wide influenza

WORLD EVENTS	CULTURE	D. H. LAWRENCE	GENERAL
3–10 Nov. General mutiny in German fleet; German Revolution; Kaiser abdicates **11 Nov.** Armistice signed at Compiegne **9 Dec.** Civil war breaks out in Russia; lasts until 1920	*Star* Miró's first exhibitions Nash: *We are Making a New World* Picasso: *Pierrot* **Music** Bartók: *Bluebeard's Castle* **Film** Chaplin: *Shoulder Arms* (First feature-length comedy) McKay: *Sinking of the Lusitania* (First feature-length animated film)	**26 Sept.** Military examination at Derby: rejected **Oct.** *New Poems* published **Nov.** DHL and Frieda ill; essays: *Education of the People*	epidemic; by 1920, 22 million will perish War casualties: approximately 8.5 million killed; 21 million wounded; 7.5 million taken prisoner and missing Education Act passed Adams: *The Education of Henry Adams* Spengler: *Decline of the West*
1919			
3 Jan. Hoover leads relief of Europe **5 Jan.** German Nazi Party founded **21 Jan.** Irish Free State declared **23 Feb.** Benito Mussolini founds the Fascist Party	**Literature** Anderson: *Winesburg, Ohio* Gide: *La Symphonie Patorale* Hardy: *Collected Poems* Hesse: *Demian* Ibanez: *The Four Horsemen of the Apocalypse* Sassoon: *War Poems*	**Jan.** Mountain Cottage: works on history; the *Times* rejects *Education* essays; possible trip to Palestine with Eders **Feb.** Very ill with flu, move to Ripley **Mar.** Murry edits *Athenaeum*,	**Deaths/births** Andrew Carnegie (1835) Pierre Auguste Renoir (1840) Theodore Roosevelt (1858) Jack Dempsey is heavyweight boxing champion of the world (to 1926)

	Art / Music / Films / Literature	Lawrence's life	Deaths/births
14–15 June First direct Atlantic crossing by airplane	Shaw: *Heartbreak House*	invites DHL to contribute	Bergson: *L'Energie spirituelle*
28 June Treaty of Versailles signed	**Art** Gropius founds Bauhaus	**May** Chapel Farm cottage: receives £20 from Rupert Brooke estate (Marsh)	Cassirer: *The Problem of Knowledge*
19 July Peace celebrations in U.K.	Modigliani: *La Marchesa Casati*	**Nov.** Leaves England for Italy; fails to get *Women in Love* manuscript for Huebsch; meets Norman Douglas and Maurice Magnus in Florence	Keynes: *The Economic Consequences of Peace*
11 Aug. Weimar Constitution	Munch: *The Murder* Picasso: *Pierrot et Harlequin*	**Dec.** Picinisco	Mencken: *The American Language*
25 Sept. President Wilson suffers a stroke	**Music** De Falla: *The Three-Cornered Hat*	**23 Dec.** Capri; manuscript of *The Lost Girl* from Germany; breaks with Brett Youngs and Mackenzies; breaks with Pinker	
	Films Gance: *J'Accuse* *Secrets of Nature* series, U.K.		

1920

	Literature	Lawrence's life	Deaths/births
10 Jan. League of Nations begins	Fitzgerald: *This Side of Paradise*	**Jan.** Capri: considers partnership with Secker; discusses publication of *Women in Love* and *The Rainbow*; needs New York agent	**Deaths/births** William Heinemann (1863)
16 Jan. U.S. Prohibition begins	Hašek: *The Good Soldier Švejk*		Amedeo Modigliani (1884)
19 Mar. U.S. Senate rejects the Treaty of Versailles	Kafka: *A Country Doctor* Lewis: *Main Street*		Tilden wins at Wimbledon

WORLD EVENTS	CULTURE	D. H. LAWRENCE	GENERAL
1 Aug. Gandhi begins civil disobedience in India campaign	Mansfield: *Bliss* Owen: *Poems* Pound: *Hugh Selwyn Mauberley* Yeats: *Michael Robartes and the Dancer*	**19–21 Feb.** Visits Magnus in Montecassino	Unemployment insurance introduced in U.K. First U.K. public broadcasting station opened by Marconi
26 Aug. Female suffrage introduced in U.S.	**Art** Matisse: *The Odalisque* Modigliani: *Reclining Nude*	**3 Mar.** Fontana Vecchia; Taormina, Sicily	Jung: *Psychological Types* Wells: *Outline of History* Whitehead: *Concept of Nature*
2 Nov. Harding elected President of the U.S.	**Music** Ravel: *La Valse* Jazz popular in Europe	**July** Possible South Seas cruise with Mackenzie	
16 Nov. End of Russian Civil War	**Film** British Board of Film Censors established	**Sept.** Florence: writes free verse	
12 Dec. Martial law proclaimed in Cork	Chaplin and Coogan: *The Kid*	**Oct.** Mountsier, New York agent; stuck in middle of *Aaron's Rod*	
23 Dec. Government of Ireland Act	Pickford: *Pollyanna* Wiene: *The Cabinet of Dr Caligari*	**20 Oct.** Fontana Vecchia	
		4 Nov. Magnus suicide on Malta	
		11 Dec. Receives copies of Seltzer's *Women in Love*; achieves first financial stability	

1921

	Literature / Art / Music / Film		Deaths/births
10 Jan. Leipzig war trials	**Literature**	**4–10 Jan.** Trip to Sardinia	Enrico Caruso (1873)
27 Feb. Riots between Communists and Fascists in Florence	Dos Passos: *Three Soldiers*	**15 Mar.** Portrait by Millicent Beveridge	Camille Saint-Saëns (1835)
8 Mar. Allies occupy Rhineland cities	Huxley: *Crome Yellow*	**4 Apr.** Takes Curtis Brown as agent	Sacco and Vanzetti found guilty
23 Mar. Germany unable to pay reparations	Moore: *Heloise and Abelard*	**9 Apr.** Leaves Taormina for Germany; meets the Brewsters at Capri	British Legion founded
31 Mar. U.K. miners strike	O'Neill: *The Emperor Jones*	**June** Finishes *Aaron's Rod*	Albert Einstein wins Nobel Prize for Physics
14 May Italian elections: 29 Fascists win	**Art**	**Oct.** Corrects *Fantasia*; trouble with Heseltine over *Women in Love*; makes alterations; reading Verga	Strachey: *Queen Victoria*
29 Aug.–16 Dec. State of emergency in Germany	Braque: *Still Life with Guitar*	**Nov.** Receives invitation from Mabel Dodge Luhan; depends on American income	
30 Sept. France evacuates Ruhr	Klee: *The Fish*	**Dec.** Wins James Tait Black prize for *The Lost Girl*	
Nov. Rapid fall of German mark	Munch: *The Kiss*		
	Picasso: *Three Musicians*		
	Music		
	Prokofiev: *The Love of Three Oranges*		
	Film		
	Griffith: *Dream Street*		
	Lang: *The Weary Death*		
	Lubitsch: *The Flame*		

WORLD EVENTS	CULTURE	D. H. LAWRENCE	GENERAL
1922			
16 Mar. U.K. formally recognises Kingdom of Egypt	**Literature** Eliot: *The Waste Land* *The Criterion* (Eliot) Galsworthy: *The Forsyte Saga*	**12 Feb.** Magnus memoir written	**Deaths/births** Marcel Proust (1871) Giovanni Verga (1840)
28 June Labour Party refuses affiliation with Communist Party	Garnett: *Lady into Fox* Housman: *Last Poems* Joyce: *Ulysses* Lewis: *Babbit*	**20 Feb.** Leaves Fontana Vecchia **23 Mar.** Ceylon: sees Prince of Wales at Kandy Perahera	Tutankhamun's tomb discovered B.B.C. established Revival of Ku Klux Klan in U.S.
2–5 July Heavy fighting in Dublin **1–8 Aug.** General strike in Italy; widespread political violence	Mansfield: *The Garden Party* O'Neill: *The Hairy Ape* Pirandello: *Enrico IV* Rilke: *Sonette an Orpheus*	**24 Apr.** Leaves Ceylon **4 May–10 Aug.** Australia: begins *Kangaroo* **4 Sept.** San Francisco	Bohr's electron theory Austin Seven popularises motoring in U.K. Bell: *Since Cézanne* Richards: *Principles of Literary Criticism*
19–23 Oct. Lloyd George coalition replaced by Conservatives **28–30 Oct.** Fascists march on Rome and form government	**Art** Klee: *The Machine Song* Miró: *The Farm* **Music** Vaughan Williams: *Pastoral Symphony*	**Sept.** Taos: meets Bynner and Johnson with Mabel and Tony Luhan **Oct.** Letter to *Laughing Horse*; occupied with Bursum Bill	Wittgenstein: *Tractatus Logico-Philosophicus*
6 Dec. Irish Free State officially proclaimed **7 Dec.** Northern Irish Parliament votes for separation **30 Dec.** Creation of the U.S.S.R.	**Film** Flaherty: *Nanook of the North* Lang: *Destiny* Murnau: *Nosferatu*	**Dec.** Del Monte Ranch with the Danes; Seltzers visit; writes to Murry after three years	

1923

	Literature / Arts	Lawrence's life	Deaths/births
11–19 Jan. France and Belgium Ruhr occupation leads to German passive resistance	**Literature** Bennett: *Riceyman Steps* Cummings: *The Enormous Room* Huxley: *Antic Hay* Mansfield: *The Dove's Nest* *Adelphi* first issued	**Jan.** Taos; *Women in Love* selling well	Sarah Bernhardt (1884) Katherine Mansfield (1888)
22 May Baldwin replaces Bonar Law	**Art** Matisse: *Still Life in the Studio* Picasso: *Seated Women* End of Dadaist movement	**Feb.** Breaks with Mountsier; completes *Kangaroo* and *Birds, Beasts and Flowers*	Royal Fine Arts Commission formed in U.K.
2 July–20 Aug. London dock strike	**Music** Bartók: *Dance Suite* Holst: *Perfect Fool*	**Mar.** Mexico City: sees bull fight	U.K. Matrimonial Acts (equal rights in divorce)
2 Aug. Harding dies and is succeeded by Calvin Coolidge	**Popular songs** *Yes, We Have No Bananas* *Tea for Two*	**May** Settles in Chapala: begins Mexican novel	U.S. recognition of Mexico (3 Sept.)
10–13 Aug. Riots in Germany	**Film** Fairbanks: *Robin Hood* Disney founds first studio	**19 July** New York	Palestine Mandate comes into force
26 Sept. Germany abandons passive resistance		**Aug.** Frieda leaves for Europe; DHL to Los Angeles	Buber: *I and Thou*
11 Oct. German mark collapses		**Sept.** Proposes collaboration with Mollie Skinner; returns to Mexico with Gotzsche	Freud: *The Ego and the Id*
8–11 Nov. Hitler's Beer Hall Putsch		**7 Dec.** England	
		c. 20 Dec. Supper at Café Royal: friends promise to go to Taos	

Deaths/births

WORLD EVENTS	CULTURE	D.H.LAWRENCE	GENERAL
1924			
23 Jan. First Labour government following general election victory (MacDonald)	**Literature** Arlen: *The Green Hat* Forster: *Passage to India* Kennedy: *The Constant Nymph*	**Jan.** London	**Deaths/births** Joseph Conrad (1857) Anatole France (1844) Franz Kafka (1883) Nikolai Lenin (1870)
1 Apr. Hitler sentenced to five years imprisonment	Mann: *The Magic Mountain* Shaw: *St Joan*	**Feb.** Murry declines going to Taos; sees old fierceness returning in Germany	Giacomo Puccini (1858) Woodrow Wilson (1856) Will Rogers at height of career
26 May U.S. limits immigration	**Art** Picasso's Abstract Period: *Mandolin and Guitar*	**11 Mar.** New York: Seltzer's business not reassuring	British Empire Exhibition at Wembley
9 Oct. Controversy on prosecution of *Workers' Weekly* defeats Labour Ministry	**Music** Gershwin: *Rhapsody in Blue*	**5 May** Moves to Kiowa Ranch given to Frieda by Mabel for manuscript of *Sons and Lovers*	
25 Oct. Zinoviev Letter urging U.K. workers to revolt published	Romberg: *The Student Prince* Puccini: *Turandot* Sibelius: *Symphony No. 7*	**July** Forster's *Passage to India*, best among English contemporaries	
29 Oct.–6 Nov. General election: Conservative victory; Baldwin returns	**Film** Fairbanks: *Thief of Bagdad* Griffith: *America* Von Stroheim: *Greed*	**Aug.** Attends Hopi Snake Dance	
4 Nov. Coolidge elected U.S. President		**10 Sept.** DHL's father dies	
		24 Sept. Completes *St Mawr*	

30 Nov.
Last French troops leave Ruhr

Nov.
Meets Somerset Maugham in Mexico City; Oaxaca

1925

16 Jan.
Trotsky dismissed as Commissar of War
3 Apr.
U.K. revalues pound
25 Apr.
Hindenburg is President of the German Republic
13 July
French evacuate Rhineland; Government inquiry into British coal strike
28 Aug.
U.K. resumes diplomatic relations with Mexico
3 Dec.
Irish boundary agreement

Jan.
Oaxaca: *Mornings in Mexico* essays
Feb.
Seriously ill; Mexican novel completed; *St Mawr* offered to Knopf
Mar.
Doctors advise return to ranch; unable to return to England
Apr.
Kiowa Ranch
May
Wants *David* produced; gets Susan the cow; suggests *Quetzalcoatl* be *The Plumed Serpent*
22 Sept.
Leaves New York for Europe
Oct.
Trip through Midlands; 1¼ million unemployed
Nov.
Villa Bernarda, Spotorno

Literature
Dreiser: *An American Tragedy*
Fitzgerald: *The Great Gatsby*
Kafka: *The Trial*
O'Casey: *Juno and the Paycock*
Woolf: *Mrs Dalloway*
Art
Gilbert: *The Shaftesbury Memorial* (Eros)
Grant: *Nymph and Satyr*
Picasso: *Three Dancers*
Music
Copland: *Symphony No. 1*
Friml: *The Vagabond King*
Lehár: *Paganini*
Film
Chaplin: *The Gold Rush*
Eisenstein: *Battleship Potemkin*
Vidor: *The Big Parade*

Deaths/births
Amy Lowell (1874)
John Singer Sargent (1850)
Flannery O'Connor (1964)
Scopes 'Monkey Trial' in U.S.; prohibition of sex education in Tennessee
Charleston fashionable dance
Female fashions: straight dresses without waistline; skirts above the knees; cloche hats
Violent controversy on education between government and clergy in Mexico
Hitler: *Mein Kampf* (I)

1926

WORLD EVENTS	CULTURE	D. H. LAWRENCE	GENERAL
Feb. Tension between Germany and Italy over South Tyrol **3 Apr.** Fascist youth organisation, 'Ballilla' **7 Apr.** First attempt to assassinate Mussolini **1 May–19 Nov.** Coal miners strike in U.K. **3–12 May** General strike in U.K. **8 Sept.** Germany joins League of Nations **25 Sept.** Campaign against Mafia in Sicily	**Literature** Gide: *Les Faux Monnayeurs* Hemingway: *The Sun Also Rises* Kafka: *The Castle* Milne: *Winnie the Pooh* O'Neill: *The Great God Brown* **Art** John: *Lady Ottoline Morrell* Moore: *Draped Reclining Figure* Munch: *The Red House* **Music** Bartók: *The Miraculous Mandarin* Berg: *Lyric Suite* Duke Ellington's first recordings being to appear **Film** Gance: *Napoleon* (triple screen projection) Hitchcock: *The Lodger* (his first thriller) Keaton: *The General*	**Jan.** Spotorno **Feb.** Ill with flu **May** Moves to Villa Mirenda; Brett returns to Taos **June** Undergoing change of life; doesn't want to write fiction **14 July** Celebrates Baroness's 75th birthday in Baden-Baden; doctors suggest inhalation cure **Aug.** Trip to England; health better **Nov.** Villa Mirenda: writing again; painting large oils	**Deaths/births** Harry Houdini (1847) Claude Monet (1840) Rainer Maria Rilke (1875) Rudolph Valentino (1895) Marilyn Monroe (1962) Queen Elizabeth II (–) Television invented by J. L. Baird Permanent wave invented Council for Preservation of Rural England founded *Electrola*, new electric recording technique, developed T. E. Lawrence: *Seven Pillars of Wisdom*

Lang: *Metropolis*
Niblo: *Ben Hur*
Barrymore: *Don Juan* (music on disc)

1927

31 Jan. Allied military control ends in Germany
21 Apr. Italian Labour Charter issued
27 May U.K. breaks diplomatic relations with U.S.S.R.
15–16 July Socialist riots in Vienna; Palace of Justice burnt
28 July Trade Union Bill passed
18 Sept. Hindenberg repudiates German war responsibility
17 Dec. Kellogg Pact

Jan. Villa Mirenda
Mar. Ill; *Lady Chatterley's Lover* finished
18 Mar.–11 Apr. Etruscan trip
May *David* produced in England; ill; resurrection picture completed
June Begins Etruscan essays; still ill
July Series of serious bronchial haemorrhages
Sept. Partially recovered
Oct. Advised to go to sanatorium; takes inhalation cure; Secker proposes collected poems;

Literature
Cather: *Death Comes for the Archbishop*
Hesse: *Steppenwolf*
Proust: *A la recherche du temps perdu*
Sinclair: *Oil!*
Williamson: *Tarka the Otter*
Woolf: *To the Lighthouse*

Art
Chagall: *Fables of La Fontaine*
Epstein: *Madonna and Child*
Gill: *Mankind*

Music
Kern and Hammerstein: *Showboat*
Shostakovich: *Symphony No. 2*

Film
Claire: *Italian Straw Hat*
De Mille: *King of Kings*

Deaths/births
Isadora Duncan (1878)
Günter Grass (–)
Lindbergh's solo flight across the Atlantic (20–1 May)
Slow foxtrot fashionable dance
Heisenberg's Uncertainty Principle
Fry: *Cézanne*
Heidegger: *Sein und Zeit*
Russell: *The Analysis of Matter*

WORLD EVENTS	CULTURE	D.H. LAWRENCE	GENERAL
	Garbo: *Flesh and the Devil* Jolson: *The Jazz Singer* (first sound film)	bored with Italy **Nov.** Decides to publish *Lady Chatterley's Lover* privately in Florence	

1928

WORLD EVENTS	CULTURE	D.H. LAWRENCE	GENERAL
7 May Parliament passes Women's Suffrage Bill (age 21) **12 May** Italian law reduces electorate by 66 percent **20 May** Leftist parties win German elections **24 June** French franc devalued **27 Aug.** Kellogg–Briand Pact signed in Paris **6 Nov.** Hoover elected President **15 Nov.** Fascist Grand Council gains increased power	**Literature** Ford: *Last Post* Hall: *The Well of Loneliness* Huxley: *Point Counter Point* Isherwood: *All the Conspirators* O'Neill: *Strange Interlude* Waugh: *Decline and Fall* Yeats: *The Tower* **Art** Matisse: *Seated Odalisque* Munch: *Girl on Sofa* O'Keeffe: *Nightwave* **Music** Gershwin: *An American in Paris* Ravel: *Bolero* Weil and Brecht:	**Jan.** Villa Mirenda: cough still a nuisance; wants to go to ranch; rewrites *Lady Chatterley's Lover* **18 Jan.** Leaves for Les Diablerets; collecting poems; ill **Mar.** *John Thomas and Lady Jane* a possible title; tries to expurgate novel for public **May** Writes to Ottoline after six years; ill; completes last proofs of *Lady Chatterley's Lover* **10 June** Leaves for Switzerland	**Deaths/births** H. H. Asquith (1852) Thomas Hardy (1840) Ellen Terry (1848) Fleming discovers penicillin Thames overflows its banks Amelia Earhart first woman to fly across Atlantic Mussolini: *My Autobiography* Shaw: *The Intelligent Woman's Guide to Socialism and Capitalism*

Threepenny Opera

Film
Eisenstein: *October*
Pudovkin: *Storm Over Asia*
Renoir: *Little Match Girl*
Steamboat Willie (first Mickey Mouse cartoon)

28 June Receives *Lady Chatterley's Lover*
Aug. Completes *The Escaped Cock*
15 Oct. To Port Cros; Aldingtons and Brigit Patmore; ill
28 Oct. Reads *Point Counter Point*
Nov. *Lady Chatterley's Lover* attacked in British press as obscene; pirated copies appear in America

Deaths/births
Edward Carpenter (1844)
Lily Langtry (1854)
Hugo von Hofmannsthal (1874)
St Valentine's Day Massacre in U.S.
Construction of Empire State Building begun

1929
31 Jan. Trotsky expelled from U.S.S.R.
11 Feb. Treaty of Lateran creates Vatican City
17 Mar. Madrid University closed after student agitation
24 Mar. Rigged Italian elections

Literature
Faulkner: *The Sound and the Fury*
Graves: *Goodbye to All That*
Hemingway: *A Farewell to Arms*
Remarque: *All Quiet on the Western Front*
Sheriff: *Journey's End*
Wolfe: *Look Homeward,*

Jan. Bandol: Mandrake Press to publish folio of paintings; copies of *Lady Chatterley's Lover* and *Pansies* seized by Scotland Yard
Mar. Not well enough to return to Taos

WORLD EVENTS	CULTURE	D.H. LAWRENCE	GENERAL
are 99.4 per cent pro-Fascist	*Angel* Yeats: *The Winding Stair*	**Apr.** Lahr publishes unexpurgated *Pansies*: Titus publishes cheap edition of *Lady Chatterley's Lover* to stop pirates	Kodak develops 16mm film Ortega y Gasset: *La Rebelion de las masas*
5 June Labour Ministry (MacDonald)	**Art** Braque: *Still Life: Le Jour* Klee: *Fool in a Trance* Mondrian: *Composition with Yellow and Blue* Nash: *March* Picasso: *Woman in Armchair* Dali joins surrealist group	**June** Rumours of DHL's death in newspapers	Russell: *Marriage and Morals*
8–29 Aug. Airship *Graf Zeppelin* flies around the world	**Music** Toscanini directs New York Philharmonic Orchestra	**July** Pictures seized by police at Dorothy Warren's showing	
28 Oct. Collapse of New York Stock Exchange	**Film** Bruñuel and Dali: *Un Chien Andalou* Dovzhenko: *Arsenal* Hitchcock: *Blackmail* (first U.K. 'talkie') Lubitsch: *The Love Parade* 'Talkies' kill silent films	**Aug.** Sees doctor; unable to walk much; Mackenzie threatens libel over *Man Who Loved Islands*	
30 Nov. Second Rhineland zone evacuated		**11 Aug.** Frieda's 50th birthday	
		Sept. Taking arsenic, phosphorus, no-salt, and fruit diet for cure; writes *Pornography and Obscenity*	
		Oct. Writes commentary on Carter's *Dragon of*	

1930

6 Feb.
Treaty between Austria and Italy

24 May
Mussolini champions revision of Treaty of Versailles

24 June
Simon Report on India

30 June
Allies finally evacuate the Rhineland

14 Sept.
Nazi Party gains in German elections

12 Dec.
Last Allied troops leave the Saar

Literature
Auden: *Poems*
Coward: *Private Lives*
Crane: *The Bridge*
Eliot: *Ash Wednesday*
Faulkner: *As I Lay Dying*
Frost: *Collected Poems*
Hammett: *The Maltese Falcon*

Art
Matisse: *Tiare*
Wood: *American Gothic*

Music
BBC Symphony Orchestra

Film
Dietrich: *The Blue Angel*
Hughes: *Hell's Angels*
Milestone: *All Quiet on the Western Front*

Apocalypse

Dec.
Harry Crosby commits suicide; agrees to see Dr Morland

Jan.
Beau Soleil, Bandol: completes *Apocalypse*; Morland insists on stay in sanatorium for two months

Feb.
Weight under 7 stone; enters sanatorium at Ad Astra

27 Feb.
Visit by H. G. Wells and the Aga Khan; Jo Davidson does head in clay

1 Mar.
Ad Astra treatment no help; moves to Villa Robermond at Vence

2 Mar.
Death of D. H. Lawrence

Deaths/births
A. J. Balfour (1848)
Robert Bridges (1844)
Arthur Conan Doyle (1859)
Ted Hughes (–)
Comic strips popular ('Blondie' series)
France begins building the Maginot Line
Schmeling named World Heavyweight Champion of the World in boxing
Bradman scores 334 runs for Australia in Headingley Test Match

Keith Sagar

6
A chronology of Lawrence's major works

The full documentation of this dating will be found in Sagar: *D. H. Lawrence: a Calendar of his Works* (Manchester University Press, 1979).

A Propos of Lady Chatterley's Lover. DHL wrote *My Skirmish with Jolly Roger* at the beginning of April 1929 as an introduction to the Paris popular edition of *Lady Chatterley's Lover*, and expanded it into *A Propos* in mid-October.

Aaron's Rod. Probably begun in November 1917. DHL worked on it fitfully until September 1919, when he probably finished an early draft. He resumed work on it in July 1920 and finished it at the end of May 1921. DHL revised the novel between August and November, and made further modifications at Seltzer's request in December and January 1922.

Apocalypse. December 1929. Revised and a new ending added January 1930.

'Bavarian Gentians'. September–October 1929.

Birds, Beasts and Flowers. The earliest poem is probably 'The Mosquito', 17 May 1920, and the latest 'The American Eagle', early March 1923.

'The Blind Man'. November 1918.

The Boy in the Bush. Begun early September 1923. Finished 14 November. Revised mid-January 1924.

'The Captain's Doll'. Late October–early November 1921.

A Collier's Friday Night. November 1909, but possibly a rewriting of a play first sketched in November 1906.

'The Crown'. September 1915.

The Daughter-in-Law. Early January 1913.

'Daughters of the Vicar'. First version, 'Two Marriages', mid-July 1911. Rewritten mid-July 1913. Possibly extended in July 1914.

David. Begun mid-March 1925. Finished 7 May.

'Education of the People'. Early November 1918–early December.

'England, My England'. Beginning of June 1915. Rewritten early December 1921.

Etruscan Places. Late April–late June 1927.

Fantasia of the Unconscious. June 1921. Revised October 1921.

The Fight for Barbara. 27–30 October 1912.

'The Flying Fish'. Late March 1925.

'The Fox'. Mid-November 1918. New ending added 13 November 1921.

The Grand Inquisitor. Introduction to. Mid-January 1930.

'Horse Dealer's Daughter, The'. Probably begun early January 1916. Finished, as 'The Miracle', early January 1917. Rewritten late October 1921.

'Hymns in a Man's Life'. 30 August 1928.

'Insouciance'. Late June 1928.

'Introduction to These Paintings'. Early January 1929. Revised early February.

'John Galsworthy'. Late February 1927.

Kangaroo. Late May–early July 1922. Revised with a new last chapter mid-October.

Lady Chatterley's Lover. Begun late October 1926. First version probably finished by early December. Second version probably begun mid-December and finished mid-February 1927. Third and final version begun 3 December 1927 and finished 8 January 1928.

Last Poems. The poems Aldington called 'More Pansies' were written between mid-May and mid-September 1929, and those he calls 'Last Poems' between late September and November.

'Look! We Have Come Through!'. The earliest poem is probably 'Moonrise' which was written by October 1911, the latest is probably 'Frost Flowers' which seems to date from April 1917.

The Lost Girl. Begun, as *The Insurrection of Miss Houghton*, early January 1913. Abandoned, half-written, in early March. DHL tried to continue it in mid-February 1920, then scrapped it and started again in early March. Finished 5 May. Revised mid-June.

'Love Among the Haystacks'. Probably early November 1911.

The Man Who Died. Part 1 of *The Escaped Cock* was written in mid-April 1927. Part 2 was written in late June and early July 1928.

'**The Man Who Loved Islands**'. Late June–early July 1926.

Memoirs of the Foreign Legion, Introduction to. Late January 1922.

Merry-Go-Round, The. December 1910.

Mr Noon. Begun 7 May 1920, but soon dropped in favour of *Aaron's Rod* until the end of November. Abandoned unfinished early February 1921.

Mornings in Mexico. 'Indians and Entertainment' mid-April 1924; 'Dance of the Sprouting Corn' 23 April; 'The Hopi Snake Dance' late August; 'Corasmin and the Parrots' 18 December; 'Market Day' 20 December; 'Walk to Huayapa' 21 December; 'The Mozo' begun 24 December and completed shortly after Christmas; 'A Little Moonshine with Lemon' November 1925.

'**The Mortal Coil**'. Probably October 1913. Rewritten late October 1916.

Movements in European History. The first few chapters were written in July 1918, the rest in December 1918 and January 1919. The Epilogue for the illustrated edition was added in September 1924.

Nettles. July–August 1929.

'**New Mexico**'. 23–4 December 1928.

'**Nottingham and the Mining Countryside**'. Probably early 1929.

'**Odour of Chrysanthemums**'. First version probably early December 1909. Revised for *The English Review* in late July 1910 and 1–2 April 1911, and again for *The Prussian Officer* in July 1914.

'**Pan in America**'. First version mid-May 1924. Second version probably June 1924.

Pansies. November–December 1928.

The Plumed Serpent. First draft May–June 1923. Second draft 19 November 1924 – 29 January 1925. Revised early June 1925.

'**Poetry of the Present**'. Late August 1919.

'**Pornography and Obscenity**'. Late April 1929. Extended early September 1929.

'**The Princess**'. Late September – 8 October 1924.

'**The Prussian Officer**'. May or early June 1913.

Psychoanalysis and the Unconscious. Second half of January 1920.

The Rainbow. DHL wrote the first draft of *The Sisters* between mid-March and early June 1913, but it is unlikely that this contained any material later developed into *The Rainbow.* The second draft of *The Sisters* certainly did. This was begun in August 1913 and abandoned, almost finished, at the end of January 1914. The early part of this draft contained material later used in the later part of *The Rainbow.* The third draft, now called *The Wedding Ring*, was begun immediately and finished in mid-May. Most of this version must have been *Rainbow* material. The final version, now called *The Rainbow*, was begun in late November 1914 and finished 2 March 1915. Revised late March, April and May 1915.

'Rawdon's Roof'. Mid-November 1927. Lengthened 22 November 1928.

'The Reality of Peace'. February and early March 1917.

Reflection on the Death of a Porcupine. All these essays except 'The Crown' were written between late June and early August 1925.

'Resurrection'. Early January 1925.

'Return to Bestwood'. Probably October 1926.

'The Risen Lord'. About 1 August 1929.

'The Rocking Horse Winner'. February 1926.

St Mawr. First version early June 1924. Second version late July–early August.

Sea and Sardinia. February 1921.

'The Ship of Death'. September/October 1929.

'Snake'. July 1920.

'Song of a Man Who Is Loved' and **'Song of a Man Who Has Come Through'.** Mid-July 1914.

Sons and Lovers. Begun, as *Paul Morel*, early October 1910. Begun again early March 1911 and abandoned at the beginning of July. Third draft begun 3 November 1911, but set aside a week later because of illness until late February 1912. Finished early April. Revised late May and early June. Fourth draft begun early September 1912 and finished mid-November.

Studies in Classic American Literature. First version begun late August 1917, beginning with Crèvecoeur. Set aside in mid-September until late January 1918. Finished early June with the last essay on Whitman. Revised August and September 1918, September 1919 and early June 1920. Final version written in November and early December 1922. Revised in early May and mid-June 1923.

'Study of Thomas Hardy, A'. Begun early September 1914. Probably finished early in December.

'Sun'. First version early December 1925. Second version mid-April 1928.

'The Thorn in the Flesh'. Mid-June 1913. Revised July 1914.

Tortoises. September 1920.

Touch and Go. October 1918.

The Trespasser. Begun April 1910 as *The Saga of Siegmund*. Finished late July. Second draft January and early February 1912.

Twilight in Italy. 'Christs in the Tirol' 2–5 September 1912; rewritten as 'The Crucifix Across the Mountains' July 1915. 'The Spinner and the Monks',

'The Lemon Gardens' and 'The Theatre' were written for journal publication between late January and April 1913, and completely recast for *Twilight in Italy* in August and September 1915. There is no record of any earlier versions of the remaining chapters, which were prepared for publication in October 1915.

The Virgin and the Gipsy. Mid-January 1926.

The White Peacock. Begun, as *Laetitia*, Easter 1906. First draft finished June 1907. Second draft finished by 4 May 1908. Third version begun late 1908, as *Nethermere*, and finished by the end of October 1909. Revised late January–early March 1910. Final revision early April 1910 – still called *Nethermere*.

Widowing of Mrs Holroyd, The. Probably early November 1910. Revised early August 1913.

'**The Woman Who Rode Away**'. Early June 1924.

Women in Love. Begun, as *The Sisters*, mid-March 1913. First draft finished by early June. Second draft begun August 1913 and abandoned, almost finished, at the end of January 1914. The third draft, now called *The Wedding Ring*, was begun immediately and finished in mid-May, but there was more of *The Rainbow* in this than of *Women in Love*. At this point DHL split *The Rainbow* off from *Women in Love* completely, and did not return to the *Women in Love* material until late April 1916. It was finished by the end of June. Another draft was written in July, and revision continued until 20 November. Further revision took place in January and November 1917, and in September 1919.

7

A Lawrence travel calendar

1885 11 September, Lawrence born at 8A Victoria Street, Eastwood, Nottinghamshire.

1887 In the late summer the Lawrences moved to the house in the Breach, now 28 Garden Road.

1891 The Lawrence family moved up the hill to 3 (now 8) Walker Street.

1902 In the early spring Lawrence spent a month convalescing after his attack of pneumonia at a boarding-house 'Sandsea', South Parade, Skegness, Lincolnshire, which belonged to his maternal aunt Nellie Staynes.

1904 In June the Lawrences may have taken a holiday in the Isle of Wight as on June 30 DHL sent a picture-postcard of Shanklin to Kitty Holderness saying 'This is absolutely the prettiest card I could get'.

Late in 1904 or early in 1905 the Lawrences moved round the corner to 97 Lynn Croft.

1905 After sitting his London Matriculation examination in early June, Lawrence and Ada took a holiday in Norfolk. They were at Great Yarmouth 12, and by 14 had reached Hunstanton via Castle Rising and Sandringham.

1906 At Lynn Croft, Eastwood, except for a fortnight's holiday in August at Mablethorpe, Lincolnshire.

1907 At Lynn Croft, Eastwood, except for holidays in August at Robin Hood's Bay, Yorkshire.

1908 At Lynn Croft, Eastwood (except for holiday in Flamborough, Yorkshire, 8–22 August) until 12 October, then to 12 Colworth Road, Croydon, where Lawrence was now schoolteaching, until the Christmas holiday, spent back in Eastwood.

1909 At 12 Colworth Road, Croydon during term time, and at Lynn Croft, Eastwood, during vacations, except for family holiday at Shanklin, Isle of Wight, 31 July–14 August.

1910 At 12 Colworth Road, Croydon, with school holidays in Eastwood. In mid-August Lawrence spent a week with George Neville in Blackpool and Barrow. He returned to his aunt Krenkow's in Leicester to find his mother ill. As she quickly deteriorated he took more and more time off school. On 3 December he became engaged to Louie Burrows. A week later his mother died. On 24 December Lawrence, his sister Ada and Frances Cooper went to Hove for a week's holiday. From there Lawrence went direct to the Burrows home in Quorn, Leicestershire.

1911 At 12 Colworth Road, Croydon in school terms until the end of September, when the Joneses moved to 16 Colworth Road. On 29 July Lawrence, Ada and Louie Burrows went to Prestatyn in North Wales for a fortnight. Lawrence spent frequent weekends at the Burrows home in Quorn.

January 1912 At 16 Colworth Road, Croydon until 6, then at Compton House, St Peter's Road, Bournemouth.

February 1912 At Bournemouth until 3, then to the Cearne, Edenbridge, Kent until 9, then to 13 Queen's Square, Eastwood.

March 1912 At 13 Queen's Square, Eastwood, except for 2–8 with Harry and Alice Dax at Shirebrook, and 25–30 with George Neville at Mount Pleasant, Bradnop, Leek, Staffordshire.

April 1912 At 13 Queen's Square, Eastwood, except for a visit to Leicester on 23, to London (Oak Lodge, St George's Road, St Margaret's-on-Thames), 25–6, and to The Cearne, Edenbridge, 27–8 (with Frieda). Back in Leicester 28 and Eastwood 29.

May 1912 At Eastwood until 3. At Metz 4–7, 8–10 at Trier, 10 at Hennef on the way to Waldbröl, Rheinprovinz (c/o Frau Karl Krenkow). There until 24, then to Beuerberg for the rest of the month.

June 1912 At the house of Alfred Weber at Icking, near Munich until August.

August 1912 Lawrence and Frieda left Icking 5 to walk to Mayrhofen, where they arrived 9, leaving 27 to walk to Sterzing am Brenner.

September 1912 Lawrence and Frieda arrived at Sterzing 2. From there they went to Riva by train, arriving 4 or 5. On 18 they moved to Villa Igea, Villa, Gargnano, Lago di Garda, which was to be their home until the end of March 1913.

April 1913 At San Gaudenzio, Gargnano, until 11, then to Verona until 14, then to Munich. By 17 at Villa Jaffe, Irschenhausen until June.

June 1913 At Villa Jaffe, Irschenhausen, until 17. By 21 at The Cearne, Edenbridge, Kent.

July 1913 At the Cearne until 9 then to 28 Percy Avenue, Kingsgate, Broadstairs, Kent, until 30, then to London.

August 1913 At the Cearne until 2, then to Eastwood until 6, then, after two nights in London, to Germany. By 9 at Villa Jaffe, Irschenhausen.

September 1913 At Villa Jaffe, Irschenhausen until 18, then to Constance. To Schaffhausen 19, whence Lawrence walked via Zurich to Lucerne, arriving 22. To Milan 26, to meet Frieda. By 30 at Lerici.

October 1913 At Lerici per Fiascherino, Golfo della Spezia, Italy. The Lawrences lived at Villino Ettore Gambrosier until June 1914.

June 1914 At Lerici until 9, then to Turin, Aosta (1)), Grand St Bernard (11), Martingny (12 or 13). By 18 in Heidelberg. By 24 in London, 9 Selwood Terrace, South Kensington.

July 1914 At 9 Selwood Terrace, South Kensington, London, with a visit to Ripley 18–22.

August 1914 On 31 July Lawrence had set off with three friends on a walking tour in the Lake District. They came down 5 August into Barrow-in-Furness to find that war had been declared. Lawrence returned 8 to 9 Selwood Terrace. By 16 the Lawrences were living at The Triangle, Bellingdon Lane, Nr. Chesham, Bucks., where they remained until January 1915.

December 1914 At The Triangle, near Chesham. In London 5–10, Ripley 10–12.

January 1915 At The Triangle, Chesham until 21, then to Hampstead for two days with the Eders. From 23 at Greatham, Pulborough, Sussex until July.

March 1915 At Greatham, Pulborough, except for 6–7 at Cambridge, and 20–21 in London.

May 1915 At Greatham, Pulborough. The Lawrences went to London 7 for four or five days, and returned by way of Brighton where they stayed two days with the Asquiths.

June 1915 At Greatham Pulborough, but for a visit to Garsington for four or five days 12, and a visit to the Asquiths at Littlehampton, Sussex 21.

July 1915 At Greatham, Pulborough until 30. Weekends of 10–11 and 17–18 in London.

August 1915 At Littlehampton, Sussex until 4, then at 1 Byron Villas, Vale of Health, Hampstead, London until December.

November 1915 At 1 Byron Villas, Vale of Health, Hampstead. 8–10 and

29–30 at Garsington.

December 1915 At 1 Byron Villas until 21. On 22 at 2 Hurst Close, Garden Suburb, London NW; 23–29 at Ripley; 30 to Porthcothan, St Merryn, Padstow, Cornwall until the end of February.

March 1916 At the Tinners' Arms, Zennor, Cornwall, until 16, then at Higher Tregerthen, Zennor until October 1917.

June 1916 At Higher Tregerthen. Lawrence's second medical examination at Bodmin 28.

April 1917 At Higher Tregerthen until 14, then at Ripley until 19, at 5 Acacia Road, London until 25, at Hermitage, Berkshire, until 27, then back to Zennor.

June 1917 At Higher Tregerthen, except for a visit to London about 19, and to Bodmin, for medical reexamination 23.

October 1917 At Higher Tregerthen until 15, then at 32 Well Walk, Hampstead, until 20, then at 44 Mecklenburgh Square, London.

November 1917 At 44 Mecklenburgh Square, London.

December 1917 At 13b Earl's Court Square, London, until 18, then at Hermitage, near Newbury, Berkshire, until 28, then at Grosvenor Road, Ripley, Derbyshire.

January 1918 At Ripley until about 11, then at Chapel Farm Cottage, near Newbury, Berkshire until the end of April.

April 1918 At Chapel Farm Cottage, Hermitage, Berkshire, except for 5–12 at Ripley.

May 1918 At Mountain Cottage, Middleton-by-Wirksworth, Derbyshire until August.

August 1918 At Mountain Cottage until 12, then at 5 Acacia Road, St John's Wood, London, until 17, then to Mersea Island, Essex, for three days, then to Chapel Farm Cottage, Hermitage, until 26, then to The Vicarage, Upper Lydbrook, Ross-on-Wye, for a tour of the Forest of Dean with Carswells.

September 1918 At Mountain Cottage, Middleton-by-Wirksworth.

October 1918 At Mountain Cotttage until 7, then to 32 Well Walk, Hampstead, until 22, then to Chapel Farm Cottage, Hermitage, Berkshire.

November 1918 At Chapel Farm Cottage until 14, except for a visit to London 11, for an Armistice party at Montague Shearman's, then at Mountain Cottage, except for a visit to London and Berkshire 23–6.

December 1918 At Mountain Cottage except for a visit to Ripley for Christmas.

January 1919 At Mountain Cottage, Middleton-by-Wirksworth, Derbyshire.

February 1919 At Mountain Cottage until the middle of the month, when

Lawrence became a victim of the influenza epidemic and was taken to his sister's at Ripley.

March 1919 At Grosvenor Road, Ripley, until the middle of the month, then back at Mountain Cottage.

April 1919 At Mountain Cottage, Middleton-by-Wirksworth.

May 1919 At Chapel Farm Cottage, Hermitage, Berkshire until July.

July 1919 At Chapel Farm Cottage until 28, except for a few days at the beginning of the month in London and at Otford, Kent, then at Myrtle Cottage, Pangbourne, Berkshire.

August 1919 At Pangbourne until 29, then at Chapel Farm Cottage.

September 1919 At Grimsbury Farm, near Newbury, Berkshire, until 15, then back at Chapel Farm Cottage.

October 1919 At Chapel Farm Cottage, except for 14–16 in Hampstead, and a trip to the Midlands the following week.

November 1919 At Chapel Farm Cottage until 4, then at 5 Acacia Road, St John's Wood, London, until 14, then to Italy. There Lawrence stayed first at Sir Walter Becker's villa, Val Salice, near Turin, 15–17. 18–19 at Lerici. On 19 Lawrence reached Florence (Pensione Balestri, 5 Piazza Mentana).

December 1919 At Pensione Balestri, Florence until 9, then in Rome until 13. At Picinisco until 22, then to Capri.

January 1920 At Palazzo Ferraro, Capri, except for a three-day excursion down the Amalfi coast at the end of the month.

February 1920 At Palazzo Ferraro, Capri, until 26, except for a trip to the Abbey of Montecassino 19–21. Then to Sicily, house-hunting.

March 1920 After house-hunting for several days with the Brett Youngs, Lawrence discovered the Fontana Vecchia, Taormina, and moved in 8 March. The Lawrences lived there until February 1922.

April 1920 At Fontana Vecchia, Taormina, until about 22. Then to Syracuse for a few days; then at Randazzo and Bronte for three days, returning 27.

May 1920 At Fontana Vecchia, Taormina until 17. The Lawrences took a trip to Malta, intending to stay two days, and were kept there for ten by a steamer strike.

August 1920 The Lawrences left Sicily 2 for Anticoli and Montecassino. On 6–9 they were in Rome; on 12 they left Anticoli for Florence, and were in Milan by 16. From there Frieda went to Germany and Lawrence went walking with the Whittleys round Lake Como. By 24 Lawrence was in Venice, where he remained until the end of the month.

September 1920 At Villa Canovaia, San Gervasio, Florence, until about 28, then to Venice.

October 1920 At Venice until 14, then back to Taormina via Florence and Rome, arriving 20.

January 1921 At Fontana Vecchia, Taormina, except for an excursion to Sardinia 4–13.

March 1921 At Fontana Vecchia, except for 11–14 in Palermo.

April 1921 At Fontana Vecchia until 9, then leaves for Palermo, Rome and Capri. In Capri at least 15–19. Then to Rome and Florence (22–3). By 27 in Baden-Baden.

May 1921 At Ludwig Wilhelmstift, Baden-Baden, Germany.

June 1921 At Ludwig Wilhelmstift, Baden-Baden, for a few days, then at Hotel Krone, Ebersteinburg, Baden-Baden.

July 1921 At Ebersteinburg until 10. Then Lawrence walked across the Black Forest, arriving Constance 15 and Zell-am-See 20 (Villa Alpensee, Thumersbach).

August 1921 At the Villa Alpensee, Thumersbach, Zell-am-See, until 25, then at 32 Via dei Bardi, Florence.

September 1921 At 32 Via dei Bardi until 21, then with Brewsters on Capri for a few days. Back at Fontana Vecchia by the end of the month until February 1922.

February 1922 At Fontana Vecchia until 20. At Palermo 20–3, 23–6 at Naples. On 26 embarked on the Osterley for Ceylon.

March 1922 The Osterley arrived in Kandy, Ceylon, 13.

April 1922 At Ardnaree, Kandy, Ceylon until 22, then at Braemore, Bullers Road, Colombo, until 24, then on board the RMS Orsova, heading for Freemantle, Western Australia.

May 1922 The Orsova arrived at Freemantle 4. At Leithdale, Darlington, until 18. Then on board the Malwa, arriving Sydney 27. On 29 the Lawrences took up residence at Wyewurk, Thirroul, New South Wales until August.

August 1922 At Thirroul until 9, then to Sydney, to embark 10 on the Tahiti for San Francisco. On 15 at Wellington, New Zealand, 20 at Raratonga, 22 at Tahiti.

September 1922 The Tahiti arrived at San Francisco 4. The Lawrences left for Lamy 8, spent a night in Santa Fe, and arrived in Taos, New Mexico 11, Lawrence's thirty-seventh birthday. On 14 Lawrence was taken on a five-day trip to the Jicarilla Apache Reservation.

October 1922 At Taos, New Mexico, U.S.A.

November 1922 At Taos.

December 1922 At Del Monte Ranch, Questa, New Mexico until March

1923.

March 1923 At Del Monte Ranch, Questa until 18. Left Santa Fe 20. El Paso 21; Mexico City 23 (Hotel Monte Carlo).

April 1923 At Hotel Monte Carlo until 27, except for trip to Puebla, Tehuacan and Orizaba 13–21. Then at Zaragoza 4, Chapala, Mexico until July.

July 1923 At Chapala until 9, then via Laredo, San Antonio, New Orleans and Washington to New York, arriving 19.

August 1923 In New York until 21, then to Buffalo until 27. Arrived Los Angeles 28.

September 1923 In Los Angeles until 25, then to Palm Springs and Guaymas.

October 1923 Left Guaymas for Navojoa, Sonora, 1. At Minas Nuevas, near Alamos, 3–4. Left Navojoa, 5. At Mazatlan, 6–9; 10–14 at Tepic, Nayarit; 16 at Hotel Garcia, Guadalajara.

November 1923 At Hotel Garcia, Guadalajara, until 16, then to Mexico City (Hotel Monte Carlo) until 21. Sailed on the Toledo from Vera Cruz 22, for England. At Havana, Cuba, 25.

December 1923 Lawrence was in London by 14, at 110 Heath Street, Hampstead. On 29 he went to spend the New Year with his family in the Midlands.

January 1924 At 110 Heath Street, Hampstead, London, until 23, except for a visit to Frederick Carter at Pontesbury, Shropshire, 3–5. Then at Hotel de Versailles, Paris.

February 1924 At Hotel de Versailles, Paris, until 6. At Ludwig-Wilhemstift, Baden-Baden, until 19. Back at the Hotel de Versailles 21. In London, Garland's Hotel, Pall Mall, by 26.

March 1924 Left London for New York 5 on RMS Aquitania. Arrived 11. Left New York 18 for Taos. Arrived 22.

April 1924 At Taos.

May 1924 Went to Lobo from Taos, to build up the ranch 5. At Lobo ranch until October.

October 1924 At Lobo Ranch until 11. Left Taos 16, left Santa Fe, 18; 20 at El Paso, 22 Mexico City (Hotel Monte Carlo).

November 1924 At Hotel Monte Carlo, Mexico City until 8. From 10 to 18 at Hotel Francia, Oaxaca, then at 43 Avenue Pino Suarez, until February 1925.

December 1924 At 43 Avenue Pino Suarez, Oaxaca, Mexico until February.

February 1925 At 43 Avenue Pino Suarez until 14. Then Lawrence, who had been struck down with malaria on 4 and had almost died, was moved to the Francia Hotel. On 25 in Tehuacan; 26 in Mexico City (Hotel Imperial).

March 1925 At the Hotel Imperial, Mexico City, until 25. After a two-day fight and after putting rouge on his cheeks, Lawrence got across the border at El Paso and arrived at Santa Fe 29.

April 1925 At Kiowa Ranch, as Lawrence had now decided to call it, Questa, New Mexico, until September.

September 1925 At Kiowa Ranch until 10, then via Denver to New York, arriving 13. Sailed 21 on SS Resolute, arriving Southampton 30.

October 1925 At Garland's Hotel, Pall Mall, London, until 8. Then at Nottingham until 14, and Ripley until 22. Then back to London, 73 Gower Street until 29. Then to Baden-Baden.

November 1925 At Ludwig-Wilhelmstift, Baden-Baden until 12. Arrived Spotorno 15 (Villa Maria). Moved into Villa Bernarda 23, where the Lawrences lived until April 1926.

February 1926 At Villa Bernarda, Spotorno, until 22. Then at Hotel Beau Sejour, Monte Carlo, until 25. Then to Capri via Ventimiglia and Rome, arriving 27.

March 1926 With the Brewsters on Capri. By 11 at Hotel Palumbo, Ravello, Amalfi. Left Ravello for Rome, 22; left Rome for Perugia and Florence, 25; left Florence for Ravenna, 30.

May 1926 At Pensione Lucchesi, Florence, until 6, then to Villa Mirenda, Scandicci, Florence, which was then the Lawrence home until June 1928.

July 1926 At the Villa Mirenda until 12. At Ludwig-Wilhelmstift, Baden-Baden 13–29. In London 30.

August 1926 At 25 Rossetti Gardens, Chelsea, London, until 6. Weekend with the Aldingtons in Padworth, Berkshire. Back in London 8. To Edinburgh 9. By 11 at Newtonmore, Inverness. From there Lawrence 'made an excursion to the west, to Fort William and Mallaig, and sailed up from Mallaig to the Isle of Skye' [Moore 931], arriving 17. Back in Newtonmore 19. To Mablethorpe, Lincolnshire 21. 28 to Duneville, Sutton-on-Sea, two miles away.

September 1926 At Sutton-on-Sea until 13, then to Ripley. In London 16–28 (30 Willoughby Road, Hampstead). Paris, 29, on the way back to the Villa Mirenda.

October 1926 Arrived back at Villa Mirenda 4.

March 1927 At the Villa Mirenda until 19, then in Rome until 21. At Palazzo, Cimbrone, Ravello, 22–28.

April 1927 At Sorrento until about 3, then to Rome until 6. At Cerveteri, 6;

7–9 at Tarquinia; 9 to Montalto di Castro, Vulci and Grosseto. On 10 (Easter Sunday) to Volterra. Back to the Villa Mirenda, 11.

June 1927 At the Villa Mirenda, except for a day or two with the Aldous Huxleys at Forte dei Marmi between 14 and 21.

August 1927 At the Villa Mirenda until 4. Then at Hotel Fischer, Villach, Austria, until 29. Then, via Saltzburg to Irschenhausen (Villa Jaffe), near Munich.

September 1927 At Villa Jaffe, Irschenhausen.

October 1927 At Irschenhausen until 5, then to Hotel Eden, Baden-Baden until 18, then back to the Villa Mirenda until January.

January 1928 At Villa Mirenda until 19 or 20. At Les Diablerets (Chalet Beau Site), Vaud, Switzerland, 21.

February 1928 At Chalet Beau Site, Les Diablerets, Switzerland.

March 1928 At Les Diablerets until 6. Then at the Villa Mirenda.

June 1928 At Villa Mirenda until 10. The night of the 10 was spent in Turin, 11 in Chambery, 12 in Aix les Bains, 13 Grenoble and 14 St Nizier. From 15 at Grand Hotel, Chexbres-sur-Vevey, Switzerland.

July 1928 At Grand Hotel, Chexbres-sur-Vevey until 6, then to the Hotel National, Gstaad until 9, then to Kesselmatte, Gsteig bei Gstaad, Bern, Switzerland until September.

September 1928 At Kesselmatte until 18, then at Hotel Löwen, Lichtenthal, Baden-Baden.

October 1928 At Le Lavandou until 15, then to La Vigie, Ile de Port-Cros, Var.

November 1928 At La Vigie, Ile de Port-Cros until 17, then at Hotel Beau-Rivage, Bandol, Var, France until March 1929.

March 1929 At Hotel Beau-Rivage, Bandol, until 11; at Hotel de Versailles, Paris, until 18; at 3 rue du Bac, Suresnes (with the Aldous Huxleys) until 25; then back to the Hotel de Versailles.

April 1929 At Hotel de Versailles, Paris until 7; 9–10 at Hotel de la Cité, Carcassonne; 11 probably at Perpignan; by 14 at Barcelona; 16 to Palma de Mallorca (Hotel Royal); by 22 at Hotel Principe Alfonso, until June.

June 1929 At Hotel Principe Alfonso, Mallorca until 18; by 22 at Pensione Giuliani, Forte dei Marmi, Italy.

July 1929 At Pensione Giuliani, Forte dei Marmi until 6; then at 6 Lungarno Corsini (with Orioli) until about 11; then at Hotel Porta Rossa, Florence, until 17; then at Hotel Löwen, Lichtenthal, Baden-Baden, until 23; then at Kurhaus Plattig, bei Buhl.

August 1929 At Kurhaus Plattig, bei Buhl, until 4; then at Hotel Löwen,

Lichtenthal, until 24; then at Kaffee Angermaier, Rottach-am-Tegernsee.

September 1929 At Kaffee Angermaier, Rottach-am-Tegernsee, until 18; then, after a few days in Munich, at Hotel Beau-Rivage, Bandol by 23.

October 1929 At Villa Beau-Soleil, Bandol, until February 1930.

February–March 1930 At Villa Beau Soleil until 6, then to Ad Astra Sanatorium, Vence, until 1 March, then to Villa Robermond, Vence, where Lawrence died on 2 March.

Bridget Pugh

8

Locations in Lawrence's fiction and travel writings

A study of Lawrence's use of place is generally seen as a mere biographical and
geographical exercise involving the identification of the source materials of
his works and having little to do with his art. In fact it is an infallible guide
to the nature of his creativity.

As the maps show, Lawrence rarely wrote about a place that he had not
visited. One is left wondering whether this was due to an inability to create
landscape, a clever writer's trick to ensure consistency by reproducing
something that was already second nature to him, or to a sheer lack of
interest in using his imaginative powers to project an external landscape
when he was more concerned with an internal one figured forth in the
interaction of his characters. Certainly his remark in the 'Introduction to
his Paintings', 1929, suggests this: 'But, for me, personally, landscape is
always waiting for something to occupy it. Landscape seems to be *meant* as
a background to an intenser view of life.'

Whatever the reason may have been for this very literal treatment of
landscape, the result is that, particularly in the novels where he could afford
to be expansive, but also in the early short stories, he always appears to
write with a map in front of him. When he dealt with the areas around
Eastwood and Cossall the map was on a large scale, and we are made so
aware of the intricacies of street turnings and the positions of houses that
we can easily identify the routes the characters took in their journeys
around these neighbourhoods. He did not alter this technique when he went
further afield, although, of course, as the scale changes the detail
diminishes. The journeys through Nottingham give street names as well as

local landmarks. In London the street names are fewer but the names of famous places, the Adelphi, the Opera or Covent Garden, establish the setting. When we come to Europe and indeed to America, the names of famous cities are strung together in an echo of journeys actually made.

It is interesting to note that every one of Lawrence's longer works contains a well-defined journey. In the first of his novels, *The White Peacock*, it is a short one – the marriage journey of George and Meg to Nottingham – in which George is seen 'to trespass that day outside his own estates of Nethermere'. Lawrence uses episodes in the journey, Meg's impulsive care for the child in the pram, the visits to the vulgar amusement park at Colwick, the Castle and the Opera, to prefigure events in the development of their marriage. We see them anew away from their workaday world. In the same way we see Paul and Mrs Morel in a different perspective when they face alien Nottingham. It is the same with Ursula and Skrebensky in London, Aaron and Alvina in Italy. And the journey of the young people in *The Virgin and the Gypsy* is used to give them an escape from the claustrophobia of their home.

Lawrence never ceased to use actual, recognisable places, as he used actual people, as the foundation of his writings. But an examination of his artistic treatment of these places shows how he moved from the straightforward reproduction of the external features of a given area in his very early writings to a use of landscape not as the customary reflection of mood and character but as an extension of both of them. One has only to read 'The Prussian Officer' to see how landscape universalises the aggressiveness of that single experience. A similar process of extension is apparent in the travel books where the constant interaction between Lawrence's preoccupations with 'life' and the appropriate aspects of the country he is purporting to describe gives added, though not perhaps always justified, authority to both his ideas and the impression of the area. It is also true in his novels, where the purely pictorial or occasionally outwardly symbolic treatment of place in early works like *The White Peacock* gives way to the use of Tevershall and the journey from it in *Lady Chatterley's Lover* to extend Connie Chatterley's sexual malaise to the sterile industrial world and present the two as facets of the same denial of natural life. This deepening and widening of his presentation of the physical world illustrates the comprehensiveness of his mature vision.

But although his artistic skill in the presentation of place developed, his use of place to find his characters was there from his earliest works. Miriam became her essential self by the white rose bush. The isolation of Alvina

Houghton is measured against the permanent community of Eastwood, the places she passed through as a nurse and the final totally alien environment of Pescocalascio, where she finds with Ciccio her true identity.

Indeed, Lawrence sought to use place not only to find his characters but to find himself. His travels and his quest for Rananim both show this. His travels and searches, providing him as they did with constantly new environments, added a new dimension to his plots. For plot in D. H. Lawrence is not just a matter of taking two couples and working out their fate 'in the manner of George Eliot'. Plot in Lawrence is also a matter of taking two or even three environments and setting them against each other in a manner that makes them not just the background of the action but part of the action itself. In Lawrence one often feels that place compels the characters to behave as they do. It is difficult to visualise Mrs Witt proposing to her groom except in a setting which by linking him with the mythical Pan gives him additional presence. And surely it was the pressure of the place she found herself in that impelled *The Woman Who Rode Away* on her sacrificial journey, even as the snow-clad mountains impelled Gerald to his death among them.

On a more practical level, place made Lawrence what he was. By his birth in Eastwood at the end of the nineteenth century Lawrence was peculiarly fitted to write not only about the last phases of the industrial revolution as it affected the mining area, but also about the decline in agriculture caused by the importation of American wheat. Moreover, in his small community he was peculiarly well placed to view the effect of the 1870 Education Act on his contemporaries. He was born into a society which was a microcosm of English life.

It might have been expected that Lawrence would have created from such material a recognisable and coherent fictitious world like Hardy's Wessex, Trollope's Barsetshire, or Faulkner's Yoknawpatawpha country. But characteristically, here as elsewhere, he avoided the strait-jacket of formal organisation. Although the physical world remains much the same in *The White Peacock, Sons and Lovers*, parts of *Aaron's Rod, The Lost Girl* and *Women in Love*, and in many of the short stories, in each of these works he used different disguises for the names of the same places in Eastwood and Underwood. The result is that the reader, instead of forming a picture of a continuing and coherent community, is under the impression that he is being offered a totally new experience in each work.

The variation in names must have been a deliberate choice, even as the use he made of them seems to have been. Although the later novels jumble together Nottinghamshire and Derbyshire names, in the early works Lawrence was

fairly consistent in disguising the names of places with which he had close
personal connections and leaving others undisguised.

Thus, in order to avoid discommoding Sir Walter Becker, Lawrence described
his visit to him as taking place at Novara, not Turin. Where such disguise
was not required he used the real names of places he visited, relying on the
involuntary associations of famous names to add to the picture he was
creating. He did not, perhaps, recognise the curious double effect this would
have on his readers. Names familiar in one continent are unknown in
another. So Lawrence must read very differently in Eastwood and Oaxaca.
But the sensuous effect of these lists of places, which sometimes read like an
incantation, must be universal, whether they reflect the Derbyshire
landscape of *The Virgin and the Gipsy* or the run from Mexico City to
Sayula in *The Plumed Serpent*.

Such lists mention a place and then dismiss it for ever. This treatment
underlines Lawrence's extremely idiosyncratic reaction to place. The areas
that inspired him were quite limited. Cornwall, where he spent some years,
is mentioned in a short story and *Kangeroo*, and there the emphasis is on
Lawrence's experiences rather than the place itself. Yet the few brief days
he spent near Pontesbury contribute quite essentially to *St Mawr*. Nine
days in Sardinia produced *Sea and Sardinia*, six weeks in Australia
produced *Kangaroo*. Richard Aldington notes in his Introduction to the
book: 'Although the first four chapters of *Kangaroo* are set in Sydney, the
Lawrences in fact spent only Saturday and Sunday there'. But Asia and
Africa went unvisited by him, and only Mexico and New Mexico in the
whole American continent inspired him to write about them.

Not only was his interest limited to certain places, it was limited to certain
aspects of those places. Despite his long sea journeys the sea appears very
infrequently in his works. *Kangaroo* has many vivid seaside settings, but
Sea and Sardinia, despite its title, is more concerned with shipboard
experiences than the sea itself. Moreover, although his topography is exact,
his description of actual land forms is fairly vague. He preferred to sketch in
the larger features of landscape and to concentrate on the minutiae,
particularly the flora, of a particular region. He had no interest in palaces
and castles, the memorials of past political power. Instead he was concerned
to present to his readers churches, cathedrals and temples, the symbols of
religious belief. It is interesting to note that in his decriptions of these places
he was often extraordinarily exact. For instance, visitors to Lincoln
Cathedral will see that the figures carved there are apparently bisexual and
could well have given rise to the argument between Anna and Will. And

modern industrial landscapes repelled him. In this reaction to place
Lawrence was essentially regressive and conservative.

Indeed, despite the outward appearance of adventurous forays to unknown
regions, Lawrence's travels often resulted in writings about different
manifestations of the same things. As Harry T. Moore pointed out in *The
Priest of Love*, Lawrence generally wrote about a village. His selection of
such a setting underlines his preoccupation with community, religion and
the natural rhythm of the seasons, for it is in such small places that these are
most clearly seen.

This lack of adventure, coupled with his frequent use of real places, throws an
interesting light on the quality of Lawrence's imagination. His was not an
inventive genius. His ability lay in taking the materials to his hand and
presenting them in a new light. It is this quality which comes out so clearly
in his descriptions of place. He reproduced actual places on paper. He was
so imbued with a sense of that place through the intensity of his observation
and the vividness of his skill in interpreting its forms that he was able to
share the experience of an actual world with his readers. And it was often
through his descriptions of an area and its dependent community that he
was able to convoy 'intuitively' the organic nature of life which he
sometimes failed to communicate in his verbal disquisitions on sex,
industrialism and the nature of being.

The familiar places described in his books gave Lawrence a concrete
framework within which to write; a framework which suited a mind which
was always happier in terms of the actual rather than the theoretical.

THE TRAVEL WRITINGS

Twilight in Italy (1915). See Maps 2 and 3

This book contains a collection of essays: 'The Crucifix Across the Mountains'
originally 'Christs in the Tyrol' (1912), 'On the Lago di Garda', 'Italians in
Exile' and 'The Return Journey'. It is particularly interesting in that it
records with pleasing freshness the impact of Bavaria and Italy on the
hitherto untravelled Lawrence and illustrates his reaction to the unfamiliar
as shown in the archetypal figures of the old woman and the monks; local
customs, and particularly local crafts like spinning, lemon-growing and
viticulture.

At the same time, the separate essays illustrate the preoccupations which
Lawrence was to explore through fiction in *The Rainbow* and *Women in*

Love: the conflicts between instinct and will as shown in the accounts of the crucifixes; the dual nature of the church as eagle and dove; the contrast between northern and southern civilisations in their attitude to the senses and the intellect; the problems of industrial society; the interaction between man, homeland and community; the nature of marriage; and the true nature of Pan as seen in Il Duro and Faustino.

In view of these two factors it is interesting to consider what these essays tell us about the places themselves. Topographically it is remarkably little. In the early essays it is often difficult to know exactly where he is from his casual references to 'The imperial road to Italy', Lake Garda, San Gaudenzio or the steamer to Descenzano. Only external references to his letters reveal that San Gaudenzio is near Gargnano. It is not until the last two essays that one is able to form a coherent impression of his journeyings from purely internal evidence. From them one can follow Lawrence from Lake Constance by steamer down the Rhine to Schaffhausen, along the Rhine valley towards Zurich to board another steamer and travel along the long lake until he 'landed somewhere on the right bank, about three quarters of the way down the lake'. Thence he passed over the hills, including the Rigi to Lucerne, where he took the steamer down the lake 'to the very last station', and onwards through Göschenen to Andermatt and up over the Gotthardt Pass down to Airolo and through the Ticino valley to Bellinzona to Lake Maggiore, Locarno and Lugano via Chiasso, ending his journey with a steamer down to Como and a train to Milan.

This recognisable itinerary of an actual walk taken by Lawrence in September 1913 brings us at last to the recognised world of a normal travel book. It is a remarkably evocative piece of writing:

> Till sunset came, very red and purple, and suddenly, from the heavy spacious open land I dropped sharply into the Rhine valley again, suddenly, as if into another glamorous world.
>
> There was the river rushing along between its high, mysterious, romantic banks, which were high as hills, and covered with vine. And there was the village of tall, quaint houses flickering its lights on to the deep-flowing river, and quite silent, save for the rushing of water.
>
> There was a fine covered bridge, very dark. I went to the middle and looked through the opening at the dark water below, at the façade of square lights, the tall village-front towering remote and silent above the river. The hill rose on either side the flood; down here was a small, forgotten, wonderful world that belonged to the date of isolated village communities and wandering minstrels.

Yet it is in the oblique approach of the early essays that Lawrence passes beyond the picturesque to describe the essence of Italy:

Another day, however, I found a broken staircase, where weeds grew in the gaps the steps had made in falling, and maidenhair hung on the darker side of the wall. I went up unwillingly, because the Italians used this old staircase as a privy, as they will any deep side-passage.

But I ran up the broken stairway, and came out suddenly as by a miracle, clean on the platform of my San Tommaso in the tremendous sunshine.

It was another world, the world of the eagle, the world of fierce abstraction. It was all clear, overwhelming sunshine, a platform hung in the light. Just below were the confused, tiled roofs of the village, and beyond them the pale blue water down below, and opposite, opposite my face and breast, the cool, luminous snow of the mountain across the lake, level with me apparently, though really much above.

I was in the skies now, looking down from my square terrace of cobbled pavement, that was worn like the threshold of the ancient church. Round the terrace ran a low, broad wall, the coping of the upper heaven where I had climbed.

There was a blood red sail like a butterfly breathing down on the blue water, whilst the earth on the near side gave off a green-silver smoke of olive trees, coming up and around the earth-coloured roofs.

It always remains to me that San Tommaso and its terrace hang suspended above the village, like the lowest step of heaven, of Jacob's ladder. Behind the land rises in a high sweep. But the terrace of San Tommaso is let down from heaven and does not touch the earth.

These two quotations illustrate the distinctive qualities of the two sections of the book. The vivid but matter-of-fact account of the German scene is taken from 'Italians in Exile', which, together with 'The Return Journey', is fairly impersonal in style. The intensely realised and very subjective description of San Tommaso is typical of the collage of pictures and impressions which are used to explore the nature of Italy in 'The Crucifix Across the Mountains' and 'On the Lago di Garda'. The two parts of the book are skilfully linked by the theme of the decline of Italy and the device of the journey either by the old Imperial route or Lawrence's own from Munich southwards towards Verona or Milan. It is a mixture Lawrence was to use again and again in both fiction and non-fiction.

Sea and Sardinia (1921). See Maps 5a and 5b

This book, originally entitled 'Diary of a Trip to Sardinia', was an account of the Lawrences' visit to Sardinia from 4 to 13 January 1921. Although Lawrence described himself as 'just finishing' it in March, it was very much altered for publication at the end of the year and for its publication in two sections in the *Dial* before this.

Lawrence himself described *Sea and Sardinia* as 'light and sketchy'. It falls into two parts – the journey from Sicily to Sardinia and the journey through Sardinia.

The first is written in the form of an internal monologue, studiedly informal, often telegraphic in style, yet providing an entertaining account of the trivia of travel. It is remarkable for underlining the fact that any description of a sea journey is eventually an account of ship-board encounters and passing landmarks.

The second section is a factual representation of the journey the Lawrences actually took in Sardinia, as map 5b illustrates. It is particularly interesting for the number and variety of its set pieces which range from descriptions of party-going children to the 'hot eyes' of almond blossom and from the process of kid-roasting to the panorama of the market:

> Peasant women, sometimes barefoot, sat in their tight little bodices and voluminous coloured skirts behind the piles of vegetables, and never have I seen a lovelier show. The intense deep green of spinach seemed to predominate, and out of that came the monuments of curd-white and black-purple cauliflowers: but marvellous cauliflowers, like a flower show, the purple ones intense as great bunches of violets. From this green, white and purple massing struck out the vivid rose-scarlet and blue-crimson of radishes, large radishes like little turnips in piles. Then the long, slim, grey-purple buds of artichokes, and dangling clusters of dates, and piles of sugar-dusty white figs and sombre-looking black figs and bright burnt figs: basketfuls and basketfuls of figs. A few baskets of almonds and many huge walnuts. Basket-pans of native raisins. Scarlet peppers like trumpets: magnificent fennels, so white and big and succulent: baskets of new potatoes: scaly kohlrabi: wild asparagus in bunches, yellow budding sparacelli: big clean-fleshed carrots: feathery salads with white hearts: long, brown-purple onions, and then, of course, pyramids of big oranges, pyramids of pale apples, and baskets of brilliant shiny mandarini, the little tangerine oranges with their green-black leaves. The green and vivid-coloured world of fruit-gleams, I have never seen in such splendour as under the market-roof at Cagliari: so raw and gorgeous. And all quite cheap, the one remaining cheapness, except potatoes. Potatoes of any sort are 1.40 or 1.50 the kilo.
>
> 'Oh!' cried the q.b., 'if I don't live at Cagliari and come and do my shopping here, I shall die with one of my wishes unfulfilled.'

It is interesting to see Lawrence and the q.b. (the queen-bee, Frieda) as viewers of the market rather than participants in it as they are in the market in *Mornings in Mexico*. It is not until the return to Palermo and the visit to the marionette theatre that one feels one is back with the whole Lawrence, at once theorising on life and immersing himself in the particular experience of the moment. This book shows him as artistic observer, as master of the apt generalisation, as on Sardinia – 'which has no history, no date, no race, no offering', but not as one eager to seek out the nature of the island. Foreignness no longer enchants him. He does not see the people he encounters as representative of a new and intriguing civilisation. In this book the individuals he meets, the officials, the sea-sick family on ship-board, the bus drivers and the bounders are petty human beings. One sees them externally as one does the whole island. But the quality of the writing leaves them as vivid pictures.

Mornings in Mexico (1927). See Maps 7 and 8

Mexico in this book refers to both Mexico itself and New Mexico. The first four essays, 'Corasmin and the Parrots', 'Walk to Huayapa', 'The Mozo' and 'Market Day' were written during Lawrence's stay in Oaxaca in December 1924. They contain references to other parts of Mexico like Guadalajara, but are clearly set in 'one little town away South in the Republic'. 'Indians and Entertainment', 'Dance of the Sprouting Corn' and 'The Hopi Snake Dance' were written earlier in 1924 and refer to the area around Taos. 'A Little Moonshine with Lemon', the European postscript, was written in November 1925. They were published separately before appearing in book form.

These essays seem to contain a clear distillation of all Lawrence had to say about his American experiences. The book, starting very simply with a look at the superficial sides of Mexico, leads us deeper and deeper into the nature of the country as Lawrence saw it, so that we have a sense of penetrating into the mysteries of Indian nature.

In the first essay, the Englishman looks at the Indian, the Indian at the Englishman and the parrot at both, each created by their own Sun and for ever separated from each other. In 'The Walk to Huayapa' Lawrence explores this difference more deeply, emphasising the remoteness of the Indians and their ambivalent attitude towards white men. He also reveals something of his own feeling of superiority towards the natives, although this is unwitting. The Indians, Lawrence claimed, had a complete absence of what we call spirit. But they were bound together by a sense of community, a blood-consciousness which made itself manifest in the excitement of the market. He deduced from meeting them that 'there is no soul, and no abiding place, and nothing is fixed, not even the Cathedral towers. The Cathedral towers are slowly leaning, seeking the curve of return'; and that 'only that which is utterly intangible matters'.

From this he goes on to consider in 'Indians and Entertainment' how the abandonment of a single god and the lack of a sense of individuality leaves the Indian at one with the universe, not external to it. His one commandment is 'Thou shalt acknowledge the wonder'. And the rest of Lawrence's book is an acknowledgement of that wonder as it is epitomised in the Indian dances – first the 'Dance of the Sprouting Corn' and secondly 'The Hopi Snake Dance'.

One might say that this is not a very good travel book, in that it reveals more of Lawrence than of Mexico. Although many of the incidents are described with literal truth, no doubt much is heightened, and the account of the Hopi Snake Dance in its final form much romanticised. Lawrence's choice of material is perhaps unduly idiosyncratic. And his musings mean that despite the vividness of his descriptions one never knows quite what part of the physical world one is in.

But despite these blemishes *Mornings in Mexico* has most of the attributes of a great travel book. It blends together a sense of novelty which brings heightened awareness, a vivid evocation of places and their inhabitants and a sense of mingled past and present which separates such writing from journalistic travel works.

Etruscan Places (1927). See Map 6

This is an account of a journey Lawrence took with Earl Brewster in April 1927.

As with *Twilight in Italy*, his *Etruscan Places* is not only a travel book but a mirror of his preoccupations of the time – his renewed interest in painting, his concern with death and resurrection, and his feeling for remote subject peoples. It was on this journey that he was inspired by the sight of a toy rooster escaping from an egg in a shop window to write 'The Escaped Cock', which uses similar material.

The book itself, with its vivid evocation of a very limited number of sites, reflects the Lawrentian method of conveying by selective description the essential truth of the nature of an area from a limited experience of it.

The book is unfinished. Although Lawrence's ill health was no doubt the reason, it is difficult to see how it could have been continued without becoming repetitive, despite the device of contrasting the modern world with the old through his disquisitions on people he met en route.

See also the essays 'Flowery Tuscany', 'New Mexico' and 'Taos'.

THE PLAYS

Collier's Friday Night, A (1906) is set in a mining town, presumably

Eastwood. The descriptions of the kitchen in the Lamberts' house is extraordinarily and often unnecessarily detailed. 'She sets them on the hearth – which has no fender, the day being Friday, when the steel fender is put away, after having been carefully cleaned, to be saved for Saturday afternoon.' It is the Lawrence home.

Daughter-in-Law, The (1913) is again set in a mining town. 'The action of the play takes place in the kitchen of Luther Gascoigne's new home' which is 'A miner's kitchen – not poor'. The scenery is very lightly sketched in.

David (begun 1925) The setting is ostensibly Biblical, but the references to a 'Sort of compound with an adobe house beyond an open place in the village'; 'An old man on a roof calling aloud and kindling a signal fire' and 'A round, pyramid-like hill, with a stair-like way to the top, where is a rude rock altar' remind one of *The Woman Who Rode Away*.

Fight for Barbara, The (1912) is set in an Italian villa. Written at Gargnano.

Married Man, The (1912) The bedroom, long low dining room, farm kitchen and bedroom suggest the Haggs, near Eastwood.

Merry-Go-Round, The (1910). The parlour, downstairs front room used as a bedroom, the foreign, titled vicar at Grunston Church all suggest Eastwood and Greasley. Lawrence's inexperience as a playwright is shown in the nonchalant direction 'Fowls pecking on the floor' as part of the scene.

Touch and Go (1918) is described as taking place in 'A large mining village in the Midlands' with 'a stumpy memorial obelisk'. The third act describes 'An old park. In the background a low Georgian hall which has been turned into offices for the Company.' This is probably Eastwood Hall.

Widowing of Mrs Holroyd, The (1910) is clearly set in Lawrence's aunt's cottage in Brinsley.

Altitude (1924) is set in Taos, at Mabel Luhan's house, and is an unfinished fragment.

Noah's Flood (1925) has no indication of setting.

THE SHORT STORIES (and other short prose fragments)

The short stories illustrate Lawrence's use of actual places as the background for his fiction. The early ones have easily identifiable settings: the later ones are sometimes generalised or symbolic. But it is always easy to relate Lawrence's actual experiences and his fictitious accounts. References are to the Penguin edition.

'Adolph' (1919) in *The Mortal Coil*. An autobiographical fragment set in Eastwood. The references to the father coming up the 'entry' and the children chasing the rabbit 'over the chapel wall' suggest that it refers to the Walker Street house. The father is pictured as finding the rabbit as he walked home from Brinsley pit.

'Blind Man, The' (1918) in *England, My England*. The Vicarage, Upper Lydbrook, Ross-on-Wye, where Lawrence and Frieda had been with the Carswells, provides the setting for this short story.

'Blue Moccasins, The' (1928) in *The Princess*. This late story presents a generalised picture of (possibly southern) small-town English country life. The heroine has travelled the world and returned to live in 'a small family mansion'.

'Border Line, The' (1924) in *The Woman Who Rode Away*. In February 1924 Lawrence and Frieda visited Baden-Baden. This story incorporates a similar journey. The description of Strasbourg Cathedral and 'the old, overhanging houses with black timbers and high gables' are clearly identifiable.

'Captain's Doll, The' (1921) in *Three Novellas*. This novella was written at Villa Alpensee, Thumersbach, Zell-am-See. The story begins in Allied-occupied Germany, passes through Munich, and ends in the Austrian Tyrol.

'Chapel Among the Mountains, A' and **'A Hay Hut Among the Mountains'** (1912) in *The Mortal Coil*. Lawrence places these stories or thinly disguised autobiographical fragments on a footpath on the way to Glashütte in the Isar valley among the Tyrolese Alps. They record experiences on the walk from Icking in August-September 1912.

'Christening, The' (1912) in *The Prussian Officer*. This short story describes in accurate detail a walk from the British School in Albert Street, Eastwood, along the Nottingham Road to Walker Street. Hilda Rawbotham must have visited John Bricknell, provision dealer, at 27 Mansfield Road to buy her cakes before turning back along the High Road (Michael Bennett).

'Daughters of the Vicar, The' (1911) in *The Prussian Officer*. This short story is believed to be set in Brinsley. The Durrants' cottage is Quarry Cottage where Lawrence's grandfather lived. Greasley (Greymeed) is 'two or three miles' away (D. H. Lawrence Society).

'Delilah and Mr Bircumshaw' (1912) in *The Mortal Coil*. The interior setting in this story makes it difficult to place. The atmosphere and situation suggest Croydon; Bircumshaw is an Eastwood name.

'Dream of Life, A' (1927) in *The Princess*. Eastwood is here called Newthorpe. The quarry was probably suggested by those out towards Annesley. The dream embraces Lawrence's American and Italian experiences, combining his viewing of Indian and Etruscan dance with earlier Biblical knowledge.

'England, My England' (1915) in *England, My England*. This gives a direct picture of Greatham, Pulborough, Sussex, with its main house and surrounding smaller buildings occupied by members of the Meynell family.

'Escaped Cock, The' (1927), ('The Man Who Died' in *Love Among the Haystacks*). Jerusalem – this is the only example of a story set in a place Lawrence had not visited. But the Congregational Chapel ensured that he knew the atmosphere from Biblical accounts. It was as much part of his heritage as the places he actually knew. Part II is set on 'the shores of Sidon' in Lebanon.

'Fanny and Annie' (1919) in *England, My England*. The Goodall home is in Princes Street, Eastwood. The ironworks are the Bennerley Ironworks, and the branch line that from Derby. The Congregational Chapel of Eastwood is here transferred to a hamlet.

'Fly in the Ointment, A' (1910) in *The Mortal Coil*. The setting for this short story is clearly Colworth Road, Croydon. 'Outside in the dark was a little yard and a hand's breadth of garden backed by the railway embankment.'

'Flying Fish, The' (1925) in *The Princess*. 'The lost town of South Mexico' referred to in this unfinished short story is Oaxaca, and the journey from it via Veracruz and Havana is one which Lawrence took in November 1923. 'Daybrook was a sixteenth-century stone house, among the hills in the middle of England. It stood where Crichdale bends to the south and where Ashleydale joins in.' Lawrence's notes to 'The Flying Fish' tell us that Crichdale is Lathkill Dale, in Derbyshire. The River Lathkill bends to the south and joins the Bradford at Alport. A sixteenth-century stone house, Haddon Hall, stands just to the north.

'Fox, The' (1918) in *Three Novellas*. The story is based on the relationship between Cecily Lambert and Violet Monk and their efforts to farm at Grimsbury Farm, Long Lane, near Newbury, Berkshire.

'Fragment of Stained Glass, A' (1907) in *The Prussian Officer* (originally 'Legend'). This early work is centred on Beauvale Priory near Eastwood. Olive Hopkin has traced out the serfs' route in a map identifying various Lawrence landmarks. It is one of Lawrence's few historical works.

'Glad Ghosts' (1925) in *The Woman Who Rode Away* (originally 'Gay

Ghosts' and then 'Ghosts of Silence'). The setting is Derbyshire, ostensibly Middleton-by-Wirksworth. Riddings is described as 'an old Derbyshire stone house, at the end of the village of Middleton: a house with three sharp gables, set back not very far from the high road, but with a gloomy moor for a park behind ... Even the little railway station, deep in the green cleft hollow, was of stone and dark and cold and seemed in the underworld'. A similar three-gabled house is to be seen near the railway station in Wirksworth (Lannah Coak and Moina Brown).

'Goose Fair' (1909) in *The Prussian Officer*. Hollow stone, the Lace Market, Sneinton Church are all parts of Old Nottingham, as the Nottingham map shows. Goose Fair is still held annually in the city. This short story is set in the time of industrial unrest after the Napoleonic Wars and reflects the situation in the city, where the castle itself was attacked and burned in the riots.

'Her Turn' (1912) in *The Mortal Coil*. This short story, set in Eastwood, clearly describes the pub also visited by Aaron in *Aaron's Rod*. It was probably The Thorn Tree (now demolished) on the Brinsley Road.

'Horse Dealer's Daughter, The' (1916) in *England, My England* (originally 'The Miracle'). 'The Hollies', formerly Eastwood House, Greasley, was a large house (now demolished) on the Nottingham Road in Eastwood (D. H. Lawrence Society). Olive Hopkin describes it as being 'on the left just after the Three Tuns Inn'.

'In Love' (1926) in *The Woman Who Rode Away*. Mathbury is an invented name. The area is presumably Wiltshire but, as in many later works, this short story could be set anywhere in the south of England.

'Jimmy and the Desperate Woman' (1924) in *The Woman Who Rode Away*. This short story is ostensibly set in Yorkshire, north of Sheffield, but its atmosphere is that of Eastwood and Olive Hopkin sets it in the Cocker Lane area, just past Eastwood Hall.

'Ladybird, The' (1921) in *Three Novellas*. The 'beautiful Elizabethan mansion' of this novella is clearly Garsington, Oxfordshire, the home of Lady Ottoline Morrell.

'Last Laugh, The' (1924) in *The Woman Who Rode Away*. The description 'Below was the yellow, foul-smelling glare of the Hampstead Tube Station. On the right the trees' suggests that this short story was set in Heath Street, Hampstead, where Lawrence stayed in January 1924.

'Lessford's Rabbits' (1908); **'Lesson on a Tortoise'** (1908) in *The Mortal Coil*. These are both autobiographical fragments reflecting Lawrence's experiences as a schoolteacher at Davidson Road School, Croydon.

'Love Among the Haystacks' (1908) in *Love Among the Haystacks*. The description of 'the old church and the castle farm, among their trees' sets this novella in Greasley. The fields were rented by the Chambers of Haggs Farm.

'Lovely Lady, The' (1927) in *Love Among the Haystacks*. The house in this short story is 'twenty-five miles out of town', but it is difficult to identify positively, despite the details of period (Queen Anne) and setting.

'Man Who Loved Islands, The' (1926) in *Love Among the Haystacks*. The story was suggested to Lawrence by Compton Mackenzie's purchase of Herm and Jethou in the Channel Islands, but never having been to the Channel Islands, Lawrence drew on his own recent visit to the Hebrides for his descriptions.

'Man Who Was Through with the World, The' (1927) in *The Princess*. In her foreword to *The First Lady Chatterley* Frieda describes Lawrence going up into the woods above the Villa Mirenda to write: 'Not far from where he sat under a large umbrella pine was the sanctuary of San Eusebio. He had a large slab of stone for his bed in a small cave and a smaller slab of stone for his table and a nice little spring nearby.' This local hermit, San Eusebio, may have suggested to Lawrence his Henry the Hermit. Though Scandicci would fit for the village Henry visits, and Florence for the town, Lawrence makes no attempt to create a specific locale.

'Mercury' (1926) in *The Princess*. This short story was written in Baden-Baden. Sagar notes in *D. H. Lawrence: A Calendar of his Works* that Lawrence reported 'a storm and torrents of rain' at the time when he was writing the story.

'Miner at Home, The' (1912) in *The Mortal Coil*. Eastwood and Shipley appear as place names without any disguise in a brief picture of the domestic impact of the strikes.

'Modern Lover, A' (1909) in *The Woman Who Rode Away*. In this short story the man is pictured as walking across the fields past Coney Grey Farm to the Haggs (Crossleigh Bank). He returns via Moorgreen Reservoir (Nethermere).

'Monkey Nuts' (1919) in *England, My England*. This short story is set in Berkshire. It was written at Hermitage, and the reference to the Bath Road, six miles away at Belbury (Newbury), confirms it was set there.

'Mortal Coil, The' (1913) in *The Mortal Coil*. An account based on an experience of Frieda's father in Germany. This contains little feeling of place, though place names and atmosphere indicate Germany.

'Mother and Daughter' (1928) in *The Princess*. This short story is set in 'one of the old Bloomsbury squares'. But, as with many of Lawrence's interior settings, it is a rather conventional reflection of the characters.

'New Eve and Old Adam' (1913) in *The Mortal Coil*. London is the ostensible setting for an autobiographical experience rendered as fiction.

'None of That' (1927) in *The Woman Who Rode Away*. This short story describes, from Venice, a series of events that occurred in Mexico. There is little sense of either place.

'Odour of Chrysanthemums' (1909) in *The Prussian Officer*. This short story is set very specifically in Brinsley. There is no attempt to disguise place names, and Selston, Underwood and Brinsley are in the correct geographical relationship to each other. The cottage appears to be the one Lawrence's widowed aunt, Mary Ellen Lawrence, lived in.

'Old Adam, The' (1911) in *The Mortal Coil*. This short story was written at 12 Colworth Road, Croydon, and the references to the child, the railway and the garden suggest that it is set there although there is little evocation of place.

'Once' (1912) in *The Mortal Coil*. This short story includes a description of a meeting that occurred on the Brühler Terrasse in Dresden. But the setting is a bedroom.

'Overtone, The' (1924) in *The Princess*. The red cliffs and the reference to the River Soar suggest the area around Quorn to be the setting of the memories in this short story. The bungalow is reminiscent of Winifred Inger's near Sawley.

'Prelude, A' (1907) in *The Mortal Coil*. This short story is set in Haggs Farm and Felley Mill (Ramsey Mill).

'Primrose Path, The' (1913) in *England, My England*. Nottingham topography is very precisely followed in this short story. Victoria Station was opposite Trinity Church. The journey past the cemetery and along the boulevard would take them via Bobbers Mill (Rollin's Mill) and Cinderhill towards Eastwood and back.

'Princess, The' (1924) in *The Princess*. The story describes a ride Lawrence himself took into the mountains beyond the Lawrence ranch at San Cristobal, near Taos, New Mexico. The lake is Columbine Lake. The ride is described in detail by Brett in *Lawrence and Brett*, 149–52. In reality, however, there is no Indian pueblo at San Cristobal, and Frijoles is the name of a river in Panama.

'Prussian Officer, The' (1913) in *The Prussian Officer* (originally 'Honour and Arms'). This short story was written at Irschenhausen. The detail and vividness suggest that Lawrence had a particular place in Bavaria in mind.

'Rawdon's Roof' (1927) in *Love Among the Haystacks*. No suggestion of place is to be found in this short story, where events occur within the house.

'Rex' (1919 or 1920) in *The Mortal Coil*. This autobiographical fragment refers to The Lord Belper, Bluebell Hill, Sneinton as The Good Omen. The 'entry' suggests the Walker Street house.

'Rocking Horse Winner, The' (1926) in *Love Among the Haystacks*. The setting of this short story is unidentifiable – 'a pleasant house, with a garden'.

'Samson and Delilah' (1916) in *England, My England*. This is the only short story set in Cornwall. Lawrence refers to Penzance and St Just-in-Penwith, and indirectly to the Botallack mines north of St Just. He also refers to the Longships Lighthouse.

'Second Best' (1911) in *The Prussian Officer*. 'Ollerton Feast' sets the scene of this short story in Nottinghamshire. It seems fairly certain that it is the area around Felley stretching up towards Bagthorpe Common.

'Shades of Spring' (1911–13) in *The Prussian Officer* (originally 'The Dead Rose'). This short story describes the journey from Eastwood to the Haggs very often taken by Lawrence in life. The forge, the trees appear to offer precise description. 'Willey-Water Farm' is The Haggs, 'The House' is Lamb Close.

'Shadow in the Rose Garden, The' (1908) in *The Prussian Officer* (originally 'The Vicar's Garden'). Jessie Chambers suggested that the garden described in this short story was one they visited at Robin Hood's Bay.

'Sick Collier, A' (1912) in *The Prussian Officer*. Scargill Street was one of the Squares in Eastwood. Like the Primitive Methodist Chapel it is now demolished. The Meadows is a district of Nottingham.

'Smile' (1925) in *The Woman Who Rode Away*. France and Italy are noted in the course of a journey to a nunnery where one nun is connected with Liguria and the Etruscans.

'Strike Pay' (1912) in *The Woman Who Rode Away*. This short story gives an accurate description of the now-demolished Primitive Methodist Chapel and the square of miners' dwellings including Scargill Street and Queen Street in Eastwood (Bestwood). 'The large natural reservoir' is Moorgreen Reservoir. The journey to Nottingham is along the Nuthall Road (here spelt Nuttall) through Bulwell.

'Sun' (1925) in *The Princess*. This story was suggested to Lawrence by Rina Secker and her little boy of twenty months, Adrian, sunbathing in the lemon groves at Spotorno below the Villa Bernarda. However, Lawrence transferred the setting to the garden of the Fontana Vecchia at Taormina in Sicily.

'Thimble, The' (1915) in *The Mortal Coil*. Indications of place in this short story – 'a castle in Scotland', 'a flat in Mayfair – are so slight that they underline Lawrence's preoccupation with other-worldliness at this time.

'Things' (1927) in *The Princess*. Paris, Florence and Cleveland are used as symbols of a kind of life rather than as places worthy of description.

'Thorn in the Flesh, The' (1913) in *The Prussian Officer* (originally 'Vin Ordinaire'). Harry T. Moore suggests that this story is set in Frieda's home in Metz, which Frieda herself described as 'a small castle ... called Rashowa'.

'Tickets Please' (1918) in *England, My England* (originally 'John Thomas'). The opening paragraphs of this short story convey the atmosphere of the villages north of Nottingham and around Eastwood (Bestwood). The first tram from Nottingham to Ripley via Eastwood ran in 1913.

'Two Blue Birds' (1926) in *The Woman Who Rode Away*. There is no clear definition of place in this satirical account of the Compton Mackenzie ménage.

'Undying Man, The' (1927) in *The Princess*. This unfinished short story is set in Spain, which Lawrence had not then visited. Its plot was suggested by Koteliansky, and it forms one of the few examples of writing not conveying direct experience in all Lawrence's works.

'White Stocking, The' (1907) in *The Prussian Officer*. The Park gates, the Castle Rock and the boulevard below indicate that Sam Adam's house in this short story was in The Park – a wealthy residential area of Edwardian Nottingham. Lace was a major industry in the city.

'Wilful Woman, The' (1922) in *The Princess*. This was the first chapter of a projected novel on Mabel Luhan. The landmarks – New York, Kansas City, La Junta, the desert, Trinidad, Lamy – indicate a journey Lawrence had not then taken. He arrived at Lamy from the west. There is some evocation of 'the high desert above the gorges of the cañons'.

'Wintry Peacock, The' (1919) in *England, My England*. The external evidence of a letter to Katherine Mansfield suggests that this short story describes the country around Middleton. Griff Low is an imaginary name.

'Witch à la Mode, The' (1911) in *The Mortal Coil*. The references to East and West Croydon, Ewell and Purley set this short story in South London, but the scenes are mainly interior.

'Woman Who Rode Away, The' (1924) in *The Woman Who Rode Away*. This short story is set in the mountains near Torreon in Central Mexico and a silver mine near Navojoa.

'You Touched Me' (1919) in *England, My England.* This short story is set in the Mellors' house in Lynn Croft, Eastwood. It was known as The Pottery House, and the pottery kilns were in the fields behind.

All the dates given are the earliest ones on which the above stories were mentioned. They are taken from Keith Sagar, *D. H. Lawrence: A Calendar of His Works.*

There are several interesting conclusions to be drawn from this analysis of the short stories.

First, it illustrates Lawrence's early and total abandonment of any attempt to write of a period other than his own, except in terms of fable or myth.

Second, it shows his movement from precise concrete description of actual places to accounts of vague generalised backgrounds sometimes combining features from several localities. From 1925 onwards the diminishing importance of pictorial description in the stories can perhaps be correlated with Lawrence's increasing concentration on painting as a means of expression.

Third, it reveals how much he relied on recent direct experience rather than memory in setting his scenes. Once he had left a particular setting he tended to forget about it (at least for fictional purposes). His imagination needed the stimulation of new scenes.

Lastly, as one might expect, the later stories, as his fatal illness gained on him, move from descriptions of the real world to a visionary one. Their tone and setting owe much to the Bible.

PLACE IN THE NOVELS

Aaron's Rod. See Map 12

Aaron Sisson was the last man on the little black railway line climbing the hill home from work.

He strode over a stile, crossed the fields, strode another stile, and was in the long road of colliers' dwellings. Just across was his own house: he had built it himself. He went through the little gate, up past the side of the house to the back.

This quotation describes Aaron's journey from the mineral railway up to the house, 99 Lynn Croft, which has been identified as his home. From there it is not difficult to trace his journey along the main street to the market place and down to the pub. Cocker House and Cocker House Road become Shottle House and Shottle House Road in the book. Plumptree Colliery is renamed New Brunswick Colliery, and the Thorn Tree Inn, The Royal Oak. All this is now demolished, but the map illustrates the precision of this description:

Shottle House stood two hundred yards beyond New Brunswick Colliery. The colliery was embedded in a plantation, whence its burning pit-hill glowed, fumed and stank sulphur . . . Shottle House was a pleasant square house, rather old, with shrubberies and lawns. It ended the lane in a dead end.

(I am indebted to the D. H. Lawrence Society for this information.)

Aaron's journey from London to Florence mirrors that taken by Lawrence in November 1919. He renamed Turin 'Novara' in the book.

Boy in the Bush, The. See Map 1

The setting is Western Australia, inland from Freemantle. Mollie Skinner was largely responsible for the background to this work.

Kangaroo. See Map 1

The first four chapters are set in Sydney, the rest in Thirroul (Mullumbimby). Chapter 12, 'The Nightmare', contains a flashback to Cornwall.

Lady Chatterley's Lover. See Map 19

The main inspiration for the setting of the third version of *Lady Chatterley's Lover* seems to have been Renishaw, the home of the Sitwells, which Lawrence calls Wragby and describes as

a long low old house in brown stone, begun about the middle of the eighteenth century, and added on to, till it was a warren of a place without much distinction. It stood on an eminence in a rather fine old park of oak trees, but, alas, one could see in the near distance the chimney of Tevershall pit, with its clouds of steam and smoke, and on the damp hazy distance of the hill the raw straggle of Tevershall village, a village which began almost at the park gates.

It is not difficult to trace the journey taken by Connie Chatterley in the book. She sets out from Wragby (Renishaw), travels south with Warsop Castle (Bolsover Castle) 'on her left, on a height above the rolling land', passes through Stacks Gate (Staveley) and sees in front of her 'hanging on the brow of the skyline Chadwick Hall' (Hardwick Hall), 'more window than wall, one of the most famous Elizabethan houses'. From there she arrived in Chesterfield (Uthwaite) with its 'pathetic little corkscrew spire of the church' and returned home conscious of Fritchley (Sutton Scarsdale, a famous Georgian mansion restored in 1784), to call at Shipley (a combination of Barlborough Hall, famous among other things for its corridors which Lawrence describes as 'ample and lovely, softly curved and full of life', and Rufford Abbey).

But, as in other books which he rewrote, traces of other versions remain in the final one. The second version of *Lady Chatterley's Lover* was set in Eastwood. The final version contains an interesting adaptation from this where all the pubs in Tevershall (Eckington are given Eastwood names and characteristics. Thus 'The Sun' 'that called itself an inn, not a pub, and where the commercial travellers stayed' must have been based on 'The Sun' at Eastwood. 'St John's Well', although given a name appropriate to the Dukeries area around Renishaw, has the appearance of Robin Hood's Well at Eastwood. And although Hucknall Torkard disappears from the final book it is interesting to see Lawrence's fictitious name for Lambclose House in *The Rainbow* reappear in the title 'the Duchess of Shortlands' in *Lady Chatterley's Lover*.

Lost Girl, The. See Map 12

Eastwood (Woodhouse) and Langley Mill (Lumley) are the setting for the early part of the book. Individual places are indicated on the map.

After stays in Doncaster, Lancaster and Scarborough, Alvina Houghton, the heroine, is described as travelling via Folkestone, Paris and Chambéry towards Turin, Genoa, Pisa, Rome and Naples, to Picinisco (Pescocalascio). See Map 4. This is a journey Lawrence took in 1919.

Mr Noon. See Map 9

Eakrast is identified as Eakring by J. T. Boulton in *Lawrence in Love*.

Plumed Serpent, The. See Map 8

The opening of the book is set in Mexico City.

Ross Parmenter notes that 'Lawrence borrowed the name of the neighbouring lake, Sayula as an alternative to Chapala, but he never went to Lake Sayula. Where he and Kate got off the train was at Ocotlan (Ixtlahuacan) ... From there he and Kate made a rowboat trip to Lake Chapala to El Fuerte (Orilla), and it was at El Fuerte that Kate and/or Lawrence took the launch'. He also notes that Coyoacan (Tlacolula), a little south of Mexico City, is the district where Kate met Mrs Morris.

Rainbow, The. See Map 13

Cossall (Cossethay) is the main setting for *The Rainbow*. Marsh Farm (now demolished) lay at the foot of the hill at Cossall Marsh, close to the colliery although hidden from it by the aquaduct. The bursting of the embankment caused the flood in which Tom drowned. The cottage next to the church (Church Cottage) was the home of Louise Burrows, to whom Lawrence was engaged. It is the home of Will and Anna Brangwen in the book. St Catherine's Church differs in certain details from the church Lawrence describes, e.g. it has never had a clock. The Vicarage in which Lydia Lensky lived is marked on the map but is now a private house.

Although the detailed description of Church Cottage makes it clearly the house Lawrence had in mind, he appears to have moved it closer to the church in the book.

St Mawr. See Maps 9 and 14

The early part of the book is set in London. It then moves to 'a tall red-brick Georgian house looking straight onto the churchyard, and the dark, looming big church' . . . 'a mile and a half from the railway station, ten miles from Shrewsbury'. This is Pontesbury in Shropshire, which Lawrence visited in 1924.

The expedition from Pontesbury was to the Wrekin. Lawrence renamed Hell Gate (the Devil's Chair) and Heaven Gate (the Angel's Chair) but retained the name Needle's Eye for local landmarks. The end of the book contains an accurate description of the Kiowa ranch at San Cristobal, near Taos, New Mexico.

Sons and Lovers. See Maps 10, 15, 11, 18 and 19

Map 10 illustrates the six mines 'like black studs on the countryside' referred to at the beginning of the book: Watnall Colliery (Nuttall), High Park Colliery (Spinney Park), Moorgreen Colliery (Minton), Bunker's Hill, Brinsley Colliery (Beggarlee), and Selston Colliery (Selby). It gives the wider neighbourhood of Eastwood.

Map 15 emphasises the strongly autobiographical nature of the work in which Eastwood (Bestwood) and the Lawrence homes − 28 Garden Road (the house in the Breach), the third house in Walker Street (Scargill Street with its ash tree outside) and 97 Lynn Croft − are the homes of Paul Morel in the book. Other landmarks include the pub The Three Tuns (The Moon and Stars) near the Wakes ground at Hilltop, and other pubs visited by Morel, the cricket ground where Mrs Morel took her young son Paul, Beauvale Brook (Beggarlee Brook), the Coal Board Offices visited by the boy Paul, the Mechanics' Institute, and the Congregational Chapel, which was the centre of his and Miriam's social life, and the station Kimberley (Keston – a Croydon name), from which Mrs Morel made her journeys to visit her sick husband. The map also illustrates the situation of the market, which Lawrence described as being 'where four roads from Nottingham and Derby, Ilkeston and Mansfield meet'.

Lawrence's Birthplace Museum and St Mary's Church, where members of his family are buried, are also underlined.

Map 11 illustrates the exactness of Lawrence's descriptions in this early work. Note how Lawrence shows Mrs Morel and Paul arriving at the station in Station Street, passing Carrington Street and St Peter's Church 'to a narrow street that led to the Castle'. The Castle does house an art collection, and is in fact a museum. The Park alongside it is an estate of Victorian houses occupied at that time by the wealthy Nottingham families. The Meadows, Sneinton and the places visited with Clara Dawes can be traced on this map.

Map 18 illustrates the countryside around Haggs Farm (Willey Farm). Map 19 gives an opportunity to see the extent of Lawrence's and Morel's expeditions to the Hemlock Stone just off the map to the south, and to Wingfield Manor via Langley Mill (Sethley Bridge) and Alfreton, returning through Crich and Whatstandwell to Ambergate Station.

Trespasser, The. See Map 9

This novel is set on the Isle of Wight, which Lawrence visited in 1909.

Virgin and the Gipsy, The. See Map 19

No doubt the whole setting is a combination of Lawrence's memories of his stay in Middleton-by-Wirksworth from May 1918 to February 1919 and his travels through the Derbyshire countryside with Ada Lawrence in October 1925. He uses obvious features of this countryside, the numerous quarries, the presence of old Roman mine workings, and the deep-wooded valleys with swiftly-flowing streams, as integral parts of the story.

It is possible that he has Cromford in mind when he describes Papplewick. Lawrence describes 'black industrialisation' (possibly of Sheffield) twenty miles to the north. The town has a stone bridge, and the Arkwright mills are also of stone. St Mary's Cromford is situated by a swiftly-flowing river, although it is without a rectory. Willersley Castle just beside it has many of the features of the setting described by Lawrence, although the house itself sounds rather like the home of the Weekleys, No. 32 Victoria Crescent, Mapperley Park, Nottingham.

While this attribution is speculative it is clear that the young people on their journey travelled from Chatsworth, 'the huge ducal house', 'with its balustraded bridge', past the church, through the gates and over the bridge in the direction of Bonsall Head. Bonsall (Bolehill) is alone among the villages in the area in the combination of the cross and turn in the road. Ada Lawrence identified Woodlinkin as Wirksworth, but Lawrence's account of the long straggling village could apply to almost any place in the area. Amberdale, she suggests, was probably Ambergate. The discussion on returning via Codnor top road or Ashbourne suggests rather long but not impossible alternative journeys.

Papplewick in Nottinghamshire no doubt gave Lawrence the name. Its setting is very different from the one here described.

White Peacock, The. See Maps 11, 16, 17 and 18

Map 11 shows how accurately Lawrence described Nottingham. If one reads the account of George Saxton's journey into Nottingham with his bride one finds that the whole account is studded with references to buildings of local note: 'The square tower of my old school [the High School] and the sharp proud spire of St Andrews'; 'Basford, where the swollen gasometers stood like toadstools'; the Castle with below it 'the sun sloping over the great river flats'; Colwick Park, the Trent Bridges, the Theatre Royal and the Victoria Hotel. When he wished to refer to the registry office in Basford he even commissioned Jessie Chambers to go and check the accuracy of his description.

Map 16 gives a broad general picture of the area covered in the book. The new Ram Inn stands opposite the old one, which is now a private dwelling. Felley Mill (Strelley Mill) has now been demolished.

Map 17 gives a detailed picture of the area around Annesley Hall. Annesley Hall was at that time owned by the Chaworth-Musters family. Their estate extended south towards the Haggs, where the Chambers were tenant farmers. Professor Chambers described the farm as being 'eaten off' with rabbits. All Saints' Church, then as now a ruin, was the *White Peacock* church. The road alongside it is as exactly described as the church.

The reference to Byron in connection with the Kennels refers to the fact that he courted Mary Chaworth-Musters when he was the very young owner of Newstead Abbey.

Cossethay in *The White Peacock* (see Map 13) is clearly not Cossall, because Cyril and Mrs Beardsall alight from the train there. The almshouse and Yew Cottage (Church Cottage in *The Rainbow*) exist in the real Cossall, which here is merely described as a village two miles from Cossethay.

Map 18 gives a detailed picture of the area around Felley Mill (Strelley Mill) and Beauvale Lodge (Woodside).

Women in Love. See Maps 9 (Quorn), 12, 18 and 19 (Kedleston)

Women in Love, because it was written and rewritten so many times, presents the same difficulty in the identification of places as *Lady Chatterley's Lover*.

It has been suggested that Beldover is Quorn, and certain features and the presence of stretches of water beyond the village make this feasible. It could as easily be Eastwood, where local inhabitants identify the Brangwen home as that occupied formerly by Willy Hopkin, and see in the directions to Somerset Drive given to Gerald Crich the directions to Devonshire Drive in Eastwood. In fact the general layout of the town and the market square with its hosiery factory, public baths and clock tower suggests the Leicestershire area, the presence of colliers the Nottinghamshire. The town seems an amalgam.

It seems obvious that the usual identification of landmarks around Moorgreen Reservoir (Map 18) is correct. Willey Green has certain features of Moorgreen, such as the railway crossing and embankment, although there is no grammar school next to the church there. Such a situation is common in many Midland towns – Ilkeston, Eastwood and Quorn, to name a few, boast schools next to churches.

The identification of Breadalby with Garsington seems to have been based on the recognition of characters and situations rather than geographical factors. Almost certainly Lawrence had Kedleston Hall in mind here. The situation is correct: 'It was a very quiet place, some miles from the high road, back from the Derwent Valley'. He mentions Corinthian pillars, which are a feature of Kedleston. An article in *Country Life* written at the beginning of the century describes the three ponds in terraces descending the valley there. And, perhaps conclusively, Kedleston lies very close to the village of Breadsall. Lawrence can be seen to have transported his recognisable people to a recognisable milieu quite foreign to them.

One is tempted to conjecture that he had done the same in *The Virgin and the Gipsy*, moving the Weekley family and their house in Victoria Crescent, Nottingham to the site of Willersley Castle in Cromford. This would certainly provide all the physical features needed for the flood, in addition to mills and a bridge, both of stone; and by coincidence a reservoir has been built since Lawrence's time which would have been able to cause this in an area that was riddled with old Roman mines.

However, these suppositions are dangerous. All my explorations have suggested that Lawrence invented nothing. There are, however, so many features in common in the Midland towns that it is not always easy to pinpoint precisely the degree of synthesis and the degree of reproduction in his accounts of places.

AN INTRODUCTION TO THE MAPS

The maps are presented with a twofold purpose – to show the extent of D. H. Lawrence's travels and to indicate as clearly as possible the precise use he made of his experiences of various places throughout the world in his writings.

The first eight maps are concerned with his journeys beyond England. They illustrate his own search for a congenial resting place, cover the areas described in his travel writings, indicate the settings of his foreign short stories, and provide some information on the background of *The Plumed Serpent, Kangaroo* and the latter part of *St Mawr*.

It has seemed practical to provide the information on Lawrence's use of place in his novels by means of the last twelve maps, rather than by lengthy descriptions. A correlation of the list of settings for the short stories with the maps will show his use of the area around Eastwood in his local short stories. A similar correlation of the maps with the text of the novels will show the actual journeys taken in *The White Peacock* and *Sons and Lovers* in Nottingham as well as the wider excursions to Lincolnshire and Derbyshire described in those books.

As the maps show, places in the early novels and in the hastily-written novels – *Aaron's Rod* and *The Lost Girl* – are very clearly identifiable. He only sought to disguise them by name, and the physical features are so clearly represented that recognition of them is straightforward. As Lawrence's writing, developed, particularly in the works which he wrote and rewrote, identification is not so easy.

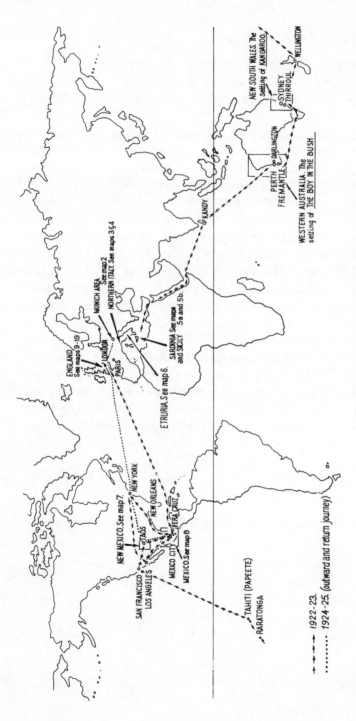

1 The Travels of D.H. Lawrence

Lawrence's visits to the Munich, Lake Garda, Lerici area before 1914, his journey from Taormina, via Kandy, Colombo, Fremantle, Darlington, Sydney, Thirroul, Wellington NZ, Raratonga, Tahiti to San Francisco, and Taos on to Mexico City, Chapala and on via New Orleans to New York back via Buffalo to Los Angeles then down the west coast of Mexico to Guadalajara, Mexico City, Vera Cruz to London in 1922–3, and his journey of 1924–5 from London to Taos via New York, on to Mexico City and Oaxaca, back to Questa, New Mexico then via Denver and New York to Southampton.

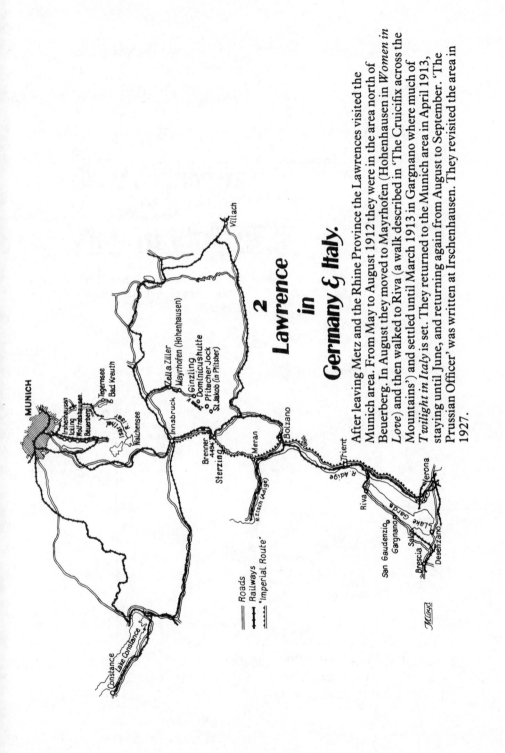

2

Lawrence
in
Germany & Italy.

After leaving Metz and the Rhine Province the Lawrences visited the Munich area. From May to August 1912 they were in the area north of Beuerberg. In August they moved to Mayrhofen (Hohenhausen in *Women in Love*) and then walked to Riva (a walk described in 'The Crucifix across the Mountains') and settled until March 1913 in Gargnano where much of *Twilight in Italy* is set. They returned to the Munich area in April 1913, staying until June, and returning again from August to September. 'The Prussian Officer' was written at Irschenhausen. They revisited the area in 1927.

Roads
Railways
'Imperial Route'

MUNICH

Constance
Lake Constance

Irschenhausen
Icking
Wolfratshausen
Beuerberg
Tegernsee
Bad Kreuth
Isar
Kochelsee
Walchensee

Villach

Zell a Ziller
Mayrhofen (Hohenhausen)
Ginzling
Dominicushütte
Pfitscher-Jock
St Jakob (in Pfitsch)

Innsbruck

Brenner
4494
Sterzing

Meran

Bolzano

Rëtsch (Adige)

Trient

R. Adige

Riva

Verona

Lake Garda

San Gaudenzio
Gargnano
Salo
Brescia
Desenzano

M Lloyd

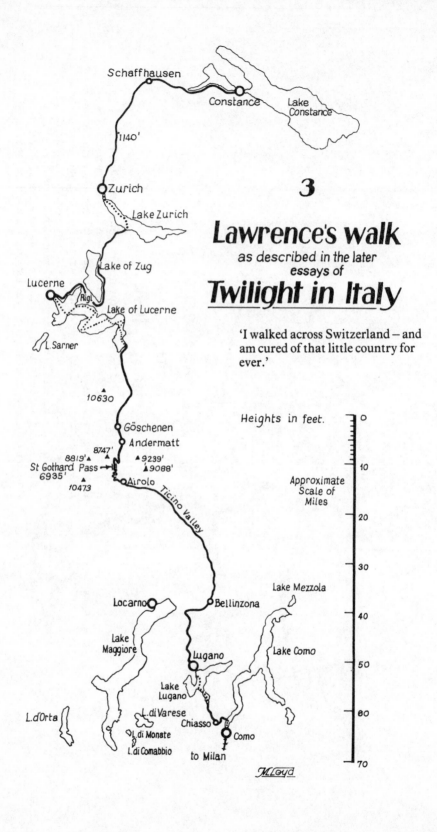

Schaffhausen

Constance

Lake Constance

1140'

Zurich

Lake Zurich

3

Lawrence's walk
as described in the later
essays of
Twilight in Italy

'I walked across Switzerland – and
am cured of that little country for
ever.'

Lake of Zug

Lucerne

Rigi

Lake of Lucerne

L. Sarner

▲ 10630

Göschenen

Andermatt

8819'▲ 8747'▲ ▲9239'
St Gothard Pass → ▲9088'
6935' ▲ 10473

Airolo

Ticino Valley

Heights in feet.

0

10

Approximate
Scale of
Miles

20

30

Lake Mezzola

Locarno

Bellinzona

40

Lake
Maggiore

Lugano

Lake Como

50

Lake
Lugano

L. di Varese

60

L.d'Orta

L. di Monate Chiasso Como

L. di Comabbio

to Milan

70

M. Loyd

4
The Lawrences in Italy

J. Lloyd

The Lawrences lived in Lerici from September 1913 to June 1914 and at Spotorno from November 1925 to April 1926. They travelled from London to Picinisco in November 1919. Aaron's journey in *Aaron's Rod* paralleled theirs as far as Florence, Alvina's journey in *The Lost Girl* coincided with theirs from Rome to Picinisco although the earlier part of it seems to have been via Genoa and Pisa.

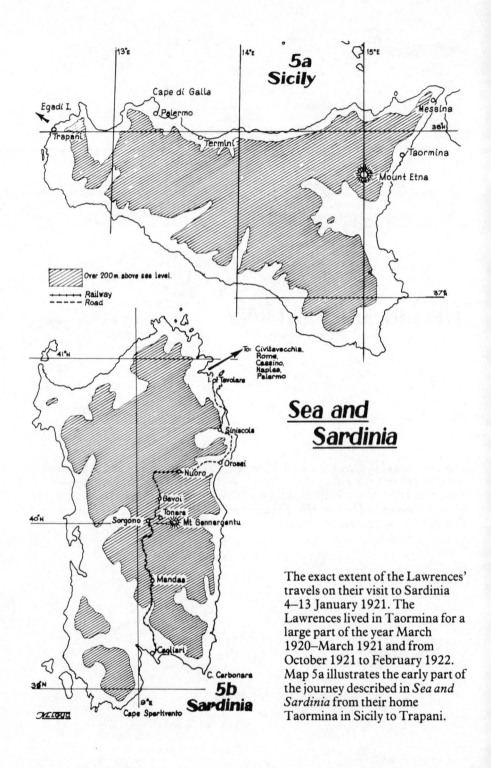

5a Sicily

Egadi I.

Cape di Galla

Palermo

Trapani

Termini

Messina

36°N

Taormina

Mount Etna

37°N

Over 200 m. above sea level.

+++++ Railway
----- Road

41°N

To: Civitavecchia,
Rome,
Cassino,
Naples,
Palermo

I. of Tavolara

Siniscola

Orosei

Nuoro

Sea and Sardinia

Gavoi

Tonara

Sorgono

Mt Gennargentu

40°N

Mandas

Cagliari

C. Carbonara

5b Sardinia

9°E

Cape Spartivento

The exact extent of the Lawrences'
travels on their visit to Sardinia
4–13 January 1921. The
Lawrences lived in Taormina for a
large part of the year March
1920–March 1921 and from
October 1921 to February 1922.
Map 5a illustrates the early part of
the journey described in *Sea and
Sardinia* from their home
Taormina in Sicily to Trapani.

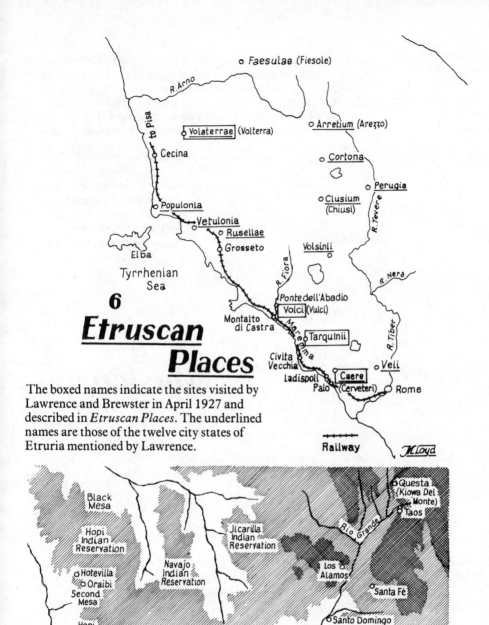

6
Etruscan
Places

o Faesulae (Fiesole)

R.Arno

to Pisa

□Volaterrae (Volterra)

o Arretium (Arezzo)

o Cecina

o Cortona

o Perugia

o Clusium (Chiusi)

R.Tevere

o Populonia

→Vetulonia

o Rusellae

o Grosseto

Elba

Tyrrhenian Sea

Volsinii

R.Fiora

R.Nera

Ponte dell'Abadio
Volci (Vulci)

Maremma

R.Tiber

Montalto di Castra

Tarquinii

Civita Vecchia

o Veii

Ladispoli
Palo

Caere (Cerveteri)

o Rome

The boxed names indicate the sites visited by Lawrence and Brewster in April 1927 and described in *Etruscan Places*. The underlined names are those of the twelve city states of Etruria mentioned by Lawrence.

+−+−+−+−+
Railway

M.Loyd

Black Mesa

Questa (Kiowa Del Monte)

Taos

Hopi Indian Reservation

Jicarilla Indian Reservation

Rio Grande

Navajo Indian Reservation

o Hotevilla
o Oraibi
Second Mesa

Los Alamos

Santa Fé

Hopi Buffs

o Santo Domingo

El Paso

o Albuquerque

M.Loyd

Over 3000 feet

Over 6000 feet

Over 9000 feet

The Lawrences lived at the Del Monte and Kiowa ranches here. The area provides the setting for 'The Hopi Snake Dance', and 'The Dance of the Sprouting Corn' (Santo Domingo) in *Mornings in Mexico*; *The Princess*; the conclusion of the novel *St Mawr*; various poems and the fragment of the play *Altitude*.

7 New Mexico

The extent of Lawrence's travels in Mexico. He and Frieda were in Oaxaca from December 1924 to February 1925. This provided the settings for the early essays in *Mornings in Mexico*. Mexico City and its suburbs is the setting for the early part of *The Plumed Serpent* and Chapala, where the Lawrences lived May–July 1923, the setting of the later part. The Lawrences' route from Mexico City to Chapala was the same as Kate's in the book. 'The Woman Who Rode Away' is partly set in Navojoa which Lawrence visited with Götzsche in October 1923. (Information for the Huayaphan map from Mr Ross Parmenter.)

from Palm Springs
Mexicali

Taos &
Questa
El Paso

Alamos

Guaymas

Navojoa

San Antonio

8
Mexico

New
Orleans

Laredo

Journey with
Götzsche.

Mazatlán

Tepic

The walk to
Huayaphan (Huayapa)
from *Mornings in Mexico*

Guadalajara

Lake Chapala
(L. Sayula)
Sayula

Ocotlán

Irapuato

El Fuerte

Querétaro

S. Felipe
del Agua

Donasi
S. Luis Beltran
S.A. Huayaphan

Mexico City
Xochimilco
Cuernavaca

Teotihuacán

Puebla

Cholula

Orizaba

Dolores

Tehuacán

Vera
Cruz

El Fort'in

OAXACA

S! Maria
Ixtotel

Oaxaca
Mitla

S! Maria
Tule

M.Loyd

9
D.H.Lawrence's
England

Robin Hood's Bay

Flamborough

Barrow

Blackpool

Prestatyn

Chatsworth
Cromford
Renishaw
Shirebrook
Lincoln
Mablethorpe
Sutton on Sea
Skegness

Middleton
Alfreton
Eakring
Leek
Ripley
Southwell
Eastwood
Nottingham
Cossall
Wrekin
Ilkeston
Pontesbury
Sawley
Quorn
Leicester

Yarmouth

Cambridge

Upper Lydbrook
Forest of Dean

Garsington
Mersea Island

Chesham
Hampstead
Bloomsbury
Pangbourne

Hermitage
Newbury
Ewell
Croydon
Broadstairs
Purley
Otford
Edenbridge

Pulborough

Bournemouth
Brighton
Hove
Littlehampton

Padstow
St Merryn
Shanklin

Longships
Lighthouse
Zennor

Penzance

K.Lloyd

In addition to the places indicated here Lawrence explored Westmorland on a
walking tour just at the outbreak of war in 1914 and visited Scotland in 1926. He
spent a fortnight or less in the places underlined. Other places on the map he was
familiar with because of longer stays or frequent short visits. This map does not show
all the places Lawrence visited but those reflected in his fiction.

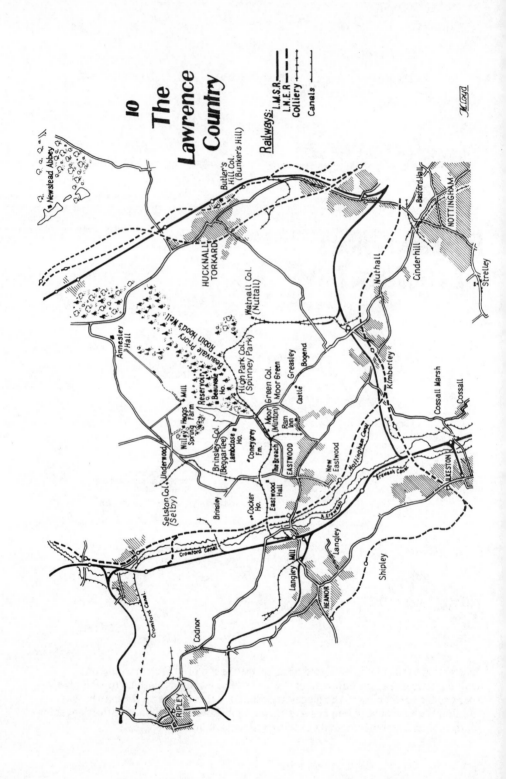

10

**The
Lawrence
Country**

Railways: L.M.S.R. ————
L.N.E.R ————
Colliery ————
Canals ————

Newstead Abbey

Butler's
Hill Col.
(Bunker's Hill)

HUCKNALL
TORKARD

Watnall Col.
(Nuttall)

Nottingham

Bestwood Hall

Nuthall

Cinderhill

NOTTINGHAM

Strelley

Annesley
Hall

Beauvale Priory

ROBIN HOOD'S WELL

High Park Col.
(Spinney Park)

Green Col.
Moor Green

Greasley

Bogend

Kimberley

Reservoir

Beauvale
Ho.

Willey
Spring
Farm

Haggs
Mill

Moor
(Minton)

Castle

Cossall Marsh

Brinsley Col.
(Beggarlee)

Lambclose
Ho.

Coneygrey
Fm.

Ram
Inn

EASTWOOD

Cossall

Selston Col. Underwood
(Selby)

The Breach

New
Eastwood

Nottingham Canal

ILKESTON

Brinsley

Cocker
Ho.

Eastwood
Hall

Erewash

Erewash Canal

Cromford Canal

Langley

Shipley

Codnor

Langley Mill

HEANOR

RIPLEY

Cromford Canal

Eastwood via Cinderhill
Bulwell
Basford

← Nuttall Rd

← Daybrook & Arnold
Arno Vale / app. 2 miles

Mansfield Rd

← Mapperley Plains
& Lambley

Woodborough
Rd
┼─ St Andrew's Church

Nottingham High Sch.
Nottingham Girls' High Sch.
Arboretum

Trinity Church (demolished)

Southwell

OLD
RADFORD

University
College
Theatre Royal
Empire

Bluebell Hill Rd

Victoria Stn (demolished)

SNEINTON
ELEMENTS

Market Place

Cossall

Unitarian Church

THE
PARK

St Peter's Church ⎫ Lace
St Mary's Church ⎬ Market
Hollow Stone ⎦ area
Sneinton Hermitage

Castle &
Castle Rock

Fountain

Station St.

Colwick Road
COLWICK PARK

Midland Stn

CastleGate
(Spaniel Row)
Carrington St
Wilford Rd

Cattle
Market

Derby

LMS

LNE

Trent Bridge

Wilford Toll
Bridge

THE
MEADOWS

R. Trent

Clifton ↓
(Clifton Grove)

II Nottingham

ℳℒoyd

Lawrence was educated at the Boys' High School here 1898–1901 and later attended University College 1906–8. He was employed at Haywood's factory, 9 Castle Gate, which is disguised in *Sons and Lovers* as Jordan's of 21 Spaniel Row. This is the only false name in all Lawrence's writings about the town of Nottingham.

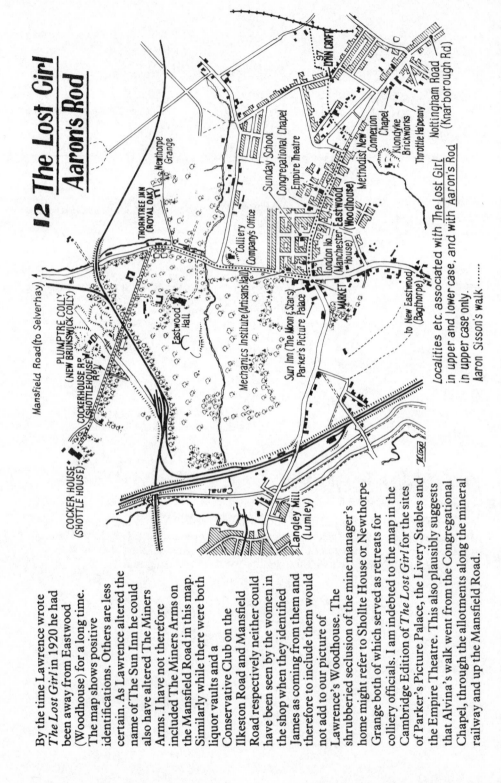

12 The Lost Girl
Aaron's Rod

Mansfield Road (to Selverhay)

PLUMPTRE COLLY
(NEW BRUNSWICK COLLY)

COCKERHOUSE Rd
(SHOTTLEHOUSE Rd)

COCKER HOUSE
(SHOTTLE HOUSE)

THORNTREE INN
(ROYAL OAK)

Newthorpe
Grange

Eastwood
Hall

Canal

Langley Mill
(Lumley)

Colliery
Company's Office

Mechanics Institute (Artisans Hall)

Sun Inn (The Moon Stars)
Parker's Picture Palace

MARKET

London Ho.
(Manchester House)

to New Eastwood
(Bagthorpe)

Sunday School
Congregational Chapel

Empire Theatre

Methodist New
Connexion
Chapel

Eastwood
(Woodhouse)

Klondyke
Brickworks

Throttle Ha'penny

LYNN CROFT

97

Nottingham Road
(Knarborough Rd)

*Localities etc. associated with The Lost Girl
in upper and lower case, and with Aaron's Rod
in upper case only.
Aaron Sisson's walk* ——

By the time Lawrence wrote *The Lost Girl* in 1920 he had been away from Eastwood (Woodhouse) for a long time. The map shows positive identifications. Others are less certain. As Lawrence altered the name of The Sun Inn he could also have altered The Miners Arms. I have not therefore included The Miners Arms on the Mansfield Road in this map. Similarly while there were both liquor vaults and a Conservative Club on the Ilkeston Road and Mansfield Road respectively neither could have been seen by the women in the shop when they identified James as coming from them and therefore to include them would not add to our picture of Lawrence's Woodhouse. The shrubberied seclusion of the mine manager's home might refer to Shollte House or Newthorpe Grange both of which served as retreats for colliery officials. I am indebted to the map in the Cambridge Edition of *The Lost Girl* for the sites of Parker's Picture Palace, the Livery Stables and the Empire Theatre. This also plausibly suggests that Alvina's walk went from the Congregational Chapel, through the allotments along the mineral railway and up the Mansfield Road.

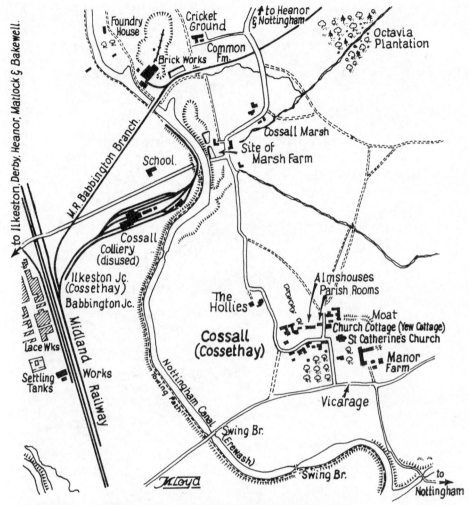

13 The Country of
The Rainbow

Cossall appears briefly as a village two miles from Cossethay (presumably Ilkeston Junction) in *The White Peacock*. The almshouses and Yew Cottage (Church Cottage) feature in this book. It is called Cossethay in *The Rainbow*. The cottage next to the church (Church Cottage) is the one in which the Burrows family lived and is described as the home of Will and Anna Brangwen in the book. Memorials to the Burrows on whom the Brangwens were modelled are in the church.

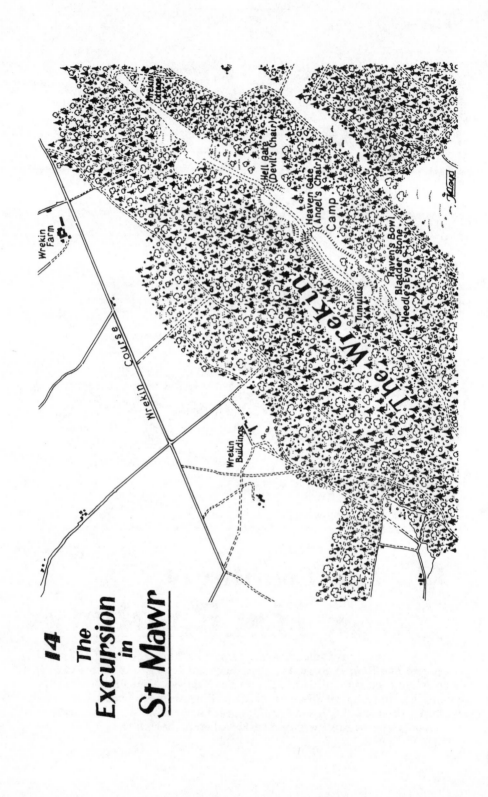

14

The
Excursion
in
St Mawr

Wrekin Farm

Wrekin Course

Wrekin Buildings

The Wrekin

Hell Gate
(Devil's Chair)

Heaven Gate
(Angel's Chair)

Camp

Tumulus

Raven's Bow

Bladder Stone

Needle's Eye

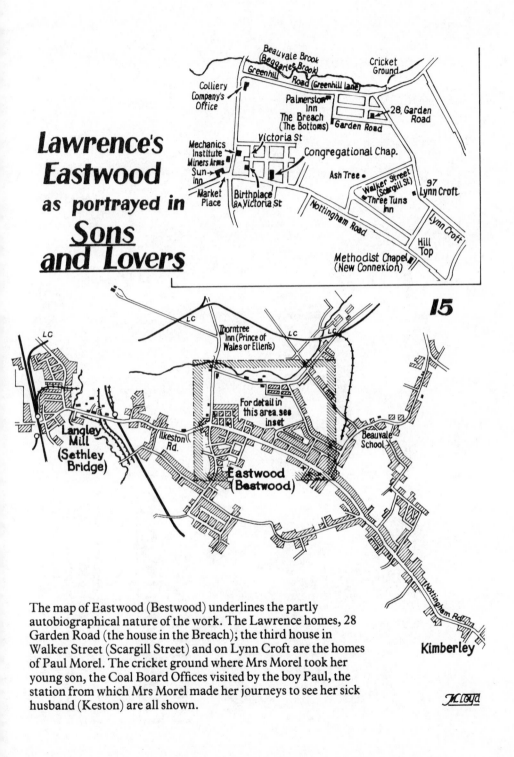

Lawrence's Eastwood as portrayed in Sons and Lovers

Beauvale Brook (Beggarlee Brook)

Greenhill Road (Greenhill Lane)

Cricket Ground

Colliery Company's Office

Palmerston Inn
The Breach (The Bottoms)

28, Garden Road

Garden Road

Mechanics Institute
Miners Arms
Sun Inn

Victoria St

Congregational Chap.

Ash Tree

Walker Street (Scargill St.)

97 Lynn Croft

Three Tuns Inn

Lynn Croft

Market Place

Birthplace 8A Victoria St

Nottingham Road

Hill Top

Methodist Chapel (New Connexion)

15

Thorntree Inn (Prince of Wales or Ellen's)

LC

For detail in this area, see inset

Langley Mill (Sethley Bridge)

Ilkeston Rd.

Beauvale School

Eastwood (Bestwood)

Nottingham Rd.

Kimberley

J. Lloyd

The map of Eastwood (Bestwood) underlines the partly autobiographical nature of the work. The Lawrence homes, 28 Garden Road (the house in the Breach); the third house in Walker Street (Scargill Street) and on Lynn Croft are the homes of Paul Morel. The cricket ground where Mrs Morel took her young son, the Coal Board Offices visited by the boy Paul, the station from which Mrs Morel made her journeys to see her sick husband (Keston) are all shown.

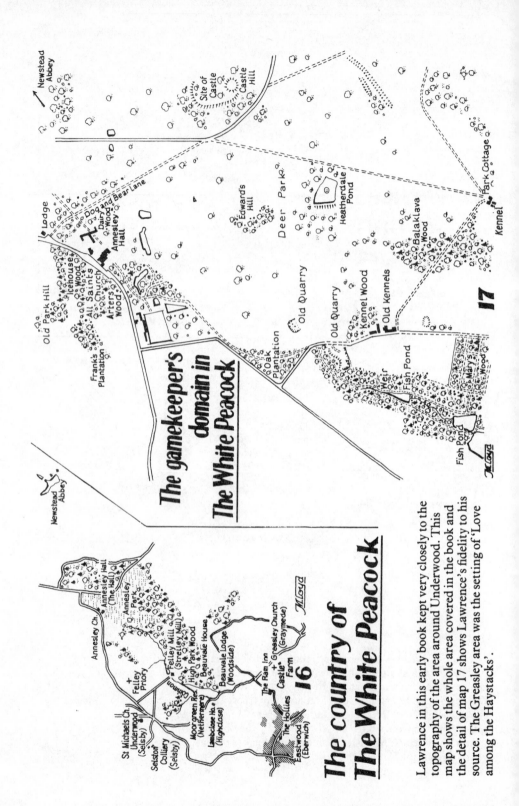

The gamekeeper's domain in The White Peacock

17

The country of The White Peacock

16

Lawrence in this early book kept very closely to the topography of the area around Underwood. This map shows the whole area covered in the book and the detail of map 17 shows Lawrence's fidelity to his source. The Greasley area was the setting of 'Love among the Haystacks'.

Map 17 labels:

Newstead Abbey

Site of Castle
Castle Hill

Old Park Hill
Lodge

Dog and Bear Lane
Dairy Wood
Amesley Hall
Icehouse
All Saints
Arters Wood
Franks Plantation

Edward's Hill

Deer Park
Heatherdale Pond

Oak Plantation
Old Quarry
Old Quarry
Kennel Wood
Old Kennels
Balaklava Wood
Park Cottage
Kennel

Weir
Fish Pond
Fish Pond
Mary's Wood

J.Lloyd

Map 16 labels:

Newstead Abbey

Annesley Ch.
Annesley Hall (The Hall)
Annesley Park

St Michaels Ch. Underwood (Selsby)
Selston Colliery (Selsby)
Felley Priory
Moor green Rd. (Nethermere)
Lambclose Ho. (Highclose)
Common
Felley Mill (Strelley Mill)
High Park Wood
Beauvale House
Beauvale Lodge (Woodside)
The Ram Inn
Greasley Church (Graymede)
Castle (Graymede)
Farm
The Hollies
Eastwood (Eberwich)

J.Lloyd

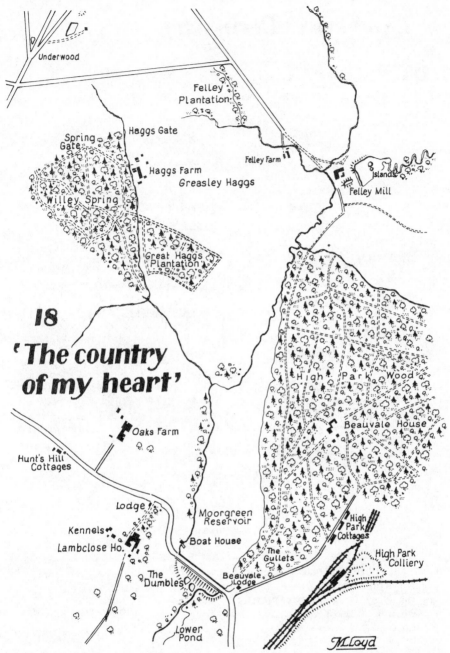

18 'The country of my heart'

Lawrence returned to this area again and again in his works. Lambclose House is 'Highclose' in *The White Peacock*. 'Shortlands' in *Women in Love*. Haggs Farm is 'Willey Farm' in *Sons and Lovers*. Felley Mill is 'Strelley Mill' in *The White Peacock*, 'the mill' in *Women in Love*. Felley Mill pond is the mill pond in *The White Peacock* and in *Women in Love* where its islands are specifically mentioned; 'Willey Water' in *Sons and Lovers*. Moorgreen Reservoir is 'Nethermere' in *The White Peacock*, 'Willey Water' in *Women in Love*. High Park Wood is 'Spinney Park' in *Sons and Lovers*.

Lawrence's Derbyshire

19

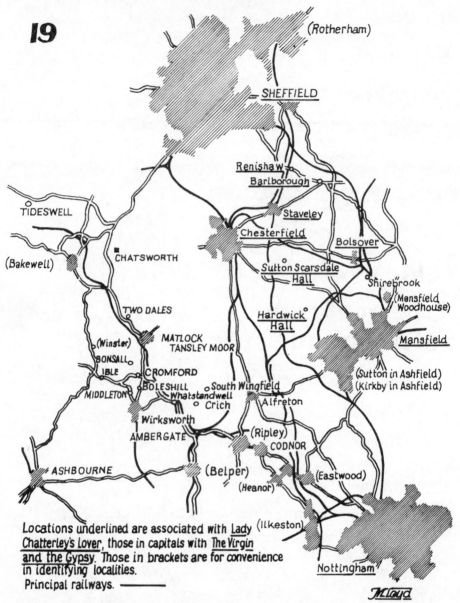

(Rotherham)

SHEFFIELD

Renishaw
Barlborough

TIDESWELL

Staveley

Chesterfield

Bolsover

(Bakewell)

CHATSWORTH

Sutton Scarsdale
Hall

Shirebrook

(Mansfield
Woodhouse)

TWO DALES

Hardwick
Hall

Mansfield

(Winster)

MATLOCK
TANSLEY MOOR

BONSALL
IBLE

CROMFORD

(Sutton in Ashfield)
(Kirkby in Ashfield)

MIDDLETON

BOLESHILL

South Wingfield
Whatstandwell
Crich

Wirksworth

Alfreton

AMBERGATE

(Ripley)

CODNOR

ASHBOURNE

(Belper)

(Eastwood)

(Heanor)

Locations underlined are associated with Lady
Chatterley's Lover, those in capitals with The Virgin
and the Gypsy. Those in brackets are for convenience
in identifying localities.

Principal railways. ———

(Ilkeston)

Nottingham

J. Lloyd

Both these books were written after Lawrence stayed in the Midlands, *The Virgin and the Gipsy* after his visit in October 1925, and *Lady Chatterley's Lover* after his visit in October 1926. They are set in Derbyshire, the first in the area around Wirksworth which was already familiar to Lawrence from his wartime stay there and the second at Renishaw near Shirebrook where Lawrence stayed with the Dax family 2–8 March 1912, when he was writing his 'colliery' novel.

Keith Sagar
and Sylvia Sklar

9

Major productions of Lawrence's plays

The productions discussed in this chapter are as follows:

Key to abbreviations of sources:

Letters *The Letters of D. H. Lawrence,* vol. I, ed. Boulton. Cambridge University Press, 1979.
Moore *The Collected Letters of D. H. Lawrence,* ed. Moore. Heinemann, 1962.
Nehls *D. H. Lawrence: A Composite Biography,* ed. Nehls. Wisconsin University Press, 1957–9.
Frieda *Frieda Lawrence: The Memoirs and Correspondence,* ed. Tedlock. Heinemann, 1961.
Ada *The Early Life of D. H. Lawrence,* by Ada Lawrence and G. Stuart Gelder. Orioli, Florence, 1931.
Delavenay *D. H. Lawrence: L'Homme et la Genèse de son Oeuvre,* by Émile Delavenay. Klincksieck, Paris, 1969.

1   *THE WIDOWING OF MRS HOLROYD*

Altrincham Garrick Society at the Unitarian Schools, Dunham Road, Altrincham. 9–13 March 1920

Cast	Mrs Holroyd	Mrs Matthews
	Blackmore	Mr Warburton
	Jack Holroyd	Master Pownall
	Minnie Holroyd	Miss Nixon
	Holroyd	Mr A. P. Hill
	Grandmother	Miss Bote
	Rigley	Rex Wynn

The Widowing of Mrs Holroyd was Lawrence's second play, written in the autumn of 1910. He sent it to Grace Crawford on 17 November 1910. At his request she forwarded it to Violet Hunt, who liked it. Hueffer then sent it to Harley Granville-Barker, who returned it saying that he had read it with interest but did not want it. Lawrence then sent the play to Edward Garnett, who in turn showed it to Iden Payne and led Lawrence to believe that Payne would put it on: 'It is huge to think of Iden Payne acting me on the stage: you are like a genius of *Arabian Nights*, to get me through. Of course I will alter and improve whatever I can, and Mr. Payne has fullest liberty to do entirely as he pleases with the play – you know that. And of course I don't expect to get money by it. But it's ripping to think of my being acted' (*Letters* I, 384). The project fell through. Garnett kept the ms. for 'nearly two years'. Lawrence sent for it in August 1913 in order to revise it for publication. He wrote to the publisher, Mitchell Kennerley: 'I saw how it needed altering – refining. Particularly I hated it in the last act, where the man and woman wrangled rather shallowly across the dead body of the husband. And it seemed nasty that they should make love where he lay drunk' (Moore, 223). Lawrence made further unsuccessful approaches to theatre people in 1914, 1915 and 1919. The following description is from Catherine Carswell: *The Savage Pilgrimage: a Narrative of D. H. Lawrence* (rev. ed. 1932; rpt. London, 1951), p. 137, pp. 141–2, pp. 144–5.

Later in the same month – February, 1920 – I received from Lawrence the announcement of a forthcoming production at Altrincham near Manchester of his first play [sic], *The Widowing of Mrs Holroyd*. The performance was to be by a company of experienced amateurs, and Lawrence was anxious to know how it went. He wished me, if possible, to see it and to write a notice which would get into print. To this end he insisted upon sending me £5 for my journey to Cheshire and back. But this, happily, I did not need, as I managed to obtain a commission from *The Times*.

... I had ... been to Altrincham to see *Mrs Holroyd*, and I confess that on my way there the undertaking began to assume the nature of a penance. Lawrence had betrayed that he was eager, even nervous, as to the results. "I have a dreadful feeling that it may be a fiasco," he had written. So too had I.

The presentation, however, was creditable, if no more. It compared favourably with the performance given in London by the "300 Club" in December, 1926, which also I saw. To do justice to the Altrincham players and the Altrincham audience, no sniggering was elicited by the scene where the dead miner's body is washed by his women. All the same I felt that in a play so realistically written and produced a body-washing scene was theatrically unacceptable. Either it must be done "off" with only the voices and the footsteps of the women to give it reality, or the stage must be darkened to a firelight glow and the whole production lifted into a plane beyond realism with movements that are classically simplified.

... Lawrence was disappointed by the general indifference to *Mrs Holroyd*, and I doubt not, though he never mentioned it, disappointed in particular by *The Times* notice.

In my anxiety I had made a bad mistake. Instead of keeping myself within 500 words, in which the praise would not have been amenable to scissors, I had run to nearly a thousand words. I was accordingly disgusted to find that in the printed version all my warmest commendations were omitted. What remained was not even good criticism. "... am afraid Mrs. Holroyd was altogether a bit of a bore and that you were miserable. Am sorry," Lawrence wrote.

The notice in *The Times* (12 March, 1920, p. 14) was as follows.

Such amateur companies as the Altrincham Garrick Society do good public service when they have the courage to produce a play like *The Widowing of Mrs Holroyd* by Mr. D. H. Lawrence. Here we have a drama in three acts by a writer of recognized distinction, a characteristically English piece of work – poignant in the extreme, perfectly simple as to situation, couched in the homeliest of dialogue – which on its publication in book form in 1914 was welcomed by all the more thoughtful critics; yet not till this week has there been a chance for author or public to see the play acted. ... [The Altrincham Garrick Society is therefore] equipped to give a straightforward well balanced rendering of any piece within the limited capacity of their stage. And straightforward, well balanced without a forced note – thus quite soberly one may describe a performance that showed up the defects as well as the qualities of Mr. Lawrence's play. Here we have an every-day situation stripped, as only a master can strip it, of all inessentials, developing and coming to a crisis of clear statement by means of every-day action and every-day speech, yet in its simplicity making an intense impression on the mind and the emotions.

Mrs Holroyd, one of the million working women of the North with a passion for all that is gracious and orderly, and – for want of a better word – spiritual, has been for years married to a man with none but crudely sensual desires, a man moreover beneath her in the social scale. She, in her conscious superiority and intolerance, has come to scorn him utterly. He, in his warmer, more confused anger, has been driven to wallow far deeper in the sensual slough than he would have done of his own nature or with a more coaxing mate. To wallow is his only means of pulling her down and heaping insult on her. And between them stand the two children, siding, of course, with the mother, yet seeing more clearly than either parent that she is their father's undoing.

For it is the man, with all his bluster, his trollops and defiance that is crushed in the conflict. He can find no separate existence, while the woman, suffering but unbroken, had decided to go off, her children with her, in the company of a sober and respectable engineer who has offered himself as her lover. It takes the death of the husband in a pit accident, at the very moment when she was wishing aloud that he might die, to show Lizzie Holroyd her own irremediable share in the man's doom. Over the dead body, with his mother's piercing accusations in her ears, she sees how ghastly her failure has been, how ruinous her fine aspirations to the father of her children.

The weakness emerging in the acted play is that we are not given enough knowledge of what Holroyd had meant to his wife in the early days of their marriage. The only clear hint comes too late from the old mother and though Lizzie's earlier autobiographical speech in contradiction rings so false that one suspects it was made false intentionally, this merely confuses the issue by a needless subtlety. It is a pity that the author (abroad just now for his health) could not for himself have seen a performance showing so clearly, here and elsewhere, what alterations are demanded by the action of his fine and stimulating play.

Perhaps Mrs Carswell saw a different performance from the reviewer in the *Altrincham Guardian* on the same date, who castigated the audience:

The Altrincham Garrick Society presented D. H. Lawrence's play on Tuesday night to a crowded but generally unsatisfactory audience. As expected at the time of the performance of 'The Will and the Way', the aspirations of the society are higher than the critical faculty of the followers, who apparently insist on regarding amateur performances as comic, whatever the theme. It cannot be ignorance, because surely after the Sankey Commission on coal mines, the most casual reader of newspapers must know that the life of a collier is a continual conflict with Nature's forces in which Nature is often the victor, and it is just as tragic when the collier is killed in the pit as when a soldier is killed on the battlefield. Yet when the body of Jack Holroyd is brought home and placed on his hearth before a sorrowing mother and weeping wife, the bulk of the audience accepted the situation as funny and utterly destroyed the work of author and players.

There is, however, hope that in due time the correct relation of audience and stage will be established, and then, perhaps, a revival of the play by the society will bring out its merits. Mr. Lawrence makes great tragedy of a sordid theme — the dismalness of life in a small colliery town, where work and drink provide the occupations of the people. Here is a picture that presents an unpleasant commentary on our civilization – a hard working community in which one member is reduced to feeling the warmth of the chimney flue to obtain some pleasure. To such a place marriage brings Mrs. Holroyd, and after thirteen years of the monotony of the life and the drunkenness of her husband, she reacts to the environment, and is prepared to go away with her lover, Blackmore, rather than continue the dull servitude of her existence.

Thus far the story is clear, and the author now uses the long arm of coincidence to kill Holroyd by a "fall of dirt". Tragic phrase – as full of death and terror as "over the top". After wishing for her husband's death, Fate takes her at her word, and removes him from her path, but we are left in doubt as to whether she accepts her freedom or not. Presumably she sees those virtues of the dead man to which she was blind while he was alive, and remains true to his idealized memory. The play is badly contructed as drama, the act endings being weak and the finale inconclusive. Nevertheless, the cast did their best, and often succeeded in rising to great heights of pathos, but never quite achieved tragedy. As a picture of existence in a small industrial town it was revealing and horrible. The brutality of Holroyd, the quiet steadiness of Blackmore, and the harrowing grief of the grandmother, for the fifth time mourning the loss of a son in the pit, were excellently played by Mr. A. P. Hill, Mr. Warburton and Miss Bote respectively. Rex Wynn's Rigley was a cameo of workmates' sympathy. "For four years we worked in th' same stall." Behind the words the picture that tomorrow it might be his turn. This scene was well done, and the shy inarticulateness of the body-bearers was well expressed by the fingering of the cape. Conscious of death in a most awful form, against it daily, in the face of the grim tragedy of their lives, they respectfully offered the sympathy of silence. The two children of Master Pownall and Miss Nixon were given without any trace of gaucherie or shyness, and the manipulation of the slab of bread and butter by the young Jack showed a sense of the stage not often possessed by many of mature years. Good, too, was the characterization of the two women of the town, typical of their sort, free, easy and generous. As for the title part, Mrs. Matthews is too good an actress to be flattered, and it is not adverse criticism to say that in this part she was more harrowing than tragic, more pathetic than strong. It may have been the disturbing factor of the audience, but the sublime height was just not reached. Why, it is hard to say with certainty, for the cast was good, the staging and production good and deserved a far better and more understanding audience. (F.E.D.)

2   THE WIDOWING OF MRS HOLROYD

Producer: Esmé Percy. The amalgamated 300 Club and Stage Society at the Kingsway Theatre, London. 12, 13 and 19 December 1926

Cast		
	Mrs Holroyd	Marda Vanne
	Blackmore	Colin Keith-Johnston
	Jack Holroyd	Peter Earle
	Minnie Holroyd	Helen Moore
	Clara	Dorice Fordred
	Laura	Margaret Cockrane
	Holroyd	Oliver Crombie
	Grandmother	Inez Bensusan
	Rigley	James Whale
	Manager	Charles Sewell
	First miner	James Trevor
	Second miner	Cyril Gaye

Lawrence was again in Italy when the next production of one of his plays took place, but he begged his friends to send him reports of it. On 13 December Rolf Gardiner wrote to him:

> I have just come back from seeing *Mrs Holroyd*. It was a very good performance and Esmé Percy had produced it in the right way. Mrs. Holroyd herself was perfect, and Blackmore and the children and all the subsidiary characters, quite splendid. But the man who played Holroyd wasn't fine or big enough, I thought; not that touch of fire and physical splendour that I feel was the hidden ore in the body of him as you meant him perhaps. The atmosphere was right and you were in the play right through; only of course they couldn't talk the Derbyshire vernacular. Bernard Shaw, who was there, said the dialogue was the most magnificent he had ever heard, and his own stuff was 'The Barber of Fleet Street' in comparison! The actors loved the play; one felt that. The bulk of the audience? I can't tell. But anyway the audiences at these shows are mostly bloody. (Nehls 3, 121)

Esmé Percy later remembered Shaw's words rather differently: 'Compared with that, my prose is machine-made lace. You can hear the typewriter in it' (John O'London, 7 February 1947). Shaw himself wrote: 'In my ignorance, I attached no importance to Lawrence until one afternoon at the Stage Society, when I saw a play by him which rushed through in such a torrent of profuse yet vividly effective dialogue, making my own seem archaic in comparison, that I was strongly interested technically' (*Time and Tide*, 6 August 1932). Lawrence was delighted with Shaw's praise: 'He ought to know about dialogue, it's very generous of him' (Freida, *Memoirs*, 147).

On 19 December Lawrence wrote to Esmé Percy:

Dear Mr Percy: Mrs Whitworth sent me photographs and press-cuttings of your production of *The Widowing of Mrs Holroyd*. I dearly wish I could have been there. You seem to have done the thing so well, and the actors, especially Miss Vanne, seem to have put such heart into it. What a bore that the audience and the critics didn't like it! – Anyhow they all say plainly it was my fault – which no doubt it was: for an audience and a critic is always the same perfection unto itself. – Why do they never have the grace to say: But alas, perhaps I was an inefficient listener!

I have to confess that it's years since I read the play myself. I wrote it fifteen years ago, when I was raw. Probably they're quite right when they say that the last act is too much taken up with washing the dead, instead of getting on a bit with life. I bet that would be my present opinion. If you've a moment to spare, tell me, will you, what you think – and what Miss Vanne thinks. – And then, if ever the play were to be done again, I'd re-model the end. I feel I should want to.

I should really be grateful for your criticism, and for that of any actors who wouldn't mind telling me how they feel.

Meanwhile many thanks to you and Miss Vanne and Colin Keith-Johnston and the others who did what they could, and evidently made the play live, even if there was no making it please the audience.

(P.S.) One of my friends thought the grandmother whined too much – and somebody else said Holroyd wasn't big enough, not the type – but people all have their own fancies. (Moore 953–4)

Marda Vanne wrote: 'I felt all the time that I was failing Lawrence. My own country, South Africa, has in it something of the doom-like quality. Perhaps that is why *Mrs Holroyd* is so real to me.' Two days later Lawrence wrote to Gertie Cooper: 'I believe most of the people found it too gloomy. I think, if it were being done again, I should alter the end, and make it more cheerful. Myself, I hate miserable endings, now. But it's so long since I wrote that play' (Ada 148).

One of the cuttings sent to Lawrence was probably from *The Times*, 14 December 1926:

Mr. Lawrence's drawing is deliberately flat. Mrs. Holroyd and her drunken bullying husband; Blackmore, who would be her lover; the miners who bring Holroyd home when he is dead, and old Mrs. Holroyd, who washes the body – all of them are less characters in drama than a group of mournful figures formally composed and little advanced from their colliery background. This curious effect is increased by an economy in the use of dialogue that amounts to a purposeful rejection of colour. Passion is suggested, but is denied its impact. Movement is not the supple, variable movement of life, but the stilled movement of a grotesque decoration. You watch the stage as if what is offered were not a play but a frieze.

In these circumstances, acting too must have a certain unaccustomed rigidity and lowness of tone. Miss Marda Vanne has very skilfully adapted herself to Mr. Lawrence's convention; she suggests, without ever openly expressing it, the conflict that is in Mrs. Holroyd's mind between a love for Holroyd which, though she has reason to hate him, will not finally die, and a love for Blackmore which, though she wishes to love him, refuses to be born. Mr. Colin Keith-Johnston makes Blackmore a kindly and attractive man, but is too open, too easy in his manner to fit perfectly into an elaborate study of imprisoned emotion. The husband (Mr. Oliver Crombie) is little more than a shadow of brutality and violence thrown across the gloomy scene, and the two drunken women whom he brings home with him – one is played with a commendable and sickening accuracy by Miss Dorice Fordred – are a part of his pattern. The only relief is brought by two children, played simply and naturally by Mr. Peter Earle and Miss Helen Moore. All else is stagnant and tormented; it lies like a burden on the mind.

On the same date there was a sensitive review (source uncertain) by Hubert Griffith:

The chief interest about Mr. D. H. Lawrence's sombre play, *The Widowing of Mrs Holroyd* (done by the 300 Club at the week-end) – and of very powerful and unusual interest it is – is that Mr. Lawrence has dared to make his characters uncertain of what they want. They are doubtful. They have, on the top, a current of desire, and they have, underneath, an opposing undercurrent of instinct. It is extremely like life.

Dramatically, of course, this is all wrong. It is outside the tradition. A perfectly simple love story should run perfectly simply. Mrs. Holroyd, the miner's wife, has a brutal husband. He comes back drunk and brings other women into the house. He is a huge, powerful, uncontrolled man, and physically neither she nor the children are safe from him. Moreover, she did not in the first place marry him for love, but to get a home. When the young engineer turns up and falls in love with her, and offers to take not only her but her children out of the country with him, technically speaking (in the playwright's world) she ought not to hesitate, but to leap at the chance.

This is the way things should doubtless go if the play were to be a popular play. But it is not the way that it is seen by Mr. Lawrence. I take it that the real interest for him is the fact that the woman cannot change – is emotionally incapable of changing – her husband as easily as she would change a pair of shoes. At the hour when she has most reason for wishing to get away from the squalid hell of his life with her, the claims of years of intimacy with him keep their hold on her. Her answers to the young engineer are doubtful, contradictory – the sentence used most often in the play is, "I don't know" – and she only yields reluctantly. And then, when the climax is precipitated, and the husband's body is brought back to the cottage after the pit accident, all she can do is to forget about the young engineer altogether and lay the body out with as tender a grief as that of the man's mother.

This is what makes the play into an achievement. It is rough and crude and stark – and Mr. Lawrence has not lessened his difficulties by choosing a set of less than normally articulate characters, who speak in short sentences and never more than half of what they are feeling. But the interest of the play remains and grows.

Ivor Brown reviewed the play in *The Saturday Review*, 18 December:

Mr. Lawrence's early piece was extremely well played at the first joint effort of the Stage Society and Three Hundred Club. The story of Mrs. Holroyd is the story of the other thing followed by love. She, a woman of some refinement, married Holroyd, a hairy ape of the mining village, because she thought the career of wife preferable to that of nursery-governess. He taught her to know better, making her the dulled slave of his kitchen and children and the target of his drunken violence. When he brought his sodden doxies into her kitchen, there was little wonder at her revolt. In the background was young Blackmore, the engineer, a different sort. Never did man proclaim his love so clearly as when he told Mrs. Holroyd that he knew not whether he loved her. An accident in the pit widowed Mrs. Holroyd, but was it despairing jealousy that drove the man to be careless? The shadow of such manslaughter lies across the love of Blackmore and the widow. It is a good situation from which the dramatist has bolted in a way disastrous to his piece. How will the lovers face that shadow, how avoid or dispel it? The question is not answered. The play ends with a lamentation over Holroyd's body, intoned by his wife and mother.

Mr. Esmé Percy's production of this piece was admirable in its force and simplicity. He had a good team. Miss Marda Vanne, as Mrs. Holroyd, made the transition from passivity to passion, from wife to lover, with a complete mastery of the quietist method. This was muted acting at its best, and Mr. Colin Keith-Johnston as Blackmore responded to it well. Another good quietist was Mr. James Whale, also to be complimented on his setting. Mr. Oliver Crombie and Miss Dorice Fordred were the hardworking representatives of noise. In this play Mr. Lawrence has shown himself a tantalizing dramatist. He has also suggested how well he might have written since if he had stuck to the life he knows instead of plunging into the theory which is clamorously acclaimed by people who have been educated beyond their intelligence.

Lawrence must have seen this review, for ten days later he wrote to Maria Huxley: 'They played my *Widowing of Mrs Holroyd* and I believe they hated it, and somebody says I ought to write about the class I come from, I've no right to venture into the Peerage – people educated above their class, etc.!' (Moore, 955). Several other reviews were extremely favourable:

The story in a sense has no end. It is not upon what happens afterwards that the dramatist wished to fix our attention, but upon the nature of the relationship between husband and wife. When she told her lover that she wished her husband was dead, that she was ready in any case to leave him and that she had never loved him, she was speaking the truth. She now feels as if she had killed him, but remorse is not the deepest feeling in her, nor is it either her trust in in the other man whom she will presently live with. As far as her conscious life is concerned, the death of her husband was merely a good riddance. The play suggests that there was some tie between them more primitive and deep than love. *The Widowing of Mrs Holroyd* is an early work of Mr. Lawrence's (1914). Since then he has attempted to formulate directly his philosophy of sex relations, often to the detriment of his art, for he has taken to preaching and obscure exposition. The germ of that philosophy is in this play; it is an interpretation of the sacrament of marriage in terms of physiological mysticism.

Dramatically, the play is remarkable for the vigour and credibility of its passions. The interludes in which the children play a part (Jack and Minnie Holroyd acted naturally) reinforce adroitly the idea of "marriage". Mr. Lawrence loves and understands his characters – Holroyd himself is no exception, though he appears before us as a drunken bully – he loves them because they live near the dark, warm heart of life. Though the play seems on the surface to be the old triangle theme, there runs through it a new conviction and an exceptional intensity. It is the sort of play the Stage Society should produce because, though it is well worth seeing, the majority of the public would take it merely as a low-life and rather sordid example of the old husband, wife and lover story. Miss Marda Vanne in the part of Mrs. Holroyd did not get the better of a refined intonation which is natural to her, but she possesses a comparatively rare gift. Whenever she is motionless her attitudes are significant; when she is still and silent her body continues to act, and she spoke with a peremptory impulsiveness admirably suited to the part. Mr Oliver Crombie's (Charlie Holroyd's) lurching, angular movement, his formidable massiveness, and his concentrated violence of utterance were just what the part required. Two other minor parts deserve printed comment; Miss Dorice Fordred's "Clara" and Mr. James Whale's "Rigley". The washing of the body, which should be the most arresting and moving moment in the play, seemed too prolonged, chiefly because Miss Inez Bensusan (Holroyd's mother) did not achieve the requisite intensity of expression. Mr. Lawrence has austerely kept his gift for lyrical expression within the bounds of naturalism. (from a review by Desmond MacCarthy, *The New Statesman*, 18 December 1926, p.310)

Mr. D. H. Lawrence's early play, "The Widowing of Mrs Holroyd", was performed last Sunday by the Three Hundred Club branch of the Stage Society. Some of the acting was extremely fine, notably that of Miss Marda Vanne as Mrs. Holroyd and Mr. Oliver Crombie as her husband. Mr. Colin Keith-Johnston was also good, while Master Earle and Miss Moore could give points to many grown-up actors. The first two acts of this play are extraordinarily good. The bare life is filled with that astonishing vitality Mr. Lawrence can put into his best work. This is not realism, but reality shorn of everything irrelevant to the emotional issue. These acts, crisp yet weighted, have that real literary quality which comes of fidelity to the truth imaginatively grasped: they are dramatic and moving. But since we were thus wrought up to the level of tragedy, the collapse of the third act was desolating. It is hard to say which was the more to blame, Mr. Lawrence, or his producer, Mr. Esmé Percy. Whenever Mr. Percy deals with death, he makes the pace funereal, which was in this case the very worst thing that could have been done. Where skilful production might have saved the play, and left us with a sense of its fine quality, here the decline was exaggerated: there crept in the gross sentimentality of a Hecuba turned oyster-wench. But the fault was partly Mr. Lawrence's: he allowed himself to be obsessed by the idea of the corpse, and left the emotional core of the play unresolved. A vague intellectual idea spoilt the impulsive unity of the rest, where the mind really had been at work. It was the idea of a corpse, not of death. The fact of death might momentarily have blotted out the passions in the play, and this effect could possibly have been obtained if the Grandmother had uttered her words as a raging outburst. Moreover, photographic, not imaginative realism, obtruded itself here. Still, it was an immensely interesting, even exciting, evening. Mr. Lawrence has made enormous strides between this play and "David", which reads like a masterpiece, and which this Society is to give us an opportunity of seeing. (from a review by 'Omicron', *The Nation and Athenaeum*, 18 December 1926, p. 422)

Mr. D. H. Lawrence is no literary trifler, but a writer under compulsion. He has a daemon who not only drives but has a rare sense of direction. It is unnecessary to describe this tense little tragedy as a masterpiece in order to express its power, or to call in the aid of prejudice to expose its weakness.

From the moment the curtain went up on the dim-lit interior of the miner's cottage, discovering the young wife brooding over her difficult problems – her estrangement from her husband and the ill-repressed passion of the young electrician – not a sentence is spoken but serves to intensify the situation and absorb the spectator's concern. Mr. Lawrence expresses character by means of dialogue that is too intense to be merely realistic, too richly charged with significance to permit of the rustling of chocolate wrappings.

The sheer technician would probably protest to him in vain that the last five minutes of the play did more to lower its fine high temperature to sub-normal than, at any earlier stage, one would have believed possible. Yet I suggest that a quicker curtain, that reduced to a gesture or two the prolonged washing of the body of the dead miner by his sad, lamenting wife and mother, would have forestalled the disastrous dissipation of the play's vital heat which the laying-out entailed. That, however, was a tactical, not a strategic weakness. The story is inconclusive, but that, no doubt is an integral factor in his realism. He employs children – usually the dramatist's easiest disaster – in a manner that I have never seen excelled. His boy and girl were beautifully acted by Peter Earle and Helen Moore. The acting of the adults was for the most part excellent. Mr. James Whale, who is always unusually good, made the small part of an awkward breaker of bad news a little masterpiece. Mr. Keith-Johnston and Mr. Oliver Crombie as Mrs. Holroyd's two loves – of comfort and despair – admirably supported Miss Marda Vanne who, in spite of a slightly devitalised accent gave a beautifully balanced and emotional performance as the play's tormented heroine. The production by the 300 Club, now allied to the Stage Society, was from every point of view distinguished. (from a review by H. H., *The Outlook,* 24 December 1926, p. 629)

The only really hostile review we have found was by St. J. E. (source uncertain) dated 19 December 1926:

Mr. Lawrence is a novelist of unusual distinction. His imagination is often inflamed with rage, but it is equally often inflamed with beauty. He is rarely quiet and never still. He beats about the world, furious here, and frantic there, but never enters or quits a place without leaving his mark on it. I seldom am able to understand what Mr. Lawrence is shouting about, but I am never in any doubt that he is shouting, and sometimes I can hear significant words in his fiercest tirades. In this play he draws a sombre but insignificant picture of life in a pit village near Nottingham.

We need not dispute about the veracity of the picture. Mr. Lawrence is himself the son of a miner and intimately knows the life he here describes. It is not prettily portrayed. How could it be? When one's view is mainly of slag-heaps, one may be pardoned for finding something intolerable in prettiness. But Mr. Lawrence has contented himself with the harsh outlines of mining life; he has given them no importance. What do we know at the end of his play? That a rough, brutalised collier, called Holroyd, turns his wife's love to loathing by drunken debauchery; that his wife, in her disgust and despair, turns for comfort to a young and seemly electrician, called Blackmore; that after humiliation and a drunken row she consents to elope with Blackmore and wishes that her husband were dead; that Holroyd is imprisoned by a fall of coal in the pit and suffocated by gas and after-damp; and that his wife, feeling that she "wished" him to his death, washes his body. That is all.

The third act was almost entirely occupied by the announcement of Holroyd's death and the washing of his half-naked corpse. There was worth in the first two acts, but there was none in the last; and the curtain fell before a bewildered audience which could with difficulty be persuaded to believe that the play was over. Insignificance was the chief feature of the piece. There were insignificant references to rats and an insignificant rat-hunt in the first act that certainly was horrible, but added nothing to the play. There was an insignificant incident when Holroyd cut his foot on a broken basin and made a to-do about bandages. There was sound and there was fury, but they signified nothing. The mind of Mr. Lawrence was not present in his play: we could not discover why he had told us these dismal facts. He has a sense of drama and dialogue unusual in a novelist, and he can, if he chooses, make himself as important a dramatist as he is already a novelist. But he must *say* something, and not rest content with a mere exhibition.

3 DAVID

Produced by Robert Atkins for The 300 Club and Stage Society at the Regent
Theatre, London. 22–3 May 1927

Cast

Merab	Veronica Turleigh
First Maiden	Dorice Fordred
Second Maiden	Doris Ashley
Michal	Angela Baddeley
Agag	Hilton Edwards
Saul	Peter Cresswell
Jonathan	Frank Vosper
Abner	Alban Blakelock
Samuel	Harcourt Williams
Jesse	Reyner Barton
Eliab	Bruno Barnabé
Abinadab	Anthony Eustrel
Shammah	Arthur Gomez
David	Robert Harris
Voice of Goliath	Norman Shelley
A Herald	Lionel Scott
First Herdsman	Charles Marford
Second Herdsman	Whitmore Humphreys
A Woman Servant	Hilda Sims
A Prophet	Val Cuthbert

David was Lawrence's last play, written in the spring of 1925. 'It is a good
play, and for the theatre', he told his agent Curtis Brown. 'Someone ought
to do it' (Moore, 845). Curtis Brown did not agree, and sent it to Knopf for
publication. But Lawrence wrote to Knopf:

I don't want it published unless it is produced. Curtis Brown thinks it would be
better if it appeared first as 'literature'. Myself, I am a bit tired of plays that are
only literature. If a man is writing 'literature', why choose the form of a play?
And if he's writing a play, he surely intends it for the theatre. Anyhow I wrote
this play for the theatre, and I want the theatre people to see it first. Curtis
Brown says it is full of long speeches that call for a whole company of Forbes-
Robertsons. There might be a whole company of even better men. I believe there
might be found Jews or Italians or Spaniards or Celts to do the thing properly:
not Teutons or Scandinavians or Nordics: it's not in their blood – as a rule. And
if the speeches are too long – well, they can be made shorter if necessary. But my
God, there's many a *nigger* would play Saul better than Forbes-Robertson could
do it. And I'd prefer the nigger. Or men and women from that Jewish theatre. –
Curtis Brown says it is not a 'popular' play. But damn it, how does he know even
that? Playgoing isn't the same as reading. Reading in itself is highbrow. But give
the 'populace' in the theatre something with a bit of sincere good-feeling in it,

and they'll respond. If you do it properly. (Moore, 845–6)

When Robert Atkins agreed to produce it for the 300 Club and Stage Society in October 1926, Lawrence, who was in England that summer, postponed his return to Italy in order to be able to help, but when the production was postponed until December, he returned to the Villa Mirenda, and wrote to Robert Atkins:

> I enclose the music I have written out for *David*. It is very simple – needs only a pipe, tambourines, and a tom-tom drum. I hope it will do.
>   Let me know when you get the thing going a bit. I hope I can come to London and help, later, if you think it really worthwhile. If only one can get that feeling of primitive religious passion across to the London audience. If not, it's no good. (Moore, 941)

Then the 300 Club decided to do *Mrs Holroyd* in December, and postpone *David* until March. Lawrence wrote: 'I shan't go to England for *Mrs Holroyd* – too wintry: but I feel I must go and give a helping hand to *David*' (Moore, 950). In the new year Lawrence's enthusiasm for returning to England rapidly faded: 'I feel an infinite disgust at the idea of having to be there while the fools mimble-pimble at the dialogue' (Moore, 964). By 8 March he had finally decided against it: 'I won't go to London for *David*. I simply won't go, to have my life spoilt by those people. They can maul and muck the play about as much as they like' (Moore, 968).
He did not go, which was, perhaps, just as well in the event.
On May 28 Lawrence wrote to Earl Brewster: 'My business is a fight, and I've got to keep it up. I'm reminded of the fact by the impudent reviews of the production of *David*. They say it was just dull. I say they are eunuchs, and have no balls' (Moore, 980). One of the reviews Lawrence had probably seen was that in *The Times*, 24 May 1927:

> It is legitimate to ask what purpose the dramatist had in mind in making use of the Biblical story, and it is fatal to the play if the question remains unanswered. What Mr. Lawrence has done here is clear enough: he has filled out the story of Saul, rather than of David with the peculiar intensity of language he invariably uses – the sort of language he cannot help using. Why he should have chosen this particular story we cannot say. . . . Impressed as we often are by the vehemence of his impassioned words, we are bound to say that the result is neither drama nor poetry. Truth to tell, this unending insistence on the verbal symbols of mysticism grows wearisome long before the last of the sixteen scenes. Flames of life and love and spirit, if they are meant for the theatre at all, need to be illustrated in common, or uncommon, action; merely to speak of them in dark hints conveys nothing. In two scenes only are we brought into the drama of Saul and David; where David and Jonathan exchange robes, taking oath of their

friendship, and where Saul is visited by evil spirits, while David sings to restore him to his kingly mind, we are conscious of more than curiosity at Mr. Lawrence's experiment. But there is hardly anything else in the play which tempts us to lose our detachment.

It is a difficult piece to act, and Mr. Peter Cresswell as Saul was called upon to bear the chief burden. His voice is rather too thick and indistinct for the passion of eloquence his part requires, and intense as was his bearing, we missed many shades of meaning in his performance. The Samuel of Mr. Harcourt Williams was not more satisfactory, although for a quite different reason; his seemed a rather careless study, entirely wanting in the nervous force one would suppose essential to a major prophet. The David of Mr. Robert Harris and the Jonathan of Mr. Frank Vosper were much better; and most satisfactory of all was the Michal of Miss Angela Baddeley, who pictured for us something of the beauty it was evident lay like a weight on Mr. Lawrence's mind. While she was on the stage we could imagine what went on in the mind of Saul. She looked very lovely and possessed of more spirit than Saul or David or the whole company of prophets.

The review by 'Omicron' in the *Nation and Athenaeum* on 28 May was far more 'impudent':

Mr. D. H. Lawrence, one of the most distinguished masters of modern prose, has seen fit to write in biblical English a long drama dealing with Saul and David which has just been produced by the Three Hundred Club. This particular production was of such an uninspired nature that one hesitates to blame the author entirely for the resultant fiasco though the fact that the play lacked all dramatic movement no doubt made it very hard to produce. . . . What on earth is the good of a twentieth century writer striving to imitate the style of the early seventeenth. The result can only be a tedious Wardour Street diction frequently interlarded with quotations from the most well-known book in English.

In October 1927 Max Mohr made some attempts to get *David* produced in Berlin. But Lawrence was no longer in a fighting mood: 'And of course the whole play is too literary, too many words. The actual technique of the stage is foreign to me. But perhaps they – and you – could cut it into shape. I shall be very much surprised if they *do* play it in Berlin. The public only wants foolish realism: Hamlet in a smoking jacket' (Moore, 1016). And that was Lawrence's last word on the theatre of his time. There were no more productions of his plays in his lifetime. He never saw a play of his on the stage.

4 *MY SON'S MY SON*

An unrevised play by D. H. Lawrence completed by Walter Greenwood.
Produced by Leon M. Lion at the Playhouse Theatre, London. First night
26 May 1936.

Cast Mrs Gascoigne   Louise Hampton
         Luther   Gyles Isham
         Joe   Valentine Dyall
         Mrs Luther Gascoigne   Sara Erskine
         Mrs Purdy   Hilda Davies
         A Cabman   N. T. Cummings
         Horrocks   Gordon Edwards

This production was revived at the Golders Green Hippodrome, first night 24
August 1936.

Cast Mrs Gascoigne   Sybil Thorndike
         Luther   Nicholas Phipps
         Joe   Christopher Casson
         Mrs Luther Gascoigne   Ann Casson
         Mrs Purdy   Nora Nicholson

This play is, of course, *The Daughter-in-Law*, which Lawrence wrote at the
beginning of 1913. When he left Germany in September of that year, he left
several manuscripts with Frieda's sister Else Jaffe, including four plays.
The Merry-Go-Round, The Married Man, The Fight for Barbara and *The
Daughter-in-Law*. He then forgot about them, and so did Else who did not
rediscover them until 1933 when she sent them to Frieda. When Frieda
returned to Taos she left the plays with Curtis Brown, who in October 1933
sent *The Daughter-in-Law* to the theatrical impressario Leon M. Lion.
Lion did not think it suitable for the London stage as it stood and
commissioned Richard Hughes, author of *A High Wind in Jamaica*, to
adapt it. Frieda could not understand why the play needed any adapting,
but Laurence Pollinger assured her that 'it was necessary that the play
should be revised in certain places if it were ever to be produced'. Hughes
had the play for eighteen months, but failed to make the adaptation, and in
April 1936 Lion handed the job over to Walter Greenwood, the author of
Love on the Dole.
Greenwood's brief was to conflate the four acts into three, elaborate Act
Three in accordance with notes provided by Lion, modify the dialect to
make the play more comprehensible, and oversee the rehearsals from the

point of view of 'the general North country atmosphere of the play'. However, it seems that Greenwood told reporters that he was in fact writing the last act of an unfinished play. Lion chose to play along with this deception, and the play was announced as 'An Unrevised Play by D. H. Lawrence Completed by Walter Greenwood'. Greenwood's work added up to making numerous small cuts and adding about three pages of new dialogue to the third act and three new scene endings in the first two acts. But the press release announced that Greenwood had written the third act according to Lawrence's rough draft. Greenwood kept up this pretense to the end of his life. The changes he made now seem to us to be crudely melodramatic and to undermine the subtleties of characterisation and relationships in the original text, which had to wait another thirty years to be performed.

Most of the reviewers preferred what they took to be Greenwood's contribution: 'Mr. Greenwood, the author of *Love on the Dole*, has finished the play. It is a pity he did not begin it. And that goes for the middle, too!' (*Sunday Times*, 21 May 1936).

> The play reflects D. H. Lawrence in every line of the first two acts and Walter Greenwood, who has more of the theatre in one of his little fingers than Lawrence could muster from a whole life's suppressed eructation, has contrived to make of the third act a living, breathing thing. A drama in one act with an introduction by D. H. Lawrence. (C.V.B.)

A few preferred Lawrence's:

> We can hardly help becoming aware, as the tale of sons and lovers nears its close, that its atmosphere has undergone a subtle change. There is still violence, but it is violence of a more familiar theatrical convention; there is still tension, but tension radically different from that which has bound together the rest of the play; there are odd incursions of sentimental comedy; and, perhaps unjustly, we attribute the change for the worse to Mr. Greenwood's natural failure to see life steadily from Lawrence's peculiar angle. But what else could a collaborator have done but give the tail of the situation left him at the end of the second act a melodramatic flourish? (*The Times*, 27 May 1936).
>
> It was clever of Mr. Greenwood to solve the problems that had been built up dramatically but not tragically. His climax is ever so slick – and D. H. Lawrence, I felt, would have gone on to the logical tragedy. Slickness had no part in his genius. (*Manchester Evening News*, 29 May 1936)

Perhaps the best comment, in the circumstances, was that of H. H. in *The Observer* (31 May 1933):

> The sabotage in the mine, which placated the dark gods in the miner's blood,

tore the fabric of truth, let in perfunctory melodrama, and procured a dubiously happy ending. Where Lawrence leaves off and stagecraft begins, is a question that need not detain us. Sufficient to say that, while the voice is the voice of Jacob, the hands are more like the hands of Esau.

Louise Hampton as the mother was generally admired, and there was praise for Giles Isham as Luther and Valentine Dyall as Joe, but D.B's reference in the *Evening Standard* (27 May 1936) to 'passages of pure Kensington which crept persistently in, and into which Miss Sarah Erskine, as Luther's wife, at last frankly relapsed' suggests that Walter Greenwood's dialect coaching had not been wholly successful.

The August revival, though it boasted Sybil Thorndike and her children in the cast, seems to have sported accents ranging from Oxford to Blackpool, and even less care seems to have been taken with the costumes: 'Returning from work in a mine, covered with a layer of coal dust and sweat, he [Nicholas Phipps] amazed me by turning the soles of his boots to the audience as he sat down – white, virgin soles that could not possibly have been anything else but brand new. (C.V.B.)'.

5   *THE WIDOWING OF MRS HOLROYD*

Adapted for television by Ken Taylor. Director: Claude Whatham. A Granada TV Network Production in the Television Playhouse series on 23 March 1961 (see Fig. 1)

Cast		
	Jack	Jimmy Ogden
	Minnie	Jennifer Quarmby
	Publican	Philip Stone
	Charlie Holroyd	Edward Judd
	Clara	Eileen Kennally
	Laura	Susan Field
	Tom Blackmore	Paul Daneman
	Lizzie Holroyd	Jennifer Wilson
	Ridgley	Peter Adamson
	Barker	Clifford Cox
	Mrs Holroyd	Marion Dawson
	Chambers	George Merritt
	Bearer	Derek Pollitt
	Designed by Peter Phillips	

The state of knowledge of D. H. Lawrence as a dramatist in 1961 is reflected in the introductory material for this production which announced it as, '. . . the first television production of any of the three [sic] plays he wrote . . .

This powerful play by D. H. Lawrence, now on television for the first time, tells the story of a woman who has to choose between two men – the handsome husband she once thought she might learn to love, and the young man in whom she sees a chance to escape from married strife.' (*TV Times*, 18–25 March 1961, pp. 13 and 33).

The following extract is from a review in *The Times* (24 March 1961, p. 18) under the heading 'Lawrence play skilfully adapted to television'.

How Lawrence would have shaped as a dramatist if he had had different opportunities and lived at a different period it is difficult to say from last night's production since it reduced the play from its original length to an hour minus commercials. The adaptation was done so skilfully and unobtrusively by Mr. Ken Taylor that one began to speculate how far he had smoothed over the rough passages and untangled knots in the construction.

Was the dialogue all Lawrence's as far as it went? It certainly sounded convincingly Lawrentian, and here at last there could be no doubt; it was crisp, spare and genuinely dramatic.

This adaptation had an important influence on the awakening of interest in Lawrence's plays. When interviewed immediately prior to the opening of his production of *The Merry-go-Round*, Peter Gill is reported as having his attention drawn to Lawrence's plays by this production.

. . . it was indirectly because of television, which in the middle sixties [sic] put on a production of "The Widowing of Mrs Holroyd". Peter Gill didn't see it, but when in 1965 he was an assistant director at the Royal Court Theatre in London and was asked to do a Sunday night production (without decor, of course) he remembered the astonished reports he had heard of Mrs Holroyd from a friend. He wrote off for a copy of the play. What came back instead was a thin green script of "A Collier's Friday Night": right author, wrong play. (from an interview with Peter Gill by Hugh Herbert, *The Guardian*, 7 November 1973, p. 8)

Ken Taylor, the adaptor for this production, and Claude Whatham, its director, were the first to join the production team for the Granada *D. H. Lawrence Series* of dramatisations of D. H. Lawrence's short stories which were transmitted from 1965 to 1967. The producer of this series was Margaret Morris who had been casting director for the 1961 Granada TV production of *The Widowing of Mrs Holroyd*.

6 *A COLLIER'S FRIDAY NIGHT*

Director: Peter Gill. A Sunday Night production without decor at the Royal Court Theatre, London on 8 August 1965. The cast included Victor Henry (Ernest), Richard Butler (Lambert), Gwendolyn Watts (Beatrice), and Clare Kelly.

A Collier's Friday Night was Lawrence's first play. In later life Lawrence wrote on the manuscript: 'Written when I was twenty-one, almost before I'd done anything, it is most horribly green.' The action takes place on a Friday night six weeks before Christmas in 1906 or 1907, and gives the impression of having been written very close to the events. However, Jessie Chambers (who is the original of Maggie in the play) said that Lawrence first showed it to her in November 1909, and that he 'certainly wrote it that autumn' (Delavenay 694). The manuscript contains several references which could not have been written before 1909, for example to the deaths of Meredith and Swinburne which took place in the spring of that year. Lawrence could, however, have rewritten in 1909 a play first sketched in 1906.

It is an astonishing production. It is on the eternal first-book theme – the plight of a sensitive young man in a warring family: but the treatment is entirely free from the self-justification and revenge that usually relegate such works to the level of juvenile.

Ernest, the young student, is not even the dominant figure: it is the *collier's* night, and the shape of the play is determined by his movements: coming home from the pit to eat and get his back scrubbed; climbing into his suit and holding a club share-out; storming back from the pub for a shouting match with his long-suffering genteel wife.

Ernest hates the sight of him, but the play treats him tenderly as he bends grimly over his plate shovelling down his supper, miserably conscious that the rest of the family are ashamed of him. Even in the midst of his desperately inarticulate harangues, he is inclined to stop and say something generous or ask humbly for a bit of pudding. The part was played beautifully by Richard Butler.

The same fair-mindedness runs through the other parts.

As a piece of construction, no doubt the play is naive: simply a representation of an evening in the lives of people Lawrence knew from long experience. But, while ignoring traditional form, it does make inventive use of common domestic incident to provide shape and suspense. And what emerges finally is a study of the economics of affection. (from *The Times*, 9 August 1965, p. 12)

This early piece was given a Sunday-night showing at the Royal Court last August and it worked beautifully. It is the least formed of all his plays, but his talent comes out much more strongly in the exact notation of working-class life (as in *The Daughter-in-Law*) than when he tries to employ an external framework (as in *The Merry-Go-Round*). Perhaps he wasn't a natural dramatist, but he wrote fine and truthful dialogue and a few superb scenes of domestic conflict and domestic peace. He was born at the right time for the regional drama revival, but in the wrong place. A few miles further north and he would have been swept into the Manchester repertory movement. But then, perhaps, we shouldn't have had the novels. (from a review of Lawrence's *Complete Plays* by Irving Wardle in *The Observer* 12 December, 1965)

This successful and well-received production laid the foundations for Peter Gill's reputation as a director of Lawrence's plays. It was recalled in March 1967 when Gill directed his first full-scale production of a Lawrence play, *The Daughter-in-Law*. 'Peter Gill's beautiful production two years ago of Lawrence's first play, *A Collier's Friday Night* exploded the idea that Lawrence the dramatist could safely be ignored' (from *The Times*, 17 March 1967).

7   *THE DAUGHER-IN-LAW*

Director: Gordon McDougall, at the Traverse Theatre, Edinburgh. First night 17 January 1967

Cast

Mrs Gascoigne	Lennox Milne
Joe	Richard Howard
Mrs Purdy	Betty Hardy
Luther	Brian Smith
Minnie	Rosemary McHale

The play represents a drab canvas of working class life in Nottinghamshire, in a testing dialect. The lives of its characters are confined by the rigid social conventions of the day: their cramped experience and small capabilities allowing them the pursuit of happiness if not its achievement. . . .
Yet despite a good production and the imaginative set the play has no real climaxes and it trudges through its plot too steadily for any dramatic excitement. (from a review in *Stage*, 26 January 1967)

The Mother-in-Law [sic] was well worth reviving. Like nearly all Lawrence's work it has its flaws, but the truthfulness and warmth of its best scenes are piercing and remarkable and make a great impact in the Traverse production.
    The ex-governess who thinks she is too good for her rough miner husband has to learn how to live with him; the miner has to understand her feelings and unlearn some of his bearishness. After the wife tells her mother-in-law some home truths, and by a somewhat Shavian trick gets rid of all her money so that she and her husband can begin again on a level of equality, there is a reconciliation, and the play ends on this precariously hopeful very moving

moment of peace and restored love.

The central quarrel scene between man and wife in Act II cuts like a knife: a painful, wonderfully penetrating encounter which shows Lawrence at his strongest. A rich Nottinghamshire dialect is used, and the whole language of the play has a notable vigour.

The production by Gordon McDougall, copes excellently with the sometimes distracting naturalism that is demanded; raked fires, real food cooking and steaming in the confined space of the Traverse. (from a review in *The Times*, 28 January 1967)

8 *THE DAUGHTER-IN-LAW*

Director: Peter Gill. First Night 16 March 1967 at the Royal Court Theatre, London.

Cast   Mrs Gascoigne   Anne Dyson
          Joe Gascoigne   Victor Henry
          Mrs Purdy   Gabrielle Daye
          Minnie Gascoigne   Judy Parfitt
          Luther Gascoigne   Mike Pratt

The ending is clearly a mechanical device and there is not the smallest conviction in the reunion. What is real in the play is the sense of incurable tension, a bond that holds the characters permanently together no matter how emotions ebb and flow. Not even Strindberg has a greater power to convey the feelings of the devitalized and humiliated male; digging his nails into his palms and retiring into a shell of self-suffering. (from *The Times*, 17 March 1967)

As the mother, Ann Dyson is formidably saturnine, a lioness who knows that if she doesn't stop licking her cubs she will eventually eat one, but can't restrain herself. Mike Pratt has just the combination of brute strength and bovine evasiveness for Luther, and Judy Parfitt is exactly right for Minnie, her bone-china intellectual pallor flushed with thwarted sensuality.

But the best-imagined character, though functionally the least necessary to the plot, is the younger son, played by Victor Henry. Clearly, he's what Lawrence thought he might have become – the soft, clever, emasculated favourite of his devouring mother. . . . In fact, this is the best production the theatre has mounted in a year or two. Gill fills it with telling detail: the clanging backgate outside, the newspapers stacked ready to spread under grimy elbows, the miner stooping for his brother to sponge coal-dust from his back before an open stove. Lawrence feared, correctly, that his contemporaries would find his plays too naturalistic and slow, but he was right and they were wrong. *The Daughter-in-Law* may not compare with his novels, but it makes most of our post-war essays in working-class drama look flimsy. (from a review by Ronald Bryden in *The Observer*, 19 March 1967)

The most remarkable thing about this production is its realism. The characters are as rounded as figures from a canvas by Courbet. The household tasks, preparing, cooking, serving and eating meals, the miner washing off the grime after a day in the pit, his clothes drying over the oven, have an absolute verisimilitude. Watching other people work – isn't that one of the pleasures of theatre-going? Most reprehensible, no doubt. . . . Whatever the explanation, the domestic work carried out in *The Daughter-in-Law* – and often carried out in silence – is enthralling. One could smell the food. . . . The play is written in archaic Midlands dialect. As much of it is incomprehensible (with the exception of Minnie) I take it to be authentic. . . . Was D. H. Lawrence a great dramatist? No, but he might have become one if he had been able to see a performance as good as this. The marital rows come blazingly to life; he could have built on that. He could have re-written the curtain lines; he could have ventured beyond strict naturalism. He knew that he was offering emotional truth: he could have learned to express it in dramatic terms. But then, where would his novels have been? The fact that it seems hardly credible that a play of the quality of *The Daughter-in-Law* could have remained unperformed is a tribute to the Royal Court Company as much as to the author. (from Frank Marcus, 'The Dominant Sex', *Plays and Players*, May 1967, p. 19)

9 THE FIGHT FOR BARBARA

Director: Robin Midgley. First night 9 August 1967 at the Mermaid Theatre, London.

Cast		
	Francesca	Cyd Hayman
	Jimmy Wesson	Stephen Moore
	Barbara Tressider	Adrienne Corri
	Angelo	Iain Reid
	Lady Charlcote, Barbara's mother	Sylvia Coleridge
	Sir William Charlcote, her father	Geoffrey Lumsden
	Dr Frederic Tressider, her husband	Robert Cartland

On 30 October 1912 Lawrence wrote to Edward Garnett: 'I've written the comedy I send you by this post in the last three days, as a sort of interlude to *Paul Morel*' (Boulton, p. 466). It dramatises the early difficulties of the eloped Lawrence and Frieda, hounded by Frieda's outraged parents and distracted husband, adding to the difficult enough problems of adjustment to each other. It was no doubt of great therapeutic value to Lawrence to present the events of this painful period as comedy and amenable to resolution.

This latest exhumation from the forgotten archives of Lawrence's plays again shows him as the British theatre's closest relative to Strindberg, and

demonstrates the power of genius to transform what in another man would be narcissistic special pleading.
... the play is essentially a duet for the lovers and, on these terms, autobiography blazes up into art. (from a review by Irving Wardle, *The Times*, 10 August 1967)

In recent days enough has been seen of Lawrence's unfamiliar stage work to suggest that there was in him a considerable dramatist. This production will not confirm that impression. But it may not altogether be Lawrence's fault. (from a review by Harold Hobson, *The Sunday Times*, 13 August 1967)

It is hard to understand Jimmy Wesson-Lawrence's fascination for Barbara (Frieda). She has less fire than irritation, is forever petulantly raving about her deserted husband, Frederic ('He loves me so, I can't bear him to suffer'), her scandalised parents and her duty. Never letting Jimmy get on with his work, she pesters him for kisses and reassurances of love. Behind the hysteria, the models are clearly locked together for life, but, dramatised, their understandable problems of loyalty, physical attraction and dependence are reduced to melodrama.
A really great actress might, conceivably, bring off this awkward role. But Adrienne Corri, who has an emotional stab at the part, is essentially two-dimensional. As Jimmy, Stephen Moore is more successful in a smaller way — solidly working-class, solidly anti-frippery.
Robin Midgley does what he can with the direction (apart from milking laughs around a nude picture on the wall, which Lawrence painted fifteen years after writing the play). He's aware of the more lasting Lawrence under the tantrums – of that finger on the delicate pulse of sexual empathy. Frederic pleads that he would spill blood for Barbara on every paving-stone in Bromley. "It doesn't do any good, if a man dies of love for me", she replies, "unless there's an answer in me".
The Fight for Barbara would have made a short story, but it doesn't sit easily on the Mermaid stage. (from a review by Helen Dawson in *The Observer*, 13 August 1967)

Well of course, it's not a very good play really. But then which of Lawrence's is? They're interesting, because they're by him, and this is more interesting than most – if you know something about Lawrence, Frieda, Frieda's first husband and the circumstances in which she ran off with Lawrence, to the scandalisation of people in general. But that must seem rather a flimsy reason for staging the play now. ...
But here Robin Midgley has had a very bright idea. Since the play, though running to four acts, can be got through at a run in an hour and a quarter, why not play it as the second half of a double bill, and then use the portion before the interval to sketch in the background and introduce us to the real-life originals of the play's cardboard cuts? ...
Mr Midgley has done his work so well ... that it crackles along at a great

pace, the ball being flung backwards and forwards from reader to reader with never a fumble. Lawrence's ideas about sex and the sexes are neatly juxtaposed with his own actions in life, and the untidy business of his romance with Frieda Weekley, nee von Richthofen, and their flight to Italy is related in selections from the writings of the three principals with a cool irony which is very appealing. . . .

[The play is] not much by itself, but fascinating in the light of what has gone before. In particular, the play tells us more than one suspects, Lawrence realised about his view of Frieda and of women in general: maybe she is meant to be attractive even though wayward and challenging in her behaviour, but she turns out as an unallayed bitch from beginning to end, so that one sympathises heartily with Wesson/Lawrence's evident desire to slap a little sense into her . . .

What might easily have been a worthy but dull act of literacy piety has been turned into an unexpectedly fascinating couple of hours in the theatre. (from a review by John Russell Taylor in *Plays and Players*, October 1967)

10   *D. H. LAWRENCE: A SEASON OF PLAYS*

Director: Peter Gill, at the Royal Court Theatre, London February–March 1968 (see Figs. *2, 3, 4*)

A Collier's Friday Night. First night 29 February

Cast	Mrs Lambert	Anne Dyson
	Nellie Lambert	Christine Hargreaves
	Gertie Coomber	Susan Williamson
	Lambert	John Barrett
	Ernest Lambert	Victor Henry
	Barker	Anthony Douse
	Carlin	Mark Jones
	Maggie Pearson	Jennifer Armitage
	Beatrice Wyld	Gwendolyn Watts

The Daughter-in-Law. First night 7 March

Cast	Mrs Gascoigne	Anne Dyson
	Joe Gascoigne	Victor Henry
	Mrs Purdy	Gabrielle Day
	Minnie Gascoigne	Judy Parfitt
	Luther Gascoigne	Michael Coles

The Widowing of Mrs Holroyd. First night 14 March

Cast	Mrs Holroyd	Judy Parfitt
	Blackmore	Mark Jones
	Jack Holroyd	Len Jones
	Minnie Holroyd	June Liversidge
	Clara	Gwendolyn Watts
	Laura	Joan Francis
	Grandmother	Anne Dyson
	Rigley	John Barrett
	Manager	Anthony Douse
	Miner	Edward Peel
	Miner	Tony Rohr
	Holroyd	Michael Coles

REHEARSAL LOGBOOK by Barry Hanson
(*Plays and Players*, April 1968)

August, 1965

A *Collier's Friday Night* is premiered as a Sunday night production without decor for the English Stage Society.

March, 1967

The Daughter-in-Law, also directed by Peter Gill, is a main-bill production. The interest created by these two productions and the reviews they receive explode the idea that Lawrence, the dramatist, may be safely ignored.

The idea of the current season of plays dates from this time. The choice of the third play, *The Widowing of Mrs Holroyd*, is made for its similarity in feeling and period to the other two. The plan is to form a small company to cover the three plays in a seven-week rehearsal period. This is not only to gain a financial saving but is done with the feeling that the best start to working towards a uniform style for the season is made with a small company, where most of the artists appear in at least two of the productions.

The scope for research on Lawrence, mining, the period, and documentary background to the three plays is enormous. For some months before the start of rehearsals, the director and his two assistants re-read all the plays, the usual books of criticism and a number of novels – *Sons and Lovers* especially.

At the same time, Shirley Matthews researches mining and social conditions of England prior to the First World War. One of the really exciting finds is a collection of photographs in the archives of the National Coal Board. These photos – by the Rev Cobb – are a brilliant record of the life of the miners Lawrence wrote about. They will be used in the programme.

Summer, 1967

Visits are made to Nottingham, Eastwood and Bestwood. It is known that Lawrence set these plays in homes he knew intimately. They are still there. The house where *A Collier's Friday Night* is set used to belong to his cousin. The house for *The Widowing of Mrs Holroyd* is found derelict in the exact relation to the Old Brinsley Pit as described in the stage directions at the beginning of the play. About the setting for *The Daughter-in-Law* we are less certain. By chance we find a house that seems to be right in every way, but it is not until one assistant reads the short story, *Annie and Fanny* – which is an early exploration of theme of *The Daughter-in-Law* – where the exact address is given, that we discover we had been right.

Quite simply, we want as full and detailed information as possible about the homes where Lawrence had set his plays. Particularly important, we want to try and stay close to the size and layout of the rooms Lawrence knew. The four sets that we have now for the three plays, designed by John Gunter, are, in fact, only very slightly larger than their originals.

To get three productions on after only a seven-week rehearsal period is going to mean simultaneous rehearsal whenever possible. The two assistants are each given particular responsibility for one production so that it is kept in rehearsal, while Peter Gill works on a third. Rehearsals are divided into four-day work periods.

With one exception – Michael Coles as Luther – all the cast of *The Daughter-in-Law* have been in the Royal Court production of 1967, so, initially, it will be possible to allot less rehearsal time to this play than to the others.

8–13 January

Rehearsal room: the Parish Hall. Like all church halls – spartan but adequate, with the remnants of Christmas decoration hanging in forlorn abandon on walls and cupboards. Quick, rough blocking. Since the design of *Collier* is a near exact replica of Lawrence's house, space is scarce. The actors mention this but the director is not sympathetic, since the Lawrences had, in fact, less space than the designer has generously allowed the actors. Half-way through the first act Peter Gill announces that he intends to insert a section from *Sons and Lovers* (regarding family affection) but that he is not going to tell anybody.

On the third day the *Collier* cast have familiarised themselves with their surroundings. They have accepted the physical limitations of the house, know where the kitchen is and Anne Dyson (Mrs Lambert) is growing increasingly concerned with her properties, which accumulate daily. Now the delicate synchronisation between action and word required by naturalism becomes apparent. The actors are told to *believe* in the physical world. Gill insists on bowls and baking tins being put down and picked up for their own value. This is difficult. In the first ten minutes of the play Anne has to butter the toast, heat the teapot, put the tea in, warm it, mash the tea, pour the tea out, serve a full meal, eat her own, serve the toast, clear the table, grease the baking tins, knead the dough to bake bread, and put the bread in the oven: the director wants this done without any rush. We are told that when running the scenes 'they must not get away with anything'. At the end of the fourth day the business is mechanical, but meaningless. Exercises are to be set. There has been refreshingly little time spent on character-probing. But now we see how the work is to be done. Gill insists on the actors listening to their parts and giving words, sentences and actions their own value.

In the last two days of this week *The Daughter-in-Law*. A problem worrying a number of the company at the first reading is that of accent and dialect. *The Daughter-in-Law* is a dialect play. The language has a form and rules of its own that can no more be ignored than those of Shakespearean blank verse. Instead of applying the accent and lessons learned from a dialect record it is decided to try to get the company to adopt a neutral stance, so that the accent emerges through listening to the author's cadences rather than through applied vowel sounds. Time after time during these rehearsals they are made to simply say the lines and listen to the rhythm of the scene and consider its place in the wider context of an action or short scene.

An improvisation is used to explore moments in the childhood of the sons, Luther and Joe. We set up a number of short scenes to build a history to the relationships. Putting the children to bed, a first cigarette, Mrs Gascoigne talking about her family, those that have grown up and left home, and those that have died. Victor Henry and Michael Coles as the brothers, aged 8 and 10 respectively, re-enacted the childhood scene with Anne Dyson as their mother. Victor 'told tales' on his brother. With his hands cupped round his mouth, refusing to speak except very privately and intimately to his Mum, Victor related what Luther had been up to. This was done brilliantly, except that what he was saying to Anne was so shocking that she was eventually forced to stop listening.

14–20 January

The Widowing of Mrs Holroyd. This is a strange and disturbing play. It is a study of a failing marriage and of a love affair which never starts. In the last scene of the play the miners bring home to Mrs Holroyd the body of her husband, killed by a freak accident in the pit. The acting of the intermediate scenes forcibly reminds one of the Moors Murders in the first instance. Gill keeps saying how disturbed he is by the play, especially the last scene in which the wife and grandmother have to wash the dead body of Holroyd. But we think he's enjoying it.

The first full company meeting was held on the Wednesday of this week. All Deirdre Clancy's designs are on show and are supported by prints of slides taken down the pits in Eastwood by the local vicar at the time Lawrence's father worked there. There are only 17 actors involved in the three plays.

22–7 January

We now move over to Petyt House in Chelsea – a beautiful rehearsal room: everyone now feels happier. The work on *Collier* proceeds and it now takes shape, although with more problems. Victor Henry, Anne Dyson and John Barrett are remarkable in that they play emotion truthfully and immediately. Beware! The text is suffering. From now on the assistants are watching to see if any of the words are altered. The director will have every single word written by Lawrence spoken. Watch Victor Henry, who has the confidence to get away with a scene which he has mentally completely rewritten. Anne Dyson has often completed the emotional meaning without actually saying the words, and John Barrett can't get the words out if he doesn't mean them when he actually says them, which is marvellous since the observation is so unerringly truthful. However, this is all going to need drilling.

During this week an exercise with George Eliot and her novel *Middlemarch* in order to explore the relationship between Ernest and Maggie. Jenifer Armitage

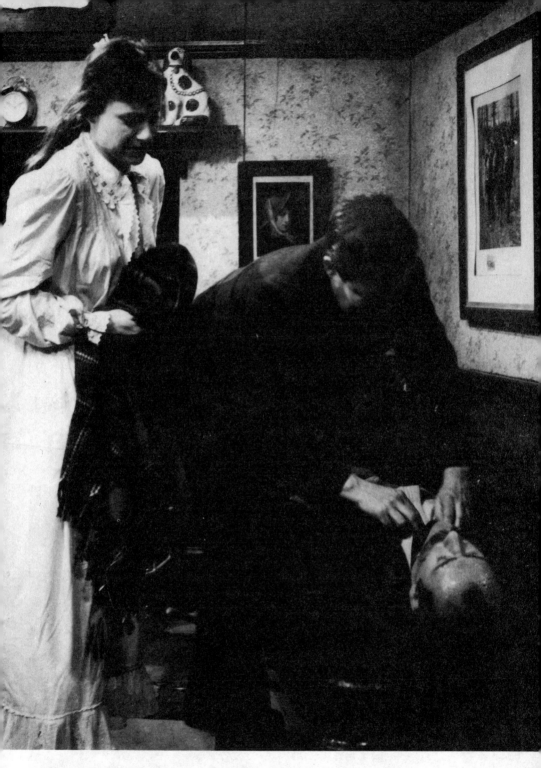

1 *The Widowing of Mrs Holroyd,* 1961 production: Blackmore and Mrs Holroyd
assist the drunken Holroyd (*photo*: Granada TV)

2 *A Collier's Friday Night*, 1968 production, Act III: Mr Lambert returns from the pub; Mrs Lambert begins a quarrel because he eats some of the grapes intended for Ernest (*photo*: Douglas H. Jeffery)

3 *The Daughter-in-Law*, 1968 production, Act II scene ii: Luther and Minnie Gascoigne's new home (*photo*: Douglas H. Jeffery)

4 *The Widowing of Mrs Holroyd*, 1968 production, Act III: the men bring in the body of Holroyd watched by his mother, his rival, Blackmore (seated left) and his wife (seated right) (*photo*: Douglas H. Jeffery)

5 *Touch and Go*, 1973 production: Gerald provokes the miners, watched by Anabel (*photo*: The Gazette Series)

(Maggie) reads a Methodist hymn to Victor Henry, who doesn't like it and says so, giving reasons. Jenifer attacks him for his inability to appreciate honest truths beautifully restated in the hymn (this improvisation is between the two of them and has nothing to do with the characters in the play). Victor continues his argument but is slightly nonplussed since, as the character Ernest, he arrogantly displays his intellectual superiority to Maggie *without* being challenged. The result is that the passionate side of Maggie is given an existence which had, previously, been dormant. Next, Jenifer reads the introduction to *Middlemarch* to Ernest; the beautiful prose seems to add to the separateness of this delicate scene in comparison with the rest.

The first four days of the week have been rewarding, the characters are dignified yet the sequence of events is still escaping everyone. The trouble is that in this play nothing develops except the evening, the characters are full of their own existence and remain so until the final curtain.

The Daughter-in-Law is run the last two days of the week. Mike Coles is the only newcomer to the cast and the play is in a good state. At the end of the week the director is very concerned that Anne Dyson may have merged all three parts she plays into one; but his fear soon vanishes.

29 January–3 February.

Holroyd Week. The play has a formal narrative structure, therefore from this point of view it's easier to control than *Collier*. But the relationships within this are strange and difficult. We know nothing about Mrs Holroyd's would-be lover except that he is an electrician on the mines. Mark Jones here plays truthfully but with an amount of reserve which makes the pace threatening. But it seems right. Mike Coles is well in command of Holroyd, and Judy Parfitt leading superbly. We note that the actors serve the text here better than in the other two plays. It is the last part of the play which causes the trouble. The final scene in which we hear of the disaster at the pit ends with the washing of the dead body. Judy Parfitt and Anne Dyson are worked up into such a state of uncontrollable emotion over this that they are physically unable to perform the operation, and indeed it's a terrifying scene.

The director understands the problem but with his total brief in the physical world he insists that they pull themselves together so they can get on with the task. All complaints from Judy and Anne are treated as excuses. 'Come on, ladies, you're washing a body, and you want to make sure it's clean, and you have to speak the lines, you can't avoid it.'

Then he goes over the scene in detail with Judy and Anne – Michael Coles lies dead on the floor, unwashed. And they set to again, but with no more success. Then Gill breaks it down into a sequence of units of physical work. Then he makes them mime this whilst saying the lines quite impersonally. Eventually Michael Coles is blacked-up and the scene starts again, but this time without words. The two women simply wash his body, concentrating only on the physical action. This affects all those watching in various ways. At first it looks sad and revolting: everyone empathises

6 (*facing*) *Touch and Go*, 1979 production: left to right, Anabel, Mr Barlow, Winifred, Oliver, Mrs Barlow, Gerald (*photo*: Oxford Playhouse)

with the two women except Gill, who has now got beyond that stage and is working towards the finished ritual. 'Look, ladies, you wouldn't weep at a dead body like that if you saw one, I tell you.'

The trouble is that Anne and Judy are crying because of each other. Finally Gill is able to command the kind of impersonal efficiency he requires from them at this stage. The text is now married to the action and the whole process has the constant quiet interruptions to give the washing the full time it needs. All attention is now focused on the relentless ritual of the washing, and by the end of the week the actresses are playing superbly: their emotion is now controlled and the job in hand assumes its proper importance. But it's true to say that it's a scene that no one in the rehearsals has become hardened to.

The week ends with a dreadful run of *The Daughter-in-Law* in the theatre. The pace has vanished; a depression has set in. The immediate corollary to this is that single words, and even whole phrases, are blurred over by a genial carelessness. Passionless, forced and muffed. God send Sunday!

5–10 February

We are now in the Scala Theatre. Immense and frightening. An assistant has been rehearsing *The Daughter-in-Law* during the last week, although Gill's comments during the course of the day would belie this. We recall the affliction of last Saturday's *Daughter-in-Law*. They have improved over the week but the spirit has gone. Why don't they prepare their performances on stage?

The next day at the Scala. A terrifying backcloth in pink, probably used for *Peter Pan* or *Cinderella*, envelopes the little *Collier* company. This has been ordered by Peter to cheer us all up. His sense of humour has never deserted him. However, things are slightly better. The director works nervously and with tremendous speed. There is very little wasted discussion in any of these rehearsals and by the end of the week *Collier* is in a fit state for some real work to start.

11–24 February.

The last two weeks of rehearsal. In the first three days we run all three plays. These are probably the most encouraging days en masse. Technically they are in very good shape, and the performances good. Monday morning starts with a passing-the-object improvisation, one of William Gaskill's lessons. The actors have to imagine an object and pass it on to the next person, who has to turn it into something else without thinking. They sit in a circle and the objects change round. The important thing about this exercise is to get the actors to naturally take what is given to them and use it, rather than any cleverness as an occupational mime. One that is particularly marvellous is where Anne Dyson passes a baby to Christine Hargreaves (Nellie), who turns it into a dog on a lead: she passes the lead to Mark Jones, who turns it into a long rope.

The second exercise is to play the whole of the first scene without words. No pig-mime is allowed, no beams or grimaces to substitute for absent speeches. Amazingly quickly, the actors are playing the scene very well, relating to each through their separate physical actions, easily preserving the flow of the scene through its different moods. When the text is used in the run-through in the afternoon, the physical flow is right; not tidy and tentative but meaningful in its own right. Then we do a section with Victor and Anne in slow motion which is marvellously funny as well as profitable. Then the return of Ernest's sister, Nellie, done at the pace of an old comic film. This work focuses the actor's energies into sustaining a physical mood throughout the scene. Its clarity and exaggeration make him more aware of his presence and that of his partners.

Gill constantly questions the actors about the sequence of the play. He regards it as important that they should be really aware of the *kind* of time they exist in. For instance, Judy Parfitt and Anne Dyson in *Holroyd* must, as actresses, not characters, be aware of the precise way in which the news of Holroyd's death is got to them and who is involved in it and at what time. There is nothing academic in this; it simply makes the actors more 'related'. Another almost daily piece of work is to turn on an actor and ask him to recreate the background of his character, answering questions from Gill quickly and fluently about the other characters. This is particularly valuable in *Holroyd* where, at the death of the husband, four members of the mining community suddenly appear on stage for a short time.

The Daughter-in-Law follows on Tuesday – a very good run.

The Widowing of Mrs Holroyd has, in fact, increased in power, the last scene having a shattering effect on its small audience. Judy and Anne play excellently. An interesting note after the run – on the relationships between Mrs Holroyd and Blackmore. Up until this time Judy has been playing with a remarkably passionate control over the events of the play. Gill realises that Mrs Holroyd was more a medium through which the emotion of the play passes: she must, from now on, not take as much responsibility for her actions or inject emotion into the part. On the other hand, Mark Jones must now draw his performance out and take over this responsibility for their relationship. The truth which he has played unerringly must now become 'observed'.

Last days.

In the last week much of the improvised work is carried on and Peter develops a passion for hymn singing (Methodist) during the mornings to prevent spiritual sloth. After the last run-through of *A Collier* an observer says she feels that most of the women are too emancipated in their performances. Peter shows annoyance at the way Jenifer (Maggie) seems not to have committed herself today. Peter asks if she has any opinions about her state in life – again in the dangerous manner of before, half as the character, half as herself. He introduces a dialectic on Female Suffrage: Jenifer becomes more angry and spirited in defence of 'Votes for Women', which, on the director's recommendation, she shouts to the gallery, obviously enjoying the experience: the remaining female members of the cast have by this time begun to talk and are led into the debate. At this point Peter launches his exercise with the dexterity of a true hustler. He get the women into a 'Die Mutter' phalanx centre stage, shouting their slogan, and the men in the auditorium to provide an unsympathetic audience: he tries to implicate the stage management but fails: the cleaners in the stalls bar are having their break and complain about the volume of noise since silence had been required for the last fortnight. The situation is ripe. The actors in the audience behave uncouthly, unsympathetically and abusively. Jeering, yelling obscenities and laughing. The women are growing all the while in nobility; they play first as themselves and then as the characters in the play. The director asks them if they'd always used the vote when they had an opportunity. They had. He asks the men. Only half of them had. Then the women demanded that the situation be reversed and that the men stand on the stage and face questioning – the point of the improvisation had been made: we can't, won't – it isn't required of us. We had the vote in 1906; they hadn't and that, to a greater or lesser extent, was their social situation. A good piece of work.

Probably what is finally impressive about Peter Gill's work is its total commitment; he loves the writer whose work he is presenting and will not allow any short-changing: the experience of the plays has to have more than just a bare approximation in the lives of his actors, and he'll pursue, bully and inspire them with an intense and generous energy to this end. What he teaches about acting is physical, practical and immediate.

Extracts from reviews of *A Collier's Friday Night*

It is an autobiographical record of his Eastwood home with no incident. The rows, rivalries and wintry affections have been going on for years and no pattern is imposed on them more dramatic than that of life itself.

It would be a big mistake to dismiss the play as artless. . . . One is left to discern the complex family bonds under the daily traffic of eating, washing, gossiping and sharing out the pay packet. . . . [the acting] reawakens one to what naturalism should be: the art of riveting the attention by telling the truth about ordinary life. (from a review by Irving Wardle in *The Times*, 1 March 1968)

. . . a detailed picture of life in his own home in Eastwood. But it is not much of a play. . . . nothing really happens but the slow passing of time . . . trivial questions are all that we are offered, as if we were watching an Edwardian edition of *Coronation Street*. (from a review by Peter Lewis in the *Daily Mail*, 1 March 1968)

Though D. H. Lawrence was not an experienced or polished playwright, with little notion of how a play should develop and resolve itself, his play – and Peter Gill's direction of it – is packed with such minute detail, such accurate observation, that one is gradually sucked into the small, slow, humdrum world of the collier.

This is a production dedicated to the truth, to the way people live, to reality. What emerges are the profound and petty jealousies of seemingly simple people, the bleak plodding sameness of their lives, the erosion of love. (from a review by Herbert Kretzmer in the *Daily Express*, 1 March 1968)

The cinema and the kitchen sink drama, not to speak of *Coronation Street*, have accustomed us to the charms of photographic realism which evidently delight Mr. Gill. He ponders dangerously on them. And since the author himself ponders, dramatically speaking, the two hours pass very slowly. (from a review by Eric Shorter in the *Daily Telegraph*, 1 March 1968)

It is a plotless play but it is not shapeless by any means. . . . It has a fine arching span that reaches from the first sight of Mrs Lambert waiting for her family's return to our last glimpse of her as she goes up to bed, all her family duties completed. I found it continually absorbing. The dialogue is wonderfully recorded, and the emotions are truly felt and transmitted warmly to the audience. (from a review by B. A. Young in the *Financial Times*, 2 March 1968)

Too much form can drain the life from a play. If everything in it derives significance only from its conclusion, nothing but that conclusion can really engage the audience's attention. Lawrence grasped this better than most professional dramatists. *A Collier's Friday Night* has no clear shape, little sense of an ending . . . It's simply a slice out of the life of a family – the family he knew best, and portrayed again in *Sons and Lovers*. Passions erupt for no obvious reason, and subside again as inexplicably, as they do in families, rising from springs too deep for neat theatrical motivation. Nothing has really changed at the end of the evening; a circle of emotions has simply become more articulate. But it's almost impossible to take your eyes from the stage at any moment. Its people are alive in every nerve.

   . . . That is all, but as in the novels Lawrence conveys that these tiny conflicts are the tips of icebergs drifting infinitely slowly to collision. The triumph of Gill's production is its evocation of the deep, animal identities beyond the apparently trivial bickerings. As the mother, Anne Dyson hangs over her child like a famished she-wolf. Even the girls who drop by carry the formidable Lawrentian charge of female antagonism. The playing is beautifully detailed and exact, particularly that of Victor Henry as the educated son and John Barrett as the miner determined to have his wife's obedience if he cannot have her love. If the two remaining plays . . . are done as well, the season should be the event of the theatre year. (from a review by Ronald Bryden in the *Observer*, 3 March 1968)

Extracts from reviews of the *Season of plays*

[The season] has revealed a dramatist of outstanding talent who, though famous in other connections, has been unaccountably neglected on the stage. . . . More generally, it has proved that naturalism, when it is the expression of integrity and high tragic vision, is extremely powerful. . . . [The final scene of *The Widowing of Mrs Holroyd*] . . . a union of naturalism and ritual which, in the depths of its grief and the dignity of its sorrow, none of the masters of ritual has surpassed and few have equalled. (from a review by Harold Hobson in *The Sunday Times*, 17 March 1968)

Anyone who cares for social realism as a means of poignant dramatic expression will go to marvel at the posthumous success of a famous novelist as a kitchen sink playwright. . . . Slow and obvious? Some may think it so. I found it true and touching. (from a review by Eric Shorter in *The Daily Telegraph*, 15 March 1968)

[The plays] have a truth and purity which makes the theatre's normal currency of charm, humour and spectacle seem vulgar. . . . You can see how he [Lawrence] does it in 'Mrs Holroyd' if you attend to the constant unobtrusive detail of washing, cleaning, and ironing. It falls perfectly naturally: what else was the life of a miner's wife? But, as Lizzie Holroyd pursues the endless purification of her house, you know without Freudian hinting or nudging symbolism why she is bound to prefer the genteel electrician who never goes underground, and also why she will never break her marriage for him. When she bends over her husband's back to wash it, the whole movement and cumulative meaning of the play gathers in her gesture like a breaking wave. (from a review by Ronald Bryden in *The Observer*, 17 March 1968)

[*The Widowing of Mrs Holroyd*] exercised an almost hypnotic spell on the audience, gradually pulling them into an appreciation of the minute by minute details of the world of the collier. (from a review by Herbert Kretzmer in *The Daily Express*, 15 March 1968)

No one who cares about the theatre can afford to miss a single one of them. . . . His plays are still life studies in which the reactions of a group of people are examined in relation to a strong central situation. (from a review by B. A. Young in *The Financial Times*, 19 March 1968)

Lawrence wrote eight plays. All of them, even the disconcertingly lush and grandiloquent Old Testament epic, *David*, deserve attention. Their historical importance is pretty obvious; where else in our early twentieth century drama do we find any comparably intelligent attempt to deal with personal relationships on stage? Shaw? Too facetious, too glibly cynical. Galsworthy then? Thin and predictable: didactic, too. Lawrence doesn't seem to impose any preconceived meaning on his plays. Rather they are, in the fullest sense of that overworked adjective, exploratory. . . . There are no villains and no heroes, no fools and certainly no wise men: only a number of people, usually rather self-righteous and invariably maladroit, trying to sort out the problems they continue to create for one another. There is continual action, reaction and re-reaction; they are the least static plays one could imagine. In short they are tremendously alive. (from Benedict Nightingale, 'On the Coal Face', *Plays and Players*, May 1968, pp. 18–19)

It is as if Lawrence were rediscovering the source of those great choric threnodies in Greek tragedy. For a short time at least, the separate members of the audience become one, not only with the mourning widow, but also with the pathetic and still vulnerable body in her arms. The wretched, wearying battle between husband and wife is over, the division between the stage and the spectators vanishes, and something like a community is created out of the shared recognition of the race's tragedy.

This scene is the illuminating climax of the play, but significantly it is followed by another in which Holroyd's mother helps the new widow to prepare the body. The mother is an old woman, already experienced in the loss of sons, and from the moment that she hears the rumour of an accident she lapses into a keening that is really a conversation with fate. "I'm sure I've had may share of bad luck, I have. I'm sure I've brought up five lads in the pit, through accidents and troubles, and now there's this. The Lord has treated me very hard . . ." So that by the time Holroyd's body is brought in she has already come to terms with his death. It is she, then, stoic in her knowledge of what has to be done, who begins to organize the details of the ritual. Seventeen actors appear in the plays, most in two productions and only Anne Dyson in the three. But there is never any question of them duplicating parts even where there are certain resemblances – as there are between the husbands and wives that Michael Coles and Judy Parfitt so beautifully realise in *The Daugher-in Law* and *Mrs Holroyd*. The same is true of John Gunter's four sets; all four are kitchens in miner's cottages, but each is very precisely the home of the people who very precisely inhabit it. The house in *A Collier's Friday Night* is where a middle-aged miner and his wife have brought up their family, just as the spruce living room with its racks of shiny plates in *The Daugher-in-Law* is the new home of the house-proud, disdainful Minnie. Into the first comes a defeated, brutalised man who sits down unwashed to suck his tea from a saucer; into the second shuffles an insecure youngster who hesitates to hang his jacket over a chair. The actors are so sunk in their roles that every unemphasised gesture is part of a personal history, a network of relationships, and a contribution to creating a portrait of a way of life that extends beyond these tiny rooms. Washing off the coal dust after a day's exhausting work, baking a pie, preparing a meal, shoving a stubbed cigarette into a pocket, and a hundred other activities are performed with an exact, unobtrusive veracity that, with the carefully spoken dialect speech convinces us that the world outside created by our imagination is as real as the smell of the stew that wafts over the footlights. . . . Despite the persistent humour, the warmth and depth of the way these characters feel for each other, this is a grim hard life they live, and to embody it as totally as these actors do must be a painful experience. But they never betray Lawrence's truth by attempting to alleviate it with sentimentality, caricature or the suggestion of false hope. They do not, in short, patronise these people.

There are many incidents in the three plays one will never forget: to name just one from each, the reconciliation between son (Victor Henry) and mother (Anne Dyson) in *A Collier's Friday Night*; the blood-chilling moment when the husband screws up the wife's treasured prints and throws them on the fire in *The Daugher-in-Law*; the ritual washing of the dead body which concludes *Mrs Holroyd*. Above all, one remembers a whole world, and this is the great achievement of Peter Gill and his dedicated cast. (from a reiew by Philip French in *The Statesman*, 22 March 1968)

Simon Gray's review of the D. H. Lawrence Season first appeared in *New Society*, 21 March 1968. Entitled 'Lawrence the Dramatist', it is reprinted in *D. H. Lawrence: a Critical Anthology*, ed. H. Coombes (Penguin, 1973) pp. 453–7.

11 *TOUCH AND GO*

Director: Peter Whelan. Presented by The Questors Theatre Company (amateur) at The Questors Theatre, Ealing, London. First night: 6 October 1973 (see Fig. 5)

Cast	Willie Houghton	Peter Sainty
	Anabel Wrath	Sherry Chester-Lawrence
	Job Arthur Freer	Michael Haines
	Oliver Turton	Roger Sherman
	Gerald Barlow	Nevile Cruttenden
	Winifred Barlow	Cathie Jones
	Mrs Barlow	Mary Jones
	Mr Barlow	Kenneth Ratcliffe
	Breffitt	David Lorraine
	Clerks	Alan Chisholm, John Davey,
	Colliers	Alan Chisholm, John Davey,
		Peter Macnamara, Mike Moriarty.
		Paul O'Connor, Tom Pritchard,
		Jack Walsh

In October 1918 Lawrence wrote to Lady Cynthia Asquith that he had written a play fired by his last sparks of hope in the world. But he had little hope of seeing it performed until, in July 1919, Douglas Goldring proposed that *Touch and Go* should be the first play to be performed by his People's Theatre Society, and the first to be published in his series *Plays for a People's Theatre*. On this understanding Lawrence let him have the play and its preface free.

In his preface Lawrence tried to define a People's Theatre. His first point is that the seats are cheap; his second that 'the plays of a People's Theatre are plays about people. Not mannequins. Not lords nor proletarians nor bishops nor husbands nor co-respondents nor virgins nor adulteresses nor uncles nor noses. Not even white rabbits nor presidents. People. Men who are somebody, not men who are something.' If there are still a few 'living individuals' among the miners and masters

> . . . then we have added another tragic possibility to the list: the Strike situation . . . Mr. Galsworthy had a peep, and sank down towards bathos. Granted that men are still men, Labour v. Capitalism is a tragic struggle . . . The man is

caught in the wheels of his part, his fate, he may be torn asunder ...
The essence of tragedy, which is creative crisis, is that a man should go through
with his fate, and not dodge it and go bumping into an accident. And the whole
business of life, at the great critical periods of mankind, is that men should
accept and be one with their tragedy. Therefore we should open our hearts. For
one thing, we should have a People's Theatre. Perhaps it would help us in this
hour of confusion better than anything.

In the event, Goldring was thwarted by a reactionary majority of his theatre
committee. *Touch and Go* was not produced, and had to wait until 1973.
The first play to be published in the series was Goldring's own *The Fight for
Freedom*, which Lawrence despised. *Touch and Go* was second.

Lawrence believed that the new machine age had turned men against men – and
men against women. *Touch and Go* is about the battle of wills between Gerald,
the colliery owner, and his miners, between himself and his parents, and
between himself and Anabel, the woman he has loved too passionately. The
clashes of character are sometimes intense, sometimes comic and in the end a
physical violence arises that threatens tragedy.

With his plea that we should 'change the system' – Lawrence talks directly to
us today in that sure, clear voice that is listened to afresh by a whole new
generation of younger admirers.

This play is so superbly actable, the dialogue full of unexpected twists and
turns, ironies and humours of real speech. The words reveal the depths of people
who are trying to communicate. And yet these words have remained unspoken
for half a century!

There are songs in the play too, and director, Peter Whelan, had taken the
liberty of adding some more. (from *Questopics*, No. 84, September 1973)

The play "Touch and Go" by D. H. Lawrence at the Questors Theatre this
week is, as its title suggests, a risky production for it has never before been
performed.

I found Saturday night's performance slow and monotonous, although the
cast gave its best.

The plot shows the playwright's usual earthy style, concerning a constant
battle of wills between Gerald Barlow, the colliery owner, and his miners,
parents and the woman of his life, Anabel.

Written in 1919, the play is set against Lawrence's home background of the
Eastwood coal mines of Nottingham. Those who have read "Sons and Lovers"
by Lawrence [this reviewer has obviously confused *Sons and Lovers* with
Women in Love] would recognise the central characters in the play.

The story opens with the return of Anabel ... who left Gerald two years
earlier for another lover. His unwillingness to take her back seems to get lost in
disputes between the Barlows, and the next minute the couple are married.

Gerald's strength of character contrasts with his father, a weak-willed man
who, unlike his son, sympathised with the miners when he ran the pit.

Mrs. Barlow . . . is a highly strung character, rowing constantly with Gerald.
The play is a continuous stream of clashes in character, sometimes intense,
sometimes comic, finally ending in violence. In the last scene Gerald and his
colleagues are attacked by the miners giving an exciting ending to an otherwise
tedious story. There is fighting and cursing although no conclusions are drawn.
(from a review in *The County Times and West Middlesex Gazette,* Ealing
edition, 12 October 1973)

12   *THE MERRY-GO-ROUND*

Director: Peter Gill. First night 7 November 1973 at the Royal Court Theatre,
London

Cast		
	Mrs Hemstock	Ann Dyson
	Nurse Broadbanks	Mary Miller
	Mr Hemstock	Alex McCrindle
	Harry Hemstock	Derrick O'Connor
	The Vicar	George Howe
	The Vicar's Wife	Gabrielle Day
	Job Arthur Bowers	David Daker
	Susan Smalley	Marjorie Yates
	Dr Foules	Oliver Maguire
	Rachel Wilcox	Susan Tracy
	Mr Wilcox	George Malpas
	Mrs Heseltine	Margaret Lawley
	Mr Heseltine	Anthony Baird
	Polly Goddard	Patricia Doyle
	Bill Naylor	Michael Melia

During the long days and nights spent sitting by his mother's bedside as she
was dying in December 1910, Lawrence, to relieve the intolerable weight of
pain, wrote a romantic, slightly farcical comedy *The Merry-Go-Round.*

Gill looked on those first three plays, he says, as though they were holy writ. He
cut a handful of lines and brought in a couple from "Sons and Lovers." That's
all. But he knew he would have to do more to "The Merry-go-Round", and he
has. He has in fact adapted it, but he doesn't put that on the credits because, he
says, he has really only done as much as he would have done in consultation with
Lawrence if he'd still been alive. (from an interview with Peter Gill by Hugh
Hebert, *The Guardian,* 7 November 1973)

The deeper the Royal Court ventures into D. H. Lawrence's plays, the more
obvious it becomes that the British theatre has been sitting on a goldmine. No
other native dramatist in the early part of the century dealt so intelligently with

personal relationships; and few (Brighouse and Houghton aside) painted such a vivid picture of British provincial life. Our debt to Peter Gill increases with each new production. . . . As in the other Lawrence plays, emotion is expressed through physical ritual as much as through words: two people simply making a bed can in Lawrence become a symbol of erotic tension. Moreover the language has a regional richness that makes many of Lawrence's contemporaries sound pallid by comparison. . . . I shall not rest till the Court gives us the remainder of the Lawrence output. (from a review by Michael Billington in *The Guardian*, 8 November 1973)

Lawrence is no less interested here than elsewhere in the full naturalistic apparatus, and in powerfully self-willed characters who do not knuckle under easily to the neat patterns of comic situation. The tone of the writing swings between outright farce and the clamped-down intensities of the companion plays. . . . The sense of reality is total, until the farcical wheels start accelerating at the end.

Besides directing, Mr Gill has adapted the play – principally by converting a lamentably unfunny pair of German moral vigilantes into the local Vicar and his lady who come over as acceptable stereotypes who do not clash with the real material. As in his earlier Lawrence shows, Mr Gill devotes microscopic attention to the detail of ordinary life: extracting dramatic life from the way a girl cuts bread (towards the stomach), and expressing a tense relationship from how the two characters make a bed. The comedy is all based on this kind of truth. . . . (from a review by Irving Wardle in *The Times*, 8 November 1973)

We've begun with the sort of situation Lawrence handles peerlessly: powerful mother near death, surly and somewhat emasculated son hovering outside her bedroom, several determined and forceful young women with their eyes on, variously, legacies and him. Is Harry Hemstock (we're asked) man enough to give himself to anyone, and, if so, will it be fickle, warm-hearted, socially suitable Rachel Wilcox or cool, maternal, 'lady-like' Nurse Broadbanks? Now, three-quarters through the play, the dramatic rewards look potentially enormous, with each of these three characters in double conflict, externally with the other two, internally with his or her own unruly emotions: some fierce new crisis is surely inevitable, and, down in the stalls, we begin to curl our toes in anticipation.

But then Lawrence abruptly changes what had appeared to be his mind and the play's mood; and, with a most uncharacteristic smirk and shrug, the putative tragedy becomes a piece of romantic fluff blown in from Shaftesbury Avenue. Harry is hastily reconciled with Rachel, his hang-ups forgotten; the nurse promises herself to a social equal, a doctor who has conveniently wandered in from her distant past; and the local baker, who was to have married Rachel, happily settles for Harry's avaricious, irritable sister. 'As you like it', remarks someone hopefully to the creak of the descending curtain, as if to remind us that Shakespeare was allowed to get away with this sort of nonsense. But I, for one, felt too cheated to be soothed by any appeal to literary authority.

(from a review by Benedict Nightingale in the *New Statesman*, 16 November 1973)

The text has been vitally boosted by Peter Gill, who has excised all manner of improbable stage-directions and extraneous snooping Poles, so as to keep the thing in its small-town perspective (plausible excuse) and keep audiences from unseemly mirth (realistic excuse); and an access of relaxation is the ruin of the play, the rib-tickling bonhomie of the last five minutes being in unacceptable contrast with the preceding couple of hours. There is perhaps something to be said for the theory that if we did not know the little ways of Lawrence's characters so well, and in particular their habit of treating serious matters even more seriously than they deserve, we might not feel so cheated when the cast of *The Merry-Go-Round* collectively perceives the folly of dark obsession and emerges, all smiles, to peddle peaceability and funny punch-lines. But no; even a complete stranger to our lad from Eastwood could hardly accept the bizarre truce he here imposes on his play's conflicts, for the basic reason that the non-aggression pact seems to have been devised offstage. A stageful of splenetic brooders is turned in a trice, as if galvanised by a whopping pay-rise or a few swift pints of black-and-tan, into a pack of rustics. One of the chiefest charms of drama is that it lets us in on the public gallery as moral issues are judged; *The Merry-Go-Round* abruptly settles out of court, a dastardly thing to do. (from a review by Russell Davies in *Plays and Players*, January 1974)

13   *TOUCH AND GO*

Director: Gordon McDougall. 5, 6, 7 and 10 November 1979 at the Oxford Playhouse. 11 November at the Royal Court Theatre, London (see Fig. 6)

Cast		
	Willie Houghton	Robert Ashby
	Anabel Wrath	Louise Jameson
	Job Arthur Freer	David Haig
	Oliver Turton	John Flanagan
	Gerald Barlow	Richard Durden
	Winifred Barlow	Alyson Spiro
	Mrs Barlow	Karin MacCarthy
	Mr Barlow	Tenniel Evans
	William	Robert Mill
	Eva	Jane Redman
	Alfred Brefitt	Godfrey Jackman
	Clerks and Miners	Steven Benton, Philip Franks, Guy Hibbert, Ian Hurley, Anthony Hyde, Godfrey Jackman, Robert Mill, David Plaut, Jamie Roberts

The first professional production of this play. In the programme Gordon McDougall wrote:

Whilst *Touch and Go* takes some of its characters and a very little of its action from *Women in Love*, (which was central to his mind in 1919) the differences are more significant than the similarities. The whole movement of dissent in the labour movement which leads to the moment at which violent revolution is possible, (but finally walked away from) is an original element in Lawrence's writing and one which, in 1919, prophetically explored the possibilities of the subsequent miners' strikes, 1926, and the fears of a Labour government. The interweaving of this with the story of Gerald and Gudrun (now Anabel) some three years on, enables Lawrence to lament a world in which his characters struggle to remain human against overwhelming forces of dehumanisation. In some cases the forces consist of the characters themselves (Oliver accuses Anabel of "dehumanising" Gerald); elsewhere they are the conditions of post-war industrialised society. The men are incapable of producing inspired leaders: Willie Houghton would rather support Gerald than see Job Arthur take over the mines. Gerald's father is a despairing figure who has opted out of life and made his peace with God, his mother a "half-demented woman", driven mad by isolation and her determination to preserve her dominating spirit. Anabel, the artist, tells Winifred, the aspiring artist, that "life works" will ultimately collapse.

The few scenes taken from the book have a distinctly different flavour: in *Women in Love* Gudrun and Winifred work in the studio at a time when Gerald desperately seeks Gudrun's affection. Now Gerald is indifferent, almost hostile to Anabel who rejected him three years previously. The struggle for Anabel and Gerald to come together seems devoid of creative feeling, compassion, compromise. Only Anabel's final desperate appeal to the miners: "he's a man as you are", has the ring of compassionate humanity which is capable of moving a society of hardened hearts.

And we are invited to view the arguments of both labour and capital with a critical judgement which reveals them both as lacking in the vital spark of humanity which in Lawrence's philosophy, can alone provide for the future. It is a bleak view of the state of relations between men and women, managers and men, which has perhaps been little tempered by the sixty years which lie between the writing of the play and its first performance.

Touch and Go shows Lawrence's thinking, his creative spark, at its very worst, and presumably it is only because it has some crude similarities to the political situation of our own day, that the director, Gordon McDougall has seen fit to give it a production. . . . The piece contains numerous, undigested raw elements . . . There isn't a character worthy of the name . . . As for the abrupt stereotyped action this is often laughable. (from a review by Garry O'Connor in the *Financial Times*, 8 November 1979)

Despite a somewhat long-drawn-out and morally and intellectually unsatisfactory conclusion, *Touch and Go* has undeniable power, moments of high drama, and an almost Shavian interplay of ideas, social, sexual and political.

There is no question that this is a piece of weight and moment, by no means dated, and much more than an interesting item of Laurentiana. (from a review by A. W. in the *Oxford Times*, 9 November 1979)

This is a brave and mighty little play in which D. H. Lawrence attempted to do battle with his personal obsessions, relating the world of power and industrial politics to the complex toil of personal relationships and unresolved sexual passions. . . .

The final scene of the play is the test of his ambitious scheme and it seems to me one of the most thrilling episodes in early 20th century drama: a clash of will between the striking miners and the young mine owner who will not concede and has strutted through the play like a peacock. The defeat of these mining men, who are merely in search of a living wage, is an eerie premonition of the 1926 General Strike, and Lawrence's divided sympathies only make it stranger. . . . The final act reveals that just as Gerald regards the struggle with the miners as a test of his potency and force, so his relationship with Anabel will always be a contest of will and strength. Richard Durden, even if dressed like a moustachioed villain, manages the sulky languor beautifully and Louise Jameson is ideally inscrutable. . . .

It is quite horrifying, but true to its time, this victory of the ruling Man who walks away, leaving the miners listless and overwhelmed by words and rank. Mr McDougall, with devastating aptness, has used the pomp and unease of Elgar's Introduction and Allegro for Strings to conclude each scene, and at the close the music sounds a note of harsh, upper class triumph. A play of flaws, but what rewards in the midst of them. (from a review by Nicholas de Jongh in *The Guardian*, 10 November 1979)

The writing always has verve, and quivers throughout with Lawrence's impassioned belief that modern industrial society is a blasphemy against a full and rich life.

But the play leaps absurdly from drawing-room sing-songs to love scenes in a park, and only finally comes to its point – a violent confrontation between the stupidly obstinate and intransigent Gerald with his striking employees, who are asking for a small wage increase and come near to murdering their boss.

However, the playwright does not know how to handle this potentially effective scene and the play ends inconclusively.

But Lawrence does win some sympathy for Gerald, who will not be bullied and would cooperate with the men if only they were represented by a leader he could respect.

He fails, however, to show why Anabel finally marries a man she herself denounces as selfish and wicked. Altogether, in fact, the play is a mess. (from a review by John Barber in the *Daily Telegraph*, 13 November 1979)

Damian Grant

10
A thematic index to
Phoenix and *Phoenix II*

It has long been a source of inconvenience to Lawrence scholars that the miscellaneous prose in the two *Phoenix* volumes is so inadequately indexed. Not only are the indexes to the two volumes in themselves very minimal, but there is no cross-reference between them. The index provided by A. A. H. Inglis to his *Selection from Phoenix* (1971) is much fuller and more helpful, but covers of course only part of the material. All of Lawrence's prose will eventually be included in the Cambridge edition, but this will not be for many years and meanwhile the familiar Heinemann volumes must remain our standard text. It is for this reason that it seems worthwhile to devise an index which will make the material more easily accessible.

The present Index of Themes therefore forms part of an attempt to index the two volumes (excluding the fiction and translations) in a complete and systematic way – the fulfilment of which will inevitably require a volume in itself. Thirty-seven words, or pairs, or groups of words have been selected to identify characteristic and recurrent themes in Lawrence's thought. These are listed alphabetically by head-word.

absolute, infinite	humanity	personality×impersonality
abstraction	idea, ideal, idealism	power
being	individual	psyche, psychology
blood×nerves	instinct, intuition	relation, relationship
body	isolation, separateness	religion
change×fixity	knowledge	self, self-consciousness
consciousness	life	sex
cosmos	love	soul
creation×corruption	machine, mechanism	time, eternity
death	materialism	the unknown
dualism	mind	word, language
ego, egoism	morality	
feeling	nature	

In the index, the heading for each word is followed by a short list of associated words which tend to recur along with the head-word: thus with 'time, eternity' we have 'past, present, future; history; memory'. Each entry then consists of (*a*) an abbreviated reference to the title of the essay quoted, the key to which is given below; (*b*) a page reference, in roman for *Phoenix* and italic for *Phoenix II*; and (*c*) an identifying quotation which places the word in its immediate context. This should enable the user of the index to 'cue in' on a theme; it also enables the index to serve as a Dictionary of Quotations. The symbol × between two words or phrases indicates a contradistinction; the symbol : : indicates a parallel opposition between two or more pairs.

It should be emphasised that the index does not pretend to fulfil the function of a concordance. Not all occurrences of a listed word are given: both because such a compilation would have been impossible without the use of a computer and (more important) because it was felt such mechanical exhaustiveness would actually be counterproductive, burying in duplicated reference those identifications of a theme which have here been selected for their sharpness and typicality.

Some fundamental concepts such as *dualism* and *relation* will be found to underlie and imply all the others; therefore listings here will be very full, and frequently overlap with other entries. Thus the statement that pagan religions 'gave the true correspondence between the material cosmos and the human soul' may be located under 'cosmos', 'materialism', and 'relation'.

Some explanation is required for the principle of selection and for apparent omissions. The words chosen relate to Lawrence's underlying ideas, his 'philosophy'; his vision of reality itself and the place of the elemental human being within that reality. A secondary list could be provided of words which relate to Lawrence's application of these ideas to human history and culture, in the commentary throughout the *Phoenix* volumes on human society and civilisation. Some of the words in the first list tend already in this direction (as the quotations in the index will show): words like *humanity, knowledge, machine, materialism, morality, personality, language* have an inevitable social and 'applied' aspect. To these one might add: *christianity, civilisation, education, industry, marriage, money, politics, science, technology, society, war,* and *work.* It has not been considered practicable to index this second list in the present publication. Nor has it been possible to include the large number of references to literary and artistic terms.

The words *God, man,* and *woman* are not indexed either, because any listing would have had to be very extensive and would result in continual overlap with more usefully specific themes. There is an important distinction to make between Lawrence's treatment of man and woman as beings, in isolation and in relationship, and the male and female principles, which govern the whole of creation, not just the human world. Entries under 'dualism', 'isolation', and 'relationship', among others, will enable the user of the index to locate the places where Lawrence returns, again and again, to the exploration of these themes.

ABBREVIATIONS

Phoenix

I   *Nature and Poetical Pieces*

WBirds	Whistling of Birds
Adolf	Adolf
Rex	Rex
PanAm	Pan in America
ManH	Man is a Hunter
Merc	Mercury
Ngale	The Nightingale
FTusc	Flowery Tuscany
EDion	The Elephants of Dionysus
David	David
Notes	Notes for *Birds, Beasts and Flowers*

II   *People, Countries, Races*

GImp	German Impressions
ChTir	Christs in the Tirol
AmList	America, Listen to Your Own
IndEng	Indians and an Englishman
Taos	Taos

AuRev	Au Revoir, USA
LGer	A Letter from Germany
SeeMex	See Mexico After
EurAm	Europe v America
ParisL	Paris Letter
FFlor	Fireworks in Florence
GerLat	Germans and Latins
NottMC	Nottingham and the Mining Countryside
NewMex	New Mexico

III Love, Sex, Men, and Women

Love	Love
AllTh	All There
MLMus	Making Love to Music
WomCo	Women Are So Cocksure
PObsc	Pornography and Obscenity
WeNeed	We Need One Another
RThing	The Real Thing
NLMe	Nobody Loves Me

IV Literature and Art

PrefIn	Prefaces and Introductions to Books (14 items)
Rev	Reviews of books (19 items)
Hardy	Study of Thomas Hardy
SurNov	Surgery for the Novel – or a Bomb
ArtMor	Art and Morality
MorNov	Morality and the Novel
WhyNov	Why the Novel Matters
JGal	John Galsworthy
InPtgs	Introduction to these Paintsings

V Education

EdP	Education of the People

VI Ethics, Psychology, Philosophy

RPeace	The Reality of Peace
Life	Life
Democ	Democracy
PStudy	The Proper Study
OBRel	On Being Religious
Books	Books
ThSelf	Thinking About Oneself
Res	Resurrection
CDPisg	Climbing Down Pisgah
DucL	The Duc de Lauzun
GMan	The Good Man
NovelF	The Novel and the Feelings
ICoSCo	The Individual Consciousness v The Social Consciousness
InPct	Introduction to Pictures

RLord	The Risen Lord
EnCiv	Enslaved by Civilization
MWork	Men Must Work and Women as Well
AuSk2	Autobiographical Sketch (1929)
Hymns	Hymns in a Man's Life
MPict	Making Pictures
PWalls	Pictures on the Walls
BMan	On Being a Man
HDest	On Human Destiny

ABSOLUTE infinite

FTusc	57	'The absolute is sunniness'
Love	151	'a belief in absolute love, when love is by nature relative'
	152	'Infinity is no arrival . . . what is the infinity of love but a cul-de-sac'
	153	'we are like a rose; we accomplish perfection, we arrive at the absolute'
WeNeed	188–95	absolutes (independence, isolation) inappropriate to human beings
PrefIn	259	'never again shall we be able to put up The Absolute Umbrella, either religious or moral or rational or scientific or practical'
Rev	379	'What must be broken is the egocentric absolute of the individual'
	382	men 'must forfeit . . . the *noli me tangere* of their own absoluteness'
	394	'Catholics . . . will swallow all the old absolutes whole'
	443	'Except in infinity, everything of life is male or female'
Hardy	446	'consciousness . . . is therefore in itself Absolute'
	454	gargoyles in the Cathedrals 'jeered their mockery of the absolute'
	463	'the fundamental, geometric conception of absolute static combination'
	510	'the Two Complementary Absolutes . . . of the Father . . . of the Son'
	513	'the Fixed Absolute, the Geometric Absolute . . . the radiant Absolute, the Unthinkable Absolute'
ArtMor	523	'each man to himself . . . an isolated absolute'
WhyNov	536	'let us have done with the ugly imperialism of any absolute'
EdP	636	'Mankind is an ostrich with its head in the bush of the infinite'; 'All our Oneness and our infinite . . . is merely instrumental to the small individual consciousness'
TwoP	*236*	'The face and breast belong to the . . . luminous infinite'
Crown	*368*	'there cannot exist a specific infinite save by virtue of the

ABSTRACTION

bodiless'

	472	Rembrandt 'must seek for the great female principle in an abstraction'
	474–5	'the abstraction from the spiritual marriage and consummation' in Turner; his art 'is only perfect by reason of abstraction from that context by which and in which it exists'
SurNov	520	abstraction 'really fatal' to new impulse in mankind
InPtgs	570	'the abstracted reality, the ego'; 'we live wound round with the winding-sheet of abstraction'
EdP	602	idea of equality 'a pure intellectual abstraction'
	664–5	'the further, abstracted, mechanical life' man's responsibility, not woman's
Democ	699	the average 'is a pure abstraction'
	704	man-in-the-street 'an abstract idea'
	705	'the abstracted, automatic, invented world of man'
	711	'the idea . . . is . . . an abstraction . . . from the living body of life'
	714	'The central Mystery is no generalized abstraction'
RTay	218	'it is all abstract, impersonal in feeling'
TwoP	230	'religion treats of the material universe as having been . . . created by some will or idea, some sheer abstraction'
LLBoy	444	love 'changes as all things change, save abstractions'
APLC	511	Buddha, Plato, Jesus taught 'that the only happiness lay in abstracting oneself from life'; 'the dry and sterile little world the abstracted mind inhabits'
	512	'We have abstracted the universe into Matter and Force, we have abstracted men and women into . . . personalities'
Insouc	534	'a deadly breach between actual living and this abstract caring'
MWork	584	'The aim is to abstract as far as possible'
	589	'trend of our civilization . . . towards a greater and greater abstraction from the physical'
	590	boy and girl 'each . . . abstracted towards real caricature'

BEING

NottM	136	'a lustrous sort of inner darkness . . . in which we moved and had our real being'
WeNeed	192	'The great I AM does not apply to human beings'
PrefIn	235	'That little laugh of achieved being is all'
	245	'the death of the naïve, pure being'
	293	'the sense of the living astrological heavens gives me an extension of my being'
Hardy	402	'the excess is the thing itself at its maximum of being'
	406	'we . . . run our flag out there in the colour and shine of

	710	'A *being* we shall not attempt to define, because it is undefinable'
	715	'the fall from ... pure being into ... materialism'
ICoSCo	761	'The moment the human being becomes conscious of himself, he ceases to be himself'
	763	'The social consciousness ... can know, but it cannot be'
TwoP	*235*	'Man is divided ... into the upper and lower man: that is, the spiritual and sensual being'
Crown	*372*	'the foam of being thrown up into consummation'
	376	'the crisis of oneness, the blossom, the utter being'
	376–7	'There are myriads of human lives that ... never come into being'
	378	'absolute is the rainbow that goes between; the iris of my ... being'
	384	'Very few men have being at all'
	410–11	'immortality is not a question of time ... It is a question of being'
RefDP	*469*	'fullness of being ... in the fourth dimension'; 'we still find ourselves in the tangle of existence and being'
	470	'The clue to all existence is being. But you can't have being without existence'; 'Being is *not* ideal ... nor spiritual. It is a transcendent form of existence'
APLC	*505*	'It is by blood that we are ... that we live and move and have our being. In the blood, knowing and being ... are one and undivided'
	512	In the mental world men 'feel the bodily presence of any other man a menace ... to their very being'

BLOOD × NERVES

IndEng	99	'The great devious onward-flowing stream of conscious human blood'
AuRev	104	'U.S.A., you do put a strain on the nerves'
	105	Aztecs 'hadn't got even as far as hot-blooded sex'
LGer	110	'Within the last three years, the very constituency of the blood has changed'
EurAm	118	'the American grips himself ... in a grip of care'
GLat	132	'the sun ... melts thoughts away, and sets the blood running with another, non-mental consciousness': 'It is the sun making the blood revolt against old conceptions'
RThing	198	'a stream ... of female life that enters my blood ... and makes me me'
PrefIn	269	'Once the blood-sympathy breaks, and only the nerve-sympathy is left, human beings become ... repulsive to one another'
	276	'There seems to be a cycle ... brutishness ... intelligence

		into communion'
InMFL	322–3	peasant's 'strong blood-presence'×Magnus: 'he had no strong blood in him', only 'parasitic lymph'
	324	" 'If there is no profound blood-sympathy, I know the mental friendship is trash' "
Crown	377	'the way of the blood, the way of power. Down the road of the blood, further and further into the darkness, I come to . . . God'; in sex 'the rocking blood goes forward, quivers on the edge of oblivion, then yields itself up'
Novel	417	Tolstoi 'to blame the column of blood, which . . . gave him all his life riches!'
	423	'Secretly, Leo worshipped the human male, man as a column of rapacious and living blood'
APLC	505	'Marriage is no marriage that is not a correspondence of blood. For the blood is the substance of the soul, and of the deepest consciousness'; 'It is by blood that we are . . . In the blood, knowing and being, or feeling, are one and undivided'; 'The blood of man and the blood of woman are two eternally different streams . . . The phallus is a column of blood that fills the valley of blood of a woman'
	506–8	'impoverishment of the blood' in modern, nervous sexuality
	507	' "personal" marriage' × 'blood-marriage': 'nearly all modern sex is a pure matter of nerves, cold and bloodless . . . in the insistence of this nervous, personal desire the blood-contact becomes frictional and destructive'
	512	each of man's relationships 'is a blood-relationship, not mere spirit or mind'
	513	'In the old England, the curious blood-connection held the classes together'
SFunk	568	'natural warm flow of the blood-sympathy' difficult to achieve
AuSk2	596	'I cannot . . . forfeit my passional consciousness and my old blood-affinity with my fellow-men and the animals and the land'
BMan	616	'Real thought . . . begins as a change in the blood'
	618	'The thought-adventure starts in the blood, not in the mind'
	620	'Suffer and enjoy the change in the blood'; 'risk your body and your blood first, and then . . . risk your mind'

BODY flesh senses the physical

GImp	71	'the tiresome split between . . . animal nature and . . . spiritual'
Love	156	'following the inmost desires of our body and spirit'

	501	'The whole process of digestion, masticating, swallowing, digesting, excretion, is a sort of super-mechanical process'
	502	'life has the two sides, of growth and of decay, symbolized . . . in our bodies by the semen and the excreta'
WhyNov	533	'We think of ourselves as a body with a spirit in it'
	534	'the sum of all knowledge . . . an accumulation of all the things I know in the body'
	535	'I . . . deny that I am a soul, or a body, or a mind, or an intelligence, or a brain, or a nervous system, or a bunch of glands, or any of the rest of these bits of me. The whole is greater than the part'
InPtgs	552	with advent of syphilis 'Man came to have his own body in horror'
	556	'the collapse of the feeling of physical, flesh-and-blood kinship'
	557	'poor high-brow bodies stand there as dead as dust-bins'
	558	'dread and hate of the instincts deep in the body'; 'modern morality has its roots in hatred, a deep, evil hate of the instinctive, intuitional, procreative body'
	559	'imagery is the body of our imaginative life'
	560	'the gleam of the warm procreative body'; Blake 'dares handle the human body'
	561	landscape art 'a form of escape . . . from the actual human body'; watercolour a 'bodiless medium'
	561–2	'Shelley is pure escape: the body is sublimated . . . Keats is more difficult – the body can still be *felt* dissolving'
	562	'truth really *felt*, in the blood and the bones. The English could never think anything connected with the body *religious*'
	562–3	'What do you paint with, Maître [Renoir] – With my penis, and be damned'
	563	impressionists 'escaped from the dark procreative body'
	564	post-impressionists discovered 'There was the body, the great lumpy body'
	569	'the crucifixion of the procreative body for the glorification of the spirit'
	572	Cézanne 'trying with his . . . consciousness to do something which his . . . body didn't want to do'
	573	'the gift of virtuosity simply means . . . you can prostitute your body to your mind'
	575	'My beliefs I test on my body, on my intuitional consciousness'
	578–81	Cézanne's attempt to regain physical contact with life
EdP	612	'never let physical movement be didactic . . . performed from the mind'
	613–20	(ch. v): defends the body against the mind

		sensual
	235	'this division is physical and actual'
	237	'the front part of the body is open and receptive ... the back is sealed, closed'; 'So the division of the psychic body is fourfold'
InMFL	*323*	' "the middle and upper classes are ... parasitic upon the body of life which remains in the lower classes" '
Crown	*369*	'First of all the flesh develops in splendour and glory'
	371	'within the withered body of our era ... the husk of the past'
	397	'the dead body of creation'
	398	'this reduction within the self is sensationalism'
	411	'the body of man is begotten and born in an ecstasy of delight and of suffering ... It is the battle-ground and marriage-bed of the two invisible hosts ... consummate, perfect, absolute, the human body'
APLC	*489*	man's reluctance 'to contemplate his own physical body'
	490	'The body is a good deal in abeyance' in modern sex
	491	'the mind's terror of the body has probably driven more men mad than could ever be counted'
	492	'life is only bearable when the mind and body are in harmony'; 'the body is ... dead or paralysed'
	493	'All the emotions belong to the body, and are only recognized by the mind'
	494–5	'the body itself hits back' at false feeling
	510	need to relate 'the body's year' to the rhythm of the cosmos: 'a need of the mind and soul, body, spirit and sex'
	511	'the gospel of salvation through ... escape from the body'
	512	Protestantism forfeited 'the togetherness of the body ... with the earth and sun and stars'; 'bodily presence' of other men now threatens us
CWom	*553*	woman's 'sureness was a physical condition'
SFunk	*570*	'Accept the sexual, physical being of yourself, and of every other creature ... Don't be afraid of the physical functions'; 'when men and women are physically cut off, they become at last dangerous'
RLord	*574–5*	'Christ rises ... in the flesh, not merely a spirit ... a man at last full and free in flesh and soul'
MWork	*582–91*	the revulsion against the physical in our civilization
	584	'this revulsion from physical effort, physical labour and physical contact'
	587	'our gross necessities' remain
	589–90	modern young 'flaunting ... the body in its non-physical, merely optical aspect'; 'physically repulsive to one another'
	590	'working man today ... has no body and no real feelings

		at all'
	591	revolution as 'a great burst of anti-physical insanity': 'the Soviet hates the real physical body far more deeply than it hates Capital'; 'the only thing to do is to get your bodies back'
MPict	*603*	painting is 'instinct, intuition, and sheer physical action'
BMan	*616–22*	man must live in the body as well as the mind
	616	'Real thought . . . a slow convulsion and revolution in the body itself'; man 'must go forward and meet life in the body'; 'the self that lives in my body I can never finally know'
	619	'the Cross . . . stands for the body, for the dark self which lives in the body'
	620	'to risk your body and your blood first, and then your mind'
	622	'the old Adam of red earth'
HDest	*623*	primitive ideas 'based on . . . reactions in the black breast and bowels'

CHANGE × FIXITY

FTusc	57	'the endless and rapid change' in the sun: 'But underneath lies the grey substratum, the permanency of cold, dark reality where the bulbs live'
AmList	88	'You can't fix a high-water mark to human activity: not till you start to die'
	90–1	need for new life-forms in America, 'surpassing . . . the old European life-form'
FFlor	124	'If anything is detestable, it is hard, stupid fixity'
WeNeed	192	'fixed ideas are no good'
	193	'The long course of marriage is a long event of perpetual change'
	194	'Sex is a changing thing, now alive, now quiescent, now fiery, now apparently quite gone'; 'If only we could break up this fixity'
PrefIn	218–22	Preface to *New Poems*: living moment × finality, perfection
	219	'Life, the ever-present, knows no finality, no finished crystallization . . . Give me nothing fixed, set, static. . . Give me . . . the moment, the quick of all change and haste and opposition'
	221	'We can break the stiff neck of habit. We can be in ourselves spontaneous and flexible as flame'
	222	'supreme mutability and power of change' × things 'set apart, in the great storehouse of eternity'
	255	'chaos' × 'form and stability, fixity'

Rev	316–17	'It is true that lilies may fester. And virtues likewise . . . If stars wax and wane, why should Goodness shine for ever unchanged?'
	343	'This world remains the same, wherever we go'
Hardy	402	'A new creature must have new air . . . to breathe'
	410	'Of anything that is complete there is no more tale to tell'
	424–5	man at work 'traverses the fixed channels and courses of life'; man in being 'must give himself up to . . . quivering uncertainty'
	429	'These old, old habits of life man rejoices to rediscover in all their detail'
	434	'repeating even the most complex motions of life will not produce one new motion'
	444–9	male motion × female stability
	444	'his motion shall portray her motionlessness, convey her static being into movement'
	445–6	'Every man seeks in woman for that which is stable, eternal . . . man, the male, is essentially a thing of movement and time and change'
	447	'So life consists in the dual form of the Will-to-Motion and the Will-to-Inertia'
	457	Raphael picture 'geometric, static, abstract'; 'The goal of the male impulse is the announcement of motion . . . endless diversity, endless change. The goal of the female impulse is the announcement of infinite oneness, of infinite stability'
	514	'In every creature, the mobility, the law of change, is found exemplified in the male; the stability, the conservatism is found in the female'
ArtMor	525	'We move, and the rock of ages moves . . . the centre shifts at every moment'; 'nothing, not even man nor the God of man, nor anything that man has thought or felt or known, is fixed or abiding'
MorNov	527	'The relation between all things changes from day to day, in a subtle stealth of change'
	528	'Philosophy, religion, science, they are all of them busy nailing things down . . . If you try to nail anything down, in the novel, either it kills the novel, or the novel gets up and walks away with the nail'
WhyNov	536	'All things flow and change, and even change is not absolute'
JGal	543	'to keep up a convention needs only the monotonous persistency of a parasite'
InPtgs	580	Cézanne's desire in art: 'to make the human form, the *life* form, come to rest. Not static – on the contrary. Mobile but come to rest . . . he *could* see that gradual flux of

		change . . . he *felt* for their changes'
EdP	592	'It has become an *idée fixe*, the idea of earning, or not earning, a living'
	614	'we are . . . born and swaddled in fixed beliefs'; 'as the land changes, his beliefs must change'; 'Man is given mental intelligence in order that he may effect quick changes, quick readjustments'
	629	'we have become too fixedly conscious. We have limited our consciousness, tethered it to a few great ideas, like a goat to a post'
RPeace	671	'the anarchy of fixed law, which is mechanism'
	672	the Red Indian 'has held himself aloof from all pure change . . . confined within bonds of an unbreakable will'
	673	'Who dares leap into the tide of new life? Who dares to perish from the old static entity . . .?'
	680	'The lark sings in a heaven of pure understanding, she drops back into a world of duality and change'
	685	vulture and condor as images of fixity
	687	'the living dead' as 'the great static evil which stands against life and against death'
Democ	712	abstraction results in 'static fixity, mechanism, materialism'
	715	'the life-activity must never be degraded into a fixed activity, there must be *no fixed direction*'
OBRel	727	'God doesn't just sit still somewhere in the Cosmos . . . He . . . wanders His own strange way down the avenues of time, across the intricacies of space'; 'the great stars and constellations and planets are all the time slowly, invisibly, but absolutely shifting their positions'; 'In the great wandering of the heavens, the foot of the Cross has shifted'
	729	'The Almighty has shifted His throne, and we've got to find a new road'
Res	738	'The world and the cosmos stagger to the new axis'
CDPisg	743–4	'The vast demon of life has made himself habits which . . . he will never break . . . these habits are the laws of our scientific universe. But all the laws of physics, dynamics, kinetics, statics, all are but the settled habits of a vast living incomprehensibility'
	744	'Young men will change their minds and their pants'
GMan	753	'our true bondage' that there is 'nothing new on the face of the earth'
CHome	*250–3*	'almost deathly sense of stillness' in England, 'intolerable shut-in-edness'
RBest	*264*	'what I am struggling for is life . . . struggling against fixations and corruptions'

	265	'What is alive, and open, and active, is good. All that makes for inertia, lifelessness, dreariness, is bad'
Crown	396	'The goodness of anything depends upon the direction in which it is moving'; 'While we live, we change, and our flowering is a constant change'
	397	imprisonment 'within the walls of unliving fact'
	405	'The ego, like Humpty Dumpty, sitting for ever on the wall'; vulture as 'static form' of eagle
	406	'the spirit incarnate of the fixed form of life'
	407	'spirit of perpetuation' as evil: 'life-forms ... now arrested, petrified, frozen falsely, timeless ... stark and static'
	408	'the vulture is beyond life or change'
	409	'This is the changelessness of the kingdoms of the earth, null, unthinkable'
	412	'Only perpetuation is a sin ... we must not think to tie a knot in Time'
	413	'The error of errors is to try to keep heaven fixed and rocking like a boat anchored within the flux of time'
	414	'This is evil, this desire for ... fixity in the temporal world'; the revelation of God is permanently changing; 'Memory is persistence, perpetuation of a momentary cohesion in the flux'; 'all our social and religious form is dead, a crystallized lie'
Aris	484	'The world is stuck solid inside an achieved form'
APLC	504	'Augustine said that God created the universe new every day'; sex 'always different, always new' in the life of man and woman
DoWoCh	539	'Humanity seems to have an infinite capacity for remaining the same'
MHouse	546	young boy 'grows up with the idea well fixed'
	547	'mass ideas ... remain, like fossils, when the life that animated them is dead'
SFunk	565	'The time of change is upon us ... And we are frightened. Because change hurts'; 'every child that is begotten and born is a seed of change'
	566	'A change is a slow flux, which must happen bit by bit'
	566-7	a vision of change in society: 'Change in the whole social system is inevitable not merely because conditions change ... but because people themselves change'
	567	'As a novelist, I feel it is the change inside the individual which is my real concern'
MWork	582	'change is of two sorts: the next step, or a jump in another direction'
	587	'Human feeling has changed ... rapidly and radically'
	588	'Can human instincts really change? They can, and in the

	281	dirtied words driven 'out of the consciousness with filth . . . haunting the margins of consciousness like jackals'
	282	'I call it a waste of sane human consciousness'
	289	'heavenly bread is life, is contact, and is consciousness'
	295	'Symbols are organic units of consciousness . . . belonging to the sense-consciousness of body and soul'
Rev	323	'the everlasting hinterland of consciousness'
	324–5	'we are pot-bound in our consciousness'
	335	W. C. Williams 'tries to bring into his consciousness America itself'
	364	Dos Passos: 'different things . . . rushing along in the consciousness'
	377–82	Review of *The Social Basis of Consciousness* by Trigant Burrow
	378	'man became cognitively conscious . . . his consciousness split'
	379	'in the first moment of his consciousness man stood, for the first time, *alone*'; 'Consciousness is self-consciousness'; man 'must strive for more consciousness, which means . . . a more intensified aloneness'
	380	'Consciousness should be a flow from within outwards'
	381	'human consciousness' × 'social, or image consciousness'
	390	effect of western ideas on 'hot and undeveloped consciousness' of Russia
Hardy	417	Clym's 'limited human consciousness'
	419	'human consciousness' × 'nature of . . . life itself, surpassing human consciousness'
	429	'But this time he is conscious, he knows what he is doing'
	430–1	'the great aim and purpose in human life . . . to bring all life into the human consciousness'
	431	'Man's consciousness . . . is his greater . . . individuality'
	434	'the whole of the human consciousness contains . . . not a tithe of what *is*'
	443–4	'the consciousness . . . is of both [male and female] . . . The consciousness . . . the truth, is eternal'
	446	'Consciousness is the same effort in male and female to obtain perfect frictionless interaction . . . and is therefore itself Absolute'
	453	'consciousness of the body came through woman'
	494	Clare's 'male impulse towards extending the consciousness'
	495	Sue 'wanted life merely in the . . . consciousness'
	499–500	Jude 'wanted . . . to find conscious expression for that which he held in his blood'
	501	Sue 'existed as a consciousness'
	504–6	Sue 'existed . . . as a point of consciousness'; Jude 'dragged

destroyed by 'the personal mode of consciousness' (625)

627–33   (ch. vii): 'primal consciousness' degenerating into 'self-consciousness'

628   'these four great nerve-centres establish the first field of our consciousness . . . our profound primal consciousness'; 'mental cognition or consciousness is . . . telegraphed from the primal consciousness into a sort of written, final script in the brain'

629   'the whole mental consciousness . . . can never be more than a mere tithe of all the vast surging primal consciousness'

634   Light 'symbolizes our universal mental consciousness'

636   the infinite is 'merely instrumental to the small individual consciousness'

643   'it is in this spontaneous consciousness that education arises'

650   activity of 'primal consciousness' a 'pure satisfaction'

655   polarity between mental and physical consciousness

657   'It is all wrong to mix up the two modes of consciousness'

RPeace   677–9   both creation and corruption part of consciousness

Democ   706   'Your *consciousness* is not *you*'

710   the ego as 'body of accepted consciousness'

PStudy   719–23   the adventure towards 'man's final consciousness'

Books   732   'Man is a great venture in consciousness'

ThSelf   735   'Perhaps it is a burden, this consciousness'

CDPisg   741   'venture of consciousness' the only adventure left to man

ICoSCo   761–4   The Individual Consciousness v. the Social Consciousness

761   'social consciousness means the cleaving of the true individual consciousness into two halves, subjective and objective'

762   'radical individual consciousness . . . is unanalysable and mysterious'

763   'social consciousness can only be analytical'

InPct   765–71   'pristine consciousness' of body × 'secondary consciousness' of mind

766   'the pernicious mental consciousness called the spirit'

767   brain mediates between 'spontaneous consciousness' and 'voluntary consciousness'

768   ideas 'units of transmuted consciousness'

769   'the body, the pristine consciousness' besieged by ideas

ArtInd   *222*   'consistent purpose working through the whole natural world and human consciousness'

TwoP   *236*   'the blood has a perfect but untranslatable consciousness of its own'

237   'when this fourfold consciousness is established in the body . . . only then do we come to full consciousness in the

COSMOS universe   sun   moon   stars   earth as plant

	510	'We must plant ourselves again in the universe'
	512	Protestantism forfeited 'the togetherness of the body, the sex, the emotions, the passions, with the earth and sun and stars'
Hymns	598	'The moon ... has shrunken a little'

CREATION × CORRUPTION new life × disintegration dissolution reduction

WBirds	5	'This is the morning of reality ... glimmering of a new creation'
Ngale	41	'the first day of creation, when the angels ... found themselves created'
Love	151	'Love is the force of creation. But all force, spiritual or physical, has its polarity'
PObsc	176	'Sex is a creative flow, the excrementory flow is towards dissolution, de-creation'
PrefIn	289	'the wonder of creation, procreation, and re-creation, following the mystery of death and the cold grave'
Hardy	426	'kings were ... producers of new life, not servants of necessity'
	502	'life has the two sides, of growth and of decay, symbolized most acutely in our bodies by the semen and the excreta'
InPtgs	573	'Any creative act occupies the whole consciousness of a man'
EdP	610–11	'the disintegration of mankind into amorphousness and oblivion'
RPeace	669	'the living drift of the unknown ... the direction of creation'
	671	'We must abide by the incalculable impulse of creation'
	673	'a living man must leap away from himself into the ... awful fires of creation'
	675–82	(ch. ii): the desire of creation and the desire of dissolution
	676	'From our bodies comes the issue of corruption as well as the issue of creation'; 'creation is primal and original, corruption is only a consequence'
	683	'slow inward corruption' of the living dead: on the 'flood of decomposition and decay': 'What has creation to do with them?'
Life	695–8	creation and the 'creative unknown'
	695	man is 'the quick of creation': 'He can but submit to the creator, to the primal unknown out of which issues the all'
	697	'I am but a flame conducting unknown to unknown, through the bright transition of creation'; 'It is a question of creative courage ... Do I fear the strange approach of the creative unknown to my door? I fear it only with pain and with unspeakable joy'

	665	man 'running on the brink of death and at the tip of . . . life'
RPeace	671	'this is the courage of death . . . to die bravely is not enough'
	673	'For we must all die. But we need not all live'
	674	'when I accept death I have . . . quiescence and resignation'; 'the activity of death . . . Our death-passion has accumulated from our fathers'
	675	'all strife between things old is pure death'
	675–82	(ch. ii): life and death, creation and dissolution
	675	'We have a winter of death . . . to surmount and surpass'
	676	'the bitter necessity to understand the death that has been'
	680	'there are ultimately only two desires, the desire of life and the desire of death'
	681	'We can never conquer death . . . Death and the great dark flux of undoing, this is the inevitable half. Life feeds death, death feeds life'
	682–7	(ch. iii): the living dead: death the purifier
	682	'the desire for death becomes single and dominant'
	683–4	'The quick can encompass death, but the living dead are encompassed . . . The righteousness of the living dead is . . . nullity'
	684	'beautiful death searches us out'
	686	'Sweet death, save us from humanity'
	687–94	(ch. iv): the two ways: of life and death
	687	will breaks up 'the systole-diastole of life and death'
	688	'the straight road of death has splendour'
	689	'there is swift death, and slow'
	692	'the great mystic truth of death'
Life	695–6	man is 'living beyond life itself and deathly beyond death . . . consummated in life and death both'
TwoP	231	'The inanimate material universe is born through death from the living universe'
InMFL	354	'I respect [Magnus] for dying when he was cornered'
Crown	374	'Death is a temporal, relative fact'
	375	'Death is part of the story'
	383	separation brings 'death and decay and corruption'
	388	war as 'the triumph of death, of decomposition'
	392	'we give ourselves up to the flux of death . . . the activity of death is the only activity'
	393	'The actual physical fact of death is part of the life-stream'
	400	'passion for the embrace with death' in war
	401–2	maimed soldier 'unloosed . . . into the light of death . . . he was surrounded by . . . people . . . seeking the death in him'
	407	'What is evil? – not death . . . but this spirit of

	perpetuation'	
	414	'we seek war, death, to kill this memory within us'
Novel	*419*	'We have to choose between the quick and the dead'
	420	'the sum and total of all deadness we may call human'
HTail	*429*	'Death . . . solves its own problems'
APLC	*492*	'The body is . . . dead or paralysed'
	510	man needs 'the renewal forever of the complete rhythm of life and death'
MHouse	*548*	'indifference is the real malady of the day . . . a deadness, an inability to care about anything'
RLord	*575–7*	vision of Christ risen from the dead: fulfilment in the flesh
PWalls	*610*	'Pictures are like flowers, that fade away sooner or later, and die'
HDest	*629*	'There is a long life-day for the individual. Then a very dark, spacious death-room –'

DUALISM division opposition polarity

WBirds	5	'We are for life, or we are for death . . . but never . . . both at once'
Rex	18	dog's 'true nature, like so much else, was dual'
Merc	36	'tree-trunks like chords of music between two worlds'
FTusc	57	north×south : : grey ×sun : : performance×change
David	62–3	fire×dew : : south×north : : Dionysus×David
Notes	65	' "from the symmetry of their mixture of fire and water, [trees] contain the proportion of male and female" '
	67	' "in the tension of opposites all things have their being" '
GImp	71	'I prefer the Frenchman who hasn't the tiresome split between his animal nature and his spiritual'
LGer	107	'The Rhine is still the Rhine, the great divider'
	108–10	division in the German soul: 'back to the savage polarity of Tartary, and away from the polarity of civilized . . . Europe'
Love	151	'the coming together depends on the going apart; the systole depends on the diastole; the flow depends upon the ebb'; 'Love is the force of creation. But all force, spiritual or physical, has its polarity, its positive and its negative'
	153–6	the dual movement of love: singleness×communion
PObsc	176	'Sex is a creative flow, the excrementory flow is towards dissolution'
PrefIn	227–9	subjective×objective self in Verga: 'In the sun, men are objective, in the mist and snow, subjective'
	242	'It is the difference between a passionate nature and an emotional'
	244	reason×passion alternatives
	252–4	DHL's 'demon'×'ordinary me': 'the demon is timeless . . .

		centres . . . with two corresponding volitional centres'
	623	separated child seeks 'corresponding pole of vitality in another'; 'the child is born and divided into separate existence'
	628	'four great nerve-centres establish the first field of our consciousness . . . four corner-stones of our psyche . . . flashing darkly in polarized interaction'
	629	'primary consciousness' × 'ideal consciousness'
	634	sunlight × starlight : : connection × separateness
	655	'our consciousness is dual, and active in duality . . . The two are never one save in their incomprehensible duality'
	657	'It is all wrong to mix up the two modes of consciousness'
RPeace	669	'There is a great systole-diastole of the universe'
	675	'The . . . division of mankind into two halves . . . is death'
	676–7	'We are not only creatures of light and virtue. We are also alive in corruption and death . . . We are angels and we are devils, both'
	679	'There is in me the desire of creation and the desire of dissolution. Shall I deny either? Then neither is fulfilled'
	680	'there are ultimately only two desires, the desire of life and the desire of death . . . the understanding is a consummating of the two in one'
	681	'even understanding is twofold . . . of life or . . . of death'
	689	'There are two roads and a no-road': life, death, and 'nullity'
	691	'Each, saint or wolf, shines by virtue of opposition'
	692–3	'Where . . . is there peace if the primary law of all the universe is a law of dual attraction and repulsion, a law of polarity? . . . There is peace in that perfect consummation when duality and polarity is transcended into absorption'; 'It is not of love that we are fulfilled, but of love in such . . . equipoise with hate that the transcendence takes place'
Life	696	'We are balanced like a flame between the two darknesses . . . of the beginning and . . . of the end'
Democ	710	conscious self × spontaneous self
	712	'You can have life two ways. Either . . . from the mind, downwards; or . . . from the creative quick, outwards'
	713	'We must discriminate between an ideal and a desire'
	714	'Man's nature is balanced between spontaneous creativity and mechanical-material activity'
CDPis	743	'dual desire . . . forth into creation, and . . . back, in death'
GMan	752	'Whoever invents morality invents . . . immorality'
ICoSCo	761–4	Individual Consciousness v Social Consciousness
	761	'the psyche splits in two, into subjective and objective reality'
	762	'Man lapses from . . . innocence . . . in two ways':

		visible between the two Infinities'
	374	'the fight of opposites . . . is holy. The fight of like things is evil'
	377	'I know I am compound of two waves'
	379–81	the tyranny of the One: 'The true crown is upon the consummation itself, not upon the triumph of one over another'
	383	the seed divides into flower and root: 'there is a red splash as the poppy leaps into the upper fiery eternity . . . below there is unthinkable silence as the roots ramify and divide'
	396	'we are balanced between the flux of life and the flux of death'
	404	'Destruction and Creation are the two relative absolutes between the opposing infinities . . . life is really in the two'
	409–15	(ch. vi): the two eternities of past and future; being as consummation of the two
	410	'The motion of the eternities is dual: they flow together, and they flow apart'
	411	the human body as 'the battle-ground and marriage-bed of the two invisible hosts . . . it is the iris of the two eternities'
	412	art as 'an absolute relation between the two eternities'
	413	'The two waves of Time flow in from the eternities'
HTail	*430*	'We live in a multiple universe'
	431	'Equilibrium argues either a dualistic or a pluralistic universe. The Greeks . . . were pantheists and pluralists, and so am I'
	434	'If it is to be life, then it is fifty per cent. me, fifty per cent. thee'
LLBoy	*444–59*	the balance between love and individualism
	444	'love, as a desire, is balanced against the opposite desire, to maintain the integrity of the individual self' . . . 'Hate is not the opposite of love. The real opposite of love is individuality'
	456	'Everything that exists . . . has two sides to its nature. It fiercely maintains its own individuality . . . And it reaches forth from itself in the subtlest flow of desire'
Ref	*470*	'All existence is dual, and surging towards a consummation'
Aris	*481*	'the vast inexhaustible duality of creation'
	482	'active life'×'quiescent life' : : sun×night
APLC	*489*	'thought and action, word and deed, are two separate forms of consciousness, two separate lives which we lead'
	497	'men are *socially* thrilled, while sexually repelled' by explicit sex
	498	'we are very mixed, all of us, and creatures of many diverse and often opposing desires'

		intuitive uncertainty'
	582	man's ego 'is his ready-made mental self'
	584	egos 'totally enclosed in pale-blue glass bottles of insulated inexperience'
EdP	637	'so-called individualism is no more than a cheap egotism'
	642	'in English the ego is very insistent'
RPeace	684	'the base absolution of the *I*'
	685	'There is an egoism far more ghastly than that of the tyrannous individual. It is the egoism of the flock'
Democ	710	'The *ego* is . . . a sort of second self'
	711	'the self-conscious ego . . . prancing and displaying itself like an actor . . . personalities and *egos* . . . are quite *reasonable*'
InPct	768	'the self-aware-of-itself has *always* the quality of egoism' . . . 'deliberate humility . . . is a rabid form of egoism'
	769	'This self-aware ego *knows* it is a derivative . . . So it must assert itself'
CHome	253	the Englishman 'enclosed . . . within the box, or bubble, of his own self-contained ego'
RevIn	283	introspection makes you 'vastly important to yourself'
Crown	367	' "I know I exist, I know I am I, because I feel the divine discontent which is personal to me" '
	380	'the egoistic God, I AM' . . . 'the crown of sterile egoism'
	381	'The ego is the false absolute'
	384	'my inferior I, my self-conscious ego'
	388	'the crowd of assertive egos' adhere to 'the null rind'
	389–97	(ch. iv): Within the Sepulchre: the ego in the tomb
	390–1	'Thus the false I comes into being: the I which thinks itself supreme . . . this is the triumph of the ego . . . the glory of the ego . . . the apotheosis of the ego . . . the unconscious undoing of the ego'; 'The ego has no feeling, it has only sentiments' . . . 'the ego in a man secretly hates every other ego'
	394	egoistic sex: 'Ego reacts upon ego only in friction'
	396	'once we fall into the state of egoism, we cannot change'
	397	'the human ego, in its pettifogging arrogance, sets up . . . absolutes'
	398	'Sensationalism . . . is the doom of egoistic sex'
	399	the ego 'vulgarly triumphant in the power of the Will'
	405	'The ego, like Humpty Dumpty, sitting for ever on the wall'
	406	'The danger lies in the fall into egoism'
	407	'static forms' of 'the achieved ego'
	409	'the I gone beyond the I'
Novel	426	'The flame of sex . . . scorches your ego'
BlesP	436	'Will is no more than an attribute of the ego'

FEELING emotion sympathy × insentience, sentiment

Italian

	296	symbols as 'units of human feeling': 'the power of the symbol is to arouse the deep emotional self'
Rev	328	'a creature born crippled in its affective organism'
	338	'she only locks up the flow of her passion tighter'
	344–5	'this degenerate insentience . . . barren of the feeling for life . . . how grateful we ought to be to a man who sets new visions, new feelings . . . quivering in us'
	349	'without a full and subtle emotional life the mind . . . must wither'
	389	'trying to *act* feelings because you haven't really got any'
	390	'the most difficult thing in the world is to achieve real feeling'
	391	Rozanov's 'real struggle to get back a positive self, a feeling self'
Hardy	398	primitive man 'making graven images of his unutterable feelings'
	416–17	Clym's 'feelings, that should have produced the man, were suppressed and contained': 'he was emotionally undeveloped'
	437	Hardy's aristocrats 'have all passionate natures, and in them all failure is inherent'
	446–7	'desire is the admitting of deficiency . . . [man's] religious effort . . . is the symbolizing of a great desire'
	455	'The female impulse, to feel and to live in feeling'
	461	Michelangelo's 'desire is to realize in his body, in his feeling'
	480	'If it were not that man is much stronger in feeling than in thought, the Wessex novels would be sheer rubbish . . . [Hardy's] feeling, his instinct . . . is . . . very great and deep'
	489	'A man is as big as his real desires'
	494	Jude 'monkish, passionate, medieval'
	498	Christian principle 'exists beyond feeling . . . only in Knowing'
	509	denial of 'the Female, the Law, the Soul, the Senses, the Feelings'
SurNov	520	novel must 'present us with new, really new feelings . . . which will get us out of the emotional rut'
JGal	539	'criticism can be no more than a reasoned account of the feeling produced upon the critic . . . The touchstone is emotion, not reason . . . A critic must be able to *feel* the impact of a work of art'
	541	sense of connection with the universe 'the last and deepest feeling that is in a man'
	545	'Sentimentalism is the working off on yourself of feelings you haven't really got'

	225	'We can feel, but we cannot transmit our feelings – we can't express ourselves'
TwoP	233	'the Cross . . . stirs us to the depths with unaccountable emotions'
RevIn	275	'This novel [*Women in Love*] pretends only to be a record of the writer's own desires, aspirations, struggles . . .'
	276	'Nothing that comes from the deep, passional soul is bad, or can be bad'
Crown	391	'The ego has no feeling, it has only sentiments'
	395	'The most evil things in the world . . . are to be found under the . . . folds of sentimentalism. Sentimentality is the garment of our vice'
LLBoy	451–8	the 'subtle streaming of desire' preferable to 'love'
	455	'Desire itself is a pure thing, like sunshine, or fire, or rain'
APLC	490	the young 'a seething confusion of sexual feelings'
	492	'the mind has a stereotyped set of ideas and "feelings", and the body is made to act up, like a trained dog'
	493	'All the emotions belong to the body, and are only recognized by the mind'
	493–7	destructive effects of 'counterfeit feeling' in sex, love, and friendship
	493	'belief is a profound emotion that has the mind's connivance'
	494	'all my friends would turn my . . . emotions to ridicule'
	495	'Sex lashes out against counterfeit emotion'
	501	'man has a double set of desires, the shallow and the profound'
	505	'In the blood, knowing and being, or feeling, are one and undivided'
	507	'sympathy of nerves and mind . . . is . . . hostile to blood-sympathy'
	513	'feeling of individualism and personality' replaces 'feeling of oneness and community'
	514	Clifford Chatterley's 'deeper emotional or passional paralysis'; essay gives 'the emotional beliefs . . . necessary as a background to the book'
GPat	537	'the strange and terrible logic of emotion'
MHouse	548	'This indifference is the real malady of the day'
SFunk	567	'My field is to know the feelings inside a man, and to make new feelings conscious'; 'feelings are a form of vital energy'
	569	'the natural warm flow of common sympathy'
EnCiv	578	'men have not learned to . . . stick up for their own instinctive feelings'
	580	'the artificial stock emotion which comes out with the morning papers'

HUMANITY mankind × the non-human

'the individual interest'

446 'Eternal, Infinite, Unchanging: the High God of all Humanity is this'

510 'It seems as if the history of humanity were divided into two epochs: the Epoch of the Law and the Epoch of Love'

514 'humanity does not continue for long to accept the conclusions of these writers ... even of Euripides and Shakespeare always'

ArtMor 524 'Cézanne ... begins to see more than the All-Seeing Eye of humanity can possibly see'

JGal 540–3 social being×human being in Galsworthy

EdP 588 'the high ideal of human existence'

590 'The system ... is only the outcome of the human psyche, the human desires'

615 'We have got to discover a new mode of human relationship ... we have got to get a new conception of man and of ourselves'

636 'Mankind is an ostrich with its head in the bush of the infinite'

637 'one human being is always more than six collective human beings'

655 'the whole system [of education] seems to be a conspiracy to falsify and corrupt human nature'

665 'Humanity can never advance into the new regions of unexplored futurity' without 'deathless friendship between man and man'

RPeace 673 'who dares have done with humanity?'

682 'When it is ... the autumn of a human epoch, then the desire for death becomes single and dominant'

684 'the word humanity has come to mean only this obscene flock of blind mouths'

685–7 'the human mass' as 'an obscene whole ... a multiplied nullity': 'Let there be no humanity ... save us from humanity ... smash the glassy rind of humanity'

Democ 704 'man has invented ... the whole ideal of humanity'

PStudy 719–23 man's role as adventurer in 'the great life'

721 'the best of the human consciousness' in new experience; 'the greater history of man'×'the lesser history'

Books 731 'miserable Israel of the human consciousness'; 'Man is a liar unto himself'

CDPisg 740–4 v. mechanical humanity

740 'the very words *human, humanity, humanism* make one sick'

741 'the graveyard of humanity'

742 'the known World ... is the Human World ... *Omnis a me humanum alienum puto* ... Here I am, without a

IDEA IDEAL IDEALISM theory thought

PanAm	23	men love 'the pomp of argument and the vanity of ideas'
	29	'The idea and the engine came between man and all things, like a death'
MLMus	160	'We are the embodiment of the most potent ideas of our progenitors ... transmitted as instincts and as the dynamics of behaviour to the third and fourth generation'
WeNeed	191–2	'It is time we got rid of these fixed notions ... We are labouring under a false conception of ourselves ... fixed ideas are no good'
PrefIn	216	'Away with all ideals'
	222	'The ideal – what is the ideal? A figment. An abstraction'
	259	dismisses 'The vast parasol of our conception of the universe'
	275	'the anguish of the idealists'
	297	'it is not Reason herself whom we have to defy, it is ... our accepted ideas and thought-forms'
Rev	317	'Idealism now is a sick nerve'
	377–8	endorses Burrow's criticism of Freud: 'he was always applying a *theory*'
	379–80	'Mankind at large made a picture of itself, and every man had to conform to the picture: the ideal ... the picture ... is just a huge idol'
	390	'the whole accumulation of western ideas, ideals ... ruined ... the very constitution of the Russian psyche'
Hardy	416–17	Clym 'could not burst the enclosure of the idea'; Eustacia 'became an idea to him'
	427	'The universal ideal ... is riches'
	429	'Those State educations with their ideals ... what are they to me?'
	434	'it may be the word, the idea exists which shall bring me forth ... But it may also be that the word, the idea, has never yet been uttered'
	445	'each man according to his need must have a God, an idea'
ArtMor	523	'the Platonic Idea ... lying in the bottom of the sack of the universe. Our own ego!'
WhyNov	537	'Men get ideas into their heads ... and they proceed to cut life out to pattern'
InPtgs	556	'We have become ideal beings, creatures that exist in an idea'
	570	'by shadow I mean idea, concept, the abstracted reality, the ego'
EdP	587	'the modern democratic ideal'; education as 'an ideal, or an idea'
	588	'the high ideal of human existence'

	713–18	(ch. iv): spontaneity×'material-mechanical' world of the idea
	713	'We must discriminate between an ideal and a desire'
	714	'impulses tend to automatize into fixed aspirations or ideals'
	715	'There can be no ideal goal for human life'
	717	'All ideals work down to the sheer materialism which is their intrinsic reality'
NovelF	756	'I carry a whole waste-paper basket of ideas at the top of my head'
InPct	768	'ideas ... are units of transmuted consciousness'
	769	'ideas ... *always* have a moral', and 'The very first idea is the idea of shame', used against 'the pristine consciousness' of body
	770	'We have got a vast magazine of ideas ... But they are practically all dead batteries'; 'I don't know of one great idea or ideal ... which is still alive today'
RTay	226	'the ideal ... emotion which many medieval artists expressed in their Madonnas'
GerEng	246	'the German desire for a world of pure idea'
	247	'The beast we have to fight and to kill is the Ideal'; 'primitive nature has ... an intuitive ethic ... much deeper than the ideal ethic'; 'our whole civilization ... is damned by the "Ideal"'
HTail	428	'the padlock of one final clinching idea'
	429	'We have pretty well caught up with the perfect Idea, and we find it a ... tombstone'
	435	'As for ideal relationships ... you might as well start to water tin pansies with carbolic acid'
RefDP	470	'Being is *not* ideal, as Plato would have it'
APLC	492	'The mind has a stereotyped set of ideas'
	503	'the Nonconformist, protestant idea of ourselves'
	511	'the idealist religions and philosophies arose and started man on the great excursion of tragedy ... Today is already the day after the end of the tragic and idealist epoch'
	512	'The idealist philosophies and religions set out ... to kill' sex
MHouse	547	'mass ideas ... remain, like fossils, when the life that animated them is dead'
BMan	620	men 'panoplied in their own idea of themselves'
HDest	623	'The millstones of the brain ... grind on the grist of whatever ideas the mind contains'; 'the difference between a primitive idea and a civilized one is not very great'
	624	'the mind and the passions between them beget the

	637	'the perfected singleness of the individual being'×'so-called individualism' which is 'no more than a cheap egotism'
	648–50	'individual self-dependence', 'aloof individuality'
RPeace	685	'It is not the will of the . . . individual we have to fear . . . but the . . . vast host of null ones'
Democ	699–704	(ch. i): The Average
	702	'the highest Collectivity has for its true goal the purest individualism, pure individual spontaneity'
	704–9	(ch. ii): Identity
	706	'you are only you'
	708	'Where do you see Being? – In individual men and women'; 'The true identity . . . is the identity of the living self'
	710	'the words *person* and *individual* suggest very different things'
	713–18	(ch. iv): Individualism
	713	'each single individual shall be incommunicably himself'
CDPisg	740	'every individual strives . . . to escape the raw edges of his own fragmentariness'; but the 'Cosmic Spirit . . . doesn't concern itself for a second with the individual'
NFeel	755	individual×collective knowledge
ICoSCo	761	'the individual is only truly himself when he is unconscious of his own individuality'
	763	'the collapse of the true individual into the social individual'
ArtInd	*221–6*	Art and the Individual
GerEng	*248*	the Englishman 'belongs to a nation of isolated individuals'
Crown	*384*	'Our ready-made individuality, our identity is no more than an accidental cohesion in the flux of time'
LLBoy	*444–59*	the tension between love and individuality
	444	'The real opposite of love is individuality'
	445	'education and the public voice urge man and woman into intenser individualism'; 'You can't worship love and individuality in the same breath'
	449	'Man is an individual and woman is an individual . . . as different as chalk and cheese'
	452	'The individual is . . . fed from beneath by unseen springs'; desire brings him 'his further, secondary existence'; 'Neither man nor woman should sacrifice individuality to love, nor love to individuality'
	452–3	'The individual has nothing . . . to do with love . . . The two individuals stay apart, for ever'
	454	'original individuality of the blood' replaced by 'dreary individuality of the ego'; 'If we were men . . . our

... of the instinctive, intuitional, procreative body'

559   'the imagination is a kindled state of consciousness in which intuitive awareness predominates'

561   'instinctive and intuitional consciousness' only 'superficially' involved in landscape painting

568   Cézanne 'wanted to live . . . to know the world through his instincts and intuitions'

570   'Our instincts and intuitions are dead'

573   'the mind works in possibilities, the intuitions work in actualities'; conflict 'between the artist's mind and [his] intuition and instinct'

574   'instinct, intuition, mind, intellect all fused' in creative act

575   'My beliefs I test on my body, my intuitional consciousness'

578   'Mankind has never been able to trust the intuitive consciousness'

579   'intuition needs all-aroundness, and instinct needs insideness. The true imagination is for ever curving round . . . to the back of presented appearance'

580   Cézanne's intuitive self

582   'ready-made mental self' × 'free intuitive self'

584   the possiblity of recovering 'live intuition'

EdP   605   'mental intelligence' obliterates 'instinctive intelligence'; need to relate 'impulsive-desirous soul' and the 'automatic *mind*'

       618–20   'the great affective centres, volitional and emotional'

       622   modern mother 'traducing . . . the deepest instincts'

       653–5   instinct at work in unconscious physical activity

GerEng   *247*   instinct, intuition and imagination: the German connection

SexL   *528*   'the intelligence which goes with sex and beauty . . . is intuition'; 'The deep psychic disease of modern men and women is the diseased atrophied condition of the intuitive faculties'

Mat   *552*   'men have tried to satisfy their deeper social instincts and intuitions' in clubs and pubs

SFunk   *565*   'We are changing . . . Instinctively, we feel it. Intuitively, we know it'

EnCiv   *578*   'men have not learned . . . to stick up for their own instinctive feelings'

MWork   *588*   'the violent change in human instinct, especially in women'

MPict   *603*   'the picture comes clean out of instinct, intuition and sheer physical action'

HDest   *623*   man 'long ago left off being an instinctive animal'

ISOLATION apartness separateness singleness

TwoP	230	'new singleness' in the process of creation
	233	'The self or soul is single, unique, and undivided'
	235	the 'struggle into separation, isolation' characteristic of our 'disintegrative' era
GerEng	247	'curious radical isolation' of the Englishman: 'he is born alone'
RevIn	248	'his own consciousness of isolation ... makes the Englishman such a good citizen'
	278	Verga 'lived in aristocratic isolation'
BPower	440	'inward isolation' a condition of power
LLBoy	453	'two individuals stay apart, for ever and ever' in love
APLC	503	'the ... protestant idea of ourselves: that we are all isolated individual souls'
	512–13	'knowing in apartness'×'knowing in togetherness'
	513	'The sense of isolation, followed by the sense of menace and fear' arises as 'the feeling of individualism and personality, which is existence in isolation, increases'
DoWoCh	541	Women 'see themselves as isolated things'
MWork	589	trend 'towards a further and further physical separateness between men and women'
AuSk2	594	'I don't feel there is any ... fundamental contact between me ... and other people'

KNOWLEDGE

IndEng	93	'I know less than nothing'
Love	156	'It is our business to go as we are impelled ... taking that knowledge for sufficient'
PrefIn	251	' "knowing oneself" was a sin and a vice for innumerable centuries, before it became a virtue ... it is still a sin and a vice, when it comes to new knowledge'
	298	knowledge×experience, of the cosmos
Rev	325	mockery of trivial 'knowledge': 'We have exhausted the possibilities of the universe, as we know it'
	378	man's 'consciousness split' when 'he began to know'
Hardy	418–19	Clym's superficial knowledge: 'He did not know that the greater part of every life is underground'
	424–6	knowledge (in the past)×being (in the present and future)
	430–1	man 'facing both ways, like Janus' in knowing and being
	434	'all the knowledge in the world' will not help us to live
	447	'the artistic effort is the effort ... of expressing knowledge'
	453–7	knowledge (male)×feeling (female): 'The female impulse, to feel and to live in feeling, is ... embraced by the male impulse – to know, and almost carried off by knowledge'
	494	'What had he, a passionate, emotional nature, to do with

LIFE living

greed

	258	'we draw our breath of life' from chaos
	285–91	the struggle for life in Dostoevsky, against material values
	285	'the mass of men ... cannot understand that *life* is the great reality'
	289	'heavenly bread is life, is contact, and is consciousness'
	290	'All life bows to the sun'
	303	'thank God for fantasy, if it enhances our life'
Rev	306	'We have faith in the vastness of life's wealth'
	312	Flaubert 'stood away from life as from a leprosy', Mann 'feels ... that he has in him something finer than ... physical life'
	325	'We are prisoners inside our own conception of life and being'
	335	W. C. Williams offers 'new and profound glimpses into life'
	345	'Life! Life exists: and perhaps men do not truly exist'
	358	men of action 'uproot the tree of life'
	364	Dos Passos novel 'is life, not a pose ... what life is, a stream of different things ... rushing along in the consciousness'
	369	Rozanov sees 'that immortality is in the vividness of life, not in the loss of life'
	377–8	'All theory that has to be applied to life' part of what 'the repressed psyche uses as a substitute for life'
	380	self-consciousness 'is truly the reversal of life'
Hardy	401	'the tick-tack of birth and death'
	404	'we must always hold that life is the great struggle for self-preservation'
	406–8	'We cannot live, we cannot *be* ... risk ourselves in a forward venture of life'
	415	Egdon Heath 'is ... where the instinctive life heaves up'
	417	Clym 'should have lived and moved and had his being'
	420	'the morality of life ... is eternally unalterable and invincible'
	423	'this vague and almost uninterpretable word "living" '
	424	'palpitating leading-shoot of life' × 'fixed channels ... of life'
	426	kings as 'producers of new life'; 'let those that have life, live'
	428	'What do we mean by living? Let every man answer for himself'
	430–1	'It seems as if the great aim and purpose in human life were to bring all life into the human consciousness'
	431	'Man is himself the vivid body of life'; 'one of the conditions of life is, that life shall continually and

progressively differentiate itself'

441 'That is the secret of life: it contains the lesser motions in the greater'

444 'Time, and Life, that is our field'

459 'In the ordinary sense, Shelley never lived'

495 Jude wanted 'to have nothing to do with his own life', Sue 'wanted life merely in the secondary, outside form, in the consciousness'

506 Jude and Sue 'knew they were sinning against life' by marrying

509 'life is life, and there is no death for life'

513 'Life is produced . . . by the combined activity of soul and spirit'

MorNov 527 'this perfected relation between man and his circumambient universe is life itself, for mankind'; art 'lives' in that 'it is beyond life, and therefore beyond death'

529 'By life, we mean something . . . that has the fourth-dimensional quality'

530 'life will always hurt'

WhyNov 533–8 the novel instinct with life

534 'Nothing is important but life'

535 'The novel is the one bright book of life'

537 'What we mean by living is . . . just as indescribable as what we mean by *being*'

538 'You can develop an instinct for life [through the novel] instead of a theory of right and wrong'

JGal 541 man 'at one with the great universe-continuum of space-time-life'

543 the social being 'Dishonest to life, dishonest to the living universe'

InPtgs 551 'The fault [the English produce so few painters] lies in the English attitude to life'

559 'imagery is the body of our imaginative life'

563 'Life isn't [concerned with purity]'

577 'Cézanne was a realist, and he wanted to be true to life'

580 his ambition to present 'the *life* form, come to rest' in art

581 Cézanne never 'as far as his *life* went' escaped mental concepts

EdP 592 'Life is the thing to be afraid of'

607 'the dark mystery of living . . . the incalculable life-gesture'; educators must have 'power for the directing of life itself'

610 'shall we hew down the Tree of Life for the sake of the leaves of grass?'

611 'We are doomed to live'

	230	'Life can never be produced or made'
	231	'The plasm of life, the state of living potentiality exists'; 'life itself . . . exists within the . . . balance of the two elements . . . we must look for life midway between fire and water'
	233	rhythm of 'newly created life' and 'life-disintegration'; 'mathematics still waits for . . . its union with life itself'
	235	'life depends upon duality and polarity'
RBest	260	'I was always weak in health, but my life was strong'
	264	'what I am struggling for is life, more life ahead'
	265	'I know our vision of life is all wrong. We must . . . have a new conception of what it means, *to live* . . . We must be sensitive to life and to its movements'; 'What is alive, and open, and active, is good . . . This is the essence of morality'
	266	'To be perfectly alive is to be immortal'
RevIn	276	the 'struggle for verbal consciousness' is 'a very great part of life'
	282	'that instinctive fighting for more life to come into being'
Crown	364	'We can't make life. We can but fight for the life that grows in us'
	374	'Life is a travelling to the edge of knowledge, then a leap taken'
	375	'It is we who are carried past in the seethe of mortality . . . the life of man is like a flower that comes into blossom and passes away'
	396	'we live . . . balanced between the flux of life and the flux of death'
	399	'The soul is still alive, while it has passion'; 'The near touch of death may be a release into life'
	403	'Life itself . . . will persist and persist'
	404	'Life is both [creation and destruction] . . . life is really in the two'
	408	'the vulture is beyond life or change'
	415	'the whole frame of our life is a falsity'
Novel	419–20	'We must choose between the quick and the dead'
HTail	427–35	life as relationship in the 'multiple universe'
	428	'What we want is life, and life-energy inside us'
	429	'we can't have life for the asking . . . the river of life flows feebler and feebler in us'; 'Let Life solve the problem of living'
	430	'We can't live by loving life, alone'
BPower	437	'From beyond comes to us the life, the power to live'; 'life does not mean length of days . . . Emily Bronte had life. She died of it'
	438	'Living consists in doing . . . what the *life* in you wants to

LOVE

Adolf	8–10	'Love and affection were a trespass upon' wild rabbit; 'We must not love it . . . he was wild and loveless to the end'
Rex	18	dog spoiled by 'that fatal need to love . . . which at last makes an end of liberty'
	21	'Nothing is more fatal than the disaster of too much love'
FFlor	126	'Love-making . . . like everything else, must be public nowadays'
NewMex	143	'it is still harder to feel religion at will than to love at will'
Love	151–6	the dual movement and manifold forms of love
	151	'Love is the happiness of the world. But happiness is not the whole of fulfilment'; we believe in 'absolute love, when love is by nature relative'; 'Love is the force of creation. But all force . . . has its polarity'
	151–2	'What worse bondage can we conceive than the bond of love?'
	152	'Love is not a goal; it is only a travelling'
	153	'Love is manifold, it is not of one sort only'
	153–4	'The love between man and woman is the perfect heart-beat of life . . . It is the melting into pure communion, and it is the friction of pure sensuality, both'
	154	'sacred love . . . knows the purest happiness'
	155	'There must be brotherly love, a wholeness of humanity. But there must also be pure, separate individuality'
MLMus	161	'To have created in us all these . . . sentiments of love . . . merely to throw us into this grotesque posture, to perform this humiliating act, is a piece of cynicism . . .'
RThing	198	'A woman does not fight a man for his love . . . she knows . . . he *cannot* love'
	199	'Love between man and woman is neither worship nor adoration, but something much deeper . . . and as ordinary . . . as breathing'
NLMe	204–7	'love of humanity' exhausted and perverted
	208	the young 'use all the precious phrases of love' for amusement
PrefIn	285	Dostoievsky's 'Grand Inquisitor finds that . . . mankind must be loved more tolerantly and more contemptuously than Jesus loved it'
Rev	306–7	the Georgians as love poets: 'we are the love poets'
	307	'Love is the greatest of all things, no "bitter blossom" . . . We believe in the love that is happy ever after, progressive as life itself'
	389–90	Rozanov's attempt to love
Hardy	410	'the first and chiefest factor is the struggle into love and the struggle with love . . . The *via media* to being, for man

InPct	770	'Love is a dead shell of an idea'
RevIn	279	Verga 'had a series of more or less distinguished love affairs'
	287	'Not being under the tyrannical sway of the idea of "love", [Gesualdo] could be fond of his wife'
Crown	370	'Love and power, light and darkness, these are the temporary conquest of the one infinite by the other'
	394	'In the name of love, what horrors men perpetrate, and are applauded!'
Novel	424	'As for the babe of love, we're simply tired of changing its napkins'
BPower	436	'The reign of love is passing, and the reign of power is coming again'
	440	'only Power can rule. Love cannot, should not, does not seek to'
	441	'The act of love itself is an act of power . . . Love itself is purely a relationship'
LLBoy	444–59	love×individuality
	444	'Love itself is . . . the relationship . . . with the rest of things'; 'Hate is not the opposite of love. The opposite of love is individuality'
	452	'we have imagined love to be . . . absolute and personal. It is neither'; 'Neither man nor woman should sacrifice individuality to love, nor love to individuality': 'the individual . . . has nothing to do with love'
	454	'And they call this marsh . . . the reign of love!!'
APLC	493	'by higher emotions we mean love in all its manifestations'
	494	'Above all things love is a counterfeit feeling today'
	495	'Sex . . . is ruthless, devastating against false love . . . it is the organic reaction against counterfeit love'
	504	'what a maiming of love when it was made a . . . merely personal feeling'; 'love is a grinning mockery . . . in our civilized vase on the table'
	507	'personal love' degenerates into 'rage and hatred'
SexL	531	'a woman may go on being quietly in love for fifty years almost without knowing it'
DoWoCh	541	'Where is the point to love? . . . There is no point'
	542	'So it is with life, and especially with love. There is no point . . . love itself is a flow'
Hymns	598	'both love and power are based on wonder. Love without wonder is a sensational affair'
HDest	624	'our love and salvation and making-good ideas'
	626	rejects 'the same idea: love, service, self-sacrifice'

MACHINE, MECHANISM

		correspondence between the spontaneous . . . soul and the automatic *mind* which runs on little wheels of ideas'
	607	rejects 'automatism' of class structure
	609–10	average man as 'the material, mechanical universal of mankind, a unit of automatized existence'
	610	'the Machine which devours us all'
	611	'The choice is between system and system, mechanical or organic'
	618–20	'The body is not an instrument', there is no 'automatic consciousness'
	630	affective centres worked 'automatically or mechanically' by the mind; 'ideal being' as 'a clever little god-in-the-machine'
	631	'A million curses on self-conscious automatic humanity'
	633	modern men 'like so many barrel-organs grinding their own sensations'
	656	'the modern athlete parading the self-conscious mechanism of his body'
	657–61	modern mechanical warfare: 'to be blown to bits by a machine is mere horror' (659)
	661	'the end of a rotten, idealistic machine-civilization'
	664	men will 'look after the further, abstracted, and mechanical life'
	665	'Men who can only hark back to woman become automatic, static'
RPeace	669	'Our life becomes a mechanical round'
	671	'the anarchy of fixed law, which is mechanism'
	688	'all relentless organization is in the end pure negation'
Democ	702	'representatives of the masses' as 'the chief machine-section of society'
	704	'the ideal world is invented . . . as man invents machinery'
	711	'an ideal is just a machine which is in process of being built'
	712	'As if creation proceeded from a pair of compasses'
	713–18	(ch. iv): spontaneity×'material-mechanical world'
	713	'an ideal is . . . like a machine control'
	714	'both desire and impulse tend to fall into mechanical automatism'
	715	the fall into 'materialism or automatism or mechanism of the self'
	717	'sheer mechanical materialism'
CDPisg	740	'Oneness and Wholeness . . . dehumanized, mechanical, and monstrous'
	744	'The universe isn't a machine after all'
NovelF	757	'Man is not a little engine of cause and effect'
InPct	767	'We are an . . . intricate clockwork of nerves and brain . . .

MATERIALISM

RefDP	*470*	'Being is ... a transcendent form of existence, and as much material as existence is'
IsEng	*558*	'The insuperable difficulty to modern man is economic bondage'
SFunk	*566*	'life will be much better ... less basely materialistic'
MWork	*591*	'the Soviet is established on the image of the machine, "pure" materialism'
PWalls	*613*	books 'a spiritual instead of a gross material property'

MIND brain intellect reason thought

NottMC	136	colliers had 'no daytime intellect. They avoided ... the rational aspect of life'
PObsc	182	'They have mentalized sex till it is nothing at all ... but a mental quantity'
	184	'Their sex is more mental than their arithmetic'
PrefIn	220–1	free verse 'is the soul and the mind and the body surging at once'
	249–50	'the workings of the unsophisticated mind ... the emotional mind ... This activity of the mind is strictly timeless, and illogical'
	265	'nothing is brought to real mental clearness' in Italian language
	277	'civilization moves on, wit and intelligence taking their revenge on insolent animal spirits': and so on, in cycle
	279	each of Pansies 'a true thought, which comes as much from the heart and the genitals as from the head': the form preferable to 'those solid blocks of mental pabulum packed ... in the pages of ... a book'
	280	'cleanse the mind, that is the real job. It is the mind which is the Augean stables, not language'
	295	value of symbols 'not simply mental'
	297	'We are full of the wind of thought-forms, and starved for a good carrot'
	301	'our present deadened state of mind ... is becoming unbearable'
Rev	346	Wells' Clissold 'a somewhat scientific gentleman with an active mind'
	349	'without a full ... emotional life the mind itself must wither'
	350	'the passionate and emotional reactions which are at the root of all thought'
	370	'you have to blame ... the craven, cretin human intelligence'
Hardy	416	quotes Hardy: ' "thought is a disease of the flesh" '
	417	'his mind, that house built of extraneous knowledge and

	765–6	'until perverted by the mind, the human body preserves itself . . . in a delicate balance of sanity'
	766	'the pernicious mental consciousness called the spirit'
	767	'All our emotions are mental'; 'Nerves and brain . . . a clockwork': 'the apparatus by which we signal and *register* consciousness': 'that strange switchboard of consciousness, the brain'
	768	mind as 'secondary consciousness'
TwoP	237	'when this fourfold consciousness is established within the body . . . we come to full consciousness in the mind . . . So we have the sacred pentagon, with the mind as the conclusive apex'
RevIn	288	'If he thought too little about his life, he helps to counter-balance those who think too much'
InMFL	322	peasant lacks 'complacent mentality' of Magnus: 'For his mindlessness I would have chosen the peasant'
	324	' "If there is no . . . blood-sympathy, I know the mental friendship is trash" '
Crown	369	'the white light, the Mind'
	378	in sexual act 'my soul is slipping its moorings, my mind, my will fuses down'
BPower	437	'All attempts to . . . intellectualize merely strangle the passages of the heart'; 'The intellect is one of the most curious instruments of the psyche'
Aris	477	natural aristocracy is 'not just brains! the mind is an instrument'
APLC	487–515	sexual life warped by the mind
	489	'the words merely shocked the eye, they never shocked the mind at all'; 'thought and action, word and deed, are two separate forms of consciousness'
	490	'After centuries of obfuscation, the mind demands to know . . . The mind has to catch up in sex . . . in all the physical acts'; 'Obscenity only comes in when the mind despises and fears the body, and the body hates and resists the mind'
	491	'It is the mind we have to liberate . . . The mind's terror of the body has probably driven more men mad than ever could be counted'
	492	'Life is only bearable when the mind and body are in harmony'; 'The mind has a stereotyped set of ideas and "feelings", and the body is made to act up'
	493	'All the emotions belong to the body, and are only recognized by the mind'; 'How different they are, mental feelings and real feelings'; our emotional self is 'all reflected downwards from the mind'; 'belief is a profound emotion that has the mind's connivance'

	497	a woman's sex is 'a power in itself, beyond her reason'; people want a 'mental substitute' for desire
	506	'affinity of mind . . . is an excellent basis of friendship . . . but a disastrous basis for marriage'
	511	'the dry and sterile little world the abstracted mind inhabits'
	512–13	'mental, rational, scientific' × 'religious and poetic' knowledge
CWom	*553*	woman's sureness 'not mental . . . a physical condition'
SFunk	*568*	'My sex is me as my mind is me'
AuSk2	*596*	'that . . . thin, spurious mental conceit which is all that is left of the mental consciousness'
Hymns	*598*	'the mind works automatically' on nature: 'intrusion of the mental processes dims the brilliance . . . of the first apperception'
PWalls	*613*	books 'something belonging to the mind and consciousness'
BMan	*616–22*	the two selves of body and mind
	616	'Man is a thought-adventurer. Which isn't the same as saying that he has intellect . . . Real thought is an experience . . . a new reality in mental consciousness'; man 'must go forth and meet life in the body. Then he must face the result in his mind'
	618	'The thought-adventure starts in the blood, not in the mind'
	620	'To be a man! To risk your body and your blood first, and then to risk your mind'
	621	'All suffering today is psychic: it happens in the mind'
HDest	*623–9*	the compulsion of thought
	623	'Man is a domesticated animal that must think . . . The mind refuses to be blank. The millstones of the brain grind on while the stream of life runs'; 'All our modern spontaneity is fathered in the mind'
	624	'let man be as primitive as primitive can be, he still has a mind'; 'the mind and the passions between them beget the scorpion brood of ideas'; 'Man *can't* live by instinct, because he's got a mind'
	625	the interdependence of mind and emotions: the 'simple trinity' of emotion, mind, idea.
	627	'The light shall never go out till the last day'
	629	'We have to germinate inside us, between our undaunted mind and our reckless . . . passions, a new germ'

MORALITY good × evil

| David | 63 | the waters of morality quench the fire of life |

NATURE organism process rhythm

		together of water and fire, to make the sun of light, the rainbow, and the perfect elements of Matter'
RevIn	285	Verga's novel 'a heavy, earth-adhering organic whole'
	286	'the splendour of the sun and the landscape' in the Mediterranean countries means that 'life pulses outwards, and the positive reality is outside'
Crown	364–415	a dense network of natural images to enforce the argument
	368	'We are fruit, we are an integral part of the tree'
	371–3	organic images for the process of life: tree, seed, womb, sea, rainbow; 'we, in the great movement, are begotten, conceived and brought forth'
	375	'the life of man is like a flower that comes into blossom and passes away'
	377–8	images of sea and flame for sex
	382–9	(ch. iii): The Flux of Corruption: plant and animal images
	392	'It is the pure process of corruption in all of us'
	394	images of organic constriction: 'the glassy envelope, the insect rind, the tight-shut shell of the cabbage, the withered, null walls of the womb'
	396	'The goodness of anything depends on the direction in which it is moving'; 'While we live, we change, and our flowering is a constant change'
	403	swan, water-lily, snake: 'corruption, like growth, is only divine when it is pure'
	406–9	vulture and eagle, baboon, hyaena, condor, carrion crow, 'these fill me with fear and horror'
	415	we need 'a new relationship with new heaven and new earth'
HTail	430	cuckoo, cow and coffee-plant as images of life
RefDP	465	'food, how strangely it relates man with the animal and vegetable world!
	467	'In nature, one creature devours another, and this is an essential part of all existence and of all being'
	469	fighting for ourselves in 'the tangle of existence and being'
	470–1	the process of germination: 'So the sun in the seed, and the earthy one in the seed take hands, and laugh, and begin to dance'
	472	'The cycle of procreation exists purely for the keeping alight of the torch of perfection in any species'
Aris	481	'the living, balanced, hovering flight of the earth'; 'Every natural thing has its own living relation to every other natural thing'
APLC	499	'the real sex in a man, that has the rhythm of the seasons and the years, the crisis of the winter solstice and the passion of Easter'

PERSONALITY × IMPERSONALITY

	554	'an overmastering fear is poison to the human psyche'
	559	'That is the great clue to bourgeois psychology: the reward business'
	578	'to introduce into our world of vision something which is neither optical nor mechanical nor intellectual-psychological requires a real revolution'
EdP	590	'The system . . . is only the outcome of the human psyche'
	618–20	locates structure of human psyche in the body, contradicting 'scientific psychology' of the mind
	622	'derangement in the psyche of the infant' due to mother-love
	624	polarity with mother 'produces the infant's developing body and psyche'
	626	'Fairies are true embryological realities of the human psyche'
	628	'the four corner-stones of our psyche . . . form the four-fold issue of our individual life'
	630–1	man 'wants to work his own little psyche till the end of time, like a clever little god-in-the-machine'; he 'sits in the machine of his own psyche and turns on the petrol'
	635	'what holds true cosmologically holds much more true psychologically'
	654	satisfaction of 'the mindless psyche' absorbed in work
GMan	752	'The eighteenth century . . . carved a pound of flesh from the human psyche'
NovelF	759	'it is no use doing as the psychoanalysts have done'
ICoSCo	761	'the psyche splits in two, into subjective and objective reality'
TwoP	227	'the relation between the sea and the human psyche is impersonal and elemental'; 'There certainly does exist a subtle and complex sympathy . . . between the plasm of the human body, which is identical with the primary human psyche, and the material elements outside'
	234	'the mystery of dual psyche, sensual and spiritual'
	235	sexual opposition 'a way of struggle into separation, isolation, psychic disintegration'; 'The duality, the polarity now asserts itself within the individual psyche'
BPower	437	'The intellect is one of the most curious instruments of the psyche'
APLC	507	rage within frustrating marriage 'part of the phenomenon of the psyche'
SexL	528	'The deep psychic disease of modern men and women is the diseased, atrophied condition of the intuitive faculties'
BMan	621	'All the suffering today is psychic: it happens in the mind'
HDest	625	'taking the human psyche, we have this simple trinity: the emotions, the mind, and . . . ideas'

RELATION relatedness the relative connection contact harmony sympathy touch

PanAm	24–6	tree as image of connection
	25	'the tree penetrates my life, and my life the tree's'
	26	'to know, with a pantheistic sensuality, that the tree has its own life . . . its own living relatedness to me'
	27	'what does life consist in, save a vivid relatedness between the man and the living universe that surrounds him?'
	29	'Once you have conquered a thing, you have lost it. Its real relation to you collapses . . . We need the universe to live again, so that we can live with it'
	30	'The contact between all things is keen and wary: for wariness is also a sort of reverence'
	31	'Life itself consists in a live relatedness between man and his universe'
FTusc	46	'Man *can* live on the earth and by the earth without disfiguring the earth'
NottMC	136	miners 'brought with them above ground the curious dark intimacy of the mine, the naked sort of contact'
NewMex	147	'This effort into sheer naked contact . . . is the root meaning of religion'
WeNeed	188–95	individual depends for his being on relationship
	190	'everything, even individuality itself, depends on relationship'
	191	'And so with men and women. It is in relationship to one another that they have their true individuality and their distinct being in contact, not out of contact'
	192	'A soul is something that forms and fulfils itself in my contacts'
	193	'the relationship of man to woman is the central fact in actual human life . . . what is sex . . . but the symbol of the relation of man to woman, woman to man?'
	194	'The relationship is a life-long change and a life-long travelling'
RThing	197	'Sex is the great uniter, the great unifier'
	198	'Man is connected with woman for ever, in connexions visible and invisible, in a complicated life-flow that can never be analysed'
	203	'It is a question of getting into contact again with the *living* centre of the cosmos'
NLMe	205	'we are more or less connected, all more or less in touch: all humanity'
	210	'Men can have a savage satisfaction in the annihilation of all feeling and all connexion'
PrefIn	221	'The utterance is like a spasm, naked contact with all

all the rest of living things, collapses'

	762	'individual feeling is only capable when there is a *continuum*, when the *me* and the *you* and the *it* are a *continuum*'
ArtInd	226	'we are for ever trying to unite ourselves with the whole universe'
TwoP	227	'the relation between the sea and the human psyche is impersonal and elemental'; pagan religions 'gave the true correspondence between the material cosmos and the human soul'
Crown	410	'God is the utter relation between the two eternities'
	412	'The perfect relation is perfect. But it is therefore timeless'; 'The true God is *created* every time a pure relationship . . . takes place'
	415	'the one glorious activity of man . . . getting himself into a new relationship with a new heaven and a new earth'
Novel	416	'In a novel, everything is relative to everything else'
	420	'the quickness of the quick lies . . . in an odd sort of fluid, changing, grotesque or beautiful relatedness'
	421	'Everything is relative'
HTail	432	'What the Greeks called equilibrium . . . I call relationship'
	433	'the strange spark that flies between two creatures . . . equilibrated, or in living relationship'
	434	'How marvellous is the living relationship between man and his object . . . the exquisite frail moment of pure conjunction'
	435	'As for ideal relationships . . . you might as well start to water tin pansies with carbolic acid'
LLBoy	444–59	equilibrium, relationship, and desire
	444	'In every living thing there is the desire, for love, or for the relationship of unison with the rest of things'
	446–7	'How can I equilibrate myself with my black cow Susan? . . . Yet a relationship there is'
	451–5	desire, as 'the reality which is inside love', occasions relationship
	457	'I go forth, delicately, desirous, and find the mating of my desire'
RefDP	469–74	the kingdom of heaven as 'the state of perfected relationship'
	469	'No creature is fully itself till it is . . . opened in . . . pure relationship to the sun, the entire living cosmos'
	471	'Blossoming means the establishing of a pure, *new* relationship with all the cosmos . . . This too is the fourth dimension . . . this mysterious other reality of things in a perfected relationship'

SELF self-consciousness

	367	'in proportion as a man gets more ... interested in himself, so does my interest in him wane'
	370	'how they love to be ... divided against themselves, these ... Russians!'
	379	quotes Burrow: ' "consciousness in its inception entails the fallacy of *a self as over against other selves*" '; we are guilty of 'The idolatry of self'
	381	'Sex does not exist; there is only sexuality ... a greedy, blind self-seeking'
	382	'The true self is not aware that it is a self'
	388	quotes Rozanov: ' "the secret (bordering on madness) that I am talking to myself" '
	391	'his real struggle to get back a positive self, a feeling self'
Hardy	403	'The final aim of every living thing, creature, or being is the full achievement of itself'
	404	'we must always hold that life is the great struggle for self-preservation': 'the old, second-rate altar of self-preservation'
	407	'we almost hate ourselves ... we are afraid to [risk] ourselves'
	408	'I am weeping over my denied self'
	410	Hardy's characters 'are people each with a real, vital, potential self ... and this self suddenly bursts the shell ... of convention'
	414	'Practically never is Clym able to act or even feel in his original self'
	415	'Let a man will for himself, and he is destroyed'
	425	man 'wants to be free to be himself'
	429	man should work 'three or four hours a day ... Then let him have twenty hours for being himself'
	431–2	the differentiation of beings into 'distinct individuals ... each one being himself'
	432–3	'A selfish person is an impure person, one who wants that which is not himself ... how can I help my neighbour except by being utterly myself?'
	471	'At last man insists upon his own separate Self'
	483	Tess 'knows she is herself incontrovertibly, and she knows that other people are not herself'
	497	'the duality of Sue's nature made her ... liable to self-destruction'
	507–9	Sue 'forswore her own being ... she annihilated herself'
	515	man 'must with reverence submit to the law of himself'
SurNov	519	'It's a funny sort of self they discover in the popular novels'
ArtMor	523	'identifying ... ourselves with the visual image of ourselves has become an instinct ... the me that is *seen*, is

		behind it'
	714	'Each human self is single, incommutable, and unique'
	715	'the fall of man ... into what we call materialism or automatism or mechanism of the self'
	716	'the first great purpose of Democracy: that each man shall be himself'
	718	'When men become their own decent selves again, then we can so easily arrange the material world'
PStudy	719–23	oblique response to Pope's 'Know then thyself'
ThSelf	735	'It's perfectly natural for every man and every woman to think about himself or herself most of the time'
	736	'We all seem to be haunted by some spectre of ourselves that we daren't face'
ICoSCo	761	'The moment a human being becomes conscious of himself, he ceases to be himself'
TwoP	235	in spiritual being 'the self excels into the universe', in sensual being 'the self is the ... centre where all life pivots'
RevIn	276	*Women in Love* is 'a record of the profoundest experiences in the self'
InMFL	360	'I am not one man, I am many, I am most'
Crown	367	' "I know I exist ... because I feel the divine discontent which is personal to me" '
	389–97	(ch. iv): the false I, the ego
	391	'This achieved self, which we are, is absolute and universal'
	395	Myshkin's 'self-analysis, self-dissolution'
	396	'the mundane egg of our own self-consciousness and self-esteem'
	398	'This reduction within the self is sensationalism'
APLC	513	'Civil strife becomes a necessary condition of self-assertion'
CWom	555	woman 'Frightened by her own henny self'
SFunk	568	'A boy divided against himself; a girl divided against herself; a people divided against itself; it is a disastrous condition'
BMan	616–22	known self in mind×unknown self in body
	616	'Each of us has two selves. First is this body which is vulnerable and never quite within our control ... And second is the conscious ego, the self I KNOW I am'; 'The self that lives in my body I can never finally know'
	619	'The Cross ... stands for ... the dark self which lives in the body. And on the Cross of this bodily self is crucified the self which I know I am, my so-called *real* self'; 'This self which lives darkly in my blood and bone is my *alter ego*'; 'We marry from the known self ... The woman of the known self is fair and lovely'

InPtgs	551–84	fear of sex and the body destructive of life and art
	551	'terror, almost ... horror of sexual life' in northern consciousness
	552	'To the Restoration dramatist sex is ... a dirty business ... Swift goes mad with sex and excrement revulsion'
	552–8	reason for this in 'the great shock of syphilis and the realization of the consequences of the disease'
	555	'The appearance of syphilis in our midst gave a fearful blow to our sexual life'
	562	Frenchman's 'conception of sex is basically hygienic'
	575	'today, the great day of the masturbating consciousness, when the mind prostitutes the sensitive responsive body'
	583	'the sex-appeal of a picture'
EdP	657	'to have your physique in your head, like having sex in the head, is unspeakably repulsive'
DucL	745–9	sexual experience in eighteenth-century France
	747	mutual attraction 'is the essence of morality, as far as love goes'
InPct	771	depraved sexuality of our day 'still the same old attack on the living body'
TwoP	234	'the divided circle ... stands ... for the sex mystery': 'the sex division is one of the Chinese three sacred mysteries'
	234–5	sex as 'delicate union' or 'tremendous conjunction', with consequences in each case
	236	'in the sexual passion the very blood surges into communion'
Crown	377–8	a version of orgasm: 'It is thus ... that I come to the woman in desire ... I am thrown again on the shores of creation'
	398	'This is the doom of egoistic sex ... the reacting of the sexes against one another in a purely reducing activity'
Novel	417	'And then to blame the column of blood, which ... gave him all his life riches!'
	423	man as 'a column of rapacious and living blood'
	426	'The flame of sex singes your absolute, and cruelly scorches your ego'
APLC	487–515	analysis of modern sexuality
	489	'I want men and women to be able to think sex, fully, completely, honestly, and cleanly'
	490	'A young girl and a young boy is a tormented tangle ... of sexual feelings and sexual thoughts which only the years will disentangle'; 'Now our business is to realize sex. Today the full conscious realization of sex is even more important than the act itself ... It means having a proper reverence for sex, and a proper awe of the body's strange experience'

	491	'young people scoff at the importance of sex, take it like a cocktail'
	495	'Sex lashes out against counterfeit emotion, and is . . . devastating against false love . . . The element of counterfeit in love at last maddens, or else kills, sex, the deepest sex in the individual'
	496	to the young 'sex means . . . plainly and simply, a lady's underclothing'
	497	'as far as sex goes, our white civilization is crude, barbaric'; men are 'socially thrilled, while sexually repelled' by sexually provocative women; 'Neither men nor women *want* to feel real desire, today'
	498	'The Catholic Church recognizes sex, and makes of marriage a sacrament based on the sexual communion'
	499	'sex is the clue to marriage and marriage is the clue to the daily life of the people'; 'the real sex in a man, that has the rhythm of the seasons and the years'
	500	'The instinct of fidelity is perhaps the deepest instinct in the great complex we call sex'; 'this question of sex and marriage is of paramount importance'
	504	'Sex is the balance of male and female in the universe . . . Sex goes through the rhythm of the year . . . ceaselessly changing'
	505	'marriage is no marriage that is not basically and permanently phallic'; 'The phallus is a column of blood that fills the valley of blood of a woman'
	506	'this is the meaning of the sexual act . . . as all the religions know'; 'sex-activity is . . . in some way hostile to the . . . *personal* relationship between man and woman'
	507	'there is probably far more sexual activity in a "personal" marriage than in a blood-marriage'; 'nearly all modern sex is a pure matter of nerves, cold and bloodless'
	508	'we can have no hope of the regeneration of England from such sort of sex'; 'the bridge to the future is the phallus'; 'The homosexual contacts are secondary'
	512	'the togetherness of the body, the sex, the emotions, the passions, with the earth and sun and stars'; 'Sex is the great unifier'
SexL	*527*	'It is a pity that *sex* is such an ugly little word . . . What *is* sex, after all?'
	528	'Sex and beauty are one thing, like flame and fire'; 'The great disaster of our civilization is the morbid hatred of sex'; 'Sex is the root of which intuition is the foliage and beauty the flower'
	529	'Nothing is more ugly than a human being in whom the fire of sex has gone out'

	530	'A... woman becomes lovely when the fire of sex rouses pure and fine in her'; 'It is a question of sex appeal in our poor, dilapidated modern phraseology'
	531	'If only our civilization had taught us how to let sex appeal flow properly and subtly'
SFunk	*568–70*	fear of sex in our civilization
	568	'this unaccountable and disastrous *fear* of sex'; 'My sex is me as my mind is me'
	569	sexual warmth as 'the most natural life-flow in the world'; 'If there is one thing I don't like it is cheap and promiscuous sex ... sex is a delicate, vulnerable, vital thing that you mustn't fool with'; 'get out of the state of funk, sex funk ... accept sex fully in the consciousness'
	570	'Accept the sexual being of yourself and of every other creature'
MWork	*589*	'The sexes can't stand one another ... The young are ... physically repulsive to one another'

SOUL

David	63	the masses 'overwhelming all outstanding loveliness of the individual soul'
ChTin	83	'There are so many Christs carved by men who have carved to get at the meaning of their own soul's anguish'
AmList	89–90	'the human soul is father and mother of all man-created beauty'
IndEng	99	'The soul is as old as the oldest day, and has its own hushed echoes'
LGer	109	'something has happened to the human soul, beyond all help. The human soul recoiling now from unison, and making itself strong elsewhere'
ParisL	119	'I had so much rather the Centaur had slain Hercules, and men had never developed souls'
GerLat	128	'the soul has changed her rhythm'
MLMus	166	Etruscan woman 'dancing her very soul into existence'
WeNeed	192	man is not 'a supreme soul isolated and alone in the universe'; 'A soul is something that forms and fulfils itself in my contacts, my living touch with people ... I am born with the clue to my soul. The wholeness of my soul I must achieve. And by my soul I mean my wholeness'
PrefIn	216	'The human soul itself is the source and well-head of creative activity'
	220–1	free verse 'is the soul and the mind and body surging at once'
	228	'The Sicilian, in our sense of the word, doesn't have any soul ... Souls, to him, are little naked people

Feelings, and our Mind': 'everything that has ever been produced has been produced by the combined activity . . . of soul and spirit'

TIME, ETERNITY past present future history memory

		conscious human blood'
LGer	110	'Whirling to the ghost of the old Middle Ages of Germany, then to the Roman days, then to the days of the şilent forest and the dangerous . . . barbarians'
EurAm	117–18	contrasting sense of the past in Europe × America
ParisL	122	'humanity like poor worms struggling inside the shell of history, all of them inside the museum'
Love	152	'What is eternity but the endless passage of time?'
	153	'We are creatures of time and space. But we are like a rose . . . we arrive in the absolute'
PObsc	183	'the last century, the eunuch century, the century of the mealy-mouthed lie, the century that has tried to destroy humanity, the nineteenth century'
PrefIn	215	'Russia will certainly inherit the future'
	218–22	Preface to *New Poems*: poetry of the present × poetry of past and future
	218	'the voice of the far future, exquisite and ethereal, or . . . the voice of the past, rich, magnificent'; 'there is another kind of poetry: the poetry of that which is at hand: the immediate present'
	219	'Give me nothing fixed, set, static. Don't give me the infinite or the eternal . . . Give me . . . the moment, the immediate present, the Now'
	219–20	'The seething poetry of the incarnate Now is supreme, beyond even the everlasting gems of the before and after'
	220	'Eternity is only an abstraction from the actual present . . . The quivering nimble hour of the present, this is the quick of Time'
	221	'The past and the future are the two great bournes of human emotion, the two great homes of the human days, the two eternities'
	222	'One realm we have never conquered: the pure present. One great mystery of time is terra incognita to us: the instant'
	249–50	Verga resists the tyranny of time: 'the mind approaches again and again the point of concern, repeats itself, goes back, destroys the time-sequence entirely, so that time ceases to exist'
	251–2	'pastness is only an abstraction . . . To the demon, the past is not past'
	254	'the demon is timeless. But the ordinary meal-time me has yesterdays'
	263	'that strange intermediate period which lies between present actuality and the revived past', where 'the past is safely and finally past'; 'It takes a really good writer to make us overcome our repugnance to the just-gone-by

	471	'perfected relationship . . . passing out of the time-space dimension'
APLC	*490*	'There has been so much action in the past . . . a wearying repetition over and over, without . . . a corresponding realization . . . After centuries of obfuscation, the mind demands to know . . . fully'
	499	the Pope 'has a thousand years' experience. Mr. Shaw jumped up in a day'
	501	man's 'great desires . . . are fulfilled in long periods of time'
	503	'the Old Church knew best the enduring needs of man, beyond the spasmodic needs of today and yesterday'
	504	'Augustine said that God created the universe new every day'
	505	the rhythm of sex throughout life, in marriage
	506	marriage 'the highest achievement of time or eternity'
	508	'the bridge to the future is the phallus'
	511	'Today is already the day after the end of the tragic and idealist epoch'
JFille	*522*	'The old lies must be questioned out of existence'
DoWoCh	*540*	'Modernity or modernism . . . comes at the end of civilizations'
SFunk	*565*	'The time of change is upon us'
	566	'The old world . . . is disappearing like thawing snow'
	567	we 'change as the years go on'
MPict	*606*	'We can call it memory, but it is more than memory'
HDest	*627–8*	'The light shall never go out till the last day . . . It is his destiny that he must move on and on, in the thought-adventure'
	629	'There is a long life-day for the individual. Then a very dark, spacious death-room'

THE UNKNOWN the beyond mystery

WBirds	6	impulse of life 'comes from the unknown upon us'
AmList	90	'You must first have faith . . . in your own unrevealed, unknown destiny'
NewMex	141	'There is no mystery left . . . Yet the more we know, superficially, the less we penetrate, vertically'
	145	'the old, old root of human consciousness still reaching down to depths we know nothing of'
Love	156	'the inmost desires of our body and spirit . . . arrive to us out of the unknown'
WeNeed	193	'marriage is a long event of perpetual change . . . like rivers flowing on, through new country, always unknown'
PrefIn	255	poetry ' "discovers" a new world within the known world'

		'unmapped wilderness'
CDPisg	744	'all the laws of physics . . . are but the settled habits of a vast living incomprehensibility'
NovelF	756	'The wild creatures are coming forth from the darkest Africa inside us'
ICoSCo	762	'The . . . radical individual consciousness . . . is unanalysable and mysterious'
TwoP	227	'The creative mystery . . . always was and always will be'
	229	'The sun is the great mystery-centre'; 'There is a mysterious duality, life divides itself, and yet there is no division in life'
	234	'the divided circle . . . stands . . . for the sex mystery'
GerEng	244	'the mystery of strange, blind, instinctive purpose'
RevIn	273	'The Apocalypse is a strange and mysterious book'
	275	'The only thing unbearable is . . . the prostitution of the living mysteries in us'
Crown	374	'Life is a travelling to the edge of knowledge, then a leap taken'
	378	sex as a 'trespass into the unknown'
HTail	430	'Life . . . enters into us from behind, when we set our faces towards the unknown'
BPower	440	'Life enters us from behind, where we are sightless, and from below, where we do not understand'
	441	'true power . . . is given us, from the beyond'
LLBoy	457	desire links us to 'the other unknown, the invisible, intangible creation'
Aris	482	'In his ultimate and surpassing relation, man is given only to that which he can never describe or account for'
APLC	506	sexual act 'is one of the greatest mysteries'
CWom	553	'the old-fashioned . . . woman was sure as a hen is sure . . . without knowing anything about it'
RLord	574	'Christ risen in the flesh! . . . We must take the mystery in its fulness and in fact'
Hymns	598	'the most precious element in life is wonder'
MPict	603	artist's image 'lives in the consciousness, alive like a vision, but unknown'
BMan	616	'The self that lives in my body I can never finally know'
	620	'*Know thyself* means knowing . . . that you *can't* know yourself'
	621	'To the unknown man in them nothing happens'
HDest	628	'the Unknown God whom we ignore turns savagely to rend us'

WORD language logos speech talk utterance

PanAm	23	men 'loved the vainglory of their own words'

David Gerard

11
Films and sound recordings relating to Lawrence

The recording on film and in sound of Lawrence's work, and of discussions of his work for educational purposes, has been a growing feature of the past two decades. An attempt is made here to list as many of these productions as it has been possible to locate, but in the absence of any universal or systematic register of audio-visual material anywhere in the world the list cannot be exhaustive. It is a beginning and it is hoped that it may stimulate more information, which the Editor would be glad to receive. Details of each title vary in accordance with information available, and there is as yet no accepted standard of description for cataloguing purposes. All enquiries about use or consultation of the materials should be made directly to the libraries or publishers concerned. The Open University holds its AV resources in an archive which is available for research; some may be available for copying or marketing. Application should be made to the Open University Library, Walton Hall, Milton Keynes, Bucks. U.K.

The heading 'Other Sources' has been used to group individual productions from a variety of publishers or distributors.

VTR = videotape.
LP = long-playing record.
Cassette = audiocassette tape.
Reel = reel tape.

FILMS

Filmed novels commercially made and distributed
The Rocking Horse Winner (Two Cities Films, 1949)
Lady Chatterley's Lover (Columbia, 1956)
Sons and Lovers (Fox, 1960)
The Fox (Warner Brothers, 1968)
Women in Love (United Artists, 1969)
The Virgin and the Gipsy (London Screenplays, 1971)

Library of Congress. Motion Picture, Broadcasting and Recorded Sound Division, Washington D.C. 20540, USA

American Indians as seen by D. H. Lawrence. 14 mins. 16mm. Colour. Released by Coronet Instructional Films. 1966.
    Frieda Lawrence discusses D. H. L's beliefs and Aldous Huxley presents passages from the works which reveal D. H. L's insights into the religious and ceremonial culture of the Indians of the South-West.
D. H. Lawrence in Taos. 40 mins. 16mm. Colour. Released by Contemporary Films/McGraw Hill. 1970.
    Written and directed by Peter Davis; narrator, Stephen Murray. Describes D. H. L's experiences at Taos, New Mexico in the 1920s. Interviews with Dorothy Brett, Willard Johnson and Joseph Foster. (McGraw Hill Films, 1221 Avenue of the Americas, NY 10020, USA)
The Rocking Horse Winner. 30 mins. Colour. Distributor Learning Corporation of America. 1977.
    Another film version, this time designed for educational use, of the famous short story. Kenneth More is the sole performer. (Learning Corporation of America, 1350 Avenue of the Americas, NY 10019, USA)

Open University. The Library, Walton Hall, Milton Keynes, Bucks, UK

D. H. Lawrence and Eastwood. 22 mins. VTR. 1″ (A 100/01) 1971.
    Graham Martin, Professor of English Literature, Open University, discusses the significance of Eastwood. Filmed on location. (Foundation Course for the Humanities.)
Forster and Lawrence. 25 mins. VTR. 1″ (A 302/15), 1973.
    Richard Hoggart and Graham Martin discuss the contrasting personal and cultural backgrounds of the two novelists. Passages from *The Fox* are read.
Industrialisation and Culture. VTR 1″ (A 100/35)
    Graham Martin outlines D. H. L's reaction to industrialisation and its effect on the evolution of his thought.
Words, Pictures and the Novel. VTR 1″ (A 302/10)
    Changes in the composition of the novel since Victorian times. *Women In Love* is cited to demonstrate how difficult it would be as a subject for graphic illustration.

Other sources

D. H. Lawrence Among His People. 23 mins. VTR 1″ (VHS/C), 1979. (College

of Librarianship Wales. Media Services Unit.)
David Gerard describes DHL's life and relationships within his family and friends.
Opening and closing sequences filmed at Eastwood; otherwise the commentary is
supported by still pictures. John Edmunds reads passages from D.H.L's letters.
Fathers and Sons. Filmstrip. Colour. 1970.
Educational Activities, P.O. Box 392, Freeport, Long Island, NY 11520, USA.

SOUND RECORDINGS

Library of Congress

The Poetry of D. H. Lawrence. LP. Spoken Arts SA 1062, 1971.
Wendy Hiller, Peter Jeffrey, David King and Peter Orr the readers. Programme
notes by Paul Kresh on slipcase.
   Contents: 'Aware'; 'Cherry Robbers'; 'Love on the Farm'; 'Green'; 'A youth
   mowing'; 'Dream-confused'; 'A winter's tale'; 'Wedding morn'; 'Piano'; 'A Young
   Wife'; 'Snake'; 'Tortoise Gallantry'; 'The Elephant is Slow to Mate'; 'Humming
   Bird'; 'Trees in the Garden'; 'A White Blossom'; 'Suspense'; 'One Woman to all
   Women'; 'New Heaven and Earth'; 'Song of death'; 'The Ship of Death';
   'Lightning'; 'A Passing Bell'; 'Twilight'.
The Psychological Genius of D. H. Lawrence. 1 hr. 30 mins. Cassette recording. Big
Sur Recordings 4620, 1970. Also issued on 5" reel.
   Lecture by Dr Malcolm Brown, recorded San Francisco, 1970.
Readings from Lawrence. LP. Folkways Records FL 9837, 1962.
   Prose and poetry selected and read by Harry T. Moore. Texts and critical notes by
   Moore inserted in slipcase.
The Trial of Lady Chatterley. LP. Nonesuch Records PPLD 206, 1961.
   A condensation of C. H. Rolph's transcripts of the trial, read by Maurice Denham
   and others from the Penguin publication. Introduction spoken by Lord Birkett.
   Text of 'Lady Chatterley's Lover and the Obscene Publications Act, 1959' by Roy
   Jenkins inserted in slipcase.
Unpublished recordings
'Kangaroo'. Read by Dylan Thomas at a poetry reading given in the home of Mrs
   Marcela Dupont, Washington D.C., 3 March 1952. (Audiotape.)
'Love on the Farm'. Read by Bramwell Fletcher during a lecture/reading in the
   Coolidge Auditorium, Library of Congress, 5 November 1962. (Audiotape.)
Poems read by Florence Becker Lennon on her radio programme *Enjoyment of
   Poetry*, Station WEVD, New York City, 1957–61. They are: 'Give us Gods';
   'Green'; 'Sane and Insane'; 'Start a Revolution, Somebody'. (Audiotape.)

City of Nottingham Arts Department, 51 Castlegate, Nottingham, U.K.

Interviews with family and friends of D. H. Lawrence, conducted by David Gerard,
City Librarian of Nottingham, 1964–8. (Audiocassettes.)
Contributors:
   Mrs Barbara Barr, daughter of Frieda and Ernest Weekley. 30 mins.
   Mr and Mrs S. Bircumshaw, Eastwood neighbours. 35 mins.

Mrs Bryce, Eastwood neighbour. 15 mins.

Mr E. C. Carlin, Eastwood neighbour. 10 mins.

Professor J. D. Chambers, brother of Jessie Chambers. 50 mins. lecture

Mrs Mabel Chatterley, friend of Connie Chatterley. 5 mins.

Mrs M. Collishaw, childhood friend. 32 mins.

Helen Corke, writer; Croydon teacher. 30 mins.

Mrs S. Cotterill, pupil teacher with D.H.L. at Ilkeston. 10 mins.

David Garnett, writer; son of Edward Garnett. 43 mins.

Stanley Hocking, Cornish farmer (interviewed by Dr Platt). 45 mins.

Mrs Alice Holditch (née Alice Hall), friend in childhood and youth (the basis for
    Alice Gall in *White Peacock*). 35 mins. (Interviewed by F. C. Tighe, 1963)

W. H. King, fellow pupil; High School. 15 mins.

W. E. Lawrence, nephew of L; son of D.H.L's brother George. 40 mins.

Charles Leeming, boy pupil of D.H.L's at British School, Eastwood. 20 mins.

Jack Lindsay, writer. 32 mins.

John Lord, friend of William Hopkin. 10 mins.

Compton Mackenzie, writer; with L in Capri. 55 mins.

Harry T. Moore, D.H.L's biographer. 30 mins.

Mrs Peggy Needham, D.H.L's niece; daughter of D.H.L's sister Emily. 14 mins.

Professor V. de Sola Pinto, Professor of English, Nottingham University; witness
    at *Lady Chatterley* trial. 20 mins.

J. C. P. Taylor, school friend, Beauvale School. 21 mins.

Mrs Julian Vinogradoff, daughter of Lady Ottoline Morell. 12 mins.

Montague Weekley, son of Frieda and Ernest Weekley. 19 mins.

Dame Rebecca West, writer. 25 mins.

Mr Westcott, headmaster of Beauvale School in the 1960s. 12 mins.

Ernest Wilson, boyhood friend. 15 mins.

Other recordings held at City of Nottingham Arts Department

BBC Radio Nottingham. Interview between Tony Church and David Gerard about
    the discovery of a slate fireplace painted by D.H.L. at 99 Lynn Croft, Eastwood.
    Interview between Tony Church and Harry T. Moore about the need to secure the
    preservation of Haggs Farm, home of Jessie Chambers. Further comments by
    Professor J. D. Chambers. (Recorded on $5\frac{3}{4}''$ reel.) July 1966.

D. H. Lawrence. A talk by Bertrand Russell. 15 mins. BBC Men of Ideas series. (Reel
    tape.) 1952.

Round Table Discussion on Lawrence. At the University of California, Los Angeles,
    March 1952. (Two 7″ reels.) Recorded by Friends of the Library, UCLA. The
    participants were: Professor Majil Ewing (Chairman); Aldous Huxley; Frieda
    Lawrence; Lawrence Clark Powell (Librarian, UCLA); Mrs Dorothy Mitchell
    (student).

Seven Arts Program, Station WERE, Cleveland, Ohio. Bob West interviews David
    Gerard, City Librarian of Nottingham, visiting Cleveland, April 1967. (7″ reel.)
    The interview examines the problems of censorship which libraries had
    experienced in the past over D.H.L's works, and explores the range and quality of
    the Lawrence Collection at Nottingham.

Open University

New Directions in the Novel. 18 mins. Reel tape, A 302/15. 1973.
Examines the reasons for the abandonment of nineteenth-century fictional techniques by early twentieth-century writers, including Lawrence. Contributor: Hugh Sykes Davies.
Personal Relationships in 'The Rainbow'. 22 mins. Reel tape, A 100/35. 1971.
Graham Martin discusses D.H.L's concern with the non-rational elements in the human make-up. Extracts from a radio talk recorded in 1952 by Bertrand Russell are included.
Psychoanalysis and Literature. Reel tape, A 100/09. n.d.
Excerpts from *The Rainbow* and *Sons and Lovers* are used to illustrate the fictional exploration of psychological states.
The Social Criticism of D. H. Lawrence. 19 mins. Reel tape, A 100/36. 1971.
Graham Martin and Stuart Hall consider D.H.L's attack on social relationships in his essays and novels. Excerpts from essays and from *The Rainbow* are read.
The Victorian Social Critics. Reel tape, A100/32. n.d.
Ian George investigates the work of Carlyle, Ruskin, Arnold and D.H.L. A passage from *Women in Love* is used in illustration.

University of Texas. Humanities Research Center, Box 7219, Austin, Texas 78712, USA.

Unpublished recordings
Helen Corke. Thirty rolls of original magnetic tape of a Malcolm Muggeridge interview with Helen Corke about her association with D.H.L. A BBC TV production entitled 'Dreaming Woman'.
Frieda Lawrence. BBC interview (no further details). 1957.
Frieda Lawrence. Reading poems by D.H.L. 7″ reel tape. n.d. The poems are: 'Red wolf'; 'Ship of death'; 'Bavarian gentians'; 'Autumn in Taos'; 'Invocation to the moon'.
Else Jaffe (Frieda Lawrence's sister). Interview by Lois and Dirk Hoffman (no further details).
Professor V. de Sola Pinto. Recording of talk entitled 'D. H. Lawrence and William Blake'. Reel tape. Delivered at Nottingham University on the occasion of the thirtieth anniversary of D.H.L's death, 1960.
Taos and Brett: a Friendship. Erik Bauersfield interviews Dorothy Brett with John Manchester at the Manchester Gallery, Taos, New Mexico, September 1966. Two 7″ reel tapes.

Other Sources

Approach to the 19th Century Novel. A7. 1971.
Includes a discussion of *Sons and Lovers* between Barry Supple and Laurence Lerner. Cassette and reel tape. (Sussex Tapes. EP Group of Companies, East Ardsley, Yorkshire.)
Approach to the 20th Century Novel. A8. 1971.
Ian Gregor and Mark Kinkead-Weekes discuss D.H.L's fiction. Text included.

Cassette and reel tape. (Sussex Tapes.)

D. H. Lawrence by Stephen Spender. 58 mins. (56 C815). 1953.

D.H.L's protest against man's preoccupation with a cerebral life and the inhibition of instinctual life. Cassette. (Audio Visual Library Services, Powdrake Rd, Grangemouth, Stirlingshire.)

D. H. Lawrence: Sons and Lovers. 28 mins. Cassette and reel, ELA 034. 1977.

Track A: The Social Background. Track B: A Study in Human Relationships. The discussion is between Angus Easson and Terence Wright. (Audio Learning, Queensway, London.)

D. H. Lawrence: The Rainbow. 28 mins. Cassette and reel, (Audio Learning, Queensway, London(ELA 041

Track A: The Brangwen Generation. Track B: Formal and Technical Aspects. Discussion between Angus Easson and Terence Wright.

D. H. Lawrence: Women in Love. 28 mins. Cassette and reel, ELA 060. 1979.

Track A: Endings and Beginnings. Track B: Technique and Innovation. Discussion between Angus Easson and Terence Wright. (Audio Learning.)

D. H. Lawrence: the Puritan Love-trip. 60 mins. Reel. 1972.

Lawrence and the treatment of sexual love in the Western tradition. (CBS Learning Systems, Box 500, Terminal A, Toronto, Canada)

Lady Chatterley's Lover. LP, Caedmon TC 1116. 1959.

Pamela Brown reads a 'distillation' of the novel. Descriptive notes in slipcase.

Listening and Writing. Two talks by Ted Hughes in which he reads 'Bare Almond Trees'. BBC RESR 19M.

Mornings in Mexico. 15 mins. 1961.

Excerpts from D.H.L's travel book. (NATL Tape Depository, University of Colorado, Boulder, Colo. 80302, U.S.A.)

Poetry 1900 to 1965. Ted Hughes reads 'Humming Bird'. Longmans 34155.

Readings from D. H. Lawrence. LP. 1969.

(Scholastic Magazines, 906 Sylvan Way, Englewood Cliffs, N.J. 07632, U.S.A.)

Sons and Lovers. 55 mins. n.d.

Dramatised excerpts from the novel with discussions of several key scenes. (Center for Cassette Studies, 8110 Webb Avenue, Hollywood, Calif. 91615, U.S.A.)

The Works of D. H. Lawrence. 15 mins. n.d.

A brief explanation by a member of the faculty of the University of Virginia arguing the reasons for his interest in D.H.L. (Scholar's Bookshelf Series.) Audio Visual Education Series, 5300 University Avenue, Minneapolis, Minn. 55414, U.S.A.)